The Political Economy of the Investment Treaty Regime

The Political Economy of the Investment Treaty Regime

Jonathan Bonnitcha

Lauge N. Skovgaard Poulsen

Michael Waibel

OXFORD
UNIVERSITY PRESS

Great Clarendon Street, Oxford, OX2 6DP,
United Kingdom

Oxford University Press is a department of the University of Oxford.
It furthers the University's objective of excellence in research, scholarship,
and education by publishing worldwide. Oxford is a registered trade mark of
Oxford University Press in the UK and in certain other countries

Published in the United States of America by Oxford University Press
198 Madison Avenue, New York, NY 10016, United States of America

British Library Cataloguing in Publication Data
Data available

Library of Congress Control Number: 2016962495

ISBN 978–0–19–871954–0 (hbk.)
       978–0–19–871955–7 (pbk.)

Printed and bound by
CPI Group (UK) Ltd, Croydon, CR0 4YY

▪ PREFACE

In 2007, the German city of Hamburg allowed a Swedish energy company to place a large coal-fired power plant on the banks of the Elbe river. The company, Vattenfall, began construction of this power plant; however, against the background of growing opposition among civil society groups and local politicians, the urban planning agency decided to impose significant restrictions on the plant's water usage in return for final approval. The measures were costly, but according to local authorities all companies operating along the river were subject to them, and they complied with European and German law.

In March 2009, Vattenfall challenged the decision based on the 1991 Energy Charter Treaty (ECT). The treaty gave Vattenfall extensive protections against a broad range of state measures and was backed up by a powerful dispute settlement mechanism: investment treaty arbitration. The ECT allowed Vattenfall to take Germany directly to international arbitration. Here, three private arbitrators could hear the dispute and potentially award significant damages to the investor. Vattenfall claimed the measures amounted to indirect expropriation and unfair treatment and asked for more than US$1.5 billion plus arbitration costs and interest.

The arbitration enraged non-governmental organizations (NGOs) and German politicians. The deputy environment minister said it was 'unprecedented how we are being pilloried just for implementing German and EU laws' (Müller quoted in Knauer 2009). Had Germany lost the arbitration and failed to comply with the tribunal's award, however, Vattenfall could have enforced the award against Germany's commercial assets around the world. Also, Germany has signed dozens of bilateral investment treaties (BITs) since 1959, and German companies have increasingly relied on the treaties to resolve disputes with foreign states. Refusing to comply with an arbitral award would question Germany's continued commitment to the investment treaty regime. In March 2011, the parties settled. Hamburg lowered the environmental requirements on the power plant in exchange for Vattenfall dropping the arbitration and German court proceedings (Verheyen 2012). In 2017, the European Court of Justice found that the original decision to authorize construction of the power plant breached EU law because it was not supported by a sufficiently comprehensive environmental impact assessment.

In 2012, Vattenfall filed a second arbitration against Germany, also based on the ECT. This time Vattenfall asked for US$6 billion, and the subject of the dispute was Germany's decision to phase out nuclear power after the 2011 nuclear disaster at Fukushima in Japan. As this book goes to press, the arbitration remains pending, but its political fallout was clear: NGOs, newspapers, and politicians across Europe were outraged that multinational corporations could bypass domestic courts and use a little-known treaty to foil Germany's phase-out from nuclear power, or at least make it a very costly reform.

The two Vattenfall arbitrations have been part of a broader trend. Since the early 2000s, foreign investors have increasingly relied on the global network of more than 3000 investment treaties to file international arbitrations against states. It is impossible to say with accuracy just how many arbitrations investors have filed, as some investment treaties allow disputes to be adjudicated in confidence. However, by 2016, we knew of more than 700 arbitrations against almost 100 states, at a rate of more than 50 arbitrations annually in the last five years. Although these figures are low compared to litigation in domestic courts, they are high compared to other international law regimes. In the World Trade Organization (WTO), for instance, its 164 member states filed less than 15 disputes annually in 2014 and 2015. As to the substance of the disputes, investors have used the treaties to ask for compensation for a very wide range of government conduct, including taxation, changes to the pricing of key utilities, public health, environmental and financial regulation, and much more.

This has made investment treaty arbitration highly controversial. Developing countries have been subject to the clear majority of arbitrations thus far, and some have attempted to renegotiate their treaties on more favourable terms. A few have decided to go further and terminate their treaties. Unilateral exit is difficult, however, as many treaties include 'survival clauses' that ensure that treaty protections remain in force for investments made prior to termination. Sometimes these clauses can 'lock in' treaty protections for up to twenty years.

In developed states, as well, investment treaty arbitration has become a salient topic because of cases such as Vattenfall. In 2014, growing public discontent led the European Commission to hold a public online hearing about its plans to include investment treaty arbitration in the Transatlantic Trade and Investment Partnership (TTIP). Of the responses, 97% opposed investment treaty arbitration, as almost 150,000 European citizens agreed with NGOs that this mechanism did not belong in TTIP or, many argued, any other international agreement.

Yet, despite the mounting criticisms, only a few states have decided to cancel their treaties altogether, and states around the world continue to negotiate treaties allowing foreign investors to file arbitrations based on far-reaching substantive protections. Investment treaties are here to stay. This raises important political, economic, and legal questions. What are the costs and benefits of investment treaties for investors, states, and other stakeholders? Are they critical instruments to promote economic and political development, or are they simply a subsidy to already powerful multinationals? Is it a good idea for private arbitrators to be able to review state regulation and award compensation to foreign investors? And why did states sign these treaties in the first place? This book tries to provide the answers.

ACKNOWLEDGEMENTS

The idea for this book was born out of a workshop that Lauge Poulsen and Michael Waibel hosted at the London School of Economics in April 2012. In writing this book over the last four years, we accumulated debts to many academic colleagues, policy-makers, and our students at Cambridge, LSE, UCL, and UNSW who generously contributed their time and expertise. We are very grateful for their help. Of course, we are solely responsible for any remaining errors.

For comments on draft chapters we are grateful to participants at the ILAP seminar at UCL, as well as to Lorand Bartels, Markus Burgstaller, Jacob Eisler, Yoram Haftel, Jean Ho, Matthew Hodgson, Steffen Hindelang, Roland Kläger, Andreas Kulick, Nikos Lavranos, William Magnusson, Ola Mestad, Federica Paddeu, Sergio Puig, Dávid Pusztai, Pedro Saffi, Stephan Schill, Andrew Sanger, Esmé Shirlow, Taylor St. John, Todd Tucker, Valentina Vadi, Ingo Venzke, Pierre-Hughes Verdier, André von Walter, Jorge Viñuales, Yanhui Wu and Rumiana Yotova.

Emma Aisbett, John Bell, Peter Harris, Donald Rakestraw, Diana Rosert, Jay Sexton, Rajesh Ramloll, and Veronika Fikfak were generous with their time to discuss different aspects of our analyses. Wolfgang Alschner, Joachim Pohl, and David Gaukrodger at the OECD, Sergio Puig, and Zoe Williams kindly shared their data.

Margherita Cornaglia, Anne-Christine Barthelemy, Damien Charlotin, Hannah Dixie, Christina Gort, Emilija Marcinkeviciute, and Veena Srirangam-Nadhamuni provided excellent research assistance, and Nicholas Turner assisted with compiling the index.

For financial support, we thank The British Academy (Small Grants Scheme SLA–U632, Lauge Poulsen and Michael Waibel), and The Leverhulme Trust (Prize PLP-2014-133, Michael Waibel).

We have been most fortunate in our editors at Oxford University Press. We thank Adam Swallow and Aimee Wright for believing in this project from the beginning, and to Katie Bishop and Aravind Kannankara for their great skill and patience in bringing it to conclusion. We are also grateful for the support of John Louth and Merel Alstein.

We dedicate this book to our children—Alasdair, Kai, Johan, and Sonia—all of whom were born while we were working on this book. So far, they seem to be coping very well without worrying about the political economy of the investment treaty regime.

Jonathan Bonnitcha
Lauge Poulsen
Michael Waibel

Sydney, London, and Cambridge
1 November 2016

■ TABLE OF CONTENTS

LIST OF FIGURES

■ LIST OF TABLES

LIST OF AGREEMENTS

Unless otherwise noted, all investment treaties are available on UNCTAD's website (investmentpolicyhub.unctad.org/IIA). Investment treaties are referred to by the treaty parties followed by the date of signature.

Treaties and other International Instruments

Domestic Instruments

Arbitration Awards

Investment arbitration awards and decisions are available at Andrew New-combe's Investment Treaty Arbitration website www.italaw.com.

Other International Decisions

National Decisions

CANADA

1 The Investment Treaty Regime in Context

Introduction

Few people had heard of investment treaties until very recently. Most of these treaties had been negotiated by mid-level government officials and with little public awareness. Parliaments and the media rarely paid much attention as compared to other globalization instruments, such as preferential trade agreements (PTAs) (Figure 1.1). Until a few years ago, investment treaties and investment treaty arbitration were examples of 'supranational governance activities that [went] virtually unnoticed' (Esty quoted in Montt 2009, 143).

Lawyers and legal scholars have appreciated the importance of investment treaties for some time. However, unlike in the international trade regime, where legal scholars have a long history of engagement with political scientists and economists (e.g. Hoekman and Kostecki 1995; Trebilcock and Howse 2005), lawyers have been slow to integrate insights about the political and economic foundations of the investment treaty regime.

This is not surprising, as there has been very little engagement with investment treaties in scholarship from politics, economics, and business. Introductions to the field of international political economy barely mention investment treaties (e.g. Gilpin 2001, 300; Oatley 2010, 205–12; Ravenhill 2011, ch. 11).[1] And while political scientists increasingly write about the investment treaty regime, the literature is still in its infancy compared with the more advanced scholarship on the trade regime. Economists have almost entirely ignored the regime—even in texts devoted to foreign investment (Navaretti, Venables, and Frank 2006, 252, 269–70)—and scholarship on international business management also tends to ignore investment treaties (for an exception, see Moran 2007). This lack of engagement leaves major gaps in our understanding of the micro- and macroeconomic underpinnings of investment treaty arbitration, as well as the practical implications of the regime for international business management and politics.

---

[1] Before the rise of investment treaty arbitration, even the main textbook on international investment policy spent less than ten pages on BITs (Brewer and Young 2000, 74–8). Cohn (2011) includes two pages on BITs.

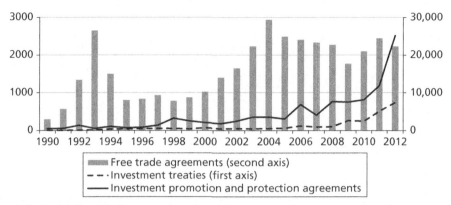

Figure 1.1 Investment treaties under the radar

Note: Figure shows number of times the phrases 'free trade agreement', 'investment treaty', and 'investment promotion and protection agreement' (the British term for an investment treaty) were mentioned in English-speaking newspapers from 1990 to 2012.

Source: Poulsen 2015, Figure 1.4.

This book seeks to fill some of those gaps. The aim is to both synthesize and push forward existing literature by integrating and contributing to legal, economic, and political perspectives on the regime. Our hope is that this will fill out the 'blind spots' of academics from different disciplines and make clear just how many crucial questions about the political economy of the investment treaty regime have yet to be adequately addressed. In addition, the book will be of use for lawyers, investors, policy-makers and stakeholders trying to make sense of these important, but little-understood, instruments governing economic globalization.

The investment treaty regime in context

The title of our book suggests that the more than 3000 investment treaties and more than 700 known investment treaty arbitrations together resemble what political scientists call a *regime* (Salacuse 2010). A regime is traditionally understood as the 'principles, norms, rules, and decision-making procedures around which actors' expectations converge in a given area of international relations' (Krasner 2009, 113).[2] This broad definition ranges from formal arrangements (e.g. international organizations and treaties) to more informal arrangements (e.g. shared norms and principles among tribunals and

---

[2] If not otherwise noted, we follow Krasner's definition of the regime components in the following text.

arbitrators), and actors include states as well as non-state actors, including foreign investors.

The notion of an 'investment treaty regime' allows us to highlight the regularities across thousands of treaties and hundreds of arbitrations, which on the surface may otherwise appear diverse. It also invites us to identify deviations within the regime and changes over time.

THREE MAIN COMPONENTS

The investment treaty regime consists of three main components: (i) investment treaties; (ii) the set of treaties, rules, and institutions governing investment treaty arbitration; and (iii) the decisions of arbitral tribunals applying and interpreting investment treaties. First and foremost is the collection of investment treaties themselves. These are treaties between two or more states that have the *protection* of foreign investment as the primary, or only, subject matter.[3] Practically all investment treaties include protections against uncompensated expropriation and discrimination against foreign investment. In practice, the vast majority also includes protections that go far beyond uncompensated expropriation and discrimination, such as rights to transfer capital, and protections against losses as a result of war or civil strife, unfair and inequitable treatment, as well as breaches of contract. In recent years, a growing minority has begun to include binding provisions on investment liberalization as well.

Treaties that include property right protections for foreign investors but do not have this as a primary concern are not considered investment treaties in this volume. The most prominent example is the European Convention on Human Rights (ECHR). Equally, we do not consider treaties that lack the common core of investment *protections*—for example, against uncompensated expropriation—to be investment treaties, even if they include some provisions dealing with the treatment of investment. Examples can be found in various agreements of the World Trade Organization (WTO)[4] and the European Union (EU).[5]

Most investment treaties are bilateral—bilateral investment treaties or 'BITs'—and they deal solely with investment protection. However, some also involve more parties and issues, such as the ECT mentioned in the preface and

---

[3] The subject matter of investment treaties is distinct from their purpose. The purpose of investment treaties is normally understood to be the promotion of foreign investment, as we discuss in the following text and later on in this book.

[4] Notably, the prohibition of some performance requirements in the Agreement on Trade Related Investment Measure (TRIMs) and mode 3 (commercial presence) commitments to liberalization of trade in services under the General Agreement on Trade in Services (GATS).

[5] Notably, rights of establishment and free movement of capital conferred by Articles 49 and 63 of the Treaty on European Union.

Chapter Eleven of the North American Free Trade Agreement (NAFTA). Investment chapters in PTAs such as NAFTA are similar in their content to freestanding BITs. In addition, the Friendship, Commerce, and Navigation (FCN) treaties signed by the United States during the Cold War also qualify as investment treaties under our definition, as they focused primarily on investment protection, and Washington saw them as treaties aimed at protecting US investors abroad (see the following text).

In recent years, the investment treaty regime has been moving towards multi-issue and plurilateral agreements. This has facilitated greater levels of 'issue-linkages' between trade, investment, and other areas across more than two parties. For instance, as this book goes to press, a large number of countries were planning to include comprehensive investor protections in the Trans-Pacific Partnership (TPP)[6] and the Regional Comprehensive Economic Partnership (RCEP).[7] The United States and the European Union have also recently attempted to negotiate a Transatlantic Trade and Investment Partnership (TTIP) with provisions on investment protection.

The investment treaty regime has become particularly important due to its dispute settlement mechanism. Early investment treaties—including post-war FCN agreements—provided only for state-to-state dispute settlement. Since the end of the Cold War, however, practically all investment treaties have included a broad and binding consent to investment treaty arbitration of disputes between foreign investors and host states. Inspired by rules governing international commercial arbitration, investment treaty arbitration gives international arbitrators broad powers to determine the scope of their own jurisdiction, to decide whether the state in question has breached the treaty ('the merits'), and to award damages.[8] Traditionally, only states were regarded as subjects of international law and thus only states had standing before international courts and tribunals. Without consent to investment treaty arbitration, most foreign investors would therefore be unable to file international arbitrations against states. So whereas not all investment treaties are backed up by this dispute settlement mechanism, consent to investment treaty arbitration has become a core design component of 'modern' investment treaties.

In addition to investment treaties, the second component of the regime is the set of complementary treaties, rules, and institutions that govern the adjudication of investment disputes in investment treaty arbitration. The

---

[6] On 23 January 2017, President Trump withdrew the United States as a signatory from the TPP. However, the other 11 prospective TPP countries, including Australia and Japan, were considering whether to pursue the TPP without the United States as this book goes to press.

[7] The RCEP is a proposed PTA between ten ASEAN members and six other states with which ASEAN has existing PTAs (Australia, China, India, Japan, New Zealand, and South Korea).

[8] We refer to investment treaty arbitration in this book, rather than the more general term 'investor–state arbitration', which also encompasses arbitrations by foreign investors against states based on investment laws and contracts. See further in the following text and in Chapter 3.

THE INVESTMENT TREATY REGIME IN CONTEXT

most important are the ICSID and the New York Conventions. Crucial to both conventions are their enforcement mechanisms: if a state refuses to pay compensation after having lost an investment treaty arbitration, investors can bring court proceedings before the courts of any member states of the conventions to seek an order allowing the investor to seize commercial assets of the non-compliant state. There are important exceptions to this system— such as sovereign immunity—but the two conventions enable courts in member states to make the investment treaty regime legally enforceable in practice.

Non-compliance may also result in diplomatic conflicts between host and home states. When Argentina postponed payment of a series of arbitration awards in the aftermath of its 2001 financial crisis, for instance, the United States suspended trade benefits to Argentina and attempted to block funding from the World Bank and the International Monetary Fund (IMF).[9] In practice, however, there have been high rates of compliance with investment treaty awards. When tribunals have awarded compensation to investors, most states have paid swiftly and in full. Although some states have sought to re-assert authority over tribunals in recent years by providing more pre-scriptive guidance *ex ante* about how the treaties should be applied and interpreted, ex post non-compliance is rare.

The rules governing investment treaty arbitration provide no real oppor-tunity for appeal—unlike, for example, domestic courts and the international trade regime. Equally, there is no requirement for foreign investors to exhaust local remedies before filing international arbitrations, which differs from other areas of international law that give private actors direct standing before international tribunals. Under the ECHR, for instance, individuals and firms can file cases before a regional court but only after having gone through domestic courts (provided such attempts would not be obviously futile). Not so for investment treaty arbitration, where investors can completely bypass domestic courts. Although drafters of investment treaties could revise these regime characteristics, they have made only few attempts thus far.

As in other areas of international law, investment treaty arbitration con-siders the state as a single actor responsible for the conduct of all its organs. The conduct of officials at any level of government can potentially result in the state breaching its investment treaty obligations. As a result, arbitrations have targeted not only acts of the executive, but also the judiciary, the legislature, specialized agencies and sub-national levels of governments (see below).[10] And since compliance with domestic law does not excuse a breach of

---

[9] According to Argentina, the delay was not due to non-compliance as such. Rather the Attorney General, Horacio Rosatti, argued that an Argentinean court had to authorize the awards. In Argentina's view, this position was not inconsistent with the ICSID Convention—which provides for the automatic recognition of the ICSID Convention awards; see Chapter 3.

[10] By contrast, the conduct of state-owned enterprises is not, as a rule, attributed to the state (International Law Commission 2007, 48).

international law, investors have brought successful arbitrations in situations where host states have complied with their own domestic laws and regulations according to its domestic courts.

Finally, the regime consists of the decisions of the tribunals themselves. While not bound by each other's decisions, as would be the case in a regime governed by a formal system of precedent, tribunals often refer to previous decisions of other tribunals. The result is the development of an informal jurisprudence that provides substantive meat to the bare bones of vague investment treaty protections. As in other regimes with strong dispute settlement systems—such as the EU or the WTO—this has resulted in interpretations that have often surprised states and other stakeholders.[11]

Arbitrators have used treaty language that states regarded as relatively unimportant at the time of treaty drafting to review a wide range of state activities. One example is tribunals' broad interpretation of the obligation to provide 'fair and equitable treatment' to foreign investors. Tribunals also determine the amount of compensation to be paid to foreign investors, and in some cases governments and other stakeholders have been surprised by the large amounts awarded. Some degree of consensus has emerged on the interpretation of these and other core questions in investment treaty arbitration, yet the jurisprudence remains incomplete and is occasionally inconsistent. This can make it difficult to know what is required of states to comply with their treaty obligations, which reduces the predictability of the regime for investors and states alike.

THE REGIME COMPLEX FOR INTERNATIONAL INVESTMENT

The investment treaty regime is not the only regime that governs investor–state relations. Foreign investors, states, and other actors involved in investment governance have to manoeuvre not only between domestic laws and regulations but also between a myriad of international arrangements, many of which have their own sets of principles, norms, rules, and decision-making procedures.

As already mentioned, there are other treaties that contain provisions dealing with the treatment of foreign investment. In addition, there are investor–state contracts, described below. There are environmental conventions, double taxation treaties (DTTs), debt rescheduling arrangements (e.g. in the Paris Club), insurance policies, codes of conduct relating to labour standards and corruption, to mention a few. All of these can be crucially important for the governance of foreign investment, which is why we do not refer to investment treaties and investment treaty arbitration as constituting *the* 'international

---

[11]   On the unintended consequences of the European Court of Justice, see Alter (1998); Burley and Mattli (1993); and Mattli and Slaughter (1995). On unintended consequences of the WTO and the International Court of Justice, see Alter (2008).

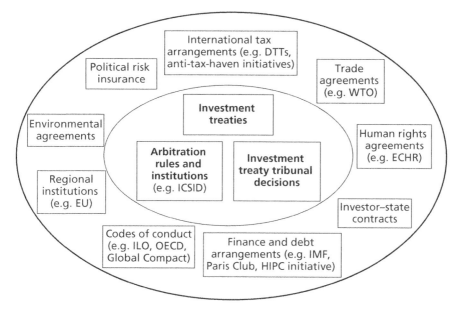

Figure 1.2 The investment regime complex and the investment treaty regime

investment regime' (in contrast to Salacuse 2010 and Simmons 2014). Rather, the investment *treaty* regime is better seen as part of a broader and loosely coupled 'regime complex' of partially overlapping institutions governing international investment.[12] We refer to this as the 'investment regime complex'.

One reason the investment treaty regime is so important, however, is that its strong dispute resolution mechanism can 'trump' other legal arrangements within the investment regime complex. While investment disputes can be resolved through a plethora of different decision-making procedures, investment treaty arbitration allows foreign investors to replace all of them with arbitration on the international plane. And when resolving investment disputes, there is little to prevent tribunals from subordinating other institutions and regimes in favour of the principles, norms, and rules enshrined in investment treaties. So while there is no formalised hierarchy within the investment regime complex, the investment treaty regime has taken centre stage.[13] Figure 1.2 provides an informal and non-exhaustive illustration.

To better understand the nature and background of the investment treaty regime, the remainder of this chapter outlines its core principles, norms,

---

[12] On this understanding of regime complexes, see Raustiala and Victor (2004) and Keohane and Victor (2011). Orsini, Morin, and Young (2013) use a slightly different conceptualization.

[13] On hierarchy in regime complexes, see generally Alter and Meunier (2009). On regime-shifting, see Helfer (2004), and on forum-shifting in dispute settlement, see Busch (2007).

rules, and decision-making procedures. Distinguishing between these different regime components is no easy exercise (Young 1986). For instance, we describe how investment treaties often include broad and vague investment protection *standards*, which arguably fall somewhere in between norms and rules. However, as an introduction, it is useful to separate each element. It also allows us to place the regime in its broader historical context.[14]

PRINCIPLES

Regime principles are basic beliefs about fact, causation, and rectitude. Three such principles underpin the investment treaty regime. The first is that international investment flows increase prosperity. The second is that protection of property rights promotes investment flows. Both principles have long historical roots, but are contested—as we return to later in the volume. Finally, the treaties proliferated after the end of the Cold War, when international law and international tribunals were seen as critical for promoting a liberal international order.

INTERNATIONAL INVESTMENT

After the Second World War, investors from developed countries expanded their international activities substantially by setting up wholly or majority-owned subsidiaries in developing countries. However, in much of the developing world, the political environment towards foreign investors was less than welcoming. Even outside the Soviet Union, economic and political theories of *dependencia* were taking hold among many post-colonial states. From this perspective, Western multinationals played a central role in what was seen as a resource transfer from poor countries to the Western 'core'. Large multinational firms were regarded as a legacy of colonial exploitation.

This ideological environment fitted well with the increasing pursuit of development strategies based on import-substitution. While not aiming to keep foreign investors out altogether, import-substitution strategies sought to carefully manage and control them to promote domestic industrialization. Dissatisfied with the ability, and willingness, of multinational companies to contribute to national development, foreign investments often became subject to screening mechanisms, performance requirements, capital transfer restrictions, high levels of taxation, and so forth (Bergsten 1974).[15] During the 1960s and 1970s, the increasingly restrictive attitude towards foreign investors

---

[14] More historical details are provided later in the book, particularly Chapter 7.
[15] A parallel development took place even in selected developed countries at the time.

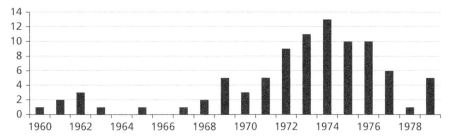

Figure 1.3 Nationalizations of oil companies, 1960–1979

Source: Author compilation based on Guriev, Kolotilin and Sonin (2011), Appendix B.

culminated in a number of large-scale expropriations of foreign capital with either little or no compensation (Figure 1.3).

This environment began to change in the 1980s. The debt crisis in Latin America and the successful growth strategies of a number of outward-oriented emerging markets led to a change in attitude towards multinationals. Occasionally prodded on by international financial institutions, many capital-importing countries began to encourage the influx of foreign capital by loosening restrictions on the establishment of international investments (Encarnation and Wells 1985). By the end of the Cold War, developing countries no longer perceived foreign capital as a threat to their sovereignty.

On the contrary, attracting foreign direct investment (FDI) became a central component of their strategies to promote economic growth and development. Unlike speculative and short-term portfolio flows, FDI involves an element of control by the foreign investor and therefore promised a stable source of capital, which in turn could result in positive spillovers to the rest of the economy, such as technological advantages and management practises. In John Williamson's ten-point list summarizing the 'Washington Consensus' towards development policies, a restrictive attitude towards FDI was considered 'foolish' (Williamson 1990, ch. 2). Even organizations such as the United Nations Commission on Trade and Development (UNCTAD), earlier sceptical about foreign investment, now saw multinationals as engines of growth that could provide critical 'help [to] make the 1990s a decade of renewed economic development' (UNCTAD 1992, iii). Most developing countries agreed, and states all over the world began to liberalize their domestic legal frameworks governing foreign investment (Table 1.1).

PROPERTY RIGHTS

Apart from opening up to foreign investment—liberalization—developing countries also began enshrining greater property right protections in their domestic legal regimes (Alvarez 2010). The premise was an old one: without

Table 1.1 National regulatory changes in domestic investment regimes, 1992–2000

	1992	1993	1994	1995	1996	1997	1998	1999	2000
Number of countries that introduced changes	43	54	49	63	66	76	60	65	70
Number of regulatory changes	77	100	110	112	114	150	145	139	150
Liberalization/promotion	77	99	108	106	98	134	136	130	147
Regulation/restrictions	0	1	2	6	16	16	9	9	3

Source: UNCTAD, Investment Policy Monitor database.

secure property rights, private investors—both domestic and foreign—would be unwilling to risk committing their capital to investment projects that might take many years to generate a return. While this idea can be traced back centuries, the rise of institutional economics gave it new prominence (North 1990).

The World Bank became a strong proponent of this principle. As Ibrahim Shihata, then the World Bank's general counsel, noted: 'serious investors look for a legal system where property rights, contractual arrangements and other lawful activities are safeguarded and respected' (Shihata 1995, 149). On this basis, the World Bank became increasingly involved in promoting legal reforms in the developing world aimed at the protection of private investment. A particularly important initiative was the World Bank Guidelines on the Treatment of Foreign Investment, which served as inspiration for many legal reforms in the developing world (Shihata 1993).

It was in this environment that investment treaties flourished. From the 1980s onwards, former communist countries began signing BITs in considerable numbers. Most Latin American and Asian countries joined the BIT bandwagon as well, making the BIT-movement a truly global phenomenon.

LEGAL INTERNATIONALISM

Finally, the investment treaty regime rests on a third principle rooted in legal internationalism (see generally Howse 1999; Koskenniemi 2002). Throughout the 1990s, states rushed to adopt a wide range of treaties, ranging from the WTO to human rights treaties and regional integration agreements. International courts and tribunals also proliferated (Alter 2014). International law and tribunals were seen as critical to tie in and push forward liberal reforms within states—a 'liberalism from above' (Sally 2002). So although the investment treaty regime may be potent and far-reaching, it 'is not a completely unique case in the history of modern international law and institutions' (Montt 2009, xx).

The proliferation of investment treaties coincided with this rise of legal internationalism. In 1988, for instance, General Secretary Gorbachev of the Soviet Union told the United Nations that he strongly supported 'the political, juridical and moral importance of the ancient Roman maxim: Pacta sunt servanda!—agreements must be honored', and noted that '[a]s the awareness of our common fate grows, every state would be genuinely interested in confining itself within the limits of international law'.[16] In 1991, when the Soviet Union collapsed, it had signed its first eight BITs a year earlier and its BIT negotiations were advanced with the United States.

Beliefs about the benefits and appropriateness of legal internationalism were not the only, or even the primary, factor that explains states' decisions to enter into investment treaties however. As we will see in Chapter 8, most developing countries had a simpler aim in mind: to promote foreign investment. The World Bank, the United Nations, international lawyers and advisors repeatedly told developing countries that, without legal protections tied to international law, foreign investors would be reluctant to invest in their countries. Most developing countries accepted the message and signed investment treaties in the hope that it would make them more attractive investment destinations. So, although commitments to international legal institutions and to the protection of property rights were both important elements of the political historical context for the rapid adoption of investment treaties, the main reason investment treaties became so widespread was the desire among developing countries to attract foreign investment.

Norms

We turn now to the norms—or standards of behaviour—of the investment treaty regime and how they are articulated in terms of rights and obligations. The regime grants foreign investors a wide range of *rights* independent of domestic laws and constitutions, which correspond to *obligations* of host states to treat foreign investment according to specified standards. In contrast, the investment treaty regime does not proscribe *obligations* for investors. Apart from domestic laws, investor obligations are left to other parts of the investment regime complex such as investor–state contracts and various non-binding codes of conduct.

INDEPENDENT INVESTOR RIGHTS

The notion that international law should guarantee foreign investors international minimum standards of treatment has a long history. In the seventeenth century, European trading powers agreed to protect foreign persons and their property in their territory according to a set of minimum standards.

---

[16] Quoted in Koh (1997, ftn. 156).

On this view, the treatment of foreign investors should not be based solely on the laws governing nationals of the host state, but also on a further set of standards independent from domestic legal regimes. Interference or outright seizure of foreign assets was prohibited during peacetime, and compensation was generally required if aliens' assets were confiscated during war (Roth 1949). All major European states accepted these basic norms, as did the United States after its independence. They were incorporated in FCN treaties, described in the preceding text, which before the Second World War dealt mostly with commercial and navigation matters but also obliged treaty-partners to uphold certain minimum standards with respect to the treatment of foreign investors.

This emerging doctrine of investment protection had been agreed upon by relatively equal parties aiming to ensure reciprocal arrangements. Extending its principles to territories outside Europe or the United States changed its political foundation (Lipson 1985, 12). As we describe in the following text, developed countries imposed Western minimum standards on developing countries through aggressive use of diplomatic protection and imperial legal enclaves, thereby moving foreign investment law 'from a base of reciprocity, to one of imposition' (Miles 2013, 21).

In response, a different set of norms emerged in Latin America, where legal scholar Carlos Calvo argued that foreign investors should not expect special treatment simply because they were foreign. Instead, host states should treat them the same way as domestic investors. Outright denial of justice would still breach international law, but the basic norm governing foreign investment should be one of national treatment (Montt 2009, ch. 1). Although targeted against Western standards, this was still a liberal investment policy— in line with the basic non-discrimination norm enshrined in the trade regime of today, for instance.[17] The Calvo doctrine appealed to Latin American and other developing countries, which incorporated it into laws, contracts, and their constitutions during the nineteenth century. Yet, most Western states continued to argue that foreign investors required certain international minimum standards over and above domestic law.

The conflict between these competing visions raged throughout much of the twentieth century. For instance, encouraged by oil-producing countries' successful establishment of control over their reserves in the 1970s, developing countries proposed a New International Economic Order in the United Nations, allowing them 'Permanent Sovereignty over Natural Resources'. A cornerstone was the 1974 Charter of Economic Rights and Duties of States, which called into question the concept of an international minimum standard

---

[17] Note that, whereas Calvo also argued that disputes relating to foreign investment should be resolved in domestic courts, WTO disputes are of course resolved through international dispute settlement.

of treatment for foreign investment. But as more and more countries adopted investment treaties in the latter half of the century (see the following text), practically all countries ended up with treaty obligations that provide foreign investors with rights independent of national laws and constitutions. So while investment treaties differ from the international investment regime during the colonial era, in that they are based on consent rather than imposed by force, their substantive provisions enshrine Western investment protection norms developed from the seventeenth century onwards.

In recent years, however, a modified version of the Calvo doctrine has resurfaced from a surprising corner. Now, some *developed* countries are beginning to question the notion that foreign investors should be given special rights. Shortly before Phillip Morris brought a controversial arbitration relating to tobacco plain packaging, the Australian government decided that foreign investors should only be granted national treatment and rejected provisions 'that would confer greater legal rights on foreign business than those available to domestic businesses' (Australian Department of Foreign Affairs and Trade 2011, 14). The United States Congress has also instructed US negotiators to apply the 'no greater rights' principle since the Trade Act of 2002. Following the controversies surrounding TTIP, the European Parliament also voted unanimously in favour of EU investment treaties granting foreign investors 'the same high level of protection as Union law and the general principles common to the laws of the Member States grant to investors from within the Union, *but not a higher level of protection*'.[18]

These recommendations are in line with those of economists who have long argued that positive discrimination leads to an inefficient allocation of resources, all other things being equal (Stiglitz 2007, 549; similarly, Bhagwati 2004, 165). Supporters of neoliberal orthodoxy too have argued against the preferential treatment granted to foreign investors under investment treaties, and instead encouraged states to base investment treaty programs on non-discrimination rules alone (e.g. Lester 2015). Thus far, however, such arguments have had limited practical importance, as developed states contend that investment treaties do not in fact offer rights above and beyond those in domestic law. In response to concerns expressed in Europe, for instance, the European Commission and Canada issued a note in 2016 that the investment protection chapter in their Comprehensive Economic Trade Agreement (CETA) would not 'result in foreign investors being treated more favourably than domestic investors'.[19] We address this discussion in Chapters 5 and 9.

---

[18] Recital 4 of Regulation (EU) No. 912/2014. Italics added.
[19] Joint Interpretative Declaration on CETA, available at: http://diepresse.com/mediadb/pdf/cetazusatztext.pdf. At the time of this writing, CETA had yet to be ratified.

NO INVESTOR OBLIGATIONS

The second core norm of the investment treaty regime is that, while investors receive far-reaching rights, they have only few, if any, obligations. Discussions about international obligations for foreign investors have a long history. Concerns about corporate (ir)responsibility were widespread during the colonial era when imperial trading companies engaged in what today would be considered egregious human rights violations, including slavery, torture, and executions. Environmental damage also often accompanied the colonial pursuit of natural resources (Miles 2013, 42–7). Unsurprisingly, however, the imperial powers were more focused on developing and expanding on the property rights of foreign investors than limiting their activities through binding and enforceable obligations.

During the 1970s, protests against the activities of multinationals reached their zenith. In 1972, the president of Chile, Salvador Allende, urged the international community to confront the 'economic power, political influence and corrupting action' of foreign investors (Allende 1972). Less than one year later, the United States had helped overthrow his government, prodded on by the International Telephone and Telegraph Company that feared expropriation of its assets (Maurer 2013, ch. 9). This, together with wider anti-corporate sentiment in both developed and developing countries, led to a series of initiatives to constrain the negative implications of cross-border investments.

One such initiative stands out. From the late 1970s and into the 1980s, the United Nations tried to promote a set of binding obligations for multinationals through its newly founded Centre on Transnational Corporations (UNCTC). The organization was explicitly established to tame and control multinationals with a plan to set up a UN multilateral investment agreement—the Code of Conduct on Transnational Corporations. Initiated in 1975, the Code was intended to combine protections for foreign investors with investor obligations. The proposal differed from investment treaties, which only included the former. Yet, the code stalled not because of disagreements over investor obligations—they were expected to be voluntary—but because of the fundamental disagreement over the protections of foreign investors, with Latin American states insisting on the Calvo doctrine (Sauvant 2015). So while the Code could have become a cornerstone of the investment treaty regime, the United Nations ultimately decided to drop it as the rise of the Washington Consensus made it appear as 'a relic of another era, when foreign direct investment was looked upon with considerable concern'.[20]

In recent years, much of the controversy surrounding the investment treaty regime has focused on the absence of binding investor obligations. But while

---

[20] US Government demarche from 1991 quoted in Braithwaite and Drahos (2000, 193).

proposals have been made to develop investment treaties with more emphasis on binding corporate responsibility rules (Miles 2013, ch. 6), they have remained largely unsuccessful thus far. This means that, while investor obligations are part of the broader investment regime complex, they are peripheral to the investment treaty regime itself. Instead, investor obligations are primarily dealt with through national laws of host states and investor–state contracts. In addition, there are a few non-binding international codes of conduct. A recent example is the UN Global Compact, which can be enforced through domestic courts in some limited circumstances (see e.g. Esdaile 2016), but which are not themselves backed up by formalized international dispute settlement. In some countries—notably, the United States—investors may also become liable for certain types of misconduct abroad—for instance, if they engage in corrupt business practices or commit serious human rights violations.

Rules

Compared with the norms of a regime, rules provide more precise prescriptions or proscriptions for action. They clarify what is forbidden, what is required, and what is permitted,[21] and thereby set specific expectations against which behaviour can be judged. In line with the principles and norms of the regime, investment treaties include rules for the protection of property rights. An increasing number of treaties also include rules on liberalization.

INVESTMENT PROTECTIONS

As described in the preceding text, almost all investment treaties include investment protections against discrimination and uncompensated expropriation. The vast majority include a raft of additional protections against other forms of state conduct adverse to foreign investment. The protections come in two forms. The first is through minimum standards of treatment, such as guarantees of fair and equitable treatment, and protection against breaches of investor–state contracts through so-called umbrella clauses. These protections are independent of how other investors and investments are treated, and are sometimes called *absolute* protections. The second is through non-discrimination protections, or so-called *relative* standards. These guarantee foreign investment treatment

---

[21] On this understanding of rules, see Ostrom (1990). Levy, Young, and Zürn (1995, 276–7) apply this understanding to international regimes.

at least as favourable as that enjoyed by domestic investors (national treatment) and foreign investors from third countries (most-favoured-nation treatment).

Some provisions entail relatively clear prescriptions about the extent of investor protection. Examples are clauses guaranteeing that investors can transfer funds relating to investments freely and without delay in an out of the host country's territory. Investors covered by the treaties are thereby entitled to exemption from any capital controls on repatriation of profits and other funds. For the most part, however, the provisions of traditional investment treaties are vaguely drafted, providing little clarity on what they forbid, require, or permit. Although they do more than merely state that foreign investors should have rights independent of host state laws—a core norm of the regime—most are so vague that they are more akin to general *standards* where it is up to tribunals to 'fill in the blanks' ex post (see e.g. van Aaken 2009).[22] Chapter 4 shows how tribunals have articulated more specific rules through interpretation and application of these standards. For now, it suffices to say that arbitrators have often given a very broad scope to investment treaty protections. Decisions have also at times been inconsistent and even contradictory. In response, many states have decided to turn towards more rules-based investment treaty models with higher levels of precision than in the past (Manger and Peinhardt 2017; Henckels 2016).[23]

If states breach the obligations they owe to foreign investors, the standard remedy in investment treaty arbitration is monetary compensation. This makes the substantive provisions of investment treaties akin to what law and economics literature calls 'liability rules' (van Aaken 2010; Bonnitcha 2014a). Such rules permit violation or interference with property rights, provided that compensation is paid to the original holder of the right (see generally Calabresi and Melamed 1972). Rights protected by liability rules are different from 'inalienable rights' that cannot be sold, violated, or transferred under any circumstances—for example, under international human rights law, a person cannot be tortured or forced into slavery regardless of whether compensation is paid. Liability rules also differ from entitlements protected by 'property rules', where the rights created by the regime can be traded openly, such as 'rights-to-pollute' under emissions trading schemes.

In investment treaties, the clearest example of a liability rule can be found in expropriation provisions, where states are allowed to take assets from foreign investors under certain circumstances,[24] but only if accompanied by compensation. Although the treaties offer no specific guidelines for how such

---

[22] On the distinction between rules and standards, see generally Kaplow (1992). On the role of precision in international law, see Abbott et al. (2000) and Abbott and Snidal (2000).

[23] On the trend towards greater precision in drafting recent investment treaties, particularly investment chapters in PTAs, see Chapters 4 and 9.

[24] Typically, if expropriations are non-discriminatory, comply with due process, and pursue a public purpose.

compensation should be calculated—a technical, but crucial question—the overall standard is typically the so-called Hull formula. This originates from the 1938 Mexican oil nationalization, where US Secretary of State Cordell Hull replied to his Mexican counterpart that the international minimum standards on expropriation required 'prompt, adequate, and effective compensation'.[25] Other investment treaty standards—such as fair and equitable treatment—do not explicitly provide that states can violate them in return for compensation. But since tribunals almost solely rely on compensation for all treaty breaches, these investment protections also function as liability rules in practice.

The prominence of monetary compensation in the investment treaty regime has become controversial in recent years (e.g. Hamby 2016b). Given the size of some awards (see the following text), an alternative default remedy would be restoring compliance of the host state's laws and regulations with its international obligation, as is the case in the trade regime. But compelling a state to comply with investment treaty obligations is arguably a more intrusive remedy than ordering it to pay compensation. For example, it may be preferable that states pay fair market value compensation for expropriations as part of a land reform, rather than being precluded by investment treaties from carrying out such reforms. Moreover, from an economic perspective, it is generally more efficient to allow states to 'pay for non-compliance' instead of compelling them to specifically perform their obligations (Posner and Sykes 2011; Pelc and Urpelainen 2015). That said, a crucial caveat is that the risk of large adverse awards may dissuade states from adopting measures that are non-compliant with investment treaties. In such cases, the practical effect of compensation as a remedy is similar to a remedy ordering compliance. This possibility is related to concerns about 'regulatory chill'—the hypothesis that the risk of investment treaty arbitration discourages states from adopting legitimate public policies (e.g. Tienhaara 2009; Pelc 2016). Chapter 9 considers the evidence for this proposition.

LIBERALIZATION

Whereas investment treaties establish far-reaching rules on investment protection, most are silent on the question of admission of foreign investment. Investment liberalization has traditionally been excluded from BITs of European

---

[25] At the time, Mexico argued in line with the Calvo doctrine that compensation was not required for general and impersonal takings, and that foreign investors should only get compensation in accordance with national laws. In practice, US oil investors in Mexico ended up with full compensation after the US government intervened (Maurer 2013).

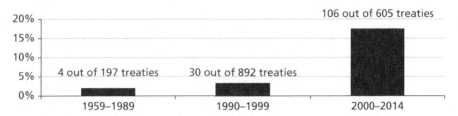

Figure 1.4 The liberalization dimension in investment treaties, 1959–2014

Note: Figure shows the share of BITs and other investment treaties that include binding liberalization provisions. The definition of 'liberalization' requires there to be references to both 'establishment' and 'acquisition', which thereby excludes some early US treaties that only mention 'acquisition' and 'expansion'. The figure does not distinguish between most-favored-nation and national treatment.

Source: Sample of 1695 English-language investment treaties. The authors thank Wolfgang Alschner for sharing this data.

states,[26] and since the bulk of investment treaties followed European templates—including many South–South BITs—the investment treaty regime has been characterised by an absence of binding liberalization rules.

Without such provisions, investors who seek international rules on liberalization must rely on other parts of the investment regime complex. For instance, the WTO agreement on services—GATS—includes some limited liberalization commitments. These are important as more than 60 per cent of global FDI is in the service sector (UNCTAD 2004). However, GATS does not cover foreign investment in the production of goods—for example, in the manufacturing and natural resources sector. In practice, this means that, even with an investment treaty in place, a host state typically has discretion over whether or not to admit foreign investments to its territory and, if so, subject to what conditions. Only if a state has allowed a foreign investment to be made in its territory does the protection of investment treaties kick in.

There are exceptions (Figure 1.4), the most important of which is the US BIT programme. US FCN agreements inspired the first US BIT model in the early 1980s, which unlike European BITs included binding provisions on both protection and liberalization. US BITs and PTAs thereby typically extend national and most-favoured-nation treatment to the pre-establishment phase, which applies to foreign investment in all sectors except those excluded in explicit reservation lists. NAFTA uses the same approach and, in recent years, a greater number of investment treaties have followed the US example—not least in investment chapters enshrined as part of broader trade agreements, such as the planned 'mega-regionals' TPP, RCEP, and TTIP.

---

[26] By contrast, the EU's trade agreements with Mexico (1997) and Chile (2002) included binding investment liberalization provisions, but no BIT-like protection provisions.

Decision-making procedures

The decision-making procedures of the investment treaty regime are highly decentralized. Unlike the international trade regime, there is no international focal point similar to that of the WTO with its secretariat and other institutions. This is the case both when it comes to negotiation of new treaties and the settlement of disputes under existing treaties.

NEGOTIATIONS

To understand the role of bilateralism in the investment treaty regime, it is useful to again consider the historical context. After the Second World War, the United States proposed an International Trade Organization (ITO), which would enshrine international minimum standards of treatment for foreign investors. This was one of a series of attempts during the early twentieth century to reach a multilateral agreement on investment protection (Van Harten 2007, 18–19; Newcombe and Paradell 2009, 15–16). However, just as developing countries had blocked previous attempts, Latin American countries and India objected to including Western investment protection standards in the ITO Charter.

Opponents of liberalization in the United States ultimately rejected the resulting compromise on this and other issues. Opponents considered that the agreement went too far, whereas proponents of an open international economic order found the agreement did not go far enough (Wilcox 1949, 145–8). Following the failure of the United States Congress to ratify the ITO, the less ambitious General Agreement on Tariffs and Trade (GATT) was put in charge of managing international trade in the post-war era. Foreign investment was completely absent from the GATT, however, and the conflict between developed and developing countries over which legal norms should govern the treatment and protection of foreign investors remained unresolved.

In response, capital-exporting states within the Organization for Economic Cooperation and Development (OECD) initiated a new round of negotiations for an international investment treaty in 1962 after a series of unsuccessful non-governmental attempts during the 1940s and 1950s. Named after its lead drafters, the Abs-Shawcross convention proposed a text founded on the international minimum standard of treatment for foreign investment (Fatouros 1961). While efforts continued through the 1960s, the convention eventually failed when it became clear that developing countries would never agree to its terms. During the 1970s, as noted in the preceding text, developing countries took advantage of their majority in the General Assembly of the United Nations to promote the New International Economic Order (NIEO), where foreign investment disputes should be settled through the application of domestic law in the courts of host states.

But what capital-exporting states failed to achieve at the multilateral level, they tried instead to gain through bilateral negotiations. Parallel to its multilateral efforts in the period after the Second World War, the United States expanded its existing network of FCN treaties and made them more focused on investment protection. While post-war FCN treaties did not become as central in the invest-ment regime complex as US policy-makers had intended (Vandevelde 2012), they did provide important inspiration for European states similarly eager to obtain favourable and legally binding standards for their investors abroad.

Having lost almost all its investments after its defeat in the Second World War, West Germany entered into a BIT with Pakistan in 1959. The treaty dealt solely with investment and was specifically customized to be negotiated between a developed and a developing country. This was to be the first of a great number of BITs signed during the 1960s, particularly by Germany and Switzerland. Given the opposition to such standards in the developing world, few developing coun-tries signed up to BITs at this time (Poulsen 2015, ch. 3). In 1974, the year of the Charter of Economic Rights and Duties of States, the international BIT network largely remained a phenomenon between Europe and Africa (Figure 1.5). Most other developing countries refrained as the North–South divide of the investment regime was entrenched. Keohane and Ooms observed at the time that:

Writing about alternative international regimes to deal with direct foreign investment may seem to be somewhat like discussing a perpetual motion machine: most people would like one for their own purposes; no one has ever built one; and discussions about their construction often take on a certain air of unreality (Keohane and Ooms 1975, 169).

Yet, the investment treaty regime was being built, slowly but steadily, treaty by treaty. During the 1980s, several new developing countries began signing investment treaties, including China. This increasing spread of BITs was partly due to growing activism among developed countries. Whereas Germany and Switzerland almost entirely dominated the early years of the BIT

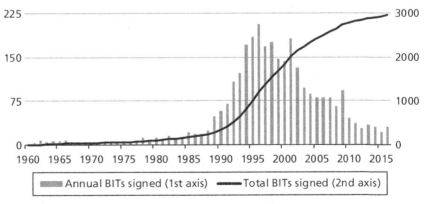

Figure 1.5 Spread of bilateral investment treaties, 1960–2016

Source: UNCTAD.

movement, this changed with the NIEO. The collective action of developing countries in the United Nations encouraged several developed countries to begin, or accelerate, their BIT programs in response.[27] This included the United States, which revived its investment protection program—now in the shape of BITs rather than FCNs.

States also attempted to conclude multilateral investment agreements, including the UNCTC Code of the 1980s (mentioned in the preceding text) and the Multilateral Agreement on Investment (MAI) under the OECD's auspices in the 1990s. The latter failed as OECD members ultimately had too little political appetite for an agreement after NGOs began campaigning actively against the initiative (Walter 2001). In recent years, various attempts of coordination have also occurred within different bargaining forums—for instance, within the OECD and UNCTAD, where networks of bureaucrats discuss and promote reforms. Overall, however, investment treaties have mostly been negotiated in bilateral or, increasingly, plurilateral forums, as multilateral attempts have failed for more than a century. This means that the bulk of the investment treaty network takes the shape of BITs, the majority of which were signed during the 1990s.

As is clear from Figure 1.5, the number of BITs signed and ratified has dropped considerably after the 1990s, the 'golden age' of the BIT movement. This is for three reasons. First, saturation—there are only so many treaties that can be signed. Second, the rise of investment treaty arbitration. As we discuss later in the book, developing countries in particular often signed up to investment treaties in the past with little appreciation of the potential liabilities (Poulsen 2015). After becoming subject to arbitrations, states are now beginning to realise the scope and potency of the regime, which in turn has prompted a slowdown in treaty adoption. A few developing countries—such as Ecuador, Venezuela, South Africa, and Indonesia—have also begun to terminate some of their investment treaties (see Chapter 8). Third, a partial shift from enshrining investment protection in BITs towards regional agreements with more parties and issues. As described in the preceding text, PTAs increasingly include investment protection chapters, and the mega-regionals such as TPP are set to reshape (and then lock in) the investment treaty regime if they are completed.

Despite the preference for preferential treaties (bilateral or regional), the investment treaty regime still has some multilateral characteristics (Schill 2009). With a few qualified exceptions, such as Ireland and Brazil,[28] practically all countries have ratified investment treaties that are highly similar. Where

---

[27] See also the collective response by OECD countries, the *OECD Declaration on International Investment and Multinational Enterprises*, 21 June 1976.

[28] Ireland is not a party to any BIT, but is a party to the ECT. It also has a 1950 FCN treaty with the United States that remains in force. Another partial exception is Brazil, which signed at least fourteen BITs in the 1990s that were never ratified since investment treaty arbitration was regarded as unconstitutional (Campello and Lemos 2015). Brazil has since signed several new BITs based on a

differences do exist in the wording of substantive protections, investors can often use most-favoured nation (MFN) clauses to 'level out' different levels of protection by importing provisions from other treaties. Moreover, because investment treaties include very broad definitions of investors and invest-ments, companies can make use of different treaties through corporate restructuring. There are important limitations to this 'multilateralization' argument, as we discuss in Chapters 2 and 4, but it does mean that the regime has more multilateral characteristics in practice than one would expect of a regime comprised largely of preferential treaties.

DISPUTE SETTLEMENT

Just as investment treaties have been negotiated with little centralized coord-ination, the rules contained in the treaties are applied through a privatized and decentralized dispute settlement system between investors and host states. To understand why, it is again useful to take a step back and consider how investment disputes were resolved before the investment treaty regime.

During the colonial era, the protection of foreign investment was largely in the hands of the home state. Within territories under imperial control, dis-putes were settled by imperial courts based on the laws of the home state. Outside formal empires, investment protection was based on international minimum standards under customary international law described in the preceding text, a breach of which could be asserted as a justification for intervention by home states. In their relationship with Latin American states in the nineteenth century, for instance, both the United States and European powers repeatedly used political and military tools to protect the assets of their investors (Lipson 1985). The practice was justified through the doctrine of diplomatic protection, whereby an injury to nationals abroad was considered an injury to their home state. The nineteenth-century version of this doctrine allowed the Great Powers to resort to force to advance the interests of their nationals abroad.

The result was that many commercial disputes turned into state-to-state conflicts at the time. The UN Charter made gunboat diplomacy unlawful after the Second World War, yet investment disputes during the Cold War occa-sionally turned into diplomatic disputes between states as well (Maurer 2013). In some cases, disputes were referred to investor–state arbitration. But unlike the recent wave of investment treaty arbitrations, consent to investor–state arbitration was typically given to *individual* investors in contracts—such as tailored concession agreements in the oil and gas sectors. On the rare occasions

very different model that does not include investment treaty arbitration. We return to the new Brazilian investment treaty program in Chapter 8.

in which states gave consent to investor–state arbitration with groups of foreign investors, it was in the context of ad hoc tribunals charged with settling disputes arising from extraordinary circumstances, such as the Iran–United States Claims Tribunal established in the aftermath of the Iranian Revolution. From the mid-nineteenth century to 1988, this 'first wave' of investor–state arbitration resulted in about 100 cases (Stuyt 1990).[29]

This was part of the background for the establishment of the ICSID Convention, signed in 1965. During the 1950s and 1960s, the World Bank kept getting dragged into such disputes, which detracted it from its broader mission (Parra 2012; St. John 2017). Given the controversy surrounding foreign investment at the time, the ICSID Convention was designed purely as a *procedural* mechanism for settling investment disputes through investor–state arbitration. Substantive investment protections were not included in the Convention and joining the Convention did not, in itself, entail the consent of a state to resolve any investment disputes through investor–state arbitration under the ICSID Convention.[30] Yet, according to the World Bank, the establishment of procedures for the resolution of foreign investment disputes through arbitration was critical, as it would 'remove disputes from the realm of diplomacy and bring them back to the realm of law' (ICSID 1970, 273).

As already described, early investment treaties did not allow foreign investors to bring arbitrations against host states, however. Instead, treaty disputes had to be submitted by the investor's home state to the International Court of Justice (ICJ) or state-to-state arbitration. Domestic laws generally did not provide advance consent to investor–state arbitration under the ICSID Convention either. In the absence of contracts providing for international arbitration, foreign investors in the early post-colonial era therefore often depended on their home state being willing to risk diplomatic goodwill and foreign policy objectives to fight for their interests abroad. Security, diplomatic, or other reasons unrelated to the investor's dispute could dissuade a state from filing an arbitration, exactly as in the trade regime (Davis 2012). As with most other regimes, early investment treaties thereby primarily established 'focal points' for mutual expectations without the backing of a strong enforcement mechanism (Poulsen 2017). This also meant that the treaties were much less central in the broader investment regime complex than they are today.

---

[29] Probably the oldest investor–state arbitration took place much before this period, involving a dispute between the French Suez Canal Company and Egypt in the mid-nineteenth century. The tribunal ordered Egypt to pay 38 million francs in damages for breaching its promise to supply forced labor to the French Suez Canal Company. Even though Egypt initially resisted complying with the award, it led to diplomatic negotiations that culminated in a convention between the company and Egypt in 1866, paving the way for the completion of the canal. For a detailed account, see Yackee (2016b).

[30] As Chapter 3 explains, some further act of consent by the host state is needed.

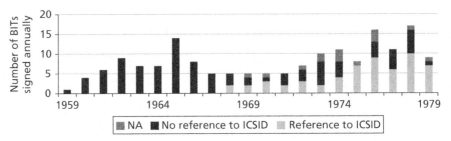

Figure 1.6 Reference to ICSID in investment treaties, 1959–1979

Source: Poulsen 2015.

This slowly began to change from 1969, when Italy entered into its BIT with Chad, allowing all investors covered by the treaty to submit disputes to international arbitration directly against its host state. In the following decade, several European states began to follow suit by including reference to investor–state arbitration under the ICSID Convention in their model investment treaties (Figure 1.6). Once the United States began negotiating BITs in the 1980s, US investment treaties also included investor–state arbitration clauses—unlike previous FCN agreements.

The decision to include investor–state arbitration provisions completed the 'modern' investment treaty and later facilitated the explosion in investment treaty arbitrations. Figure 1.7 plots the rise in investment treaty arbitration. Although it captures the majority of cases and decisions, some investment treaties and arbitration rules allow proceedings to be kept confidential, so we do not know the precise number of investment treaty arbitrations. What we do know, however, is that this 'second wave' of investor–state arbitration has been far more wide-ranging than the first.[31] Unlike investor–state contracts, the consent to arbitration enshrined in investment treaties allows *all investors* covered by the treaty to file arbitrations against the host state without having to first go through domestic courts. This reduces the transaction costs to investors of securing consent to investor–state arbitration, as investors no longer have to negotiate contracts on an individual basis (on reduction of transaction costs as a core regime function, see generally Keohane 1984). Since investment treaties tend to include very broad definitions of 'investors', consent by host states to arbitration in investment treaties opens up for thousands of potential claimants. Not only multinational firms, but their shareholders, financial

---

[31] The wave analogy is not perfect. Investors today still use some of the same instruments that they used to file arbitrations during the first wave of investor–state arbitration (most notably investor–state contracts), and states signed some of the treaties that investors use to file arbitrations during the second wave before the end of the Cold War. Finally, investor–state arbitration can also be based on consent in domestic laws. See Chapter 3.

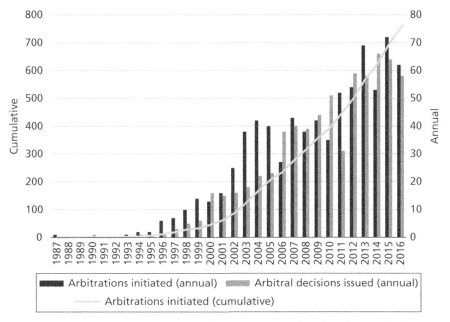

Figure 1.7 Known investment treaty arbitrations, annual registrations and decisions (1987–2016)

Note: Figure does not include investor-state arbitration under contracts or domestic investment laws. Only ICSID provides data on all its investment treaty arbitrations, and the figure may thereby underestimate the number of non-ICSID arbitrations.
Source: UNCTAD.

institutions, state-owned enterprises, and individuals too can file arbitrations. The wide definition of 'investments' equally expands the scope of the regime by covering disputes not only over FDI, but also portfolio investments, contracts, intellectual property rights, and much more. So given the scope of potential claims and claimants, the 'standing offer' by states in investment treaties to arbitrate disputes with a broad range of foreign investors was a revolutionary development (Alvarez 2011b).

Giving foreign investors the right to file claims against governments has proven highly controversial in recent years. Critics argue that foreign investors are already privileged in many countries, so it is not clear why they should have access to a separate legal mechanism to resolve disputes. Concerns are also raised that giving investors the right to file arbitrations can result in adventurous legal arguments that states would not pursue in state-to-state proceedings out of concern that such arguments might be used against them in later disputes. Suggestions have been made to instead rely on state-to-state dispute settlement—as in the WTO and early investment treaties—as this may filter out the most controversial arbitrations. In its recent investment treaties,

Brazil decided to exclude investor–state arbitration and instead allow only state-to-state arbitrations for this very reason. Proponents of the current regime, however, object to proposals to return to a system of state-to-state dispute settlement because it would unduly 'politicize' investment disputes (e.g. Baetens 2015, 9). We return to this discussion in Chapters 7 and 8.

Aside from the identity of the claimants, another important feature of investment treaty arbitration was alluded to in the preceding text. Whereas contract arbitration is based on specific rights and obligations negotiated on a case-by-case basis—often specified in hundreds of pages—investment treaty arbitration is based on broad and vaguely drafted investment protections. For this reason, investment treaties were rarely longer than seven or eight pages until recently. This has given arbitrators considerable flexibility in determining the nature of state liability, and the end result has made the second wave of investor–state arbitration cover a much wider range of state activity. Very few arbitrations have been won because of direct expropriation,[32] as investors have used investment treaties to address a much broader range of concerns about executive, legislative, and judicial acts—such as transparency, predictability, and fairness in government decision-making.

Arbitrations have been most prevalent in industries in which foreign investors make large, immobile investments—such as utilities and natural resources (Table 1.2). However, investors in manufacturing, finance, and various service industries have also used investment treaties to seek compensation. Most arbitrations have been brought by investors from developed countries against developing and transition states. Countries such as Argentina, Venezuela, and the Czech Republic have been subject to dozens of arbitrations. Increasingly, however, investors also bring arbitrations against developed countries. Canada has been subject to more than 20 arbitrations under NAFTA, and Spain has been subject to more than 30 arbitrations under the ECT. If investment treaty arbitration is included in either the TPP or TTIP, this may be a hint of what is yet to come.

At the time of writing, investors have won 27 per cent of concluded arbitrations, while states have successfully defended 36 per cent.[33] This 'win–loss' ratio is often used by both proponents and critics of the regime to make claims about the balance, fairness, or alleged bias of investment treaty arbitration. However, because investors are likely to take their probability of success into account when deciding whether to bring particular disputes to investment treaty arbitration, this win–loss ratio tells us little in and of itself.

---

[32] See Figure 4.2.

[33] These figures do not add up to 100 per cent because 24 per cent of cases settled prior to a final decision, an outcome which potentially also involves some payment of compensation by the host state. A further 10 per cent of cases were discontinued, and the remaining tribunals found liability but awarded no damages.

Table 1.2 Distribution of investment treaty arbitrations by country and sector

Most frequent industry	Most frequent host state	Most frequent home state of investor
1. Electricity and gas supply (153)	1. Argentina (59)	1. USA (148)
2. Mining, oil, and gas (130)	2. Venezuela (41)	2. Netherlands (92)
3. Manufacturing (115)	3. Czech Rep. (34)	3. UK (67)
4. Construction (70)	3. Spain (34)	4. Germany (55)
5. Financial services & insurance (69)	4. Egypt (28)	5. Canada (44)
6. Water and sewerage (45)	5. Canada (26)	6. France (41)
7. Transportation and storage (41)	6. Mexico (25)	7. Spain (38)
7. Telecommunications (41)	7. Russia (24)	8. Luxembourg (34)
8. Real estate (39)	8. Poland (23)	9. Italy (30)
9. Agriculture, forestry & fishing (30)	8. Ecuador (23)	10. Switzerland (24)
10. Professional services (16)	9. India (21)	
	9. Ukraine (21)	
	10. Kazakhstan (17)	

Note: UNCTAD codes many arbitrations as belonging to several industries; particular overlaps exist between arbitrations involving power utilities and the oil and gas industry. UNCTAD counts only arbitrations that have been formally brought, not notices of intent.
Source: UNCTAD, as of April 2017.

To illustrate this point, consider a situation in which arbitral tribunals interpret the provisions of investment treaties expansively. Investors are likely to respond by pursuing a wider array of cases that have an arguable chance of success in light of such expansive interpretations, including cases that ultimately fail. Such a system does not necessarily produce a higher ratio of investor 'wins' than would be the case in a system where arbitral tribunals interpret provisions narrowly and investors choose only to pursue those cases that have an arguable chance of success in light of such narrower interpretations. Questions of fairness, balance, and bias must therefore be assessed on other grounds than simple win–loss ratios, and this book provides some of the tools to conduct such analyses.

Among known arbitrations, tribunals have often awarded far less than what investors claim, yet some states have had to pay hundreds of millions of dollars in compensation, and a few awards have exceeded US$1 billion (Table 1.3). Not surprisingly, developing countries have borne the brunt of costs thus far, but the settlement between Germany and Vattenfall described in the Preface is an example of how investment treaty arbitration is no longer a one-way street. In fact, members of the OECD have lost or settled about 45 per cent of their arbitrations, despite having well-developed legal systems and functioning political institutions (Wellhausen 2016a). In 2017, for instance, an arbitral tribunal made an award of 128 million Euro plus interest against Spain.

Apart from the costs of compensation, the legal fees in investment treaty arbitration are very significant. Each party typically pays US$4–5 million per case, although some arbitrations have involved much higher fees (Hodgson 2014).

Table 1.3 Amount of compensation in investment treaty arbitration

	Claimed	Awarded by tribunal	Agreed in settlement
Less than US$1 million	5	11	0
US$1–9.9 million	38	34	2
US $10–99.9 million	150	47	15
US $100–499.9 million	158	19	9
US $500–999.9 million	53	3	5
US $1 billion or over	78	6	2
Not available	204	2	61

Note: Number of arbitrations. The data only includes known investment treaty arbitrations where UNCTAD had information about the amount of compensation claimed, awarded, or agreed to in settlement.
Source: UNCTAD, as of September 2016.

Even when states 'win' an arbitration, they often have to pay their own legal fees, as there is no established 'loser pays' principle in the regime.[34] The high legal costs mean that primarily large investors use investment treaty arbitration. And although there are plenty of examples of small- and medium-sized firms filing arbitrations, the bulk of compensation has indeed been granted to companies with billions in annual revenue and to wealthy individuals (Van Harten and Malysheuski 2016).

The dispute settlement mechanism is not just costly and wide-ranging; it is also uncertain. As tribunals are not bound to follow each other's rulings and there is no real possibility for appeal, we have already mentioned how some decisions have been inconsistent—and occasionally contradictory. In an early case, a US investor—Ronald Lauder—first lost his arbitration against the Czech Republic based on the Czech–US BIT. Within ten days, however, he won US$350 million in the same dispute, as he had filed a parallel arbitration through his Dutch holding company based on the Czech–Netherlands BIT. The facts of the case were the same, and the relevant treaty language was very similar, yet the two tribunals reached contradictory conclusions. This is an extreme case, but it serves to highlight the sometimes unpredictable nature of investment treaty arbitration for both states and investors.

Finally, apart from the scope and potential costs of investment treaty arbitration, the mechanism is notable for the identity of the adjudicators. The vast majority of cases have been decided by a small cadre of private lawyers. Table 1.4 highlights the emergence of elite arbitrators who together sit on the majority of tribunals in investment treaty arbitrations. Almost all are Western men, and fewer than half are experts in public international law. The delegation of adjudicative powers to such a small group of relatively homogenous individuals, most of whom have been lawyers in private practice, has prompted considerable controversy in recent years.

---

[34] However, recent US and EU investment treaties (e.g. CETA) do establish a 'loser pays' presumption in relation to costs.

Table 1.4 Most frequently appointed investment arbitrators

Arbitrator	Nationality	Gender	Specialist in public international law	Full-time practitioner	Number of appointments (% of known investment treaty arbitrations)
Brigitte Stern	France	Female	Yes	No	76 (11%)
Gabrielle Kaufmann-Kohler	Switzerland	Female	No	Yes	46 (7%)
Francisco Orrego Vicuña	Chile	Male	Yes	No	44 (6%)
Charles Brower	United States	Male	Yes	Yes	42 (6%)
Yves Fortier	Canada	Male	No	Yes	42 (6%)
Albert Jan Van den Berg	Netherlands	Male	No	Yes	35 (5%)
Marc Lalonde	Canada	Male	No	Yes	34 (5%)
Christopher Thomas	Canada	Male	No	Yes	33 (5%)
V.V. Veeder	United Kingdom	Male	No	Yes	30 (4%)
Karl-Heinz Böckstiegel	Germany	Male	No	No	30 (4%)
Bernard Hanotiau	Belgium	Male	No	Yes	28 (4%)
Bernardo Cremades	Spain	Male	No	Yes	26 (4%)
Rodrigo Oreamuno Blanco	Costa Rica	Male	No	Yes	25 (4%)
Piero Bernardini	Italy	Male	No	No	24 (3%)
Jan Paulsson	Sweden/France	Male	Yes	Yes	24 (3%)
Vaughan Lowe	United Kingdom	Male	Yes	No	24 (3%)
Stanimir Alexandrov	Bulgaria	Male	Yes	Yes	24 (3%)
Philippe Sands	United Kingdom/France	Male	Yes	Yes	23 (3%)
Juan Fernandez-Armesto	Spain	Male	No	Yes	22 (3%)
Pierre-Marie Dupuy	France	Male	Yes	No	20 (3%)
Toby Landau	United Kingdom	Male	No	Yes	20 (3%)

Note: Total number of arbitrations at time of this writing was 696. Column 5 refers to the arbitrators' professional career as a whole. None of these individuals maintain a full-time private practice alongside their many arbitral appointments (for time and conflict reasons).

Source: UNCTAD Investment Policy Hub and Waibel and Wu (2012).

One criticism involves the fees of the arbitrators. In a US$100-billion dispute against Russia, the three arbitrators charged almost US$9 million for their services, and their assistant received US$1.7 million (*Yukos v. Russia* 2014, paras. 1859–66). Although this is again an extreme case, it is highly unusual in any regime of public international law to have its adjudicators work for profit. Some critics suggest that such financial rewards give arbitrators an incentive to increase the judicial scope of the regime to facilitate more arbitrations. In addition, concerns have been raised whether arbitrators subordinate norms and values from other regimes—such as the environmental regime—and instead focus exclusively on investor rights in the adjudication of disputes. As one investment arbitrator has put it, 'the more [people] find out what we do and what we say, and how we say it, the more appalled they are' (V.V. Veeder quoted in Poulsen 2015, 4).

We return to these, and related, concerns in the concluding chapter of the book. For now, it suffices to say that these concerns were particularly pronounced in the context of the TTIP controversy, where the European Commission decided to promote a revised form of investor–state dispute resolution with an appellate body and a standing investment tribunal. The model involves a greater degree of institutionalization and state control of investment treaty arbitration. At the time this book went to press, the EU had successfully included its model in some agreements that were yet to enter into force—including in treaties with Canada and Vietnam. Importantly, however, the EU's new system for investor–state dispute resolution retains most of the main characteristics of investment treaty arbitration: investors enjoy standing to bring arbitrations against states before international arbitral tribunals; they need not exhaust local remedies; and the system will remain ad hoc on a treaty-by-treaty basis. The EU envisages this system of standing treaty-based investment tribunals as providing a stepping stone to the estab-lishment of multilateral investment court with jurisdiction to decide investor-state disputes arising under any investment treaty. The prospects of the EU's proposal for a multilateral investment court remain uncertain. But if such a court were established, it would constitute a significant departure from the treaty-by-treaty basis of dispute settlement within the investment treaty regime.

Although proponents of traditional investment treaties regard the new model of standing treaty-based investment tribunals as a 'seismic shift' (Nappert and Lavranos 2016), in our view the EU's proposal is a good example of how states have responded to criticisms of the regime through incremental reform rather than radical reconfiguration of the regime. While the regime's rules and procedures are increasingly subject to contestation and change, the principles, norms, and decision-making procedures have fundamentally remained the same.[35] So although the investment treaty regime could unravel if more states decide to withdraw, the regime is here to stay for now.

Conclusion

Proponents of investment treaty arbitration argue that host states are to blame for the recent explosion in arbitrations. Had they not behaved in arbitrary, discriminatory, or predatory ways towards foreign investors, arbitrations would not have been filed in the first place. On this view, the investment treaty regime increases the cost for states of failing to conform with norms of 'good governance' and the 'rule of law', which, in turn, should help spur

---

[35] See generally, Hasenclever, Mayer, and Rittberger (1996, 180).

prudent domestic reforms in the countries that need them most. In addition, without signing up to strong investor protections backed up by a neutral dispute resolution mechanism, many countries would be unable to attract much-needed foreign investment.

Critics are not persuaded by these arguments. They argue that foreign investors are already privileged in many developing countries, and that tribunals have often awarded compensation over and above what is reasonable. Moreover, the unpredictable nature of a dispute settlement system premised on ad hoc arbitration and the financial stakes involved for arbitrators themselves renders investment treaty arbitration unsuitable for settling disputes arising from the exercise of state authority. This is particularly the case, critics argue, as there is no convincing evidence that the treaties are economically or politically useful for host countries.

To provide a deeper understanding of these ongoing debates, this book integrates the legal, economic, and political perspectives on the past, present, and future of the investment treaty regime. As a starting point, the following chapter outlines the basic economics of foreign investment as well as the legal foundations of what it means to be an 'investor' and an 'investment' in the investment treaty regime.

2 Foreign Investment

Economic and Legal Foundations

Introduction

This chapter examines two foundational questions relating to foreign investment: why firms engage in foreign investment, and how inward foreign investment affects host states.[1] We then examine the scope of the investment treaty regime's coverage of different types of 'investors' and 'investments'. The chapter makes a simple yet often overlooked point: while investment treaties cover practically all forms of investment and all types of foreign investors, the economic drivers and effects of different types of investments vary significantly. This is important to keep in mind for later chapters addressing the law, economics, and politics of investment treaties.

It is commonplace to distinguish between foreign direct investment (FDI) and foreign portfolio investment. The distinction is based on control. If an investor controls a foreign enterprise, the investment is considered a direct investment; if the investor does not control a foreign enterprise, it is a portfolio investment. Standard statistical definitions of FDI require an investor to hold a minimum of 10 per cent of the voting power in a foreign enterprise, which is assumed to confer control (OECD 2008).[2] Examples of foreign portfolio investment include loans to foreign enterprises, financial products such as derivatives and futures, and minority shareholdings in foreign enterprises that do not confer a degree of control. This chapter focuses primarily on FDI. However, because investment treaties also cover many types of portfolio investment, we briefly discuss the economic effects of portfolio investment as well.

---

[1] We do not discuss the economic impact of outward foreign investment on home states. For recent contributions, see, for example, Desai, Foley, and Hines (2005; on US FDI), Arndt, Buch, and Schnitzer (2010; on German FDI), and Lee (2010; on Japanese FDI). Chapter 7 considers the politics of investment treaties in developed countries, and touches upon the political implications of the distributive effects of outward investment.

[2] Conceptualizing and measuring FDI poses challenges, to which we return in Chapter 6 when discussing FDI's impact of investment treaties.

Why do firms engage in foreign direct investment?

To understand the relevance of investment treaties for firms' investment decisions, a subject covered in Chapters 5 and 6, we need to understand why firms invest abroad in the first place. This, in turn, requires us to draw upon insights from the disciplines of both economics and international business. Prior to the 1960s, theories of foreign investment were typically extensions of economic models of international trade. It is therefore useful to begin with one of the most influential models of international trade: the Heckscher–Ohlin (H–O) model. Economic theories of international investment have progressed a long way from the H–O model, yet it nevertheless provides a useful starting point in assessing the drivers and patterns of foreign investment.

The simplest form of the H–O model involves two countries using two factors of production, capital and labour, to produce two types of goods.[3] Factors of production are assumed to be immobile, so the only possible economic exchange between the two countries is through trade. The model predicts that the capital-abundant country will export the good that is relatively capital-intensive to produce and import the good that is relatively labour-intensive. This trade in goods creates net economic benefits for both countries, but there are distributive effects *within* countries due to changing returns to capital and labour: owners of capital in the capital-abundant country and workers in the capital-scarce country become better off from trade, whereas owners of capital in the capital-scarce country and workers in the capital-abundant country are left worse off.

Now consider what happens if we assume that capital is mobile between countries and that international trade is costly, perhaps because there are tariffs or transaction costs associated with exporting and importing (Mundell 1957). In this case, capital owners will seek the higher returns available in the country that is initially capital-scarce, resulting in a flow of capital from the capital-abundant country to the capital-scarce country. The economic implications of these movements are, in important respects, identical to international trade within the basic H–O model.[4] Specifically, the flow of capital from the capital-exporting to the capital-importing country equalizes factor prices between both countries, leading to the same welfare and distributive effects as trade with the basic H–O model. The only significant difference between factor price equalization through international trade and

---

[3] A detailed exposition of the H–O model can be found in textbooks on international economics (e.g. Krugman, Obstfeld, and Melitz 2014). We focus only on a couple of core assumptions and insights relevant to this chapter.

[4] This theory has become known as the 'Mundell equivalency'.

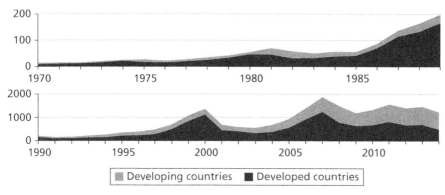

Figure 2.1   Global inward FDI flows, 1970–2014

Note: 'Developing countries' includes 'transition economies'. Figures in billions of US$ (current prices).
Source: UNCTAD.

factor price equalization through international capital movements is the location of production.[5]

Although the H–O model has considerable clarity and intuitive appeal, its predictions are difficult to reconcile with observed patterns of international investment flows. First, a core prediction from the H–O model is that capital flows from capital-abundant to capital-scarce countries. Yet, during the last 100 years, FDI flows have largely occurred *between* countries that are relatively capital-abundant (Lipsey 1999).[6] Developed countries are not just the most important source of FDI; they were also the primary destination for FDI until the 2000s (Figure 2.1). Although developing countries do receive a larger share of global FDI inflows than their share of global income, investments in the developing world are concentrated in relatively advanced developing countries. Least-developed countries attract only a slightly higher share of inward FDI than their (very low) share of world income, despite being scarce in capital (Markusen 2008).

Second, whereas the H–O model predicts that capital-abundant countries engage in outward foreign investment and capital-scarce countries receive inward foreign investment, countries typically engage in both (see Table 2.1). Developing countries accounted for a miniscule share of outward FDI for most of the twentieth century, but have become more important

---

[5] In comparison to factor price equalization through international trade, factor price equalization through international capital movements results in a larger share of production in the capital-scarce country. A portion of the return to capital owned by the capital-exporting country is then earned through foreign production. However, the returns to labour and capital in each country are unaffected.

[6] Although information is scarce, previous eras of international business activity also involved FDI between countries with similar factor endowments, for example, in Europe during the Middle Ages and cross-Atlantic flows during the nineteenth century (Jones 1996).

Table 2.1 FDI flows, selected economies, 1970–2010

	1970s		1980s		1990s		2000s		2010s	
	In	Out	In	Out	In	Out	In	Out	In	Out
USA	1.3	7.6	16.9	19.2	48.4	31.0	314.0	142.6	198.0	277.8
UK	1.5	1.7	10.1	7.9	30.5	17.9	121.9	235.4	49.6	39.4
Germany	0.8	1.1	0.3	4.7	3.0	24.2	198.3	56.6	65.6	126.3
Japan	0.1	0.4	0.3	2.4	1.8	50.8	8.3	31.6	−1.3	56.3
China	0.0	0.0	0.1	0.0	3.5	0.8	40.7	0.9	114.7	68.8
Hong Kong	0.0	0.0	0.7	0.1	3.3	2.4	70.5	70.0	82.7	98.4
India	0.0	0.0	0.1	0.0	0.2	0.0	3.6	0.5	27.4	15.9
Korea	0.1	0.0	0.0	0.0	1.0	1.1	11.5	4.8	9.5	28.3

Note: Figures in billions of US$ (current prices).

Source: UNCTAD (2015a).

sources of FDI over the last decade and a half. By 2014, developing countries accounted for 35 per cent of global outward FDI (UNCTAD 2015a), and countries like China and India had billions of dollars of both inflows and outflows. Traditional models that focus only on factor endowments fail to explain this two-way character of FDI flows.

A third deviation from the predictions of the basic H–O model is that much FDI is attracted not just to countries with high per capita incomes, but also to large markets (Brainard 1997; Markusen and Maskus 2002). In fact, market size is one of the most—if not the most—robust predictor of inward FDI (Chakrabarti 2001). For instance, the European Union's large integrated market is important *in itself* in attracting inward FDI. Approaches solely focusing on relative costs of capital resulting from different factor endowments have difficulty explaining this phenomenon.

A fourth and final observation, which goes some way to explaining the correlation between market size and inward FDI, is that a significant share of foreign investment is not motivated by different costs of production—as the H–O model predicts—but by the ability to sell goods in host countries. This is often called 'market-seeking' FDI, where production plants are set up abroad to service local markets. The investment is 'horizontal' in the sense that it replicates activities performed in the home market in a foreign market (Markusen 1984). This contrasts with 'efficiency-seeking' FDI, where different stages of a production process are integrated across borders in a 'vertical' supply chain (Helpman 1984; Helpman and Krugman 1985, ch. 12). Horizontal FDI is often made through mergers and acquisitions of enterprises in the host country, whereas vertical FDI is often conducted through 'greenfield' investments, where foreign investors establish new production facilities in the host country. The distinction between horizontal and vertical motives is porous in practice, and they often interact in ways that make predictions difficult (e.g. Yeaple 2003),[7] yet the distinction nevertheless remains analytically useful for some purposes.

In short, until the 1960s, FDI was typically seen through the lens of one of the most influential neoclassical frameworks to explain international economic exchange—the basic H–O model. Yet, this model failed to account for the significant share of global inflows to capital-abundant states, the two-way character of FDI flows, the attraction of FDI to large markets, and the significant share of horizontal FDI among countries with similar factor endowments.[8] As Chapters 7 and 8 show, these characteristics of international investment flows are also important for the *politics* of the investment treaty regime. For now, however, it suffices to say that, because of these shortcomings of the basic H–O framework, current work on foreign investment focuses not just on *country-specific* locational factors—as in traditional trade models—but also on *investor-specific* factors relating to ownership and organization within *imperfect markets*. This is the subject of the next section.

Foreign direct investment and the firm

When considering the motives of individual firms, the presence of FDI offers a puzzle. Setting up operations abroad is often costly. For market-seeking FDI, where production plants are replicated abroad, the firm may forego economies of scale associated with keeping production within the same plant ('plant-level economies of scale') (Navaretti, Venables, and Frank 2006, ch. 2). For instance, rather than producing extra cars in an existing plant at home, firms incur costs to set up new assembly plants abroad. For efficiency-seeking FDI, where different stages of production are separated in vertical production networks, the firm forgoes 'economies of integration' by increasing the costs of intra-firm trade. For instance, shipping different car components around the world is expensive and increases the complexity of production. Moreover, foreign firms can suffer from barriers due to language, culture, and exclusion from local business networks. This is all before one considers the potential political risks of operating abroad that investment treaties are designed to protect foreign investors from (e.g. uncompensated expropriation). So why is it that firms incur the costs and risks associated with FDI, rather than locating all production in their home market and supplying foreign markets through

[7] In the following section, we introduce other types of FDI—specifically, natural-resource-seeking FDI and asset-seeking FDI—which do not fit neatly within the categories of 'vertical' or 'horizontal' FDI.
[8] Another reason why basic versions of the H–O model perform poorly under empirical testing is that capital flows are assumed to be homogenous—that is, portfolio and FDI are treated as equivalent. We will not deal with this here (although see the following discussion on the economic impact of portfolio investment).

exports or, alternatively, licensing out production to local firms that already operate within foreign markets?

In contrast to theories of international trade, there are few general theories of FDI that purport to answer this question. Instead, there are various partial theories and many empirical contributions, which are often statistically fragile (Chakrabarti 2001). Particularly influential is Dunning's Ownership-Location-Internalization (OLI) framework, which is an attempt to summarize and classify a complex set of relationships between multiple variables that explain patterns of FDI (Dunning 1988; 2001). As such, it has difficulty generating testable predictions, but is nevertheless a useful way of organizing the review of the vast and heterogeneous literature on foreign investment in the following text.

The OLI framework asserts that three cumulative factors determine the extent, form, and pattern of FDI: (i) firms' ownership of products or production processes that give firms market power; (ii) locational advantages from operating in a foreign country rather than the home country; and (iii) internalization benefits from exploiting these advantages within the organizational structure of a firm rather than through arm's length agreements with foreign firms (such as licenses). All three factors must be present for FDI to be worthwhile.

OWNERSHIP ADVANTAGES

Ownership advantages are firm-specific assets that a multinational enterprise (MNE) can effectively apply to production in different countries, and which confer a *relative* advantage on the investing firm as compared to other firms. Some of the early works on internationalization of production focused on how these ownership advantages generate monopoly power for multinationals (Kindleberger 1969; Hymer 1976).[9] More recent economic models of FDI also incorporate firm heterogeneity arising from ownership advantages (e.g. Helpman, Melitz, and Yeaple 2004).

Ownership advantages can result from unique access to production inputs whether at home (e.g. raw materials) or abroad (e.g. international capital). More important, however, are 'intangible assets' such as intellectual property rights, superior production processes, or unique market access through established sales networks. These ownership advantages can result in economies of scale at the level of the firm—'firm-level economies of scale'—as replicating production processes does not require the firm to replicate its firm-specific assets as well (Markusen 2002). Toyota, for instance, can bring its brand,

[9] Marxist approaches to foreign investment rest on similar notions: market imperfections in industrialized countries generate monopolization tendencies, which in turn spur large corporations to engage in foreign investment (Brewer 2002, 261–5).

Table 2.2 Foreign-owned vs. national plants in the United Kingdom, average 1996–2000

	Foreign owned	UK owned
Size (number of employees)	485.16	203.45
Productivity I (value added/employee)	44.60	29.60
Productivity II (output/employee)	151.99	81.85
Capital intensity (capital/employee)	98.81	43.24

Note: Average for the pooled 1996–2000 sample. Productivity I, Productivity II, and Capital Intensity in thousands of pounds sterling.

Source: Criscuolo and Martin 2003, table 4.

technology, and expertise on research and development to any new manufacturing plant it sets up or acquires abroad. These firm-level economies of scale can counterbalance the reduction in plant-level economies of scale associated with FDI.

Assessing ownership advantages is no easy task due to the scarcity of data on economic performance at the firm level. One potential indicator of ownership advantages is a comparison of the productivity of foreign-owned firms with domestically owned firms. Table 2.2 compares UK-based plants in manufacturing, mining, and utilities. From this basic comparison, it might appear that foreign-owned firms are more productive than UK-owned firms.

However, differences between foreign-owned and domestically owned firms could arise from firm size. Foreign-owned firms tend to be larger than domestic firms, many of which operate only in their home market (e.g. Horst 1972). Moreover, foreign-owned firms are concentrated in sectors that are more intensive in capital, technology, and research than the economy as a whole. The importance of these factors is reflected in studies which show that differences in productivity are primarily explained by whether firms have operations in multiple countries (i.e. multinational vs. single-country firms), regardless of whether they are locally or foreign owned.[10] This supports the view that firms invest outside their home markets because they possess ownership advantages.

Related to the higher productivity of multinational firms is the often-repeated stylized fact that foreign-owned firms tend to pay higher wages than domestic firms. Affiliates of US multinationals, for instance, pay 40 per cent higher wages in high-income countries and about double the local

---

[10] For example, there is little difference between the productivity of UK plants owned by foreign MNEs and the productivity of UK plants owned by UK MNEs (Criscuolo and Martin 2009). Other studies have found similar results (e.g. Doms and Jensen 1998; Benfratello and Sembenelli 2002). Some studies do identify productivity advantages of *foreign* firms after controlling for factors such as size, multinationality, and capital intensity (e.g. Conyon et al. 2002), whereas others find none (e.g. Benfratello and Sembenelli 2002). No study has found that *multinationals* perform worse than firms without foreign operations (Navaretti, Venables, and Frank 2006, 43).

average wage in low-income countries (Graham 2000). Again, this could be due to a range of factors other than productivity advantages, such as greater propensity for foreign ownership in different sectors or domestic regions (e.g. special economic zones) than average domestic firms. Yet, even after controlling for these, and other factors, the higher wages of foreign-owned firms seem to persist (Aitken, Harrison, and Lipsey 1996; Lipsey and Sjöholm 2001). The wage premium of foreign-owned firms is at least in part due to higher productivity (Conyon et al. 2002; Brown, Deardorff, and Stern 2004, 318), which again suggests that these firms do in fact have ownership advantages.

Preferential treatment given by home states to firms operating abroad is another source of ownership advantage. Notably, state-owned or state-controlled enterprises often benefit from cheap credit and other benefits that provide a competitive advantage in both home *and* foreign markets. The utility sector is a good example. State-owned enterprises (SOEs) enjoying monopolies and/ or significant government subsidies dominate the sector (Capobianco and Christiansen 2011). As described in the following text, these ownership advantages have important policy implications for the investment treaty regime, as many SOEs invest abroad and most investment treaties cover such investments.

LOCATIONAL ADVANTAGES

Market power associated with ownership advantages is an insufficient reason for firms to engage in FDI. If Toyota is more efficient than an Indian car manufacturer, it can outcompete the Indian firm by simply exporting cars to India. The second condition for FDI is therefore the presence of locational advantages from operating abroad, such as the lower costs of production available in the host country or the ability to avoid tariffs on imports. In the absence of such advantages, firms will operate solely within their home markets and supply foreign markets through exports (Blonigen 2005; Faeth 2009).[11] Importantly, however, different types of locational advantages are important for different types of FDI. This is crucial for ongoing debates about the 'locational advantage' that investment treaties provide—something we return to in Chapter 6. Here, we briefly review four sources of locational advantages: (i) proximity to foreign markets; (ii) domestic investment policy,

[11] We single out particularly important aspects of this large literature. We exclude, for instance, the literature relating to risk diversification in terms of markets and products (for an early work, see Rugman 1977). Equally, we do not discuss the role of economic and financial crises (for a review, see Poulsen and Hufbauer 2011), industry agglomeration (for a review, see Navaretti, Venables, and Frank 2006, 147–9), 'oligopolistic reactions' (Knickerbocker 1973), regime type and property rights (Henisz 2000; Jensen 2003; Li and Resnick 2003; Choi 2009; Li 2009; Kerner 2014), labour rights (Busse, Nunnenkamp, and Spatareanu 2011), labour markets (Javorcik and Spatareanu 2005), and corruption (Wei 2000).

including investment subsidies and taxation; (iii) regional integration; and finally (iv) specific assets such as availability of natural resources and technology.

First, some scholars have argued that a proximity–concentration trade-off applies to market-seeking FDI (Brainard 1997). A firm gives up the *concentration* of production, by replicating plants abroad, but achieves *proximity* to a foreign market. By contrast, an exporting firm gives up proximity to foreign markets, while keeping production concentrated in one domestic plant. One implication of this theory is that higher costs of international trade should lead to more market-seeking FDI. Some FDI-inducing costs to trade are imposed by states, such as tariffs (Belderbos 1997; Blonigen 2002; Nunnenkamp and Spatz 2002), whereas other costs are inherent in exporting, such as transportation and communication (Buckley and Casson 1981; Markusen 1984).

For efficiency-seeking FDI, the impact of trade barriers is very different. Recall that the core locational advantages that drive vertical FDI are the availability and cost of inputs to production—as trade models predict. The availability of cheap labour is often important, but other factors fall under this category as well. Whereas trade costs can encourage horizontal FDI, they are bound to discourage vertical FDI by increasing the costs of intra-firm trade of intermediate goods (Hanson, Mataloni, and Slaughter 2001). While trade is a substitute for horizontal FDI, it should to be a complement for vertical FDI—for instance, in manufacturing and assembly. This is important, as about one-third of world trade happens within firms and 80 per cent of all trade involves multinationals (UNCTAD 2013). It is also relevant to consider in the context of broad economic integration agreements that include both trade liberalization and investment protection provisions (see Chapters 1 and 6).

A second locational factor that is relevant to both types of investments is that many states have reduced *barriers to investment* significantly.[12] Much of the increase of FDI into the developing world since the 1980s is due to deep reforms in their investment policies (see Chapter 1). Removal of restrictions on inward foreign investment in service sectors, for instance, prompted significant market-seeking FDI in telecommunications, energy, and transport (sectors that are all heavily represented in investment treaty claims, as Chapter 3 shows).

Many countries have gone beyond removing barriers to investment and also provide direct and indirect subsidies to foreign investors, such as preferential tax treatment, support services, infrastructure, as well grants and preferential

---

[12] The removal of barriers to investment is not, in itself, a locational advantage. Even if all barriers to foreign investment are removed, there must be some additional location advantage to investing abroad for foreign investment to occur. However, assuming that other underlying locational advantages are present, the removal of barriers to investment is a locational factor that makes foreign investment more likely.

loans (Johnson et al. 2016). For instance, 70 per cent of African countries use tax holidays to attract FDI (Cleeve 2008). Western countries also use direct and indirect subsidies in an attempt to attract FDI, particularly at the sub-national level (see e.g. Neven and Siotis 1993; Jensen et al. 2014). Although such incentives may offer locational advantages for multinationals at the margin, they can be economically detrimental for host states overall if they fail to effectively address market failures, in which case they would also distort competition with like domestic investors (see e.g. Blomström and Kokko 2003). As Chapter 5 underscores, this debate about investment subsidies is important for the investment treaty regime as it has parallels with the analysis of the economic benefits of investment treaties.

Aside from broader investment regulation and specific incentives, some studies have associated higher taxes with lower levels of FDI (Loree and Guisinger 1995; Hines 1999; De Mooij and Ederveen 2003). Yet, it is difficult to establish causal effects, as findings are bound to vary not just by types of investments but also types of taxes.[13] Aside from the extent of the fiscal burden, uncertainty arising from potential changes in a state's tax regime over time and the administrative burden of complying with tax laws may also affect FDI (UNCTAD 2015a, ch. 5). Moreover, any negative effect of higher taxation on inward FDI must be weighed against potential benefits of tax-funded public services, such as education and infrastructure, which are important for many multinationals (Madiès and Dethier 2012). Still, the relevance of taxation for multinationals is important to keep in mind—not least when considering the FDI impact of investment treaties as compared to, for instance, double-taxation treaties (see Chapter 6).

A third locational factor is the extent to which the host state is part of a broader, regionally integrated market (Chase 2003; Manger 2009).[14] For market-seeking FDI, regional integration is important in allowing access to bigger markets. For efficiency-seeking FDI, regional integration reduces trade costs and thus encourages vertical integration within the region. A well-known example is the growth of US FDI into Mexico after the adoption of NAFTA in 1994. Regional integration also benefits export-platform FDI. After the establishment of the European Single Market, for instance, small European countries such as Ireland became more attractive as export platforms, particularly if

---

[13] A more fundamental problem is distortion in the underlying data arising from the ability of firms to shift profits by engaging in transfer pricing (see e.g. Gresik 2001). In addition, multinationals engaged in tax evasion or avoidance are attracted to low-tax jurisdictions (Desai, Foley, and Hines 2006; UNCTAD 2015a, ch. 5). Many US multinationals, for instance, have an incentive to move their headquarters abroad ('inversions') to avoid paying US corporate taxes on unrepatriated profits earned outside the United States by their subsidiaries.

[14] Rugman argued in several contributions that most multinationals are not global but primarily regionally oriented (Rugman and Verbeke 2004; Rugman 2005). If true, this should further increase the importance of regional integration agreements.

they had lower factor costs or tax rates than other countries in the region (Navaretti, Venables, and Frank 2006, ch. 8).[15] A major challenge in assessing the impact of regional integration on FDI is to separate out the effect of domestic reforms and distinct elements of regional cooperation (e.g. trade liberalization, investment liberalization, and free movement of labour) under-taken at the same time (Blomström and Kokko 1997). As Chapter 6 shows, a similar challenge arises with many studies assessing the impact of investment treaties on FDI.

Finally, we turn to two other types of FDI that we have yet to introduce—namely, those that seek to secure assets. The first type is 'natural-resource-seeking' FDI, where firms invest abroad to access primary commodities. This was the dominant form of FDI during the colonial era (Jones 1996), but it constitutes a smaller portion of global foreign investment today. In 2012, 12 per cent of global inward FDI stock was in primary industries—most of which is in extractive industries—compared with 26 per cent in manufactur-ing and 63 per cent in services (UNCTAD 2015a).[16] In some countries, however, natural-resource-seeking FDI projects still dominate, such as parts of Africa, Central Asia, and Latin America. Examples from 2005 are included in Figure 2.2.

Some locational considerations are the same for natural-resource-seeking and efficiency-seeking investments. For instance, openness to trade should be important, as primary commodities must be exported back to the parent firm or onward to global markets. Similarly, policy openness to FDI in natural resource sectors matters. Other locational considerations differ, however, as natural-resource-seeking investment is critically dependent on the availability of primary commodities. This means that resource-seeking investors often tolerate conditions that would dissuade foreign investors in manufacturing or

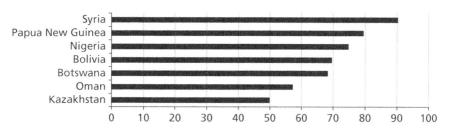

Figure 2.2 Share of extractive industries in the inward FDI stock of selected economies

Source: UNCTAD.

---

[15] Recall from Chapter 1 that Ireland is one of the very few developed countries without any investment treaties.

[16] Seven per cent remain unspecified.

services sectors, such as corruption or political instability. While studies of whether more stringent environmental regulation increases or decreases inward FDI in the aggregate have yielded mixed results (Brunnermeier and Levinson 2004), 'dirty' industries such as oil and gas could be more likely to favour jurisdictions with lax environmental standards at the margin (Copeland and Taylor 2004).[17]

Natural-resource-seeking investors may regard the value of investment treaties differently than other types of investors. In this respect, it is noteworthy that, despite its relatively small share of global FDI, roughly one in four investment treaty arbitrations relate to foreign investments in natural resources (see Table 1.2). This could be due to the high sunk costs and relatively long time horizons associated with these investments, as well as the potential negative impacts of natural resources on the 'quality' of governance in some contexts (Dupont et al. 2015). We return to these questions in Chapters 5 and 6.

The second type of asset-seeking investment is 'strategic asset-seeking investment', where firms invest abroad to acquire assets such as brands or technology (Makino, Lau, and Yeh 2002). Note that this type of investment fits poorly with the OLI framework overall as firms go abroad to seek, rather than exploit, firm-level ownership advantages. Yet, it has proven particularly important for developing country firms investing in developed countries to overcome latecomer disadvantages (Makino, Lao, and Yeh 2002; Cui, Meyer, and Hu 2014). It often takes place through mergers and acquisitions. For instance, Japanese acquisitions in the United States during the 1980s were motivated by the desire to access technology (e.g. Kogut and Chang 1991). A more recent example was when Lenovo, a Chinese firm, acquired parts of IBM (Rui and Yip 2008). As many investment treaties explicitly cover intellectual property as an 'investment' (also see below), the investment treaty regime could have important implications for firms investing abroad primarily to seek strategic assets.

INTERNALIZATION ADVANTAGES

Even when firms are internationally competitive and foreign countries have immobile locational advantages large enough that a commercial presence is useful, firms can benefit from these advantages without FDI. Rather than keeping the cross-border production process within the 'boundary of the firm'—i.e. internalization—firms can outsource activities within the production process (Rugman 1980). If there are no *internalization* benefits from retaining control over their ownership advantages, foreign firms will simply

---

[17] The evidence for this proposition is mixed and subject to significant data constraints. An influential study finds no evidence that environmental standards are important drivers of FDI for 'dirty' industries (Javorcik and Wei 2004).

license proprietary technology and other advantages for use by domestic firms at arm's length.

Many firms *do not* internalize the entire production process within a single corporate group. For example, Apple, Fujitsu-Siemens, and Lenovo all use a Taiwanese company, Inventec, to design, build, and distribute electronics products from its production plants in the Czech Republic, Malaysia, and Mexico (UNCTAD 2011, 129).[18] Identifying why, and under what circumstances, firms internalize their cross-border activities is the most important aspect of FDI theory. The extent of internalization also has important implications for the positive spillovers from foreign investment to the host economy, an issue we discuss in the text that follows.

Rooted in insights from the economics of organization and the theory of the firm (e.g. Coase 1937; Williamson 1981), we can see a multinational corporation as a special case of a firm with several plants (Buckley and Casson 1976, 36). Even when it is possible to rent out or license skills, technologies, and other assets to external partners, there are reasons for keeping production within a single firm or corporate group. Motivations for internalization vary depending on the type of investment; so here we will focus on the core distinction between horizontal (market-seeking) and vertical (efficiency-seeking) investments.

In general, market-seeking investors internalize cross-border activities to protect proprietary assets (e.g. brands, intellectual property) (see e.g. Horstmann and Markusen 1987). Coca Cola, for instance, prefers to pay for the establishment of parallel production facilities in the countries in which it intends to sell its products, rather than share its proprietary concentrate with external partners. In contrast, vertically integrated firms generally internalize activities within a single production chain to ensure the quality, compatibility, and security of supply of intermediate products (Caves 1996, 13). The alternative—namely, organizing a production chain through a series of external contractual relationships—can be difficult as writing, monitoring, and enforcing the contracts themselves are often costly.[19]

These theories of the reasons for internalization suggest a counterintuitive relationship between locational advantages and FDI, in that they imply that weak protection of intellectual property and contracts should *increase* the

---

[18] In 2010, the value of outsourced service provision and manufacturing conducted under third-party contracts was over US$1 trillion. Franchising and licensing each accounted for an additional US$300 billion, and management contracts for around US$100 billion (UNCTAD 2011).

[19] These concerns are related to the 'hold-up problem' that Chapter 5 discusses in more detail in relation to 'contracting' with host states (see, generally, Grossman and Hart 1986; Hart and Moore 1990). One example of incomplete contract monitoring and enforcement was when Mattel, a US multinational, was forced to recall millions of toys produced by contractors in China because of concerns with product safety (Walter and Sen 2009, 182).

likelihood of FDI.[20] In practice, however, the relationship between intellectual property protection and FDI is likely to be ambiguous. For even when production is internalized within the firm, concerns about imitation mean that foreign investors rank protection of intellectual property high among their priorities when considering where to invest, particularly in research-intensive industries (see generally, Javorcik 2004). Equally, vertically integrated firms are interested in contract enforcement insofar as least some of their activities are dependent on local partners, as is usually the case (Henisz 2000; see also Ahlquist and Prakash 2010).

In sum, we can understand FDI as the result of the interaction of three factors: ownership advantages, locational advantages, and internalization advantages. All three factors must be present for firms to invest abroad. However, different types of ownership, locational, and internalization advantages are relevant for different types of firms investing in different sectors. Understanding that different advantages are relevant to different types of investment is important when considering the impact of investment treaties on firms' decisions to invest abroad, a question we return to in later chapters.

The economic impact of foreign direct investment

Apart from understanding why firms invest abroad, the economic impact of such investments is also a critical question for the investment treaty regime. Countries often enter into investment treaties with the expectation that they would stimulate foreign capital flows, which in turn would promote the economic development of both host and home states (see Chapters 7 and 8). Moreover, different views on the economic impact of foreign investment influence proposals to reform the investment treaty regime. For example, some supporters of investment treaties equate criticism of investment treaty arbitration with opposition to FDI (Schwebel 2009, 269), and some NGOs campaigning against investment treaties are also staunch critics of multinational corporations.

Here, we focus only on the economic impact on host states, which is subject to a large and heterogeneous literature.[21] The impact of FDI is likely to vary considerably. An investment by Microsoft in Denmark and an investment by a Chinese oil company in Nigeria are very different propositions. As Moran notes, '[t]he idea that FDI has some generalized positive or negative impact on

---

[20] Recall that investment treaties can be used to protect intellectual property as an 'investment'. However, unlike investor–state contracts, commercial contracts with private partners cannot be enforced through investment treaties.

[21] On the economic impact on home states, see the references in footnote 1.

host-country growth does not make sense' (Moran 2011, 3). And indeed, there is only weak support for large exogenous effects of FDI on economic growth in the aggregate (Borensztein, De Gregorio, and Lee 1998; Carkovic and Levine 2005; Alfaro et al. 2010). Aggregate studies of the relationship between FDI and growth are likely to mask significant variations in the economic impact of different types of FDI in different circumstances (Nair-Reichert and Weinhold 2001). For this reason, recent empirical research is more nuanced, focusing on the circumstances in which FDI is beneficial from a host country perspective.

One potential benefit of FDI is through market reallocation of resources to more productive firms (Melitz 2003; Helpman et al. 2004). This is a core theoretical gain from international investment liberalization, but surprisingly few studies on FDI have tried to isolate it (Alfaro 2014; for an exception, see Alfaro and Chen 2015). In principle, however, the expansion of more productive firms should benefit a host country, even if those firms are foreign and their expansion displaces their less efficient domestic competitors.

In addition to direct benefits, FDI can also create indirect benefits, or 'spillovers', from foreign to domestic firms. The most well-known spillovers from FDI are the diffusion of knowledge and technology. These spillovers are thought to have an independent, positive causal impact on economic growth (Balasubramanyam, Salisu, and Sapsford 1996). A first type of spillover is horizontal. Here, domestic firms gain from technology and knowledge 'leakages' from foreign firms *within* the same industry. This can happen because of demonstration effects, where domestic firms emulate the production processes of foreign affiliates (Bengoa and Sanchez-Robles 2003), or because of worker mobility, where foreign firms train workers who then change jobs and work for local firms.[22] The latter effect is consistent with the finding that foreign-owned firms tend to invest more in educating workers than locally owned counterparts (te Velde 2002; on wage differentials, see earlier). A second type of spillover is vertical. Here, domestic firms gain from engaging directly with foreign firms *across* industries, which in turn can occur through backward linkages (foreign firms buy from domestic suppliers) and forward linkages (foreign firms sell to domestic purchasers).

Evidence suggests that horizontal FDI spillovers are often small or nonexistent (Iršová and Havránek 2013). This is consistent with the internalization rationale for FDI (mentioned earlier), where foreign firms guard ownership advantages to protect their competitive position (Javorcik 2004).[23] There is

---

[22] There are also illicit forms of technology and knowledge 'leakage' through industrial espionage. We do not cover these here.

[23] Some studies even find that FDI is correlated with a decline in the productivity of local firms (e.g. Konings 2001). One possible explanation is that local firms lose market share as a result of competition from foreign entrants, meaning that they lose their ability to benefit from economies of scale in production (Aitken and Harrison 1999).

much stronger evidence to support the existence of positive vertical product-ivity spillovers associated with backward linkages (e.g. Javorcik 2004; Kugler 2006). This could be because foreign firms have an interest in sharing technol-ogy and quality-control techniques with their suppliers (Moran 2007). Recent work has also identified significant 'forward' vertical spillovers among local firms that use inputs supplied by foreign-owned firms (Newman et al. 2015).

Increasingly, scholars are careful to acknowledge that spillover effects depend on host country characteristics (Blomström and Kokko 2003).[24] Diffusion of technology, for instance, requires absorptive capacity among domestic firms. In one influential study, Borensztein, De Gregorio, and Lee (1998) concluded that FDI had a positive impact on growth but only in countries with highly educated workforces. According to this analysis, coun-tries such as Afghanistan or Eritrea are unlikely to exploit FDI spillovers (see also Xu 2000). Similarly, Alfaro et al. (2010) find that local entrepreneurs depend on well-functioning local financial markets if they are to take advan-tage of FDI-induced knowledge and technology spillovers (see also Hermes and Lensink 2003; Javorcik and Spatareanu 2009). Along the same lines, other work has highlighted the importance of trade policy, arguing that FDI does not spread knowledge and technology in highly distorted economic environ-ments (e.g. Balasubramanyam, Salisu, and Sapsford 1996).

The impact of FDI can also vary across sectors and industries. Due to data limitations, most economic studies focus exclusively on aggregate FDI flows or stocks. Alfaro and Charlton (2007) are an exception. They use a range of difference metrics, such as skill requirements for employees, as proxies for the 'quality' of FDI in different sectors and industries and find that higher-quality FDI has a greater positive impact on economic growth. These findings are consistent with firm-level data from the United Kingdom, where intra-industry spillovers are absent in the aggregate, but present for high-skill industries (Girma, Greenaway, and Wakelin 2001; see also Kathuria 2000 for India).

More generally, we should expect greater positive spillovers in sectors where there are close linkages between domestic and foreign firms—such as labour-intensive manufacturing—than in sectors where there is less scope for linkages—notably, natural resource extraction (UNCTAD 2001, 138). This is reflected in concerns about 'enclave' economies where foreign firms entirely *internalize* their production with little, if any, engagement with the local economy. As an extreme example, consider the following description by a

---

[24] The majority of studies cited in this paragraph do not seek to isolate spillover effects. Rather, they examine the extent to which the impact of inward FDI on economic growth in the aggregate is conditional on the presence of various other factors. However, the existence of spillovers provides a possible explanation for findings that the impact of FDI on economic growth is conditional on other factors.

journalist of a US$1.5 billion natural gas facility in Equatorial Guinea that Marathon Oil, a US firm, built and operated:

The plant—like many oil installations in the developing world—could have been on the moon for all the benefit it offered local business... Instead of buying cement from a Malabo company that might not deliver on time, Marathon built a small cement factory on the construction site. Raw materials were imported, and the factory would be dismantled when construction ended. The trailers in which (foreign workers) lived were prefab units—no local materials or local had been used to build them. The plant had its own satellite phone network, which was connected to the company's Texas network—if you pieced up a phone you would be in the Houston area code, and dialling a number in Malabo would be an international call. The facility also had its own power plant and water-purification and sewage system. It existed off the local grid (Maass 2009, 35–6).

Such examples are consistent with evidence that investments in extractive sectors are more likely to have negative effects for host states with little institutional and regulatory capacity (Hendrix and Noland 2014).[25]

Equally, there may be important differences with respect to the home state of the investor. For example, Chinese firms investing in infrastructure and extractive industries in Africa are widely believed to employ more migrant workers from the investor's home country (i.e. China) than comparable Western firms (e.g. Alessi and Xu 2015). There is insufficient data to confirm this hypothesis, however, or to explore its implications for the impact of Chinese outward FDI. This reflects a wider lack of research on the differential impacts of FDI according to the home state of the investor (for exceptions, see Girma and Görg 2007; Javorcik and Spatareanu 2011).

A final factor is the investor's mode of entry. Neto, Brandão, and Cerqueira (2010) find that FDI made through greenfield investments has a greater positive economic impact on host states, through greater capital formation and productivity growth, than FDI through mergers and acquisitions. Other studies report similar findings (Harms and Méon 2011). Although limited data prevents strong conclusions (Alfaro 2014), these findings are relevant for the study of the investment treaty regime as well, since investment treaties protect foreign investors irrespective of their mode of entry.

The central conclusion emerging from this section is simple: while FDI *can* play an important role for economic development in host states, its impact is contingent on host state and investment-specific conditions. Investment treaties, however, grant protections to practically all foreign investors and investments—the subject of the next, and final, section.

---

[25] For broader arguments considering other challenges associated with managing natural resources in such countries, see, for example, Ross (2012).

'Investments' and 'investors' covered by investment treaties

To appreciate the *legal* architecture of the investment treaty regime, it is not enough to understand the nature of the procedural rights (Chapter 3) and substantive rules (Chapter 4) of the regime. We also need to identify the investments and investors that fall within its coverage. In light of the previous sections of this chapter, the scope of coverage of investment treaties is also critical when assessing the *economic* effects of the regime.

Each investment treaty defines the range of foreign 'investments' and 'investors' that fall within the coverage of the treaty in question. In principle, one would expect these legal definitions to align with the types of actors and assets that states wish to attract and protect. In practice, however, there is a significant incongruity between the legal coverage of investment treaties, which protect almost every type of economic asset owned or controlled by a foreign 'investor', and policy debate about investment treaties, which proceeds on the assumption that the purpose of investment treaties is to attract FDI (Bonnitcha 2016).

INVESTMENTS

Investment treaties almost always define the range of 'investments' that they cover. The vast majority contain broad definitions that encompass a very wide range of economic assets. Most treaties refer to 'every kind of asset' owned or controlled by a foreign investor, followed by an open-ended list including tangible property, debt and equity, bonds, contractual rights, intellectual property rights, and concession contracts. Other investment treaties use closed lists, but the lists are often so long that they cover practically every type of asset as well. Most treaties cover investments made both before and after the treaty entered into force.[26] Aside from provisions dealing with investment liberalization (see Chapter 4), exclusion of certain sectors from the scope of the treaty's coverage is rare.[27] The vast majority of investment treaties do not distinguish between 'high-quality' and 'low-quality'—or 'sustainable' and 'unsustainable'—investments. Instead, they cover practically all assets owned or controlled by foreigners.

---

[26] Coverage of pre-existing investments typically extends only to state conduct in relation to such investments after the treaty has entered into force. As a rule, investment treaties do not allow foreign investors to challenge the conduct of the host state that took place prior to the treaty's entry into force.
[27] One sectoral exclusion found in some investment treaties concerns government procurement. ACIA Article 3(4)(c) completely excludes government procurement from the scope of the agreement; NAFTA Article 1108(7)(a) contains a partial exclusion of government procurement.

Investment treaties' coverage extends well beyond FDI to include assets that fall within the standard definition of portfolio investment—including share-holdings of less than 10 per cent, loans, and other contractual rights that do not confer control over an enterprise. Notably, some tribunals have also held that sovereign debt also falls within the coverage of investment treaties (e.g. *Abaclat v. Argentina* 2011). Such broad coverage of the investment treaty regime has important economic implications, as most research on portfolio investments is sceptical of their benefit to host states (see e.g. Prasad, Rajan, and Subramanian 2006; Kose et al. 2009). The absence of control over an enterprise in the host state means that portfolio investment is less likely to involve the transfer of technology, skills, and know-how into the host state than FDI (Colen, Maertens, and Swinnen 2013). Flows of portfolio investment are also more volatile than FDI (Albuquerque 2003), which can leave a country vulnerable to rapid withdrawal of funds during times of crisis (Stiglitz 2000; Reinhart and Reinhart 2008). Countries with inadequate regu-latory and institutional frameworks are also prone to deeper and longer financial crises after liberalizing their capital account to short-term portfolio flows (e.g. Ostry et al. 2010).[28] This is relevant for the investment treaty regime as well, as investment treaties not only protect portfolio investments, but also liberalize the capital account for 'investors' covered by the treaties through clauses that permit the free transfer of funds (see Chapter 4). It is partly for these reasons that some recent treaties wholly or partially exclude portfolio investments from coverage—such as the 2015 Brazilian and Indian model BITs. These are exceptions, however, and the vast majority of investment treaties in force extend coverage to a wide range of portfolio investments.

Another systemic implication of broad definitions of 'investment' is that they generally allow shareholders—including minority, indirect, and non-controlling shareholders—to file investment treaty arbitrations in relation to the treatment of an enterprise in the host state in which they hold shares (e.g. *Enron v. Argentina* 2004).[29] This significantly increases the number of potential claimants in relation to any particular investment dispute. In this respect, the investment treaty regime differs from almost all advanced domes-tic legal systems, which contain strict limitations on the ability of shareholders to file claims for reflective loss (such as declining value of shares) arising from the treatment of an enterprise in which they hold shares (Gaukrodger 2014a).

---

[28] It is partly for this reason that the IMF revisited its policy on capital account liberalization following the global financial crisis in 2008, and is now more open to the use of capital controls as an appropriate policy response to financial crises in some circumstances (IMF 2012; see also Rodrik 2010).

[29] A small minority of tribunals have attempted to articulate some limits to this principle. For example, the tribunal in *Standard Chartered v. Tanzania* (2012, paras. 230–2) held that 'passive' indirect ownership of shares in an enterprise did not fall within the scope of the UK–Tanzania BIT. In the view of the tribunal, some 'active' contribution to the investment by the investor was required.

In addition to definitions of the 'investments' covered by individual investment treaties, some arbitral tribunals have held that the ICSID Convention places further limitations on the types of 'investments' in relation to which investment treaty arbitration is possible under the ICSID Convention. Insofar as the ICSID Convention imposes such limitations, a question that remains controversial, they do not affect the scope of investment treaties themselves. Such limitations are relevant only in arbitrations under the ICSID Convention.[30]

Article 25 of the ICSID Convention provides for arbitration in claims arising 'directly out of an investment'. Although the term 'investment' is not defined in the ICSID Convention, some arbitral tribunals have held that it has an inherent meaning, which may be narrower than the range of 'investments' covered by a particular investment treaty. Specifically, some tribunals have held that the concept of an 'investment' in the ICSID Convention refers to:

(a) a contribution,
(b) of a certain duration over which the project is implemented,
(c) which involves the sharing of the operational risks, and
(d) a contribution to the host State's development (*Salini v. Morocco* 2001; *Bayindir v. Pakistan* 2005).

According to this view, arbitration under the ICSID Convention is only possible if the purported 'investment' possesses these characteristics.

On this basis, tribunals have occasionally refused to allow claims in cases in which the foreign investor's activity in the host state did not, in the tribunal's view, make a contribution to the host state's development. For example, in *Malaysian Historical Salvors v. Malaysia* (2005), the tribunal held that a contract granting a foreign firm the right to locate and salvage cargo from a shipwreck in Malaysia was not an 'investment' within the meaning of the ICSID Convention because it did not make a significant contribution to Malaysia's economy. However, the tribunal's reasoning was exceptional, and the decision was annulled in 2009.[31] The vast majority of tribunals have held either that there is no requirement that an 'investment' must contribute to the development of the host state, or that, if such a requirement does exist, that it is easily satisfied.

---

[30] We examine the role of the ICSID Convention in establishing a framework for investment treaty arbitration in more detail in Chapter 3. In short, most investment treaties provide for arbitration under the ICSID Convention, although a foreign investor initiating an arbitration generally has a choice of whether to bring the arbitration under the ICSID Convention or some other set of procedural rules—for example, the UNCITRAL Rules.

[31] ICSID Annulment proceedings allow the losing party to seek the review of awards on a limited number of procedural grounds. A successful annulment sets aside the original award. See Chapter 3.

INVESTORS

Investment treaties also cover a very broad range of foreign 'investors', grouped under two types: individuals (natural persons) and juridical entities (legal persons). With respect to the first category, investment treaties generally cover all individuals who are nationals of the home state according to that state's laws. Investment treaty arbitrations concerning foreign investments owned or controlled by individuals are in the minority, although their prevalence varies by region. Among cases against countries of South and East Asia and the Pacific, for instance, the share is only 7 per cent (ICSID 2015). In contrast, individuals have brought almost 20 per cent of the ICSID cases against African and European states (ICSID 2016a; ICSID 2016b.) One well-known example of an investment treaty claim brought by an individual involves German entrepreneur Franz Sedelmayer under the Germany–USSR BIT, alleging mistreatment of his security services firm in Russia.[32]

Juridical entities bring the majority of investment treaty claims. Most investment treaties define the set of legal persons falling within a treaty's coverage to include all juridical entities constituted in the 'home' state.[33] As such, companies qualify as 'investors' of the state in which they are incorporated, even if they do not have any significant business operations in that jurisdiction. This approach reflects standard legal principles, according to which a company is considered to have the nationality of its place of incorporation. A minority of investment treaties impose the additional requirement that a company must have its headquarters—or a significant commercial presence—in the 'home' state to be considered an investor of that state.[34]

The practical effect of treaty provisions that recognize all legal entities incorporated in a given state as 'investors' covered by the treaty is to expand the potential scope of application of any one investment treaty. Figure 2.3 depicts three scenarios. In the first scenario, a company decides to invest in a foreign country through a wholly owned subsidiary company incorporated in a third state, perhaps because the structure has tax benefits. In this case, the subsidiary in the third country qualifies as an 'investor' under the BIT between the third country and the host state and can therefore file an investment treaty arbitration against the host state. For example, one tribunal allowed a Dutch subsidiary of Mobil Corporation, a US company, to file an arbitration against

[32] Sedelmayer owned a US-incorporated company, which made the investment in Russia. The US company did not qualify as an 'investor' under the Germany–USSR BIT. Moreover, Russia and the United States have signed an investment treaty, but that treaty never entered into force. However, as a German national and owner of the company that made the investment in Russia, Sedelmayer qualified as an (individual) 'investor' under the Germany–USSR BIT.

[33] For example, Article 1(b) of the 2004 Dutch Model BIT, which simply refers to legal persons constituted under the law of the home state—a very broad definition.

[34] For example, Article 1(2)(b) of the France–Mexico BIT.

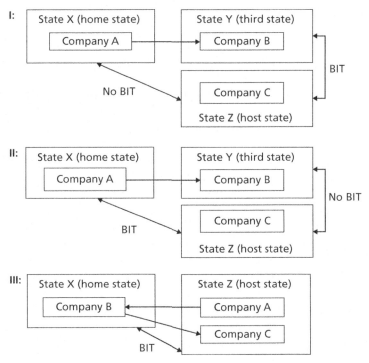

Figure 2.3 Corporate structuring and investment treaty coverage

Venezuela, despite Mobil admitting that it had restructured its investment by inserting the Dutch intermediary into the chain of ownership *after* the investment was originally made, solely to obtain coverage of the Netherlands–Venezuela BIT (*Mobil v. Venezuela* 2010). This restructuring was necessary because there was no investment treaty between the United States and Venezuela.

A second scenario is when investments are owned via subsidiaries incorporated in third countries that do *not* have a BIT with the host state, whereas the home state of the 'parent company' does. This scenario is illustrated in part II of Figure 2.3. In such situations, the ability of the investor (Company A) to bring an arbitration against the host state (State Z) based on its indirect ownership of the underlying investment depends on the terms of the treaty in question (e.g. *HICEE v. Slovakia* 2011). However, in the absence of clear limitations in the treaty in question, arbitral tribunals have generally allowed investors to bring arbitrations based on indirect ownership of foreign investments.

A third scenario involves a domestic investor structuring an investment in its 'home' state via a foreign-incorporated company to obtain investment treaty coverage. For example, in a case against Ukraine, a Lithuanian-incorporated company 99 per cent owned by Ukrainian nationals was held to fall within the definition of a Lithuanian 'investor' under the Lithuania–Ukraine BIT. The tribunal considered that the Ukrainian nationals' control of the company was irrelevant. This type of arbitration is also possible where the shareholders of a company incorporated in the host state are companies incorporated in a foreign country and the shareholder companies are ultimately owned and controlled by nationals of the host state in which the investment is located. For example, in the largest investment treaty arbitration to date, a company incorporated in the Isle of Man (United Kingdom) that owned shares in the Russian oil company Yukos (2014) successfully brought an arbitration under the ECT against Russia following the nationalization of Yukos, even though the claimant company had no substantial business operations in the Isle of Man and was ultimately controlled by Russian individuals.

These definitional issues relating to the coverage of investment treaties have profound policy relevance for the investment treaty regime. Formally, investment treaties are preferential agreements negotiated between two or more countries. However, the ease with which investors can engage in 'treaty shopping'—the structuring of an investment to bring it within the coverage of at least one investment treaty—raises questions about whether the regime is preferential in practice. The practice of treaty shopping poses practical challenges for states. States are not necessarily aware of how the ownership of particular investments in their territory is structured and, therefore, will not be in a position to determine, in advance, which investments fall within the coverage of any given investment treaty. On this basis, some scholars and commentators argue that rational host states should assume that obligations contained in any one of their investment treaties are 'owed to every State and every company' operating in their territory (Legum 2006, 4). According to this view, the possibility of treaty shopping transforms a web of formally preferential investment treaties into a *de facto* multilateral investment treaty regime (Schill 2009).

Such claims of multilateralization must be carefully qualified. As noted in the preceding text, the definitional terms of investment treaties vary. Some do require investors to have a genuine link with the 'home' state, thereby limiting the scope for treaty shopping. The extent to which the existing network of investment treaties functions as a genuinely multilateral regime also depends on how common the practice of treaty shopping is.[35] This is an empirical question, on which little research has been conducted. However, evidence of low levels of awareness of investment treaties among foreign investors, which is discussed in Chapter 6, suggests that treaty shopping is not a routine practice

---

[35] Investors may not only or even primarily shop for the most advantageous investment treaty. Tax considerations are likely to be more important in practice. But little empirical research has been done on this question.

among foreign investors.[36] Finally, investment treaty tribunals themselves have articulated at least some limits to the practice of 'abusive' treaty shopping. In *Philip Morris v. Australia* (2015), the tribunal concluded that Philip Morris transferred its Australian business to a Hong Kong subsidiary for the purpose of bringing an arbitration under the Australia–Hong Kong BIT at a time when a dispute about Australia's tobacco plain packaging legislation was already foreseeable. The tribunal held that 'abusive' restructuring of this sort was impermissible, and dismissed Philip Morris' claims.

A distinct issue is the *types* of juridical entities that qualify as 'investors' under investment treaties. In general, investment treaties do not limit the types of juridical entities that qualify as 'investors', either based on the business that an entity is engaged in, or an entity's ownership and corporate governance arrangements. As such, banks, hedge funds, and private equity firms all fall within the coverage of investment treaties. These financial actors are, themselves, significant foreign investors. From 1990 to 2003, for instance, US banks acquired almost US$25 billion in FDI (Goldberg 2007), a figure that does not include their much larger holdings of portfolio investment. And private equity funds now account for about one in four of cross-border mergers and acquisitions worldwide (UNCTAD 2015a, 15).

Moreover, investment treaties do not generally require a juridical entity to be owned by private individuals to fall within the coverage of investment treaties (Feldman 2010). As mentioned in the preceding text, SOEs also fall within the treaty definition of covered 'investors' under most investment treaties. The investment treaty regime's coverage of SOEs has significant systemic implications. SOEs own or control roughly US$2 trillion worth of foreign assets and 15,000 foreign affiliates (UNCTAD 2014). To put these figures in perspective, there are approximately 100,000 MNEs with almost 900,000 foreign affiliates in world economy, and these foreign affiliates held assets worth US$102 trillion in 2014 (UNCTAD 2014). As a rule, sovereign wealth funds (SWFs) also qualify as 'investors' under investment treaties. SWFs currently control over US$100 billion of foreign investment (UNCTAD 2014). Because the investment treaty regime was originally intended to protect and promote *private* investment, the coverage of these types of 'sovereign investors' has attracted considerable attention in recent years (see e.g. Alvarez 2012a; Feldman 2016; Poulsen 2016).

---

[36] At the time of this writing, a very large share of foreign investment stocks is not formally protected by investment treaties, as there is no treaty between the EU and the United States. These two economies are by far the largest sources and destinations of foreign investment (OECD 2015a). To date, there is no evidence that it is common practice for transatlantic investment to be structured to bring it within the protection of other EU or US BITs. On this basis alone, at the time this manuscript went to press, the investment treaty regime cannot be said to be genuinely multilateral.

Conclusion

This chapter has examined the motivations for and effects of foreign investment. It showed that the economics of FDI is complex and, to some extent, contested, and that different types of foreign investments have different drivers and effects. In other contexts, states' investment policies reflect these insights. For example, many countries target investment promotion activities in particular industries, on the assumption that the targeted industries are more likely to generate economic benefits (Harding and Javorcik 2011). In contrast, virtually all investment treaties provide blanket protection to practically all foreign investments, including investments falling outside standard definitions of FDI.

The analysis in this chapter suggests that the economic effects of investment treaties depend not just on *whether* investment treaties affect the volume of foreign investment—something that Chapter 6 reviews—but also on *how* and *why* investment treaties impact *different types* of foreign investment in *different countries*. These are important conclusions to keep in mind, as the next two chapters turn attention to the legal rights granted to foreign investors in the investment treaty regime.

3   **Investment Treaty Arbitration**

Introduction

The resolution of investment disputes through international investor–state arbitration is central to the investment treaty regime. This mechanism operates outside the host state's own legal system and allows foreign investors to obtain binding monetary awards against host states, backed by international enforcement. As Chapter 1 describes, the rapid growth in the number of disputes brought to investor–state arbitration under investment treaties since the late-1990s has transformed the investment treaty regime from an obscure field of international law to a central part of the investment regime complex. Investment treaty arbitration is also the focus of the strongest criticisms of the investment treaty regime.

The focus of the chapter is on investment *treaty* arbitration, where a host state's consent to investor–state arbitration is contained in an investment treaty. In addition, we also touch on two other modes of consent to investor–state arbitration already introduced, namely investor–state contracts and domestic investment laws. The first section explains the basic features of investment treaty arbitration, drawing attention to the similarities and differences between investment treaty arbitration and other dispute resolution processes—such as domestic and international courts, investor–state arbitration based on contracts, as well as state-to-state arbitration.[1] The second section describes different institutions and arbitral rules for investment treaty arbitrations. It outlines the phases of investment treaty arbitrations and core features of the arbitration process, such as the choice of remedies. The third section deals with issues that arise following the conclusion of an investment treaty arbitration—notably, the review, enforcement, and compliance with arbitral awards. The fourth section evaluates two potential alternatives to investment treaty arbitration—alternative dispute resolution (ADR) and litigation in domestic courts.

---

[1] For an in-depth treatment of the law of investment treaty arbitration (discussed in this chapter) and of substantive investment law (discussed in Chapter 4), see e.g. Dolzer and Schreuer (2012) and McLachlan, Shore, and Weiniger (2017).

Features of investment treaty arbitration

Unlike domestic courts with defined, mandatory jurisdiction over particular classes of cases,[2] arbitration is a binding, private dispute resolution mechanism, based on the *agreement* of the disputing parties to submit a dispute to a particular person or persons for resolution (Mattli 2001, 920; Mustill 2004, 209; Lazareff 2005, 478). Arbitrators have resolved disputes for thousands of years on this basis (Westermann 1907; Ræder and Synnestvedt 1912; Hale 2015). The arbitrator listened, considered the facts and legal arguments, and then rendered a final and binding decision (Blackaby and Partasides 2015, 1–2).

Modern arbitration can be divided into three basic categories, based on the *types of parties* involved:

(i) *Arbitration between private parties, such as individuals or companies.* This includes both purely domestic disputes—for example, with regard to employment—and disputes that have a significant international dimension, notably disputes arising from international business transactions. This latter type of arbitration is known as *international commercial arbitration.*

(ii) *Inter-state arbitration for disputes between states*—for example, in disputes concerning who has sovereignty over territory.

(iii) *Investor–state arbitration between a private party and a state*, the focus of this chapter.

THREE MODES OF CONSENT TO INVESTOR–STATE ARBITRATION

Arbitration in all its forms is based on an agreement between the disputing parties. This requirement of party consent is the first characteristic of investor–state arbitration. States typically consent to arbitration *before* an investment dispute has arisen, in one of three ways: (i) investment contracts (investor-state contracts); (ii) domestic laws—typically investment laws; and (iii) investment treaties. Figure 3.1 shows the frequency of these three modalities of consent in arbitrations under ICSID rules (see further in the text that follows).

In addition to the consent of the state, the consent of the investor is also needed to settle disputes through investor–state arbitration. In the case of investment contracts, the contract contains the advance consent of both the investor and the state to resolve disputes arising under the contract through

---

[2] One caveat is that the parties to a contract can agree to submit disputes arising under that contract to arbitration, or to a particular state's courts, to the exclusion of other states' courts. Nevertheless, the basic principle remains that the jurisdiction of domestic courts is not based on party consent. For example, the ability of a pedestrian to sue the driver of a vehicle that has injured him or her in an auto accident does not depend on an agreement between the pedestrian and the driver to resolve disputes in court.

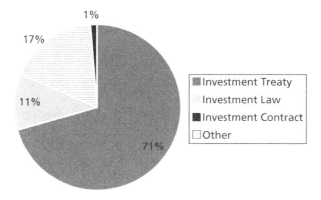

Figure 3.1 Instruments of consent in ICSID arbitrations (1972–2016)

Source: Author compilation from the ICSID website, based on 573 ICSID Cases, as of August 2016.

arbitration. In contrast, an investment law or an investment treaty contains only the advance consent of the state to arbitrate certain categories of disputes with a specified—but typically very broad—class of investors (see Chapter 2). This form of arbitration is known as 'arbitration without privity', because the offer to arbitrate by the host state is not addressed to a particular actor with which the host state already has a legal relationship (Paulsson 1995). Instead, an individual investor consents to arbitration only after the investment dispute has arisen by initiating the arbitration, thereby satisfying the requirement of mutual consent by accepting the host state's *standing offer* of arbitration.

There are two important implications from this temporal gap between a host state's advance consent to arbitration in investment treaties or investment laws and the acceptance of this offer by an individual investor. First, investors typically retain the option of using other dispute resolution mechanisms prior to initiating the arbitration.[3] This is unlike investment contracts, which often contain advance agreement of the parties to use arbitration as the exclusive process for resolving all disputes arising under the contract in question. Second, the question of whether host states can withdraw consent to arbitration prior to acceptance by the investor arises only with respect to 'arbitration without privity'. The prevailing view is that, in principle, host states can withdraw their consent in investment treaties or investment laws before investors accept the offer to arbitrate.[4] With investment laws, such withdrawal takes effect immediately. However, in the case of consent to arbitration contained in an

[3] The terms of the host state's consent to arbitration may limit such choice. For example, so-called 'fork-in-the-road' clauses contained in some investment treaties preclude an investor from bringing a claim to investment treaty arbitration if the investor has already litigated that claim before domestic courts (see Schreuer 2004b).
[4] *Ruby Roz v. Kazakhstan* (2013, paras. 152–6). However, the *Rumeli v. Kazakhstan* tribunal (2008, para. 335) qualified the host state's consent to arbitrate in an investment law as an 'acquired right'.

investment treaty, the rules on treaty termination[5] and the 'survival clauses' in investment treaties circumscribe the ability of a state to withdraw its consent to arbitrate by unilaterally terminating the treaty in question. Survival clauses typically allow arbitration with respect to investments made prior to the host state's termination of the investment treaty for a further 5–20 years (Harrison 2012; Voon and Mitchell 2016). As Chapters 1 and 9 discuss, these clauses limit the ability of states to unilaterally reform or exit from the investment treaty regime.

The use of investment contracts and domestic investment laws as modes of consent to investor–state arbitration predates consent to investor–state arbitration through investment treaties.[6] Most important are investor–state arbitration clauses in investment contracts. Such clauses remain standard practice in many sectors, particularly for investments that depend on a project-specific agreement between the host state and the investor—for example, investments in extractive industries or infrastructure (Yackee 2008c; Brower and Schill 2009).

As described in Chapter 1, early investment treaties—including FCN treaties—did not contain consent to investor–state arbitration (Yackee 2008b; Roberts 2014). Rather, they provided solely for state-to-state arbitration. The first investment treaty with consent to investor–state arbitration was the 1969 Chad–Italy BIT, but it is only since the 1980s that investment treaties have commonly consented to investor–state arbitration (Yackee 2008b). Moreover, early versions of investor–state arbitration clauses in investment treaties were often narrow. For example, Russian investment treaties prior to the 1990s and Chinese investment treaties prior to 1998 seemingly allowed for investment treaty arbitration only in a narrow range of disputes 'concerning the amount of compensation' payable in the event of expropriation (Gallagher and Shan 2013; Ripinsky 2013).[7]

The remainder of this chapter hones in on investment *treaty* arbitration, although many of our observations apply equally to investor–state arbitration based on contracts or investment laws.

SELECTION OF ARBITRATORS BY THE DISPUTING PARTIES

As is the case with most forms of arbitration, in investment treaty arbitration, the disputing parties appoint the arbitrators in the dispute. There are normally three arbitrators. The investor bringing the arbitration appoints one

---

[5] The default rule in the Vienna Convention on the Law of Treaties (VCLT) provides for twelve months' notice. Investment treaties can provide for other rules. Importantly, they commonly include survival clauses. States can still withdraw, but the investment treaty remains in force for a certain period of time.

[6] Cf. the *Suez Canal Company* arbitration described in Chapter 1.

[7] Investor–state tribunals have been divided, however, on whether questions such as whether expropriation occurred in the first place are excluded from the tribunal's jurisdiction under such clauses. In addition, some investors have been able to circumvent these limitations by relying on the most-favoured nation provision of the treaty in question (see Chapter 4).

arbitrator, the host state defending the arbitration appoints another arbitrator and the two parties (or their party-appointed arbitrators) then try to agree on the appointment of a third, presiding arbitrator. Although different investment treaties designate different sets of arbitral rules to govern investor–state arbitrations, all arbitral rules governing investor–state arbitrations share this same basic model of party appointment. This is a major point of contrast to domestic courts, in which tenured judges who are not appointed by the disputing parties for their particular dispute decide cases (see Table 3.1).

The investment treaty itself, or the arbitral rules designated by the investment treaty to govern the arbitration, also specify a default appointing authority—typically an arbitral institution or individual, such as the secretary general of ICSID or the secretary general of the Permanent Court of Arbitration (PCA). The appointing authority only steps in to appoint arbitrators if the disputing parties fail to appoint an arbitrator within the timeframe provided by the relevant arbitral rules (e.g., in the case of ICSID arbitrations, within 90 days from the day on which the secretary general has dispatched the notice that ICSID has registered the request for arbitration), or if the parties are unable to agree on the appointment of the presiding arbitrator. Such institutional appointments are a backup to prevent a party that has consented to arbitration from frustrating the process by subsequently refusing to cooperate (Schwebel 1987, ch. 3). With the United Nations Commission on International Trade Law (UNCITRAL) and the PCA rules, the appointing authority also decides on challenges to individual arbitrators—for example, on grounds of bias (see the following text). For these reasons, the appointing authority is an important consideration when deciding between competing arbitration rules.[8]

Irrespective of who appoints them, all arbitrators are subject to requirements of neutrality and impartiality. A party can challenge the appointment of a person whom it believes lacks these prerequisites for sitting as an arbitrator.[9] Either the other two arbitrators or the appointing authority deal with such challenges. But although arbitrators do occasionally withdraw voluntarily prior to a formal decision on the challenge, challenges to arbitrators are rarely successful in investment treaty arbitration in practice. For example, in *EDF v. Argentina* (2008), Argentina challenged the appointment of an arbitrator who also served as a non-executive director of UBS. The Swiss bank held 5 per cent of the shares of a company that the claimant's parent company effectively controlled. A collective investment vehicle for Swiss pension funds affiliated with UBS held 1.5 per cent of the shares in the claimant's parent company. The arbitrator did not disclose her UBS board position when she accepted her

---

[8] Other factors, such as the duration and costs of proceedings and the enforceability of the resulting awards (which we review in the text that follows), may also come into play.

[9] Equally, an arbitrator's lack of independence or impartiality is grounds for annulling or denying recognition to an award under the New York Convention (see Section 4 in the text that follows).

appointment as an arbitrator. The two co-arbitrators found that these facts did not call into question the arbitrator's ability to exercise independent judgment, and rejected the challenge.

Typically, neither investment treaties nor the arbitral rules governing investor–state arbitration provide for additional requirements relating to the age, experience, or professional qualifications of the arbitrator. In theory, the pool of potential arbitrators is therefore limitless (Pauwelyn 2015). In practice, however, parties almost always appoint practising lawyers or academics from within the small, club-like community of international investment law (Puig 2014; see generally Dezalay and Garth 1996; Mattli and Dietz 2014, ch. 1). Chapter 1 showed the high rate of re-appointments in investment treaty arbitration from a very small pool of individuals. This preponderance of 'repeat arbitrators' stems from the incentive of each party to appoint arbitrators from inside this community to maximize the ability of 'their' arbitrator to persuade their co-arbitrators, as newcomers may carry less weight in the deliberations of the tribunal (Queen Mary School of Arbitration 2010; Kapeliuk 2012, 276). The culture and incentives created by an elite, club-like transnational community of investment arbitrators has, however, become controversial—something we return to in Chapter 9.

The mandate of arbitrators is to resolve a particular dispute based on the applicable investment treaty. Once a tribunal issues its final award, the arbitrators' appointments terminate, and the lifecycle of the arbitral tribunal comes to an end. While arbitral tribunals arguably exercise governance functions and develop international investment law—something we return to in Chapter 9—their ephemeral existence contrasts markedly with national or international courts, which are permanent and whose decision-makers are appointed for fixed terms or for life (Mackenzie 2010). Table 3.1 illustrates

Table 3.1 Security of tenure of different adjudicators

Court/tribunal	Length of term	Possibility of reappointment	Appointing mechanism	Concurrent roles
US Supreme Court	Life	Not applicable	US president on advice of the Senate	Excluded
German Constitutional Court	12 years	No	Bundestag and Bundesrat elect eight judges each	Only minor professional activity (e.g. teaching)
ICJ	9 years	Yes	UN General Assembly and Security Council	No formal rules; at the discretion of the ICJ president
WTO Appellate Body	4 years	Yes	Dispute Settlement Body	Permitted, subject only to checks on impartiality and conflicts of interest
Investor State Tribunal	Appointed for each dispute	Yes	Disputing parties/appointing authority	Permitted, subject only to checks on impartiality and conflicts of interest

these central distinctions between judges and arbitrators, using the German Constitutional Court and the US Supreme Court as examples of domestic courts, and the WTO Appellate Body and the International Court of Justice (ICJ) as examples of international courts.

INVESTOR STANDING TO BRING ARBITRATIONS AGAINST STATES

Apart from requiring the consent of both disputing parties and relying on party-appointed arbitrators, a third characteristic of investment treaty arbitration is the ability of investors to bring arbitrations directly against a host state without the involvement of, or the need for approval by, their home state (Sykes 2005). Traditionally, only states had the ability to bring disputes to international courts and tribunals. The investment treaty regime is at present the only international regime in which non-state actors have direct standing against governments based on treaty commitments without the need to exhaust local remedies (see next subsection).[10] The scope of the protections under investment treaties (see Chapter 4) and the number of potential claimants (see Chapter 2) mean that direct standing in investment treaty arbitration has revolutionized the resolution of investment disputes and led to an upsurge in investment treaty arbitrations.

Whereas tribunals established under investment treaties have jurisdiction over claims by investors against the host state, the opposite is typically not the case.[11] The scope for host states to formulate counterclaims against investors—that is, claims closely linked to the principal claims of the investor—is very limited (Kryvoi 2012; Bjorklund 2013). As a rule, states wishing to file claims against investors are limited to commencing separate domestic proceedings, and these proceedings are unlikely to influence the outcomes of parallel or subsequent investment treaty arbitrations. This makes investment treaties asymmetrical in two important respects: (i) only host states have obligations vis-à-vis investors; and (ii) only host states give *advance* consent to arbitration (Alvarez 1997; Muchlinski 2011; Dumberry and Dumas-Aubin 2013; Muir Watt 2014). We return to this issue in Chapter 9.

Investor standing in investment treaty arbitration raises important questions that will be addressed in this book. Two are worth highlighting at this point. Firstly, a core *legal* question surrounding investor standing is about the exact nature of the rights created by investment treaties. In particular, are the substantive rights of investment treaties granted directly to foreign investors, or is the ability of investors to bring investment treaty arbitrations solely a

---

[10] Direct standing of private parties is also a feature of regional human rights regimes such as the ECHR, but subject to a stringent requirement to exhaust local remedies; see the text that follows.

[11] As for contractual arbitration, the rights of the host state against the investor depend on the terms of the contract.

procedural entitlement to enforce the home state's substantive rights under the investment treaty (Douglas 2003; Roberts 2015)? This debate has important implications for the ability of home states to intervene in investment treaty arbitrations and their ability to settle the claims of their nationals (Alvarez 2011b). For instance, if the substantive rights in investment treaties belong to the home state rather than investors, the United States could agree to waive all investment treaty claims by US investors against Argentina arising from Argentina's financial crisis as part of a global settlement between the United States and Argentina, and could do so without the consent of the US investors. If, instead, the substantive rights belong directly to the investors themselves, the home state could not waive these claims without their consent. This question remains unresolved among legal scholars.

A second core question is why investors should have the right to file investment treaty arbitrations against states in the first place. One potential answer is that direct investor standing reduces the need for the investor's home state to play a role in enforcing compliance with the provisions of investment treaties.[12] Consider the comparison with the trade regime, for instance. In the WTO system, only states can bring complaints that another state has breached its obligations under WTO law. Exporters can only protect their interests by convincing a state to initiate proceedings in the state's own name. To take a prominent example, in 2011, tobacco company Philip Morris's Hong Kong–based subsidiary initiated investment treaty arbitration against Australia relating to tobacco plain packaging (*Philip Morris v. Australia* 2015). In parallel, tobacco companies enlisted the backing of Cuba, the Dominican Republic, Honduras, Indonesia, and the Ukraine to bring WTO complaints against Australia.[13] In the investment treaty regime, by contrast, investors do not have to rely on their home state to file claims against host states.

The comparison with state-to-state dispute resolution is particularly relevant as virtually all investment treaties include not just investor–state arbitration provisions, but also state-to-state arbitration provisions that allow a state party to an investment treaty to bring disputes with another state party 'concerning the interpretation and application of the treaty' to arbitration.[14] In addition, Chapter 1 described how early investment treaties *only* included state-to-state dispute settlement provisions, where disputes could be submitted at the ICJ, for instance. Also, a handful of recent investment treaties do not contain consent to investor–state arbitration either, and provide only for state-to-state dispute settlement. Examples include the investment chapters of the Australia–US FTA

---

[12] Chapter 8 considers whether investment treaty arbitration has 'depoliticized' investment disputes.
[13] *Australia—Tobacco Plain Packaging* (WTO 2012; 2013). Both Philip Morris International and British American Tobacco supported the complaining states with legal advice (Thompson 2012). In May 2015, the WTO Panel granted Ukraine's request to suspend its proceedings with Australia. The four other WTO disputes are still pending as this book goes to press.
[14] Cf. Article 37 (1) of the U.S. Model BIT 2012.

(AUSFTA), the Australia–Japan FTA, and the Brazil–Mozambique BIT. At present, it is unclear whether these rare and isolated examples mark the beginning of a wider trend toward the negotiation of investment treaties without investor–state arbitration.

Proponents of state-to-state dispute settlement note that, since state claimants (acting on behalf of their investors) are repeat players, they have an incentive not to advance legal arguments that are likely to 'backfire' in future arbitrations that might be brought against them. By contrast, investors may be more prone to advance 'adventurous' legal arguments as host states cannot commence arbitrations against them and they therefore only have 'offensive' interests in investment treaty arbitration (see Chapter 1). In addition to reducing the number of arbitrations—as there are fewer potential claimants—state-to-state dispute settlement may thereby also be an effective 'filter' on particularly controversial claims. Similar arguments are made in favour of more specific state filters on investment treaty arbitrations, such as investment treaty provisions barring investors from bringing certain types of claims unless both state parties agree that the dispute should not be resolved by domestic legal proceedings (e.g. Kleinheisterkamp and Poulsen 2014). Such a filter is included in NAFTA, for instance, for investment disputes involving taxation (Park 2001).

In contrast to these arguments, proponents of investor standing are concerned that the return of states as gatekeepers could 're-politicize' investment disputes (e.g. Brower and Blanchard 2014; European Federation for Investment Law and Arbitration 2014), a discussion we return to in Chapter 8. For the time being, however, there are only four known state-to-state arbitrations under investment treaties to date (Roberts 2014). In some cases, home states have also used the treaties as 'focal points' for informal settlement negotiations (Poulsen 2017),[15] but direct investor standing remains a core—if not *the* core—characteristic of the modern investment treaty regime.

NO NEED TO EXHAUST LOCAL REMEDIES

A fourth feature of investment treaty arbitration is that investors normally do not have to exhaust local remedies before commencing arbitration. 'Exhaustion of local remedies' refers to the requirement of customary international law that non-state actors must first attempt to resolve a dispute through the legal system of the host state before they can turn to international tribunals, provided that the local remedies are in fact reasonably available (i.e. that

---

[15] For instance, Noble Energy, a US investor, raised the possibility of invoking the Israel–US FCN treaty in a dispute involving oil and natural gas rights in Israel (Wrobel 2010). Equally, European officials suggested in the 1970s that their investment treaties had been useful in resolving investment disputes informally, despite an absence of investor–state arbitration provisions (Poulsen 2016, 111).

domestic courts are not obviously dysfunctional or biased). For example, an individual can only bring proceedings against a state to the European Court of Human Rights (ECtHR) once domestic legal procedures in that state have run their course, or if pursuing redress through domestic proceedings would be obviously futile. The requirement to exhaust local remedies also applies to the ability of a home state to exercise diplomatic protection on behalf of its nationals (see Chapter 1). The exhaustion requirement is a powerful mechanism to accord deference to national legal systems, in that it gives national legal systems the opportunity to correct any potential violations of international law before the home state can raise the claim at the international level (Alvarez 2011a, 77).

In investment treaty arbitration, by contrast, the default rule is that local remedies need not be exhausted. In theory, investment treaties could require the exhaustion of local remedies as a condition of access to investor–state arbitration, but thus far state parties have hardly ever included such a requirement.[16] A minority of investment treaties requires a foreign investor to attempt to resolve a dispute in the host state's courts for a minimum period of time (e.g. a waiting period of 18 months) prior to initiating arbitrations (Pohl, Mashigo, and Nohen 2012), but this is still a far less onerous requirement than the obligation under customary international law to *exhaust* reasonably available local remedies.

PROCEDURAL FLEXIBILITY

A fifth feature of investment treaty arbitration is the absence of detailed and prescriptive rules governing the conduct of proceedings. The disputing parties have broad flexibility to decide how the arbitration should be conducted, subject only to mandatory requirements of the arbitral rules they have chosen to govern the arbitration (see the following text) and mandatory procedural rules imposed by the treaty. This means that parties generally have the flexibility to agree on the location of hearings, the degree of confidentiality, the timeline for the arbitration, who can and cannot be called as witnesses, and the rules governing document production. If the disputing parties cannot agree on these issues, the arbitral tribunal has broad discretion to decide on how it conducts the proceedings. Regardless of whether the parties decide these issues by agreement, or the arbitral tribunal decides, tribunals generally specify detailed rules for the conduct of each arbitration by issuing procedural orders.

In contrast, civil cases before domestic courts are typically governed by a set of mandatory procedural rules dealing with issues such as the location of proceedings, admissibility of evidence, document production, etc. (Blackaby and Partasides 2015, 21). The competent court is limited in its ability to vary

---

[16] An exception to the general trend is the 2016 Indian Model BIT, where a foreign investor has to exhaust local remedies for a period of five years before commencing investment treaty arbitration; Articles. 15.1 and 15.2.

these rules from one dispute to the next. Compared with domestic courts, therefore, arbitration gives more procedural flexibility and a correspondingly lower degree of predictability as to how the disputing parties and the tribunal choose to conduct the proceedings.

CONFIDENTIALITY OF PROCEEDINGS

A sixth and final feature of investment treaty arbitration is the opacity of proceedings. Court proceedings are almost always public, whereas arbitrations are traditionally held behind closed doors.[17] In investment treaty arbitration, the default position is that proceedings are private and the submissions of the disputing parties are confidential. This default position can differ if the treaty providing the basis of consent specifies that certain aspects of the proceedings and submissions should be public or, alternatively, if the disputing parties agree to make them public.

In practice, the only aspect of investment treaty arbitrations that is now routinely publicly available is the end product, namely, the arbitral award (but again only with the agreement of the parties). ICSID publishes a list of all past and pending investor–state arbitrations registered with it. Thus, certain basic information about each ICSID arbitration is a matter of public record. While ICSID accounts for 62 per cent of publicly known investor–state arbitrations (more than two-thirds of which are based on treaties; see Figure 3.1), information about non-ICSID arbitrations that remained confidential is uncovered from time to time, through freedom of information requests or when investors seek enforcement of awards before national courts (Balcerzak and Hepburn 2015). In 2015, for example, Investment Arbitration Reporter, a specialized reporting service, unearthed more than 12 pending, non-ICSID treaty arbitrations against Poland (Hepburn 2015).

The lack of transparency in investment treaty arbitration has been controversial. We return to this in Chapter 9, but for now note that the sustained criticism about the confidentiality of investment treaty arbitrations has prompted a recent trend towards greater transparency (Shirlow 2016). This is so both within investment treaties as well as arbitration rules. For example, new investment treaties and model BITs of Canada, the European Union, and the United States now routinely include provisions overriding the default presumption of confidentiality of proceedings.[18] On the institutional side, as

---

[17] The degree of transparency in domestic proceedings varies. For example, written pleadings are not publicly accessible for the Court of Justice of the European Union; in some countries, the identity of litigants is concealed; not all judgments are easily accessible either online or in libraries, particularly insofar as developing countries are concerned; and courts in countries that belong to the French legal family tend to offer sparse reasoning—see Lasser (2004) and Bell (2006).

[18] 2004 Canada Model BIT, Article 38; CETA, Annex 29-A, para. 38 to Chapter 29; EU–Vietnam FTA 2016, Annex 1 to Chapter 13; US Model BIT 2012, Article 29.

mentioned in the preceding text, ICSID permits proceedings and awards to be published with the consent of both parties. However, the most important recent change has been the new transparency rules within UNCITRAL.[19] The central provisions of the new rules provide the following: (1) essential information about the dispute must be published, including the parties' pleadings and the tribunal's orders and decisions; (2) limited exceptions apply—for example, to protect confidential business information or security interests; and (3) arbitral tribunals must exercise their discretionary powers in a way that balances the public interest in transparency and the parties' interest in a fair and efficient resolution of their dispute. However, these rules apply only prospectively, that is, to investment treaty arbitrations under treaties concluded on or after 1 April 2014. As a result, they crucially do not cover arbitrations under several thousand older investment treaties unless the state parties to those treaties agree to extend the application of the transparency rules. A potentially important treaty-based mechanism to extend their application to pre-2014 treaties is the 2015 Mauritius Convention on Transparency. By becoming parties to the Mauritius Convention on Transparency—drafted alongside the UNCITRAL Transparency Rules— states agree to extend the application of the UNCITRAL transparency rules to all their existing investment treaties. As this book went to press, the Convention was set to enter into force in October 2017, but since only three states had ratified it will have limited practical effect at first.[20]

HOW DOES INVESTMENT TREATY ARBITRATION DIFFER FROM OTHER MODES OF CONSENT TO INVESTOR–STATE ARBITRATION?

Except for recent initiatives relating to transparency, the features of invest- ment treaty arbitration that we have just examined—the need for consent, party appointment of arbitrators, direct standing for investors, no exhaustion of local remedies, choice of arbitral institutions, and arbitral rules—are char- acteristic of all investor–state arbitrations, regardless of the mode of consent. This is important for the discussions in the subsequent chapters about the extent to which other legal instruments, such as investment contracts, operate as effective substitutes for investment treaties in practice. Already now, however, it is important to make clear that an agreement in an investment contract to submit disputes to investor–state arbitration gives foreign investors access to a similar dispute settlement mechanism to that provided under investment

---

[19] UNCITRAL Rules on Transparency in Treaty-based Investor–State Arbitration 2014 ('Rules on Transparency').

[20] The Convention has attracted 18 signatures by 2017 (including by Canada, Germany, the Netherlands, the United Kingdom, and the United States)—but has only been ratified by Canada, Switzerland, and Mauritius. As a result, the Convention was only set to apply to the BIT between Mauritius and Switzerland at the time of writing.

treaties (Yackee 2008c, 123). The two significant differences between investor–state arbitration under an investment contract and investor–state arbitration under an investment treaty are as follows:

(1) In the case of investment contracts, foreign investors must, themselves, negotiate the inclusion of consent to investor–state arbitration. In contrast, in the case of investment treaties, foreign investors can rely on procedural rights conferred by a treaty between the host state and their home state. The inclusion of consent to arbitration in investment treaties is likely to involve lower transaction costs than the case-by-case negotiation of consent to arbitration in investment contracts.[21]

(2) The substantive rights and obligations contained in investment contracts may differ materially from the set of protections that investment treaties commonly provide to foreign investors.[22] As an investment contract can include a range of project-specific provisions, it is potentially superior from an investor's perspective.

Consent to investor–state arbitration contained in the domestic law of a host state can also provide foreign investors with access to the same dispute settlement process as consent to investor–state arbitration contained in an investment treaty.[23] From the perspective of the investor, however, consent to investor–state arbitration contained in a law is less secure, because the prevailing view is that host states can unilaterally withdraw advance consent to arbitration by legislative amendment at any time prior to the investor initiating arbitration. Later in this chapter, we discuss other potential substitutes to investment treaty arbitration, including mediation, state-to-state arbitration, and domestic court proceedings.

Arbitral rules and institutions

Investment treaties normally allow a foreign investor a choice between different sets of arbitral rules when commencing investment treaty arbitration. This section first considers the menu of options that investment treaties provide to foreign investors. Second, it examines the relationship between arbitral

---

[21] In theory, such reductions in transaction costs could benefit both foreign investors and the host state. Foreign investors may also be able to benefit from consent to arbitration in investment treaties in situations where they would lack sufficient bargaining power to insist on the inclusion of consent to arbitration in an investment contract. In contrast to reductions in transaction costs, such shifts in bargaining power primarily alter the *distribution* of the benefits of foreign investment between the host state and foreign investor, and do not create net benefits. See Chapter 5.

[22] That said, in theory, the parties could draft an investment contract to include substantive rights equivalent to those normally found in investment treaties.

[23] Chapter 8 provides some early examples of host state consent in domestic laws.

institutions and the two most important sets of arbitral *rules* in investment treaty arbitration—the ICSID Convention and the UNCITRAL Rules, both of which have been mentioned several times already. Third, it describes the different phases of a typical investment treaty arbitration, and finally it evaluates the available remedies.

CHOICE AMONG ARBITRAL RULES IN INVESTMENT TREATY ARBITRATION

The two most important sets of arbitral rules in investment treaty arbitration are the ICSID Convention, as supplemented by the 2006 ICSID Arbitration Rules (the two always go together); and the 2010 UNCITRAL Arbitration Rules.[24] Because investor–state arbitration under the ICSID Convention is contingent on both the host state and the home state of the claimant investor being party to the ICSID Convention, ICSID offers a second set of arbitral rules in which either the host state or the home state (but not both) is party to the ICSID Convention—the ICSID Additional Facility Arbitration Rules. Even though these Rules are nearly identical to the ICSID Arbitration Rules, they are not subject to the special regime for review and enforcement of arbitral awards that applies to arbitrations conducted under the ICSID Convention (Bishop, Crawford, and Reisman 2014, 281; see further the section on compliance and enforcement of arbitral awards). Other non-ICSID arbitration rules, such as the 2012 International Chamber of Commerce (ICC) Arbitration Rules and the Stockholm Chamber of Commerce (SCC) Arbitration Rules, play only a minor role in investment treaty arbitral practice. They are mostly used in international commercial arbitration.

Many investment treaties allow for arbitration under a range of different sets of arbitral rules (Pohl, Mashigo, and Nohen 2012). Under such treaties, the choice between the arbitral rules lies with the foreign investor initiating the arbitration,[25] and over time the trend has been towards offering investors more choice (Gaukrodger and Gordon 2012, 54). How exactly investors have made use of this is ultimately unknown due to the rules on transparency mentioned in the preceding text, but the arbitration rules of ICSID are seemingly the most popular in investment treaty arbitration, and UNCITRAL Rules are the second most used (UNCTAD 2014).

---

[24] UNCITRAL amended the Rules in 2013 to incorporate the UNCITRAL's Rules on Transparency in Treaty-based Investor–State Arbitration.

[25] For example, the Energy Charter Treaty allows investors to bring investor–state arbitrations using either the ICSID Convention or the ICSID Additional Facility (as relevant), the UNCITRAL Rules, or the SCC Rules. Likewise, NAFTA offers investors a choice between either the ICSID Convention or the ICSID Additional Facility (as relevant), and the UNCITRAL Rules.

RELATIONSHIPS BETWEEN ARBITRAL RULES AND ARBITRAL INSTITUTIONS

Depending on the arbitral rules governing the arbitration, an arbitral *institution* may assist the arbitral tribunal. The role of the arbitral institution is to support the tribunal in administering the arbitration. For example, an arbitral institution may provide a channel of communication between the parties and the tribunal, ensure safe custody of documents relating to the arbitration, and provide logistical and technical support for hearings and meetings of the tribunal. An arbitral institution is a distinct entity from the arbitral tribunal, which it supports. In this important respect, arbitral institutions differ from standing international courts such as the International Criminal Court, the ICJ, and the WTO Appellate Body.

In investment treaty arbitration, the most prominent arbitral institution is the ICSID Secretariat, whose main task is to administer arbitrations conducted under the ICSID Convention or under the ICSID Additional Facility Rules. The Secretariat plays no formal role in the development of the substantive rules protecting foreign investors, but may play a more prominent role behind the scenes—for instance, through institutional appointments of arbitrators, advice to tribunals on precedents, assisting tribunals with the editing of drafts, and so on (Tucker 2015, 84–6). The role of the ICSID Secretariat may thus be underappreciated in current literature and policy debates, even if it is not as influential as the WTO Secretariat. The latter services not only the WTO's dispute settlement body but also the WTO bodies that negotiate and develop WTO rules, monitors compliance, and often 'nudges' WTO panels to ensure consistency in WTO jurisprudence (Pauwelyn 2015).

In contrast to the ICSID Convention, the UNCITRAL Arbitration Rules do not require that a particular arbitral institution administer investor–state arbitrations, meaning that the parties can select an arbitral institution. However, the UNCITRAL rules enjoy a privileged link with the PCA—which is the default appointing authority. Despite its name, the PCA is not a court. Rather, it is an arbitral institution that supports the administration of arbitrations conducted under various sets of non-ICSID arbitral rules. Investment treaty arbitration can also be conducted under the UNCITRAL Rules or another set of arbitration rules without the support of any arbitral institution—so-called ad hoc arbitration.

THE PHASES OF INVESTMENT TREATY ARBITRATIONS

Investment treaty arbitrations involve a combination of written submissions and hearings at which the disputing parties (normally represented by lawyers) present their arguments orally to the tribunal. It is up to the tribunal to decide whether to divide the arbitration into separate phases ('bifurcation') or to deal with a series of issues in a single round of written submissions and hearings. With this caveat in mind, this subsection describes the different phases of a typical investment treaty arbitration: (i) the initiation of the arbitration by the investor through a notice or request for arbitration; (ii) the establishment of the tribunal through the appointment of the arbitrators and the determination of the 'seat' of arbitration; (iii) the jurisdictional phase; (iv) the merits phase; and (v) the quantum phase.

Investment treaty arbitrations begin when an investor lodges a 'request' or 'notice' of arbitration. Here, the investor outlines the basis for its arbitration—for example, the investor asserts that it is covered by a particular investment treaty, that the host state has breached particular provisions of that investment treaty, and that the host state has given its advance consent to investor–state arbitration of disputes under that investment treaty.

The second phase is the establishment of the arbitral tribunal, in which the parties appoint their arbitrators (see section on the features of investment treaty arbitrations in the preceding text). One crucial issue at this phase of the proceedings is the seat of arbitration. The seat of an arbitration is a legal concept distinct from the location where the hearings are held. Rather, it refers to the domestic legal system that has supervisory jurisdiction over the arbitral proceedings. The choice of seat is important because the courts of the seat of the arbitration have the power to review and set aside awards (Fouchard et al. 1999, 225–7; Born 2009, 351).

The disputing parties generally have the freedom to choose the seat of arbitration. If they are unable to agree, the tribunal decides.[26] In practice, the seat of arbitration is normally a third state—that is, a state that is neither the host state nor the investor's home state—with a developed legal system and a policy of supporting arbitration. However, investor–state arbitrations conducted under the ICSID Convention do not have a seat, as the Convention establishes a special international system for investor–state arbitration that is outside the supervisory jurisdiction of any country's courts. This has important implications for the review and enforcement of awards rendered under the ICSID Convention, which are explained in the following text.

In the third phase of proceedings, the tribunal determines whether the investor bringing the arbitration falls within the coverage of the basis of the arbitration—for example, the investment treaty in question—and within the scope of the advance consent to arbitrate given by the host state. In investment treaty arbitration, this invariably requires the tribunal to determine whether the claimant qualifies as an 'investor' that possesses an 'investment'

---

[26] For example, the UNCITRAL Arbitration Rules vest the authority in the arbitral tribunal to decide on the seat based on the circumstances of the arbitration, unless the disputing parties have otherwise agreed.

under the investment treaty in question.[27] There may also be issues concerning the geographic and temporal scope of the investment treaty—for example, a tribunal would not normally have jurisdiction over a dispute arising from actions by the host state before the treaty in question entered into force (although this depends on the wording of the treaty). If the tribunal finds that the investor has failed to satisfy any of these jurisdictional requirements, the substantive provisions of the investment treaty are inapplicable and the arbitration concludes.

If the tribunal finds that it does have jurisdiction over the dispute, proceedings move to a fourth phase, concerning the 'merits' of the investor's claim(s). In this phase, the tribunal determines whether the host state has breached the substantive provisions of the investment treaty in question. If the tribunal finds that the host state has not breached the investment treaty, the arbitration concludes. If the tribunal finds that the host state has breached the investment treaty, proceedings move to a fifth phase, which may be joined to the merits. In this phase, the tribunal decides the amount of compensation that the host state must pay to the investor. This phase often raises complex questions of valuation, to which we return in Chapter 4.

COMPENSATION AS THE MAIN REMEDY

We now turn to the question of remedies. As remedies give teeth to legal rights, they are crucial for understanding the impact of investment treaty regime on both investors and host states. As mentioned in Chapter 1, the main remedy in investment treaty arbitration is monetary compensation.[28] Chapter 4 examines the legal principles governing the award of compensation and the three main valuation methods. For now, we look at compensation and its main alternative, 'specific performance'. We also compare the role of compensation as the standard remedy in the investment treaty regime with remedies for analogous claims in domestic law and remedies in other international regimes.

The remedy of compensation involves investor–state tribunals ordering host states to pay a sum of money to investors to put them in the same position as if the state had not breached the investment treaty. Host states remedy their breach of the treaty by paying compensation, but the challenged state measure(s) remain in place. By contrast, the remedy of specific performance involves tribunals ordering the host state to follow a particular course of conduct to ensure that the state complies with the provisions of the investment

---

[27] Section 4 of Chapter 2 deals with these issues in detail.
[28] Legal scholars disagree about whether arbitrators have the power to award specific performance—see Schreuer (2004a); Douglas (2010); Hindelang (2011); and Sabahi (2011, chs. 4–5). Some investment treaties expressly exclude such non-monetary remedies (e.g. NAFTA, Article 1135).

treaty in question.[29] These orders can be directed at the annulment or amendment of a particular law, or the annulment of a particular administrative act, and so on.

The central role of compensation as a remedy in investment treaty arbitration differs from the combination of remedies typically available to investors in analogous legal claims under domestic legal systems. Remedies vary in domestic law depending on the cause of action. In domestic legal systems, compensation is the default remedy in some circumstances—for example, in cases of expropriation and breach of contract by a state entity (Bell 2006). By contrast, the typical remedy with respect to unlawful administrative action is normally the quashing of the administrative action in question (Montt 2009; van Aaken 2010; Gaukrodger and Gordon 2012, 79–87). An order quashing administrative action 'sets aside' the measure, yet it leaves the state free to adopt other measures that may still be contrary to the interests of the investor, subject to the constraint that these new measures must now comply with the requirements for lawful administrative action prescribed by the legal system in question (Elliott, Beatson, and Matthews 2010, 434; Lewis 2015, 6.002–19).

The role of compensation as the primary remedy in the investment treaty regime also differs from some other parts of the investment regime complex with strong dispute settlement mechanisms (see Chapter 1). For instance, if taxation of a taxpayer is in breach of a double taxation treaty (DTT), the typical remedy under domestic law is that such tax cannot be levied—akin to an order of specific performance. Equally, in trade disputes, a successful (state) claimant is unable to obtain compensation for either past or future losses caused by breach of a treaty obligation by another state. Instead, remedies are focused on restoring compliance (Dixit 1987; Bagwell and Staiger 2002). The WTO's Dispute Settlement Body orders the WTO member state concerned to prospectively conform its conduct to the provisions of the WTO regime—that is, it orders specific performance. By contrast, the ECtHR is one part of the investment regime complex that in principle does grant compensation for the deprivation of property rights. Yet, the basis on which compensation is calculated in human rights claims is different from that in investment treaty arbitration, resulting in lower compensation in comparable claims.[30]

---

[29] That said, orders of specific performance can leave some discretion to the state as regards implementation.

[30] See generally Shelton (2004, ch. 9) and Varuhas (2016, ch. 5). Empirical work on the ECHR remains limited. A recent exception is Altwicker-Hamori, Altwicker, and Peters (2016).

Review and enforcement of awards

The existence of an arbitral tribunal comes to an end when it issues its final award. Yet, this is not necessarily the end of the dispute. Once a tribunal has issued an award, both the investor–claimant and the host state have the option to seek review of the award. Moreover, if an arbitral tribunal has ruled in favour of the investor and the host state refuses to comply, the question of the enforcement of arbitral awards comes to the fore. The first part of this section examines the different mechanisms for reviewing awards in investment treaty arbitration within and outside the ICSID system. The second part looks at different mechanisms for enforcement.

REVIEW AND ANNULMENT OF ARBITRAL AWARDS

If a disputing party is dissatisfied with the outcome of an investment treaty arbitration, it can seek review of the arbitral award. ICSID and non-ICSID systems of review differ in some respects, but both focus on *procedure*—that is, whether the arbitral proceedings were conducted properly. In this sense, the review of arbitral awards differ from appeals against court judgments in domestic legal systems, which also allow the losing party to partially challenge the *substance* of decisions of lower courts. The result is that annulment committees and courts have upheld some awards, even when they took the view that the reasoning of the initial tribunal was 'wrong' as a matter of substantive law. For example, the annulment committee in *CMS v. Argentina* (2007) explained that, given its limited mandate, it could not annul parts of the arbitral tribunal's award even though it 'contained manifest errors of law' (para. 158).

The ICSID Convention is unique in that it establishes an entirely self-contained and internationalized mechanism for investor–state arbitration (Born 2012, 417; Dolzer and Schreuer 2012, 239). There is no possibility of review of, or appeal against, awards rendered under the ICSID Convention in domestic courts.[31] The only possibilities for review are those set out in the ICSID Convention itself, the most significant of which is the annulment of an award. There are five grounds for annulment of an ICSID arbitral award: (i) improper constitution of a tribunal; (ii) manifest excess of power; (iii) corruption of the tribunal; (iv) serious departure from a fundamental rule of procedure; and (v) failure to state reasons on which the award is based.

---

[31] Note, however, that an investor may still need to rely on the courts of a host state to enforce an award under the ICSID Convention, and that the ICSID Convention does not affect sovereign immunity from enforcement. Certain classes of state-owned assets are immune; see the following text.

When a dissatisfied party requests annulment of an award under the ICSID Convention, the ICSID Secretariat establishes a dedicated ad hoc committee to consider the request. A successful request for annulment quashes the award in whole or in part. This is a more limited remedy than an appeal. In domestic legal systems, courts of appeals can often partially or fully substitute their own views for those of the lower courts. In contrast, if the request for annulment succeeds in full, the award disappears and the parties are back to square one. If an investor still wishes to pursue the claim within the ICSID system, the only option is to commence proceedings again before a newly constituted tribunal (which is likely to last three years or more, see Table 3.3).

The threshold for annulments of arbitral awards under the ICSID Convention is high. In the 182 treaty and non-treaty disputes under the ICSID Convention that tribunals have decided on the merits to date, the 'losing' party requested an annulment in 53 cases (29 per cent). Ad hoc annulment committees have annulled five arbitral awards in whole and seven arbitral awards in part to date. This equals 24 per cent of cases in which a disputing party requested an annulment (and 6 per cent of all awards).[32]

Arbitral awards besides those made under the ICSID Convention are subject to review by the courts of the seat of arbitration. As in the ICSID system, a successful challenge to an arbitral award in the courts of the seat of arbitration results in the award being 'set aside' or 'vacated'. The grounds of review depend on the law of the seat of arbitration, yet the laws of jurisdictions commonly designated as seats in investment treaty arbitration (e.g. England, France, or Singapore) establish similar grounds for review. It is normally limited to procedural questions—for example, whether the tribunal was properly constituted and whether the tribunal conducted the hearings fairly and impartially—and to the question of whether the tribunal exceeded its jurisdiction. The 'merits' of arbitral awards are again not subject to review. In the words of a US court: 'The whole point of arbitration is that the merits of the dispute will not be reviewed in the courts, wherever they be located' (*Intl. Standard Elec. v. Bridas* 1990, 178).

COMPLIANCE AND ENFORCEMENT OF ARBITRAL AWARDS

For the most part, host states subject to investment treaty claims comply voluntarily with arbitral awards.[33] Reputation effects likely play an important role in encouraging compliance with arbitral awards, although this has not been subject to empirical testing thus far (see generally, Guzman 2008). If host states do not comply with arbitral awards, the investor in question has three

---

[32] Author's calculation, based on ICSID website, September 2016.
[33] Gaukrodger and Gordon 2012, 73. That said, data on compliance remains limited.

options: (i) to settle—often for a significantly lower compensation than in an award, but with a high likelihood of prompt payment, (ii) to enforce the arbitral award through domestic courts—that is, to attempt to seize assets belonging to the debtor state[34] that are located outside its territory, and (iii) to lobby the home state of the investor to exert political pressure on the debtor state. The feasibility of the second and third options has important practical implications for the relative bargaining power of the parties in any settlement negotiations.

At any stage of an investment dispute, the disputing parties can settle on agreed terms. Settlements can result from negotiations between the parties prior to an arbitration, or can follow an award on jurisdiction or liability.[35] As is common in commercial litigation, more than one-third of all ICSID arbitrations settle (Hafner-Burton, Puig, and Victor 2016). This figure significantly understates the role of settlements in the investment treaty regime, however, because they only count cases in which a dispute has settled *after* arbitration proceedings have been commenced. It is not uncommon for the parties to settle before registration, although there is little empirical evidence on this aspect of investor–state disputes.

When the disputing parties settle before any decision of the arbitral tribunal, the agreed compensation is often below the market value of an investment, reflecting the uncertainty over the investor's prospects in the arbitration.[36] For example, in 2012, Argentina expropriated Repsol's stake in the Argentine company YPF. Repsol brought an arbitration against Argentina under the Argentina–Spain BIT, claiming US$12 billion in compensation.[37] In 2014, Repsol and Argentina agreed on compensation comprising Argentine sovereign bonds with a face value of US$5 billion plus a further US$1 billion in cash (Settlement Argentina-Repsol 2014). The advantage of this settlement arrangement for Argentina was that it did not have to draw on US$5 billion in foreign reserves immediately. Repsol too derived advantages from receiving a fixed

---

[34] In this sub-section, we use the term 'debtor state' to refer to an uncooperative host state that has refused to pay the compensation it owes to an investor following an investment treaty arbitration.

[35] For example, *Abaclat v. Argentina* (2011) in respect of Argentina's sovereign default in 2001 settled five years after an award on jurisdiction. See Caputo (2016); Goldhaber (2016). The settlement was for 150 per cent of the bond's nominal value. For bondholders who bought at par, this was not a generous settlement, given the interest payable over fifteen years from default to settlement. Conversely, for bondholders who bought substantially below par after the default (say for 30 per cent), the settlement was generous.

[36] Settlements sometimes also contain non-monetary terms—e.g. the state's agreement to amend/revoke a particular measure, or to apply it in a certain way to an investment—such as *Vattenfall I v. Germany* (2011), discussed in the Foreword. This is another reason why settlements may result in lower monetary compensation than a case where the investor entirely exits the host state.

[37] For tactical reasons, investors' claims for compensation generally err on the high side. So Repsol's stated value should not be taken as firm evidence of the expropriated investment's real value.

amount of compensation earlier than if it waited for the conclusion of the arbitration (Maurer 2013).

The second option of enforcement refers to the seizure of assets to satisfy an amount owed under an award. Enforcement of an arbitral award is not automatic. It requires the award holder to identify assets of the debtor state outside its territory (assets located within the debtor state are typically of little use when that state is refusing to comply), and then to seek the cooperation of courts in the jurisdiction(s) where the assets of the debtor state are found. Thus, the enforcement stage is another point of interaction between investment treaty arbitration and domestic judicial systems.

The process of enforcing an ICSID award differs somewhat from the process of enforcing an award rendered under any other set of arbitral rules. All state parties to the ICSID Convention must automatically recognize awards rendered under the ICSID Convention as final and enforceable. In contrast, an investor who has obtained an award under any other set of arbitral rules must first seek 'recognition' of that award by the courts of the jurisdiction in which it is seeking enforcement (Reed, Paulsson, and Blackaby 2011, 15). The influential New York Convention on Recognition and Enforcement of Foreign Arbitral Awards facilitates recognition. It has 156 state parties and establishes common rules for the recognition of arbitral awards. Nevertheless, such recognition outside the ICSID system is not automatic. The provisions of the New York Convention allow a debtor state to argue that awards should not be recognized on procedural grounds similar to those for setting aside awards (see the preceding text). The process of obtaining recognition of an award entails further costs and possible delays.

Once an investor has obtained recognition of an award by the courts of the state where it is seeking enforcement, it faces further practical challenges in identifying non-immune assets of the debtor state. In most states where enforcement is sought, sovereign immunity from enforcement means that only *commercial* assets of a debtor state are subject to seizure. Embassies and warships are immune, for instance, and the same applies to other property used for governmental purposes, such as central bank reserves.[38] By contrast, commercial property of a state—such as commercial planes or buildings—does not generally benefit from sovereign immunity. This creates difficulties in practice, as debtor states typically have most of their non-immune, commercial assets within their own borders.

In some cases, claimants challenge the immunity of state assets. For example, Chapter 1 described how Argentina stalled on paying some arbitral awards against it, and in one case the investor sought to seize US$300 million of Argentina's reserves at the Bank for International Settlements. The investor

---

[38] Central bank reserves are a particularly important category of assets (in volume terms) held partly abroad; see *NML v. Bank for International Settlements* (2010).

was unsuccessful, however, as the highest Swiss court, supported by the Swiss government, upheld the immunity of these reserves (*NML v. Bank for International Settlements* 2010).[39] In other cases, a debtor state may actively move assets between or within jurisdictions so that they are sheltered from the reach of investors seeking to enforce arbitral awards. For instance, in the US$50 billion award in favour of Yukos mentioned in Chapter 1, Russia frustrated Yukos' attempts to seize buildings by affixing plaques to them and thereby claiming that the buildings were part of the Russian embassy (The Economist 2016).

Nevertheless, some attempts to enforce arbitral awards against debtor states succeed. In *Walter Bau* (2009), Thailand failed to comply with an UNCITRAL award against it. The claimants then sought to enforce the award in Germany, where a court ordered the seizure of a Thai prince's aircraft at Munich airport. Thailand subsequently deposited the value of the award (€38 million/US$45 million) into an escrow account in Germany in exchange for the release of the royal Boeing 737 (Nottage and Thanitcul 2016).[40] Similarly, in 2006, German courts ordered the Russian state to sell an apartment complex in Cologne—previously used by the KGB—to the benefit of Franz Sedelmayer, a German investor with an outstanding investment treaty award against Russia (described in Chapter 2). Hence, while it is often difficult and time-consuming, the ability of investors to confiscate debtor states' commercial assets worldwide is a powerful enforcement mechanism underwriting the investment treaty regime.

Finally, a third option is for investors to lobby their home state to act on their behalf against the debtor state. Even though home states cannot exercise formal diplomatic protection while ICSID disputes are pending (Article 27 ICSID Convention), diplomatic protection is possible if host states fail to pay arbitral awards. For example, following lobbying by two investors who had obtained awards against Argentina in investment treaty arbitrations, the United States voted in 2012 to withdraw or suspend World Bank and Inter-American Development Bank loans to Argentina until Argentina paid the investors (Cotterill 2013).[41] The United States also suspended trade benefits previously available to Argentina under the WTO's Generalized System of Preferences (Rosenberg 2013), and Argentina ultimately settled with both investors (along with three others) in October 2013.

---

[39] To date, all significant attempts by Argentina's creditors to enforce their awards against Argentina's assets abroad have failed.

[40] In October 2016, the German Bundesgerichtshof, the highest German court, upheld the enforceability of the award.

[41] Ecuador, for instance, criticised the close affinity of ICSID with the World Bank and the US government (see Chapter 8).

Alternative dispute resolution and domestic courts as alternatives

Despite the salience of investment treaty arbitration, it is important to recall that only a minority of investment disputes ever reach investment treaty tribunals. Negotiation remains the dominant method of resolving investor–state disputes (Salacuse 2003; Waibel 2010a; Merrills 2011), some of which lead to settlements (Echandi and Kher 2013). When negotiations fail, multiple methods of dispute resolution are usually available besides investment treaty arbitration.[42] We have already described in the preceding text how investor–state arbitration based on contracts and, less commonly, domestic laws can be potential substitutes, as can state-to-state dispute resolution. We now hone in on two other alternatives: (1) alternative dispute resolution (ADR), such as mediation or conciliation, and (2) litigation in domestic courts of host states.

ADR AS AN ALTERNATIVE TO INVESTMENT TREATY ARBITRATION

Both mediation and conciliation are structured methods to assist disputing parties in finding an agreed solution to their dispute. In both cases, the parties appoint a neutral individual or individuals to evaluate the arguments and evidence, and to recommend ways to resolve their dispute (Merrills 2011). The recommendations of a mediator or conciliator are not binding, unless both parties accept those recommendations. In contrast, in arbitration, the parties agree in advance to accept the decision of the arbitrators as binding, without knowing what the decision will be.

ADR is used in some parts of the investment regime complex—for instance, when the World Bank finances or insures foreign investors. The International Finance Corporation (IFC) thus encourages ADR when foreign investors run into commercial disputes with local firms, and the Multilateral Investment Guarantee Agency (MIGA) is occasionally used as a mediator in investor–state disputes. Many investment treaties build in elements of ADR in their investor–state provisions as well. Nine out of ten require some form of pre-arbitration dispute settlement process (Gaukrodger and Gordon 2012), such as attempts at amicable settlement, cooling-off periods (often six months), and—in some instances—initial referrals to domestic courts. However, investment treaties

---

[42] Political risk insurance is not a method of resolving investment disputes, but can be an effective way of insulating foreign investors from host country political risk. See further Peinhardt and Allee (2016).

rarely provide for a mandatory period of mediation or conciliation prior to arbitration.[43]

Proponents of ADR argue that mediation and conciliation help preserve the relationship between the disputing parties, unlike adversarial methods of dispute settlement such as litigation and arbitration.

Existing research on this thesis is limited. The high costs of investment treaty arbitrations (see Chapter 1 and the following text) could also encourage the use of mediation (Coe 2005; Franck 2007; Salacuse 2007). Notwithstanding these potential benefits, ADR has not played a major role in resolving investor–state disputes to date. ICSID has only registered nine conciliation requests (as compared to 573 ICSID arbitrations).[44] And although there is no comprehensive data on the number of investor–state disputes that have been resolved through ADR, there is little anecdotal evidence that ADR plays a meaningful role apart from a couple of dozen disputes that MIGA mediated (Perera 2008).[45]

The absence of obligations to engage in mediation or conciliation as a pre-requisite to investment treaty arbitration cannot, in itself, explain why investors and states fail to use these methods more frequently, as it remains possible for the disputing parties to resort to these methods at any point by mutual agreement. Instead, there are two plausible explanations. One possibility is that the incentives facing government officials in host states discourage the use of mediation or conciliation. Wälde is worth quoting at length:

Host country officials shirk from the responsibility for the settlement that comes with mediation. They rather, for self-protective reasons, prefer a high loss blamed on other parties (tribunal, counsel) to a lower-value settlement payment or a creatively designed renegotiated deal for which they have to take personal responsibility. This is the so far largely unresolved principal impediment to mediation (2008–2009, 534–5).

While this explanation may go some way to explain the unpopularity of these methods for resolving investor–state disputes, it has not yet been subject to any empirical verification (on blame-shifting in international economic disputes, see generally Allee and Huth 2006; Davis 2012).

The second, and arguably more persuasive, explanation is that since mediation and conciliation are not binding, they are rarely an adequate substitute for binding methods of dispute resolution such as arbitration and litigation (Schwebel 2007; Reisman 2009). Non-binding methods of dispute resolution are premised on the assumption that there are solutions to disputes that satisfy

---

[43] Exceptions include the Thai Model BIT of 2012 and CETA 2015, Article 8.20.
[44] Author calculations from ICSID website, as of September 2016.
[45] The World Bank, and MIGA specifically, has been involved in settling a much larger number of disputes informally. MIGA assisted Ethiopia in resolving a large number of expropriation disputes dating back to the 1970s, MIGA (2002).

both parties, and that a wise outsider who can dispassionately appraise the dispute can identify these mutually beneficial solutions. This may happen on occasion in foreign investment disputes, but the premise is difficult to reconcile with the broader observed patterns of disputes. A major reason why there are investor–state disputes that the parties fail to settle themselves is because their objectives are mutually incompatible. If mutually beneficial solutions existed, one would expect the parties to be able to negotiate settlement privately without any need for mediation or conciliation. We observe this trend in the practice of investment disputes, where negotiations and settlements play a large role (Hafner-Burton, Puig, and Victor 2016), but mediation and conciliation do not.

In sum, when there are no solutions that are better than both parties' best alternative options outside the mediation/conciliation process, persisting with attempts to find a mutually agreeable solution through ADR risks simply adding to the cost and duration of investment disputes. (This is akin to the role of parties' 'best alternative to a negotiated agreement' in defining the range of mutually beneficial solutions in a negotiated settlement (see generally Fisher, Ury and Patton 2011).) The following, and final, sections will therefore assess a more relevant alternative to investment treaty arbitration, namely litigation in domestic courts.

LITIGATION IN DOMESTIC COURTS AS AN ALTERNATIVE TO INVESTMENT TREATY ARBITRATION

Foreign investors can typically litigate before the domestic courts of the host state (or the domestic courts in third countries if their investment contracts so provide). To evaluate the importance of investment treaty arbitration as a method of resolving investment disputes, it is therefore necessary to compare it with the role of domestic courts in settling investment disputes in practice.

There is at present no reliable evidence on the percentage of investment disputes that investors choose to submit to investor–state arbitration, whether based on consent in contracts, laws, or treaties. It is likely that the percentage varies across countries depending, among other factors, on the reputation of the relevant host state's judiciary for independence and impartiality. Figure 3.2 attempts to give an idea of the relative importance of domestic courts in settling investment disputes for selected member states of the Council of Europe—that is, countries where the ECHR applies. From 1990 to 2015, claimants brought over 8800 cases based on Article 1 of the First Additional Protocol ('A1P1')[46] to the ECHR against the now 47 member states of the Council of Europe. The number of A1P1 cases provides a rough proxy of the investment disputes that domestic courts have decided across the member states of the Council of Europe, because the ECtHR only has jurisdiction over

---

[46] A1P1 is the property rights provision of the ECHR. It provides that: 'Every natural or legal person is entitled to the peaceful enjoyment of his *possessions*'.

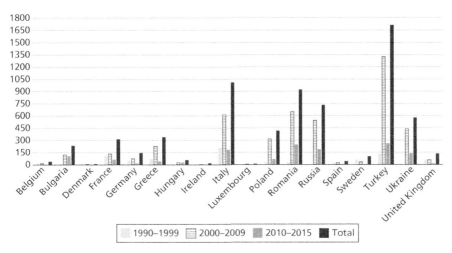

Figure 3.2 Right to property disputes before the ECtHR (1990–2015)

Source: Author compilation from the HUDOC database of the ECtHR, as of May 2016.

disputes if the claimant has first exhausted local remedies (see Section on the features of investment treaty arbitrations in the preceding text). On the one hand, these statistics systematically underestimate the number of investment disputes in national courts, because many disputes resolved in national courts do not subsequently result in proceedings before the ECtHR. On the other hand, the statistics could overestimate the number of *foreign* investment disputes in national courts, because individuals and companies can bring arbitrations against their own states to the ECtHR. We are unable to determine the combined effect of these factors.

The average number of property disputes from 1990 to 2015 is 16.5 per country. For most countries, this is ten times (or more) the number of investment treaty arbitrations per year. As Figure 3.2 shows, this average masks considerable variation across countries. Over the 25-year period, the number of such disputes ranges from two in case of Andorra, to 134 for the United Kingdom, 145 for Germany, 734 for Russia, 921 for Romania, and 1010 for Italy. Turkey accounts for the highest number of disputes (1714). Even though this data suggests that domestic courts play a much more important role than investment treaty arbitration, at least insofar as most developed countries are concerned, the incidence of investment disputes before the domestic courts is an important issue for future research. It is therefore useful to consider how investment treaty arbitration measures up to domestic litigation in terms of costs, duration, effectiveness, and neutrality, as these factors affect the attractiveness of investment treaty arbitration vis-à-vis litigation in domestic courts.

NEUTRALITY OF INVESTMENT TREATY ARBITRATION

From the perspective of foreign investors, one of the major attractions of investor–state arbitration, including investment treaty arbitration, is that it offers a mechanism for the binding resolution of investment disputes outside the direct control of the host state.[47] In this sense, investor–state tribunals are 'neutral'. From the perspective of investors, the neutrality of investment treaty arbitration is theoretically appealing for at least two reasons. First, a neutral forum for the resolution of investment disputes is particularly relevant for host countries in which the judiciary is insufficiently independent from the other branches of government or where judicial corruption is widespread (e.g. Henderson 2006). Domestic courts may also be subject to political constraints in the polity of which they form part and which could influence their decisions (e.g. Firth, Rui, and Wu 2011). Second, some domestic courts may be biased against foreign claimants, particularly because host states are invariably respondents in investment treaty arbitration.

There is only limited empirical work on foreign bias in domestic courts. Existing work is largely limited to civil litigation in US courts (e.g. Clermont and Eisenberg 1996; Tabarrok and Helland 1999; Moore 2003). Also, the *perception* of bias of domestic courts may be just as important as the reality of bias. To the extent that foreign investors collectively believe that investor–state arbitration is a more neutral mechanism for resolving investment disputes than domestic courts, the host state's consent to investor–state arbitration (through a treaty, or otherwise) could to lead to more FDI than if the host state simply agreed to litigation in its own courts.[48] The extent to which foreign investors hold these views is an empirical question that requires further study. Some evidence suggests that foreign investors are hesitant to litigate in the host country's courts (e.g. PWC and Queen Mary 2013), but it is not clear whether comparable domestic investors are any better off litigating in the same courts (see generally, Aisbett and Poulsen 2016). Understanding when, and under what circumstances, foreign investors are treated worse, the same, or better in domestic courts than in investment treaty arbitration is an important subject for future research.

In addition to research on the neutrality of domestic courts, some empirical work has studied the neutrality of investment treaty arbitration. We examine some of this work in Chapter 9, but none of it calls into question the basic contention that investment treaty arbitration is a process for dispute resolution

---

[47] The point of comparison between investor–state arbitration and litigation is typically with courts *in the host country*. However, it could equally be the courts of a third country. The choice of a third country is common with respect to financial instruments, typically the courts of England or New York (e.g. with respect to financial instruments in *Abaclat v. Argentina* 2011 described earlier).

[48] Chapter 6 examines the link between investment treaties and FDI flows in greater detail.

that is outside the *direct* control of both host states and foreign investors. This does not necessarily mean, however, that investment treaty arbitration is 'depoliticized'. Importantly, recent empirical work suggests that investment treaty tribunals are sensitive to political signals that states send—particularly those states that are vocal, influential, and developed (Langford and Behn 2016).

The NAFTA arbitration *Loewen v. United States* (2003) illustrates several of these observations. After a failed business deal between Canadian company Loewen and a local business partner in the United States, the latter sued Loewen in Mississippi state court. It fell to a civil jury to decide the case. The jury returned a verdict with damages that were thirty times what the claimant had asked for, based in no small part on the 'anti-Canadian prejudices' that the lawyer acting for the Mississippi company managed to stir up among the jurors during trial (Hamby 2016c). This serves as a reminder that a lack of neutrality in adjudication can be a concern even in countries with well-developed judicial institutions.

Yet, the very same dispute also raises questions about the perceived neutrality of investment treaty arbitration. In *Loewen v. United States* (2003), the US government 'leaned on' Judge Mikva, the arbitrator it nominated to avoid a ruling against the United States. US Department of Justice officials told the this arbitrator: 'You know, judge, if we lose this case we could lose NAFTA', to which Mikva replied: 'Well, if you want to put pressure on me, then that does it' (quoted from Schneiderman 2010, 404). The tribunal subsequently ruled against Loewen on a jurisdictional technicality in a case many expected the United States to lose had it proceeded to the merits, given the conduct of the Mississippi state court.

COSTS OF INVESTMENT TREATY ARBITRATION

In addition to neutrality, it is important to consider the costs of domestic court litigation compared to investment treaty arbitration. There are two main, direct costs of investment treaty arbitrations: legal advice (including legal representation) and tribunal costs.[49] While costs vary greatly from one case to another, they are high. The *average* total cost of investment treaty arbitrations is over US$10 million, more than 80 per cent of which the disputing parties typically spend on legal advice (Gaukrodger and Gordon 2012). As Table 3.2 shows, the *median* legal fees of investors amount to US$3.2 million, and US$2.7 million for host states. The median tribunal cost is almost US$0.5 million, with ICSID tribunals being 10–20 per cent cheaper than UNCITRAL tribunals (Hodgson 2014). ICSID arbitrator fees are capped,

---

[49] In addition, there may be potential reputation costs for the host state due to investor–state arbitration (Allee and Peinhardt 2011).

Table 3.2 Costs of ICSID arbitrations (1972–2011)

	Arbitration costs	Claimant legal costs	Respondent legal costs	Total cost
Average	1.2	4.3	8	13.5
Median	0.5	3.2	2.7	6.4
Minimum	0.04	0.03	0.2	0.3
Maximum	20.9	24.4	218.6	263.6

Note: Figures are in US$ millions. Calculations do not include several multi-billion-dollar awards issued since 2011 (e.g. Yukos).

Source: Based on 79 ICSID cases (1972–2011); Hodgson (2014).

whereas UNCITRAL arbitrator fees are not. Note that these figures do not include several multi-billion-dollar awards since 2011.

The average figures in Table 3.2 are higher than the medians due to some large outliers. An example of a very expensive investor–state arbitration is the unusually complex and lengthy *Yukos v. Russia* arbitration mentioned previously. It is too recent to be covered by the data in Table 3.2, but Yukos's legal costs for this arbitration alone[50] were close to US$80 million, of which US$10 million was for experts (*Yukos v. Russia* 2014, para. 1847). Russia, which retained a US law firm to defend the arbitration, incurred legal costs of US$27 million.[51] As mentioned in Chapter 1, each of the three arbitrators received close to US$2 million in fees, and their assistant earned more than US$1 million.

There is no comprehensive empirical evidence available on the relative costs of investment treaty arbitration versus civil litigation in domestic courts. The costs of the latter depend on the nature of the dispute, the cause of action invoked, and the state in which the claim is brought. Another factor is the cost of appeal, which may add to the relative costs of domestic court proceedings when compared to the limited possibilities for review of awards in investment treaty arbitration. Yet, evidence from English and US commercial cases suggests that the cost of litigating commercial cases in the United Kingdom and the United States until the point of final resolution—that is, including any appeal—is lower than the average total cost of investment treaty arbitration since the 2000s. For example, the average cost order of the UK Commercial Court from 2008 to 2018 was around US$0.8 million, and the lawyer fees were around US$1.5 million (author's calculations based on Jackson 2010). Civil litigation costs of Fortune 200 companies in the United States were around US$2 million per case over 2004–2008 (Lawyers for Civil Justice 2010). These figures from the United States and the United Kingdom are remarkably similar (US$2 million versus US$1.5 million in average total costs). As such,

---

[50] Not counting significant costs for enforcements proceedings in various jurisdictions.

[51] Some states typically use mostly in-house lawyers (which are significantly cheaper) (e.g. Argentina, Australia, and the United States).

investment treaty arbitration is not necessarily cheaper than litigation in domestic courts, and is possibly more expensive (Blackaby and Partasides 2015, 35).

High costs have given significant impetus to third-party funding in investment treaty arbitration, as it has for litigation in domestic courts.[52] Third-party funding refers to the financing of the arbitration by an entity that has no prior interest on the litigation. They typically work on a contingency basis so that the third-party funder obtains a significant percentage of any damages awarded to the investor (often in the range of 20–40 per cent), and nothing if the arbitration fails. For instance, Burford Capital financed Rurelec's investment treaty arbitration against Bolivia with US$15 million, and earned a US$11 million profit on the transaction (Burford 2014).

Third-party funding can improve access to international dispute settlement for foreign investors which lack sufficiently deep pockets to finance the arbitration themselves (e.g. Steinitz 2011). At the same time, third-party funding and its impact on the incentives to bring arbitrations, as well as the lack of transparency around funding arrangements, has been one of the most controversial features of investment treaty arbitration over the last decade (Gaukrodger and Gordon 2012). Critics denounce it as 'ambulance-chasing' (Sornarajah quoted in Hamby 2016d). How third-party funders shape investor–state arbitrations is an important area for future research, but for our purposes the core point is again that the cost of investment treaty arbitration compared with litigation in domestic courts is an important consideration when evaluating the relative benefits of the two dispute settlement mechanisms.

THE DURATION OF INVESTMENT TREATY ARBITRATION

The speed of proceedings is another oft-cited advantage of investment treaty arbitration over litigation in domestic courts. As Table 3.3 shows, the average duration of ICSID arbitrations is 3.6 years (Sinclair 2009).[53] The longest phases of all ICSID arbitrations (including those based on contract and laws) are from the constitution of the tribunal to the hearing(s) (1.7 years), and from the last hearing to an award on the merits (1.3 years). On average, arbitrations with dissenting opinions take considerably longer (Sinclair 2009). Annulment proceedings on average add another 2.7 years to the total duration. These averages mask considerable variation. The longest ICSID arbitrations

---

[52] Litigation and arbitration funding has developed into an industry of its own; see e.g. Justice Not Profit (2015). Examples of third-party funders include Burford Capital and Omni Bridgeway.

[53] No comprehensive data is available for investor–state arbitrations under UNCITRAL rules.

Table 3.3 Duration of ICSID arbitrations

	Average duration (years)	Median duration (years)	Minimum duration (years)	Maximum duration (years)
Registration to constitution of tribunal	0.8	0.5	0.01	9.0
Constitution of tribunal to last hearing	1.7	1.5)	0.1	5.6
Latest hearing to award	1.3	1.0	0.1	8.4
Subtotal	3.6	3.2	0.7	12.2
Award to annulment decision	2.7	2.3	1.1	9.6
Total (including annulment)	6.3	6.3	1.1	13.3

Note: Based on 198 ICSID cases and 40 annulment requests, excluding settled cases (on average, it takes 5.1 years from registration to settlement, 2.5 years longer than for decided cases). The table includes contract, treaty, and investment law arbitrations, as well as ordinary ICSID and Additional Facility arbitrations.

Source: Waibel and Wu dataset, drawing on Sinclair (2009).

have taken more than 10 years to resolve (including annulment), whereas the shortest lasted for no more than 1.5 years.

The lack of information on the average duration of comparable proceedings in domestic courts makes it difficult to assess whether investment treaty arbitration is in fact a speedier alternative to litigation in domestic courts. Table 3.4 provides data on the duration of domestic civil litigation in select jurisdictions. English, German, Swiss, and US courts take on average between 14 months and 18 months to resolve standard commercial disputes. By contrast, Italian and Indian courts on average need 3 and 4 years, respectively.

When comparing Table 3.3 and Table 3.4, note that the average investor–state tribunal takes 3.6 years from the date of the request for arbitration to handing down an award. Notably, this is more than twice the duration for litigation in domestic courts in selected developed countries. At the same time, it is comparable to the average duration of litigation in Italian or Indian courts.

To illustrate the variable length of domestic civil litigation and investment treaty arbitration, consider the following two disputes that were adjudicated both before domestic courts and investment treaty tribunals. The first is *Chevron v. Ecuador* (2010). The investment treaty arbitration arose out of the extreme delays in trying to resolve commercial disputes in Ecuador. From 1991 to 1994, Texaco Petroleum, later a subsidiary of Chevron Corporation, began seven proceedings against Ecuador. In 2006, with the proceedings before Ecuadorian courts still unresolved, Chevron commenced investor–state arbitration under the US–Ecuador BIT. It argued that delays in the Ecuadorian court proceedings meant that Ecuador had failed to provide an 'effective means of enforcing rights' with respect to Chevron's investments. In 2010, four years later, the arbitral tribunal ruled in Chevron's favour.

Table 3.4 Average length of civil litigation

Country (overall 'Doing Business' ranking in brackets)	Average length (in years) to obtain and enforce final judgment (Doing Business 2016)	Average length (in years) to obtain first-instance decision (ICLG 2016)	Average length (in years) to obtain decision (2013 data)		
			First	Second	Final
England & Wales (33)	1.2*	1.5	0.9		
France (14)	1.1	–	0.8	0.9	0.9
Germany (12)	1.2	0.8	0.5	0.6	
Italy (111)	3.1	3.5	1.5	3.0	3.3
India (178)	3.9	7.5	–	–	–
United States (21)	1.0	1.5**	–	–	–
Switzerland (46)	1.1	1.5	0.4	0.4	0.3

* United Kingdom as a whole; ** denotes California only

Source: Author compilation, based on Doing Business (2016); International Comparative Legal Guides (ICLG) (2016); and OECD (2013).

By contrast, American pharmaceutical Eli Lilly brought a NAFTA arbitration against Canada in September 2013 following failed domestic litigation.[54] The Canadian court litigation had commenced in 2009 and 2010, and, in less than two years, the courts found that the company's pharmaceutical patents were invalid. This included an appeal by Eli Lilly. By contrast, the NAFTA arbitral tribunal held the main hearing only in May 2016—almost three years after the proceedings were commenced—and issued its award in March 2017.

Empirical research has yet to study in detail whether, and under what circumstances, domestic court litigation is quicker, slower, or the same as investment treaty arbitrations. One explanation for the relatively long duration of investment treaty disputes is that they may be significantly more complex in legal and/or factual terms than standard commercial litigation in domestic courts. However, the dispute against Canada referenced in the preceding text indicate that, in some instances, domestic courts may resolve comparable claims concerning the same set of facts more quickly.

Conclusion

This chapter surveyed the basic features of investment treaty arbitration, a method of resolving investment disputes based on the consent of the disputing parties. We examined important characteristics of investment treaty arbitration, such as party-appointments of arbitrators for each dispute and standing

[54] *Eli Lilly v. Novopharm* (2011); *Eli Lilly v. Novopharm* (2012); *Eli Lilly v. Novopharm* (2013).

of private investors. The chapter also introduced the UNCITRAL and ICSID Arbitration Rules, and the role of arbitral institutions in resolving investment treaty disputes. We examined the different phases of investment treaty arbitrations—including the jurisdictional, merits, and damages phases—as well as the review and annulment of arbitral awards and the 'translation' of international arbitral awards into domestic legal systems through the process of enforcement. Finally, we compared and contrasted investment treaty arbitration with potential alternatives: investor–state arbitration based on contracts and domestic laws, inter-state arbitration, ADR, and domestic court litigation. Against this background, Chapter 4 now turns to the substantive standards of protection commonly found in investment treaties.

4   Standards of Investment Protection

Introduction

This chapter introduces the substantive obligations in investment treaties. Although the treaties differ, most offer a common core of six substantive protections to foreign investors: most-favoured nation treatment (MFN); national treatment (NT); fair and equitable treatment (FET); a guarantee of compensation for expropriation; an umbrella clause; and a free transfer of funds clause. While investment treaties contain other substantive protections—such as the guarantee of full protection and security—many of these provide overlapping protection from host state conduct that would also breach one of the six core standards. Table 4.1 shows how common the main provisions are in investment treaties.[1]

In any given investment treaty arbitration, investors typically claim that the host state breached two or more substantive protections of the investment treaty. At the heart of most arbitrations are three so-called 'absolute' standards of protection: expropriation, the umbrella clause, and FET—standards that have no analogue in the international trade regime (Kurtz 2016, 79). The application of these three standards is normally decisive for outcomes in investment treaty arbitration, with FET playing a particularly important role. Table 4.2 shows how often investors have alleged breaches of substantive protections, how often investment tribunals have upheld each type of claim, and the success rate for each.

This chapter proceeds as follows. The first section examines MFN and NT, two 'relative' standards of protection. As described in Chapter 1, they are relative standards in the sense that their application requires a comparison of the way a state treats one foreign investment with the way it treats one (or more) other investments. The second section turns to four 'absolute' standards of protection: expropriation, FET, umbrella clauses, and free transfer of funds. They are 'absolute' in the sense that they require host states to guarantee foreign investors certain standards of treatment, regardless of how they treat

---

[1] We cross-checked the percentages by hand-coding a representative sample of 400 of the treaties used in Table 4.1. The percentages are similar to other studies. For example, Pohl, Mashigo, and Nohen (2012) find that only 6.5 per cent out of 1660 investment treaties do not include investor–state arbitration.

Table 4.1 Frequency of investment treaty provisions

	Investment treaties containing provision (%)
Most-favoured-nation treatment	95%
Expropriation	95%
Investor–state dispute settlement	90%
Fair and equitable treatment	90%
Free transfer of funds	80%
Full protection and security	70%
Losses sustained due to insurrection, war	70%
National treatment	60%
Arbitrary, unreasonable, and/or discriminatory treatment	45%
Umbrella clause	45%
Exceptions	10%
Performance requirements	5%

Source: Author compilation from 1602 investment treaties from UNCTAD's International Investment Agreements Navigator, last updated by UNCTAD in July 2016.

Table 4.2 Breaches of investment treaty provisions alleged and found in known investment treaty arbitrations

	Alleged/share of 739 arbitrations	Breach found	Success rate
Fair and equitable treatment	368/50%	93	36%
Indirect expropriation	331/45%	47	20%
Full protection and security	197/27%	19	13%
Arbitrary, unreasonable, and/or discriminatory treatment	163/22%	24	19%
Umbrella clause	107/14%	13	17%
National treatment	106/14%	8	13%
Most-favoured-nation treatment	84/11%	0/21	0%/41%
Direct expropriation	81/11%	19	42%
Other	50/7%	9	22%
Free transfer of funds	27/4%	2	10%
Performance requirements	12/2%	3	30%

Note: In the 'found' column for MFN, the '0' relates to better treatment granted to the investor/investments of a third nationality other than by virtue of another investment treaty; '21' refers to better treatment based on a third investment treaty where investors used the MFN clause as a stepping stone to another substantive guarantee (on this distinction, see the following text). Success rates are calculated as a percentage of decided cases (not shown). These rates exclude settled, pending and discontinued cases, which column 1 includes.

Source: Author compilation from 739 known investment treaty arbitrations in UNCTAD's Investment Dispute Settlement Navigator, with a few corrections of the coding by the authors. Last updated by UNCTAD in September 2016.

other investments. As investment treaty protections are often formulated in vague, imprecise terms, arbitral tribunals have a great degree of discretion in their interpretation and application. Consequently, each section considers how arbitral tribunals have interpreted and applied the six core treaty provisions in practice.

The third section examines carve-outs that remove certain state measures from the scope of application of investment treaties, defences that can justify or excuse breaches of investment treaty protections, and the standard of review that tribunals apply when examining host state conduct. Together, these three issues have a significant impact on the scope of a host state's obligations under investment treaties. The fourth and final section discusses the calculation of compensation or damages if host states have breached investment treaties.

Relative standards of protection: MFN and NT

This first section introduces the two relative standards: MFN and NT. MFN and NT protect foreign investors from discrimination based on the nationality of the investor. With the exception of using MFN to import provisions from *other* investment treaties (see Table 4.2), MFN and NT have only played a peripheral role in the investment treaty regime. This is in contrast with the international trade regime, where relative standards of treatment are the core, and is arguably for three reasons. First, with respect to national treatment, Chapter 1 described that the trend in investment policy since the 1990s has been for states to provide established foreign investors with equal treatment, and, in some cases, better treatment than domestic investors. Second, the narrow prohibition of discrimination on grounds of nationality leaves host states leeway to distinguish between investors based on other criteria supported by legitimate policy objectives—for example, imposing more stringent environmental requirements on investment in sectors that have greater environmental impacts. Third, the MFN and NT provisions of most investment treaties apply only after an investment has been made in the host state ('post-establishment'). This leaves host states free to impose discriminatory requirements on the admission and establishment of new foreign investment ('pre-establishment').

This section begins by examining the application of these twin non-discrimination standards to investments that host states have already admitted, before turning to the more recent extension of NT and MFN obligations to the pre-establishment phase. This shift has major policy implications and promises a greater role for NT and MFN in the future (see further Chapter 6).

POST-ESTABLISHMENT MFN AND NT

NT and MFN clauses bar host states from drawing nationality-based distinctions among investors. MFN prevents host countries from treating foreign investors of one nationality better than foreign investors of another nationality. NT prevents host states from treating its own investors better than foreign investors. Both clauses are typically broadly formulated, and traditionally apply to all state conduct affecting foreign investment. They are not normally subject to significant exceptions.

Both clauses prohibit *de jure* and *de facto* discrimination. *De jure* discrimination refers to the situation when a legal instrument—for example, a law of the host state or another investment treaty (see the following text)—provides less favourable 'treatment' to foreign investors on grounds of nationality. *De jure* discrimination is simple to identify, as it arises from explicit nationality-based distinctions contained in legal texts (Schill 2009, 218–21)—for example, a law that explicitly imposes more onerous regulatory requirements on investors of one nationality than investors of another nationality. In claims for *de jure* discrimination, the main issue has been the types of 'treatment' that fall within the scope of the relevant treaty provision.

By contrast, *de facto* discrimination refers to the factually disparate treatment of investors/investments of different foreign nationalities in cases where relevant laws and policies do not expressly discriminate between investors by nationality. As the burden of complying with laws that are not explicitly discriminatory often falls more heavily on some investors than others, identifying *de facto* discrimination raises more complex and controversial questions than *de jure* discrimination. A particular source of controversy has been whether a law that purports to address a legitimate policy aim, such as the protection of the environment or public health, amounts to *de facto* discrimination because the burden of complying with that law falls more heavily on foreign investors than domestic investors. The following section discusses these issues.

POST-ESTABLISHMENT MFN

MFN clauses appeared in the earliest investment treaties (e.g. the Germany–Pakistan BIT of 1959), and more than 90 per cent of investment treaties contain them (Table 4.1).[2] To illustrate the implications of the MFN provision, consider the following combined MFN/NT clause in the Austria–Kazakhstan BIT (2010).[3]

Each Contracting Party shall accord to investors of the other Contracting Party and their investments or returns treatment no less favourable than it accords to its own investors and their investments [NT] or to investors of any third country and their investments or returns [MFN] with respect to the management, operation, maintenance, use, enjoyment, sale and liquidation as well as dispute settlement of their investments or returns, whichever is more favourable to the investor.

---

[2] An exception to this trend is the Japan–Singapore FTA (Brown 2013, 360).

[3] In early investment treaties, both MFN and NT are frequently combined in a single provision. More recent investment treaties tend to contain separate and more detailed clauses, including exceptions—for example, Articles 3 and 4, US Model BIT 2012.

Under this MFN clause, Kazakhstan agrees to treat Austrian investors and investments at least as well as investors and investments from third countries. Austria made a reciprocal MFN commitment to Kazak investors. As such, Austria could not give more favourable treatment to US investors in an investment treaty or in an Austrian law than it gives to Kazakh investors. For example, if an Austrian law granted subsidies to established US investors in a particular sector, *established* Kazakh investors in that sector would be entitled to the same subsidy on account of the MFN provision of the Austria–Kazakhstan BIT. Crucially, for *de jure* discrimination, it is enough that a *hypothetical* investor in like circumstances be entitled to better treatment as a matter of law (Schill 2009, 519). A Kazakh investor would not need to identify a US investor operating in Austria that actually benefits from the subsidy.

There are at least three points of contrast between MFN obligations in the trade and investment treaty regimes.[4] First, in the investment regime, MFN obligations are bilateral, owed only to investors with the nationality of the other treaty party (here, by Austria to Kazakh investors and vice versa). In contrast, in the trade regime, MFN obligations are multilateral, owed by each WTO member to all 163 other WTO members (WTO 2016). Second, the scope of the MFN obligation in the trade regime operates 'within the relatively confined framework of the WTO covered agreements' (McRae 2012, 19). For example, the GATS allowed WTO members to provide for MFN exemptions on accession. Third, built-in exceptions to MFN in investment treaties are rare, unlike in trade agreements. For example, Article XXIV of the GATT carves out FTAs and custom unions from the operation of the MFN clause to the extent necessary for their formation (Bhagwati 2008)—a very significant limitation of MFN, given the proliferation of FTAs.[5]

Whereas MFN has played an important role in the trade regime (Kurtz 2016), its role in the practice of investment treaty arbitration has been limited. To date, no investment tribunal in a publicly available award has found that a host state breached MFN by treating a foreign investment from one state worse than a foreign investor from a third state (see Table 4.2, cf. also Caron and Shirlow 2015, 400). Thus far, MFN has exclusively functioned as an enabling device to import more favourable provisions from another investment treaty. This is by far the most important practical effect of MFN provisions in the modern investment treaty regime, and therefore the focus of the paragraphs in the following text.

---

[4] The comparison in this paragraph is between the WTO and investment treaties, leaving aside the MFN provisions of trade in goods and trade in services chapters of PTAs. Note that few disputes under PTAs are resolved in formal dispute settlement, with the exception of NAFTA and Mercosur (Davey 2007). See generally Allee and Elsig (2015).
[5] Similar carve-outs are found in some investment treaties—for example, those based on Singapore's de facto model BIT (Ho 2013, 637)—but are surprisingly uncommon.

Although most investment treaties share a common core of substantive protections, there is a degree of variation in such provisions between treaties. This heterogeneity of obligations, coupled with the reference to all 'treatment' in typical MFN clauses, has opened up space for arguments that the (higher) level of protection promised to foreign investors of a third state by an investment treaty between the host state and a third state qualifies as 'treatment' under MFN clauses. Under this interpretation of MFN, host states are bound to extend the most advantageous protections granted to the foreign investors of *any* of its treaty partners to a foreign investor that is covered by an investment treaty containing an MFN clause. Accordingly, some tribunals have allowed foreign investors covered by one investment treaty to invoke more generous substantive and procedural obligations contained in a host state's other investment treaties.

In this way, MFN clauses serve to 'multilateralize' substantive and potentially procedural guarantees across the investment treaty network (Schill 2009). The effect is to harmonize upwards states' obligations to foreign investors to the highest level of protection provided in *any* treaty of the host state. As a result, a state may owe foreign investors in its territory a combination of obligations that are more onerous than those found in any one investment treaty (considered individually) to which it is a party. Despite being made up of bilateral treaties, MFN provisions thereby give the investment treaty regime a multilateral flavour. Apart from the practical implications, this is also important for how empirical researchers test the effects of investment treaties, something we return to in Chapter 6.

One of the known investment treaty arbitrations in which the investor successfully relied on the MFN to import substantive protections from another investment treaty is *White Industries v. India* (2011). An Australian investor in India sought compensation under the Australia–India BIT for the Indian court system's 8-year delay in enforcing a commercial arbitration award against an Indian state-owned company. The Australia–India BIT did not contain any provisions explicitly dealing with judicial processes; however, it did contain a standard post-establishment MFN provision. The tribunal accepted the investor's argument that the investor was entitled to use this MFN provision to rely on a provision of the Kuwait–India BIT, in which India guaranteed to provide Kuwaiti investors with an 'effective means of asserting claims and enforcing rights with respect to investments'. The tribunal held that India breached this standard.

This importation of substantive provisions from other investment treaties contrasts with how MFN provisions work in the trade regime. Even more controversial, however, is whether MFN clauses allow investors to invoke more favourable *procedural* dispute settlement guarantees in other treaties (Banifatemi 2009; Douglas 2010; Maupin 2011). The answer again turns on the range of 'treatment' that the MFN provision in question covers, and, more precisely, whether MFN clauses cover variations of arbitral procedure, and the extension of subject matter and temporal jurisdiction. As most MFN provisions do not specify whether 'treatment' includes procedural rights conferred by other treaties, it has fallen to arbitral tribunals to resolve this matter.

As Table 4.3 shows, arbitral tribunals are divided on whether MFN can be used to invoke more favourable dispute settlement procedures in other investment treaties. For example, in the case of *Maffezini v. Spain* (2000), a foreign investor successfully used an MFN provision in the Argentina–Spain BIT to circumvent a procedural requirement in that BIT to exhaust local remedies—that is, to litigate first in the Spanish domestic courts—before commencing arbitration. Another Spanish BIT did not contain this procedural requirement. The tribunal's rationale was that such procedural advantages under this second BIT were 'essential for the adequate protection of the [substantive] rights they sought to guarantee' and, therefore, fell within the range of 'treatment' covered by an MFN clause of the Argentina–Spain BIT (para. 55). Other tribunals have disagreed with this reasoning, however, and stressed the undesirability of displacing specifically negotiated procedures between the two state parties (*Plama v. Bulgaria* 2005).

Table 4.3 Use of MFN to import different types of provisions

Type of MFN question	MFN invocation successful?		
	Yes	No	Dissent
Change arbitral procedure	11	3	4
Extend temporal scope	0	2	0
Expand subject matter scope	1	11	3
Import substantive obligations	9	1	0
Better treatment	0	13	0
Totals	21	30	7

Note: *Change in arbitral procedure*: investor attempts to invoke more favourable dispute settlement procedures in another investment treaty. *Extend temporal scope*: investor attempts to invoke the broader temporal coverage of another investment treaty. *Expand subject matter scope*: investor attempts to invoke the broader range of 'investments' or government measures covered by another investment treaty. *Import substantive obligations*: investor attempts to invoke substantive protections contained in other investment treaties. *Better treatment*: the investor alleges that the host state offered better treatment—other than in a third investment treaty—to investments/investors of a third nationality. The table is limited to decided cases that are publicly available (a significant number of pending and settled cases in which investors invoked the MFN clause but no further information is available is left out). For the last two categories—the importation of substantive obligations and better treatment—the table only includes cases where the tribunal reached a finding on the investor's MFN claim (i.e. it excludes cases in which the tribunal declined jurisdiction and also cases such as *Bilcon v. Canada* (2015) in which the tribunal did not decide the MFN claim). In addition, in four cases in the fourth category, tribunals did not allow the investor to bypass exceptions based on the MFN clause, or found that the investor failed to show that another BIT was more favourable. In another dozen cases, tribunals did not decide the claim that investors could use the MFN clauses to import substantive provisions.

Source: Authors' coding of arbitral awards. The first three rows draw on Box 2 in Maupin (2011, 172), extended and updated by the authors.

Foreign investors have also attempted to use MFN provisions to expand the coverage of an investment treaty to include types of disputes and investments that fall outside the coverage of the treaty in question, but within the broader jurisdictional parameters of another of the host state's investment treaties. There is virtually no support among tribunals for the use of MFN clauses to expand an investment treaty's jurisdictional scope in this way. This is because an investor is only able to benefit from the MFN provision of an investment treaty if it first establishes that it falls within the scope of that treaty's coverage. An investor that falls outside the coverage of an investment treaty is simply not entitled to the benefit of that treaty's MFN provision, meaning that it has no entitlement to demand more favourable treatment of any sort provided by a host state's other investment treaties.

The extent to which MFN provisions allow investors covered by one investment treaty to benefit from the more favourable substantive and procedural provisions of other investment treaties has been controversial. In response, some states have begun to draft MFN provisions in new investment treaties more precisely.[6] For example, the Austria–Kazakhstan BIT cited in the preceding text expressly extends MFN to dispute settlement—a reaction to arbitral awards that excluded procedural matters from MFN clauses. Conversely, the MFN provisions of other new investment treaties, such as the TPP, explicitly prevent the importation of procedural provisions from other investment treaties.[7] Some new treaties, such as CETA, go even further and prevent the importation of *both* substantive and procedural treaty provisions.[8] Such limits on importation of terms from other investment treaties are essential if a state wishes to enter into new investment treaties that grant lower levels of protection than its existing treaties. Moreover, the approach in CETA is similar to how MFN clauses operate in the trade regime. If CETA is ratified and future investment treaties were to follow this approach, the operation of MFN clauses in the trade and investment regime could converge (see Kurtz 2016).

POST-ESTABLISHMENT NATIONAL TREATMENT

Although a standard provision in modern investment treaties, NT was less commonly included in investment treaties in the early years of the regime than

---

[6] In Chapter 9, we return to *greater precision* as one technique by which states have reasserted control over the investment treaty regime.

[7] Article 9.5 (3) TPP 2016.

[8] Article X.7 CETA 2016: 'For greater certainty, the "treatment" referred to in Paragraph 1 and 2 does not include investor-to-state dispute settlement procedures provided for in other international investment treaties and other trade agreements. Substantive obligations in other international investment treaties and other trade agreements do not in themselves constitute "treatment", and thus cannot give rise to a breach of this article, absent measures adopted by a Party pursuant to such obligations'.

MFN (see Table 4.1). Some countries—such as China—still subject NT pro-visions to qualification or limitation (Gallagher and Shan 2013, 160). The purpose of NT provisions is to ensure a 'level playing field' between domestic and foreign investors (Dolzer and Schreuer 2012, 198). The metaphor of a *playing field*—also influential in the international trade regime—invokes a relationship between competitors. Notwithstanding the widespread accept-ance of the *playing field* metaphor, economic ideas about the nature and extent of competitive interactions among various investors and investments have played a surprisingly limited role in how arbitral tribunals interpret and apply investment treaties' NT provisions.[9]

NT has only played a minor role in the practice of the investment treaty regime to date. Insofar as NT claims have been brought to arbitration, most involve allegations of *de facto* discrimination (Bjorklund 2010, 411; Henckels 2015, 78). Among known cases, only eight tribunals have decided NT claims in favour of investors (see Table 4.2). All were under investment treaties that extend NT to the pre-establishment phase. And, with one exception, all were concerned with *general* measures affecting the *importation* of foreign-produced goods such as discriminatory taxes or quantitative restrictions—the traditional domain of trade law.[10]

Foreign investors need to meet two conditions to succeed in claims of *de facto* discrimination in breach of a guarantee of NT. They have to show that their investment has (i) been treated less favourably; than (ii) a comparable domestic investment. With respect to element (ii), the central question is whether particular domestic investments can reasonably be compared to the foreign investment in question. In answering this question, arbitral tribunals have also considered whether there is a reasonable justification for treating the foreign investment less favourably. For example, if a host state imposes more onerous environmental conditions on a foreign-owned gold mine than it imposes on a domestic-owned gold mine, this would normally breach NT. However, if the differences in environmental conditions resulted from a more polluting extraction technique used by the foreign-owned firm, or because the foreign-owned mine operated in a more ecologically sensitive area, an arbitral tribunal might regard these investments as not comparable. On this basis, a tribunal might regard any difference in treatment of the two mines as justified and, therefore, not a breach of NT.

---

[9] We examine the implications of economic ideas for the interpretation and application of NT provisions in Chapter 5.

[10] The only exception thus far is the arbitration *Bilcon v. Canada* (2015). It concerned a Canadian environmental review panel's rejection of a foreign investor's proposal for a new mining project. The NT claims at issue did not unequivocally concern post-establishment protection. Six of the NT claims were under the NAFTA and two under US investment treaties (both of which extend NT to the pre-establishment phase). We return to the distinction between general and specific measures in Chapter 9.

Arbitral tribunals have differed on the choice of comparator in NT claims. For example, in *Methanex v. US* (2005), the tribunal held that the treatment of a foreign investor should be compared to the treatment of domestic investors in the most similar situation. As such, it compared the treatment of a Canadian methanol producer to US-owned methanol producers and found no breach of NT. In reaching this conclusion, the tribunal held that the more beneficial treatment given to US *ethanol* producers was not relevant as a comparator. In contrast, in *Cargill v. Mexico* (2009), the tribunal found that Mexican producers of cane sugar were relevant comparators when considering the treatment of US-owned producers of high-fructose corn syrup operating in Mexico. (Both cane sugar and high-fructose corn syrup are used to sweeten soft drinks.) On this basis, a tax that applied to high-fructose corn syrup—but did not apply to cane sugar—breached NT. The tribunal in *Occidental v. Ecuador I* (2004) took an even broader approach to the choice of comparator in NT claims. It held that Ecuador's imposition of value-added tax on oil exports—but not on the export of other products—breached NT, even though the tax applied equally to oil exports by both foreign and Ecuadorian-owned companies. This is because the tribunal found that Ecuadorian companies in the mining, seafood, and cut flowers sectors were relevant comparators in assessing the treatment of a foreign investor in the oil sector, because all were involved in producing goods for export.[11]

Differences in treaty language are relevant in clarifying the basis for comparison in NT claims. As is typical of European BITs, the non-discrimination provision in the Austria–Kazakhstan BIT in the preceding text does not provide any guidance on the choice of comparator in NT, leaving the question entirely to the tribunal. NAFTA states that a foreign investor/investment should be compared to a domestic investor/investment 'in like circumstances', but leaves it up to the tribunal to determine when investors are 'in like circumstances'.[12] The TPP, which was signed but had not entered into force at the time of publication,[13] contains the further clarification that a determination of whether investors/investments are in like circumstances 'depends on the totality of the circumstances, including whether the relevant treatment distinguishes between investors or investments on the basis of legitimate public welfare objectives'.[14] This clarification directs tribunals to consider the justifications for any differences in treatment—for example, that the more onerous environmental conditions imposed on a particular foreign investment may be justified by its more serious environmental impacts.

---

[11] Other tribunals consider the extent to which the firms compete with one another—for example the *SD Myers v. Canada* case examined in Chapter 5.

[12] Articles 1103 and 1104 NAFTA 1992.

[13] As mentioned in Chapter 1, the TPP's prospects were uncertain at the time of writing, following President Trump's withdrawal of the US signature on 23 January 2017.

[14] Footnote 14 to Article 9.4 TPP 2016.

INVESTMENT LIBERALIZATION: NT AND MFN
IN THE PRE-ESTABLISHMENT PHASE

As noted in Chapter 1, investment treaties historically did not limit states' ability to restrict or prohibit new foreign investment. While many older investment treaties require host states to 'encourage and admit' new foreign investment, these provisions are expressly subordinated to the host state's law, and toothless in practice.[15] Even today, about 90 per cent of investment treaties, including virtually all European BITs and the Energy Charter Treaty, do not contain binding provisions governing the admission of new foreign investment (UNCTAD 2015b, 3).

However, investment treaties increasingly do extend guarantees of NT and MFN to the entry and establishment of foreign investment. Such provisions are standard in recent Canadian, US, and Japanese BITs (Joubin-Bret 2008, 11). They are also an increasingly common feature of multilateral investment treaties[16] and the investment chapters of multi-issue preferential trade agreements (PTAs) (see Table 4.2).[17] Under this approach, non-discrimination extends to the 'admission', 'establishment,' and 'acquisition' of investments, as opposed to only applying to the 'management', 'conduct,' and 'operation' of investments (post-establishment). For example, NAFTA Article 1102 states that each state 'shall accord NT with respect to the *establishment, acquisition,* expansion, management, conduct, operation, and sale or other disposition of investments'.

The application of NT and MFN provisions to the pre-establishment phase is sometimes described as creating 'market access' obligations (e.g. Sacerdoti 1997, 321–31; DiMascio and Pauwelyn 2008, 56). However, the use of the term 'market access' in this context is confusing. Provisions such as NAFTA Article 1102 do not prevent states from placing restrictions and conditions on the admission and establishment of new investment in their territory, so long as such restrictions and conditions do not discriminate by nationality.[18]

Nevertheless, the application of NT to the pre-establishment phase potentially prohibits the use of restrictions on new foreign investment in the pursuit of other policy objectives. For example, many states limit foreign investment in strategic industries on national security grounds; regulate foreign investment in the media sector to ensure plurality; limit the ability of foreign

---

[15] For example, Article 3, French Model BIT 2006: 'Each of the Contracting Parties encourages and admits, *in accordance with its legislation* and the provisions of the present Agreement, investments . . .'.

[16] For example, Article 5, ASEAN Comprehensive Investment Agreement, 2009.

[17] For example, Articles 9.4 and 9.5, TPP 2016; Article X.4, CETA 2016.

[18] Moreover, the term 'market access' in trade treaties refers to a specific set of obligations concerned with the elimination of quantitative restrictions (e.g. Article XVI, GATS; Chapter 10, Article X.4, CETA). 'Market access' provisions in this specific sense of the term differ from pre-establishment MFN and NT.

nationals to own land; impose joint venture requirements on foreign invest-ment in particular sectors to encourage technology transfer to local firms; and place restrictions and conditions on foreign investment to protect local firms from foreign competition. Absent relevant exceptions, such measures breach NT in the pre-establishment phase.[19] For instance, Singapore applies an additional buyer's stamp duty of 15 per cent to foreign nationals buying land.[20] As a result of the unqualified NT obligation in the Singapore–US FTA 2001, US citizens are entitled to the same treatment as Singaporeans, and, consequently, do not need to pay the higher rate of tax (unlike, for example, Chinese, Indonesian, or Malay citizens purchasing property in Singapore) (Vaughan 2013).

Pre-establishment NT and MFN obligations have played no role in invest-ment treaty arbitration to date. Time will tell whether they acquire greater importance. Yet, even in the absence of claims brought to arbitration, the extension of MFN/NT obligations to the pre-establishment phase could have powerful behind-the-border effects in requiring host states to remove or amend discriminatory restrictions on foreign investment. We return to the issue of the impact of investment treaties on state decision-making in Chapters 5, 6, and 9—an important area for further research.

Absolute standards of protection

We now turn to four 'absolute' standards of protection: expropriation, FET, umbrella clauses, and free transfer of funds. These standards of protection are 'absolute' in the sense that they require host states to guarantee certain stand-ards of treatment to foreign investors and investments covered by the treaty, regardless of how other investors and investment are treated. We focus on these four absolute standards, as they typically capture breaches of other substantive protections as well—such as the prohibition of arbitrary, unreasonable, or discriminatory measures, which overlaps significantly with FET and NT.

NO EXPROPRIATION WITHOUT COMPENSATION

Expropriation refers to state conduct that deprives investors of title to prop-erty, or otherwise substantially deprives investors of their investments.[21] Investment treaties allow states to expropriate foreign investments, but this right is subject to the payment of compensation (see again the discussion of

---

[19] Figure 8.4 shows exceptions to pre-establishment national treatment in selected US treaties.
[20] Inland Revenue Authority of Singapore (2016).
[21] We use the terms 'nationalization' and 'taking' as synonyms for 'expropriation'.

'liability rules' in Chapter 1). Recall from Chapter 2 that most investment treaties cover a broad range of investments, including intangible rights (e.g. intellectual property rights) and financial instruments (e.g. bonds and hedging contracts). As such, the application of investment treaties' expropriation provisions extends beyond the expropriation of physical assets such as factories and mines.

The legal principles governing expropriation of foreign investment are rooted in customary international law. Customary international law acknowledges a state's right to expropriate foreign-owned property subject to three conditions: the expropriation must (i) serve a public purpose; (ii) be carried out with due process of law; and, most importantly, (iii) be accompanied by 'full' compensation—a standard understood to refer to an investment's fair market value (see section on 'Compensation and Damages' in the following text). The duty to pay compensation is by far the most important condition in practice; although many expropriations comply with conditions (i) and (ii), investors frequently contend that host states fail to pay full compensation.

These standard conditions are also found in most investment treaties. For example, Article 5 of the 2008 UK Model Investment Treaty provides:

Investments of nationals or companies of either Contracting party shall not be nationalized, expropriated or subjected to measures having effect equivalent to nationalization or expropriation in the territory of the other Contracting Party except for a public purpose related to the internal needs of that Party on a non-discriminatory basis and against prompt, adequate and effective compensation.

As with almost all investment treaties, Article 5 distinguishes between direct expropriations ('investments... shall not be nationalized [or] expropriated') and indirect expropriations ('or subjected to measures having effect equivalent to nationalization or expropriation'). Both are equally compensable.

Direct expropriation involves a transfer of title or physical seizure of an investment. The expropriation comes about in a single act, and is usually easy to identify. As direct expropriations without compensation are becoming rare (see Chapter 1), only about one in ten of the more than 700 known investment treaty arbitrations have alleged a violation of this provision (Table 4.2). Instead, the more important question in arbitral practice is how to identify *indirect* expropriation. Investors have alleged indirect expropriation in 45 per cent of all known investment treaty arbitrations (Table 4.2),[22] and the subject has proven highly controversial (Fortier and Drymer 2004; Ratner 2008, 229, 482–4; Schneiderman 2008, 75; Shirlow 2014). Several considerations are important for this distinction, which we review in the following text.

---

[22] The 2008 UK Model BIT, Article 5, for instance, describes indirect expropriation as 'measures having effect equivalent to nationalization or expropriation'.

As a starting point, it is important to clarify that mere reductions in the profitability of an investment are insufficient for an indirect expropriation to have occurred; what is needed is a loss of such magnitude that it very substantially lowers the value of an investment. For example, in one recent case, a tribunal concluded that significant reductions in the feed-in tariffs that Spain paid to foreign-owned solar plants did not amount to expropriation (*Charanne v. Spain* 2016).[23] Equally, even though Argentina's modification of gas distribution licenses in the early 2000s in the aftermath of its financial crisis had a negative impact on the businesses of foreign investors, a tribunal found that the impact was not severe enough, nor sufficiently permanent in duration, to amount to indirect expropriation (*LG&E v. Argentina* 2006, para. 200). Similarly, host states can significantly increase levels of taxation without the resulting tax burden amounting to an indirect expropriation (*Paushok v. Mongolia*, para. 332).

While arbitral practice unanimously supports the view that state conduct can only amount to indirect expropriation if it results in a substantial deprivation of the investor's investment, there is an ongoing controversy about how to draw the line between indirect expropriation and a state's non-compensable exercise of regulatory powers to meet public policy objectives. There are many cases in which state conduct has a substantial negative impact on an investor's business but in which the state asserts a justification for such interference on public policy grounds. Examples from previous arbitrations include a host state cancelling an investor's operating license citing the failure of the investor to meet mandatory environmental standards (e.g. *Tecmed v. Mexico* 2003), and a state banning the sale of an investor's product citing public health risks (e.g. *Chemtura v. Canada* 2010). Some tribunals have articulated implicit exceptions to the concept of indirect expropriation—namely, that non-discriminatory regulatory measures in pursuit of legitimate policies *never* amount to indirect expropriation regardless of the magnitude of loss, or interference with, an investment (e.g. *Methanex v. US* 2005, Part IV, Chapter D, para. 7).

More generally, there are two stylized approaches in determining whether a measure affecting a foreign investment amounts to indirect expropriation and, therefore, obliges the host state to compensate the investor. The first approach looks exclusively to the *effect* of the state conduct on the investment, including the degree of economic loss that the conduct causes to investors and the extent to which it interferes with the investor's legal rights to use and enjoy the property (Schreuer 2006; Hoffmann 2008). This view accepts that state conduct must have created a 'persistent or irreparable obstacle' to the operation of the investment (*Generation Ukraine* 2003, para. 20.32), but permits little or no

---

[23] At the time of writing, more than 30 similar arbitrations were pending against Spain concerning its modifications of feed-in tariffs for solar energy.

consideration of the state's regulatory purpose. This 'effects' approach was particularly influential in early investment treaty arbitral decisions. For example, in *Metalclad v. Mexico* (2000), the tribunal held that a local government's refusal to issue a construction permit to a landfill that had been approved by all other levels of the Mexican government amounted to an indirect expropriation. In the words of the tribunal, the local government's inaction was a 'covert or incidental interference with the use of property which has the effect of depriving the owner, in whole or in significant part, of the use or reasonably-to-be-expected economic benefit of property even if not necessarily to the obvious benefit of the host State' (para. 103).

A second approach adopts a narrower view of indirect expropriation, granting states greater latitude to regulate foreign investment for legitimate public purposes. Alongside the intensity of interference with the property of the investor, this approach considers the *purpose* and *characteristics* of host state measures. For example, in another case against Mexico, the tribunal considered Mexico's decision to discontinue its practice of granting tax rebates on cigarette exports to a foreign investor. In addition to noting that the measure had not deprived the investor of control over its investment, the tribunal observed that the change in practice affected *all* cigarette resellers and was justified by the purpose of discouraging tobacco smuggling (*Feldman v. Mexico* paras. 112–16, 136–7). Taken together, these factors meant that Mexico's measure did not amount to indirect expropriation.

The 'effects' approach to indirect expropriation has been especially controversial, as critics argue that it provides greater protection to foreign investors than is provided to private property rights in most developed legal systems (Montt 2009). In response to these, and other, criticisms, a newer generation of investment treaties define the concept of 'indirect expropriation' more precisely, thereby reducing arbitral tribunals' interpretative discretion (Nikièma 2012; Moloo and Jacinto 2013). The first and most influential clarification was a new annex to the 2004 US Model BIT, which clarifies that non-discriminatory regulatory measures will only amount to indirect expropriation 'in rare circumstances'.[24] It also directs arbitral tribunals to distinguish between indirect expropriation and legitimate, non-compensable regulation based on three factors:

(1) the degree of interference with property rights;
(2) the character of the government measure—that is, its purpose and context; and
(3) the interference of the measure with reasonable and investment-backed expectations—notably, expectations related to the use of the investment.

---

[24] Annex B on Expropriation, US Model BIT 2004. Canadian investment treaties follow a similar approach.

These three factors are adapted from the US Supreme Court's jurisprudence on indirect expropriation, notably the decision in *Penn Central Transportation Co. v. New York City' (1978)* (Sanders 2010). The US government's decision to define 'indirect expropriation' based on the way that concept is understood in US law followed a Congressional direction to the US Executive in 2002 that US investment treaties should not provide protection to foreign investment beyond that found in US law (Gagné and Morin 2006). The annex on indirect expropriation has been included in all subsequent US investment treaties. It has also diffused into the treaty practice of other states. Similar text clarifying the meaning of indirect expropriation is now found in investment treaties as diverse as the ASEAN Comprehensive Investment Agreement (ACIA), the Comprehensive Economic and Trade Agreement (CETA) between Canada and the EU, the China–Japan–Korea trilateral investment treaty, and the TPP.[25]

FAIR AND EQUITABLE TREATMENT

We turn now to the most important substantive protection in the investment treaty regime, FET. Consider the following sample clause:

'Each Contracting State shall in its territory in every case accord investments by investors of the other Contracting State fair and equitable treatment'.[26]

As with most FET clauses, this short and open-ended formulation provides broad interpretive discretion to investment tribunals. Whereas the outcome in early investment treaty arbitrations often turned on the application of indirect expropriation, the interpretation and application of FET provisions has been decisive in most disputes since 2000. (This is an important point for empirical scholarship on investment treaty arbitration, some of which still focuses primarily on indirect expropriation; e.g. Pelc 2016). Investors have invoked the FET standard to challenge the entire gamut of state conduct, including changes to legislation of general application, decisions of executive agencies of the host state specifically addressed to the investor in question, and the actions of the host state's judiciary.

One important point of contrast between FET and the concept of indirect expropriation is that host states may breach FET even if the impact of state conduct on the foreign investor falls short of a 'substantial deprivation' of an investment necessary for expropriation. Moreover, in contrast to NT and MFN, a host state's action may breach FET even if it is non-discriminatory. Investment tribunals 'regularly apply [FET] in a broad manner, using it as a yardstick for the conduct of the national legislator, of domestic administrations, and of domestic courts' (Schill 2009, 79). For this

---

[25] Annex 2, ASEAN Comprehensive Investment Agreement 2009; Annex 8-A, CETA 2016; protocol to the China–Japan–Korea trilateral investment treaty 2012; Annex 9-B, TPP 2016.
[26] Article 2(2), German Model BIT 2009.

reason, the FET standard has begun to eclipse the operation of other substantive protections.

The meaning of FET is the subject of disagreement between arbitral tribunals, states, and academics. In practice, arbitral tribunals have played a major role in elaborating the meaning of FET through the interpretation and application of FET in individual disputes (on the 'law-making' functions of tribunals, see Chapter 9). Tribunals have considered a range of factors in determining whether host states have breached FET, including: (i) the extent to which state conduct interferes with or alters a foreign investor's legal rights under domestic law; (ii) the extent to which state conduct breaches promises made to foreign investors; (iii) the extent to which state conduct is consistent with standards of procedural fairness and due process; (iv) the extent to which state conduct pursues a legitimate policy objective; and (v) the likely effectiveness of the state conduct in achieving its intended policy objective.

Given these interlocking factors, the exposition of the FET standard in legal texts is almost always organized around a discussion of the different 'elements' of FET—that is, more specific legal principles that apply to particular categories of cases. However, no two academic commentators propose the same taxonomy of 'elements' (cf. Newcombe and Paradell 2009, 275; Dolzer and Schreuer 2012, 145; Vandevelde 2012, 190; Paparinskis 2013, 239; Salacuse 2013, 388; Bonnitcha 2014a, 161). In this section, we organize discussion of the FET standard under the following three headings: (i) denial of justice and due process, (ii) arbitrary or unreasonable conduct, and (iii) legitimate expectations.

Denial of justice and due process

This first dimension of the FET standard refers to requirements of procedural fairness in administrative and judicial proceedings. It includes procedural requirements such as investors' rights to make submissions to decision-making processes affecting their interests, to unbiased and impartial decision-making, and to knowing the basis and reasons for state decisions so that investors can challenge them (Schill 2010, 158). Arbitral consideration of whether a state has breached this element of the FET standard looks to the *process*, as opposed to the outcome, of proceedings affecting the foreign investor.

Take the example of *Loewen v. United States* (2003), described in Chapter 3. Here, Loewen argued that its treatment in the Mississippi court system amounted to a breach of FET by the United States. For unrelated reasons, the arbitral tribunal found that it lacked jurisdiction over this claim. However, it explained that, if it had had jurisdiction over the dispute, it would have found that the serious procedural irregularities in Mississippi state court's conduct amounted to a denial of justice in breach of the FET provision of the investment treaty (para. 137; see also Paulsson 2005, 186).

Arbitrary or unreasonable conduct

A second dimension of FET is the prohibition on 'arbitrary' or 'unreasonable' state conduct that interferes with a foreign investor's investment. Although they are not always consistent, arbitral tribunals normally use the term 'arbitrariness' to mean a lack of a rational policy justification for measures adversely affecting a foreign investor (e.g. *Noble v. Romania* 2005, para. 177; Paparinskis 2013, 241).[27] Used in the sense of lack of rationality, 'arbitrariness' overlaps with concepts such as 'reasonableness' and 'proportionality', which also direct a tribunal's attention to the strength of a state's policy justifications for conduct affecting foreign investors. These issues also overlap with the degree of deference that arbitral tribunals should show to states' policy judgments, an issue that we consider in more detail in the next section.

Tribunals have taken radically different views about the extent to which FET entitles a tribunal to evaluate the strength of policy justification for measures that affect foreign investors. The tribunal in *SD Myers v. Canada* (2000) took the view that tribunals applying the FET standard do not have:

> ...an open-ended mandate to second-guess government decision-making. Governments have to make many potentially controversial choices. In doing so, they may appear to have made mistakes, to have misjudged the facts, proceeded on the basis of a misguided economic or sociological theory, placed too much emphasis on some social values over others and adopted solutions that are ultimately ineffective or counterproductive (para. 261).

In contrast, other arbitral tribunals have taken a more active role in evaluating the justifications for state conduct under challenge. For example, in *Occidental II*, the tribunal engaged in detailed scrutiny of whether Ecuador was justified in terminating a concession contract in response to Occidental's prior breach of that contract. It concluded that Ecuador's decision to terminate was disproportionate, because Ecuador could have responded to Occidental's breach of contract in ways that were less damaging to Occidental's interests (*Occidental v. Ecuador II* 2012, para. 452). The extent to which arbitral tribunals should use the FET standard as a tool to review the policy justifications for state conduct remains a controversial issue.

---

[27] In contrast to this usage, the arbitral tribunal in *Bilcon v. Canada* concluded that the conduct of a Canadian environmental review panel breached the FET standard because it was 'arbitrary'. However, the tribunal used the term 'arbitrary' to refer to *procedural* failures relating to the way Canada carried out the review. The tribunal said that it was not expressing an opinion on whether a decision to approve or not approve the project was justified (paras. 602–3).

Legitimate expectations and stability of the legal framework

A third dimension of FET is the protection of investors' 'legitimate expectations'. Investment tribunals differ in the weight they give to legitimate expectations under FET, and in how to distinguish those expectations protected by investment treaties from those that are not. Among tribunals that see an important role for legitimate expectations under FET, most recognize that there are two significant limitations: (i) that the investor's expectations must be based on a *specific* commitment made by the host state to the investor; and (ii) that these expectations must be *reasonable* in light of the circumstances.

A comparison of the various arbitral awards arising out of the Argentine financial crisis of 2001 illustrates the first requirement of a specific commitment. Prior to the crisis, the Argentine peso had been pegged to the US dollar, and a range of investment contracts were denominated in dollars. When Argentina dismantled the currency convertibility regime, it modified the terms of gas distribution licenses of foreign investors. The licenses had specifically guaranteed the payment of gas tariffs to investors in US dollars and indexed to the US gas market. In a series of cases, the foreign license holders successfully argued that Argentina's actions had breached their legitimate expectations by violating these specific commitments (e.g. *LG&E v. Argentina* 2007, para. 134).

Continental Casualty, a US insurance company operating in Argentina, also challenged the dismantling of the currency convertibility regime and the forced pesification of dollar-denominated contracts and debt. It argued that it had a legitimate expectation that the regime would remain in place, and that this expectation was derived from Argentinian legislation establishing the currency convertibility regime and ministerial pronouncements (*Continental Casualty v. Argentina* 2008, para. 252). However, the tribunal held that, in the absence of a specific commitment addressed directly to the claimant that the regime would be maintained, the claimant could not have any legitimate expectation that the regime would continue in force. Similarly, in *Charanne v. Spain* (2016), the arbitral tribunal found that the Spanish legislative framework for investment in the solar sector, though aimed only at a limited number of investors, did not create specific commitments vis-à-vis each solar investor, and therefore could not create a legitimate expectation of a stable legal framework. In the tribunal's view, any other conclusion would have unduly constrained the host state's right to regulate (paras. 493).[28] At the time of writing, several dozen pending solar arbitrations turn on whether other tribunals reach the same conclusion.

---

[28] See Chapter 9 for further discussion on the impact of investment treaties on host states' exercise of regulatory power in practice.

Second, representations by themselves are insufficient—they must also generate *reasonable* expectations. A good example of unreasonable expectations is *Thunderbird v. Mexico* (2006). The US company Thunderbird asked the Mexican Interior Ministry whether its gaming machines were lawful under Mexican law. Based on Thunderbird's description of its machines, the ministry informed Thunderbird that its business venture would be lawful. However, Thunderbird had not accurately described its machines, and Mexico subsequently closed down the company's gaming facilities. In light of Thunderbird's misrepresentation, the tribunal concluded that Thunderbird had no legitimate expectation that it could operate gaming facilities in Mexico.

Finally, related to legitimate expectations is the controversial notion that major changes to the legal framework of a host state made after a foreign investment was established could violate FET. The legal issue here is whether foreign investors have a 'legitimate expectation' of a stable regulatory environment, even absent expectations based on specific commitments. In one view, the host state's legal framework as such is an important source of expectations on the part of the investor (Dolzer and Schreuer 2012, 115). This has some support among arbitral tribunals (e.g. *Occidental v. Ecuador* 2004), but it remains an outlying view. Several investment tribunals have criticized the view that FET entails a general guarantee of stability of the legal environment (*LG&E v. Argentina* 2007, paras. 66–7; *Suez v. Argentina* 2010, para. 224).[29]

The broad range of protections that FET confers on foreign investors, coupled with a success rate of 37 per cent for investors, has made this open-ended standard the most important, albeit controversial, substantive guarantee in the modern investment treaty regime. It allows for compensation even in disputes where no expropriation, discrimination, or denial of justice has taken place. To its champions, the quasi-constitutional standard of FET embodies the rule of law in the investment treaty regime (Schill 2009, 333–8), whereas to critics it has 'disempower[ed] governments from modifying their laws, even in reaction to new threats to the public welfare' (Alvarez 2011a, 248).

State responses to concerns about FET

States have been slow to respond to developments in arbitral jurisprudence in ways that clarify the meaning of FET (cf. Alschner 2016). An exception is the authoritative interpretation issued by the three NAFTA state parties in July 2001 (NAFTA Notes of Interpretation 2001). It stated that FET does not go

---

[29] As Chapter 5 shows, stringent guarantees of a stable and predictable legal framework are problematic from an economic perspective.

beyond the requirements of customary international law. This joint intervention by Canada, Mexico, and the United States was a response to the expansive
interpretation of FET by the arbitral tribunal in *Pope & Talbot v. Canada* in
June 2001. However, this joint interpretation did not clarify the standard of
protection required by customary international law, which is itself a subject of
disagreement and uncertainty, and has done little to resolve the debate.

Against this background, a new trend of defining FET more precisely within
the text of investment treaties is beginning to emerge. For example, Article X.9
of CETA contains the following exhaustive list of the 'elements' of FET:

(i) denial of justice;
(ii) fundamental breach of due process, including a fundamental breach of
transparency;
(iii) manifest arbitrariness;
(iv) targeted discrimination on manifestly wrongful grounds, such as gender,
race, or religious belief; and
(v) abusive treatment of investors, such as coercion, duress, and harassment.

These 'elements' overlap with those considered in this chapter, except that a
breach of legitimate expectations is not recognized as a freestanding ground
for violation of the FET standard.[30] If and when CETA enters into force, it
will be important to examine whether these clarifications narrow tribunals'
application and interpretation of the FET provision, or whether the specific
introduction of a term such as 'manifest arbitrariness' broadens the scope of
the provision in some cases.[31]

UMBRELLA CLAUSES

The fifth substantive protection we consider is the umbrella clause, included
in roughly half of all investment treaties (Table 4.1; UNCTAD 2007, 73;
Sinclair 2013).[32] A typical umbrella clause can be found in the Switzerland–
Pakistan BIT

---

[30] A subsequent paragraph of CETA explains that a tribunal may consider whether a state's action
has breached legitimate expectations, but only as part of an inquiry into whether one of the five
specifically enumerated elements of FET has been breached.

[31] The EU Commission's proposal for the investment chapter in TTIP follows the same model—see
Article 3, European Commission (2015b).

[32] The model BITs of Austria, Canada, China, Colombia, Germany, Italy, Korea, Latvia, Russia,
Singapore, and the United States do not contain umbrella clauses, whereas the Japanese, Dutch, Swiss,
UK, and French models do. However, the majority of US investment treaties contain umbrella clauses
even though the US model treaty does not. The first group accounts for circa 1000 investment treaties,
and the second for circa 600.

[E]ither Contracting Party shall constantly guarantee the observance of the commitments it has entered into with respect to the investments of the investors of the other Contracting Party.[33]

This clause spans a protective 'umbrella' over the 'commitments' or 'obligations' that host states have assumed with regard to foreign investments. In doing so, it functions as a type of 'catch-all' provision, potentially requiring host states to comply with a myriad of obligations beyond those set out in the investment treaty itself—most notably, obligations contained in investor–state contracts.[34] However, as is the case with FET, the precise effect of umbrella clauses is much contested (Crawford 2008; Sinclair 2013).

The practical significance of debates about the effect of the umbrella clause is best illustrated with an example. Country A signs a contract with foreign investor B to build a power plant in A. This contract is governed by the law of A. Country A alleges that B did not build the power plant to the contractually agreed specification, and refuses to pay the final instalment for construction of the plant. As a result, either A or B—or both—may be in breach of the investment contract and may pursue contractual remedies in the forum that they agreed to use for the resolution of contractual disputes. This forum could be domestic courts or contractual arbitration, but, whichever forum is chosen, the court or tribunal would have to resolve the dispute on the basis of the rights and obligations in the *contract*. Umbrella clauses may change this situation in two respects: first, with respect to the forum in which disputes are resolved; and, second, with respect to the applicable law.

The first controversy is whether umbrella clauses override an express agreement between A and B to resolve contractual disputes in another forum. In one view, an umbrella clause allows a foreign investor to commence investment treaty arbitration in respect of obligations in an investment contract, even if that contract contains an express agreement between the investor and the host state to resolve contractual disputes in a different forum (e.g. *Eureko v. Poland* 2005, paras. 93, 246). The effect of this interpretation is to give investor B a better deal than it bargained for in the investor–state contract, because B is allowed to enforce some obligations contained in its investment contract while avoiding the effect of other obligations contained in the contract—namely, the obligation to submit disputes to an agreed forum. However, on a second, narrower interpretation, the parties' *exclusive* choice of forum in an investment contract remains binding (e.g. *SGS v. Philippines* 2008). The effect of this interpretation is that B cannot turn to investment treaty arbitration insofar as contractual breaches are concerned. (B retains the right to bring claims that

---

[33] Switzerland–Pakistan BIT 1995, Article 11. The dispute in *SGS v. Paraguay* (2012) was based on this umbrella clause.

[34] We do not examine the extent to which umbrella clauses allow foreign investors to invoke a host state's non-contractual obligations that they have expressly assumed—for example, a host state's obligations to foreign investors arising from human rights treaties that the state has entered into.

A has breached other investment treaty provisions—e.g. claims of compensation for expropriation—to investment treaty arbitration). Insofar as claims for breach of contractual obligations are concerned, B is limited to the forum it agreed to with A.

A second controversial issue is the extent to which umbrella clauses alter the content of the underlying obligations contained in investment contracts. On an expansive first view, umbrella clauses 'internationalize' investment contracts, so that the governing law is no longer the domestic law originally chosen by the parties in their contract (*Noble v. Romania* 2005). One practical implication of this interpretation is to prevent A from relying on defences to claims of breach of contract recognized in the chosen domestic law—for example, a defence available under the law of A that A's non-payment of investor B is justified by B's failure to build the power plant to agreed specification. Critics of this expansive interpretation argue that its effect is to 'transform the obligation which is relied on into something else' (*CMS v. Argentina, Annulment* para. 95). An alternative, narrower view is that umbrella clauses do not alter the governing law of a contract (*SGS v. Philippines* 2004). According to this view, the question of whether an investment contract was breached depends on the chosen domestic law; but the effect of the umbrella clause is to give the authority to decide this question to an arbitral tribunal established under an investment treaty.

Arbitral tribunals have adopted diverging interpretations of these clauses, and the issues remain unsettled. Whether they adopt the narrow or the expansive approach has significant implications; the expansive view greatly limits the ability of host countries to renegotiate, unilaterally modify, or cancel investment contracts, including in response to breaches of investment contracts by foreign investors.

FREE TRANSFER CLAUSES

We now turn to the last of the six core provisions discussed in this chapter. Free transfer of funds clauses guarantee foreign investors that they can carry out all transfers related to investments freely and without delay. They were at the heart of the investment treaty regime when states created it in the 1960s and 1970s, and were of major importance to foreign investors, given how widespread capital controls were at the time (Paparinskis, Poulsen, and Waibel 2017). Uniquely among the core substantive standards in investment treaties, free transfer clauses are not primarily about protecting investment, but about *liberalizing* inward and outward transfers. As states have largely refrained from imposing new restrictions on the transfer of funds since the 1990s (Eichengreen 1998; Simmons 2000; Abdelal 2007; Henry 2007; Mukherjee and Singer 2010), foreign investors have rarely invoked free transfer provisions in arbitrations (see Table 4.2). Only two tribunals have found that host states breached the free transfer clause.[35] Nevertheless, the provision is potentially crucial as investors consistently rate the ability to transfer funds freely as a high priority when making international investments (Drake and Nicolaïdis 1992; Freeman 1999; Sauvé and Steinfatt 2001; US Chamber of Commerce 2011).

Consider the following free transfer clause from the Ecuador–US BIT:

Each Party shall permit all transfers related to an investment to be made freely and without delay into and out of its territory.

Subsequent sections of the article clarify that the term 'all transfers' covers current payments, profits, and repatriation of capital. The broad scope of this obligation contrasts with the more limited obligations of states under the multilateral IMF Articles of Agreement.[36] Whereas the IMF Articles of Agreement require IMF Member States to allow free transfers in relation to current transactions (Article VIII(2))—for example, a foreign investor's transfer funds out of the host state to pay for imported inputs used in their operations in the host state—the IMF Articles permit states to restrict inflows and outflows that pertain to the host country's capital account (Article VI (3)). As such, the main effect of free transfer clauses in investment treaties is to constrain host states from using capital controls that are permissible under the IMF Articles. For this reason, investment treaties arguably liberalize the capital account by the backdoor (Waibel 2010b; Siegel 2013), and could chill the use of capital controls in times of crisis. This is an example of a potential negative 'spillover' from the investment treaty regime to other parts of the investment regime complex (see Chapter 9).

Capital controls have long formed part of a state's macro-prudential regulatory toolkit to maintain financial stability (Kant 1996; Ostry et al. 2010; Korinek 2011; Broner and Ventura 2016). Yet, only around 10 per cent of investment treaties create exceptions for restrictions on the transfer of funds during balance-of-payments crises or other macroeconomic emergencies.[37] By contrast, the vast majority of investment treaties do not contain any exceptions for balance-of-payments crises or other macroeconomic emergencies (UNCTAD 2007, 62; Poulsen 2011b, 196). The issue came to a head in the drafting of the US Model BIT 2012, with input from an advisory panel. Notwithstanding a call by more

[35] *Achmea v. Slovakia* (2012) and *Pezold v. Zimbabwe* (2015). In *Achmae*, however, this breach was subsumed within FET (para. 286).

[36] The IMF is the major international organization in the monetary sphere. It has 189 member states. Virtually all states are members, with Cuba and North Korea being the only notable exceptions.

[37] See Table 4.2. Canadian, French, and UK investment treaties often include a balance-of-payments exception. Cf. Article 6 of the French 2006 Model BIT provides: 'When, in exceptional circumstances, capital movements from or to third countries cause or threaten to cause a serious disequilibrium to its balance of payments, each Contracting Party may temporarily apply safeguard measures to the transfers, provided that these measures shall be strictly necessary, would be imposed in an equitable, non-discriminatory and in good faith basis and shall not exceed in any case a six months period'.

than 250 economists to strike a better balance between investor protection and financial stability in future US investment treaties (Hausmann et al. 2011), the US Treasury took the view—without explanation—that US treaties already provided sufficient flexibility for host states to manage risks associated with rapid reversals in capital flows (Geithner 2011).

Carve-outs, defences, and the standard of review

No discussion of international investment law would be complete without consideration of carve-outs, defences, and the applicable standard of review. *Carve-outs* refer to matters that are expressly excluded from the scope of an investment treaty's application, whereas *defences* refer to treaty provisions and legal principles that justify or excuse state conduct that would otherwise amount to a breach of substantive investment treaty law. The *standard of review* refers to the extent to which tribunals reconsider factual and policy judgments by host states while determining whether a host state's conduct breaches investment treaties. As will become clear, the role of all three legal features in balancing host state regulatory autonomy with investment protection is much in flux.

CARVE-OUTS

Carve-outs are the simplest and most direct way in which host states can limit the applicability of substantive treaty obligations or, more rarely, the availability of dispute resolution (Russo 2015). These provisions may exclude certain economic *sectors* from the scope of treaty obligations, or they may exclude certain types of *state measures* from the scope of treaty obligation. Carve-outs have not been a standard feature of the investment treaty regime and were entirely absent from early investment treaties. When included, the most common carve-out concerns taxation measures. For example, Article 21 of the US Model BIT 2012 exempts taxation measures, except for the obligation to provide compensation in the event of expropriation. Other carve-outs are rare.[38] In recent years, some countries have specifically carved out tobacco control measures in response to Philip Morris' challenge of Australia's and Uruguay's plain packaging legislation.[39] Yet, the vast majority of investment

---

[38] Article 1108(7)(a) NAFTA ('Reservations and Exceptions') and Article 14(5)(a) 2012 US Model BIT ('Non-Conforming Measures') carve out procurement from MFN and NT, but not the other substantive protections; Annex 10-B, Chile–US Free Trade Agreement, 6 June 2003, and Annex X, CETA, provide that *only* MFN and NT apply to the restructuring of sovereign debt—see further Waibel (2007a).

[39] Examples include Article 29.5 TPP and the 2016 Amendment of the 2003 Singapore–Australia PTA, Article 22.

treaties do not contain *any* carve-outs for the environment or public health, perhaps because such carve-outs would remove a broad range of measures from the scope of the treaty's substantive obligations. Environmental, public health, and other similar considerations have not played significant roles as defences either—as discussed in the next section.

Among investment treaties that extend the application of NT and MFN to the pre-establishment phase, sectoral carve-outs from the application of these provisions are common. This reflects the ubiquity of discriminatory restrictions and conditions attached to new foreign investment under the national laws and policies of many countries. For example, NAFTA contains schedules of measures and economic sectors that are excluded from pre-establishment NT and MFN.[40]

DEFENCES AND EXCEPTIONS

Defences also limit the operation of the investment treaty's substantive guarantees in practice. They allow host states to pursue regulatory objectives in ways that would otherwise be inconsistent with investment treaty obligations (Henckels 2015, 81). The term 'defences' is generic and covers general and specific exceptions in investment treaties, as well as circumstances recognized in the customary international law of state responsibility as 'precluding wrongfulness' of state conduct that is otherwise in breach of international obligations—for example, situations of necessity (Paddeu 2014).[41] However, the term does not cover every limit on the application of an investment treaty. For example, some arbitral tribunals refused to hear claims brought by foreign investors who acquired their investments by bribing state officials and to hear claims relating to investments made in violation of the host state's laws (e.g. *Phoenix Action v. Czech Republic* 2009, paras. 102–3).[42]

Only around 10 per cent of existing investment treaties include exceptions (see Table 4.1). Many of these relate only to specific provisions—for example, exceptions to free transfer of funds clauses in case of criminal offenses, provided the host state's law is applied equitably, non-discriminatorily, and

---

[40] Exemptions include pre-existing discriminatory measures and measures undertaken in particular economic sectors specified each state's schedules such as transportation, energy, legal services, and social services. Drafting such schedules requires a high level of negotiating capacity and policy coordination between different arms of government. Lack of necessary capacity may be the reason why, in some investment treaties, developed countries have more extensive reservations to pre-establishment national treatment than developing countries (Cotula 2014; see also Chapter 8).

[41] Articles 20–25 of the Articles on State Responsibility provides for six circumstances precluding wrongfulness: (1) consent, (2) self-defense, (3) countermeasures, (4) force majeure, (5) distress, and (6) necessity.

[42] Such limitations are occasionally described as 'defenses' (e.g. *World Duty Free v. Kenya* 2006), but are better understood as jurisdictional limitations on the range of 'investors' and 'investments' covered by investment treaties, akin to those considered in Chapter 2.

in good faith.[43] General exceptions are rarer still, and the most common among them excuse only measures that are 'necessary' to protect 'public order' or a state's 'essential security interests'.[44] Such clauses are often called 'non-precluded measures' provisions. In contrast to the investment treaty regime, the international trade regime contains a much broader range of general exceptions designed to safeguard states' ability to pursue specified policy objectives even in non-emergency situations. For example, Article XX of GATT includes exceptions for measures 'necessary to protect human, animal or plant life or health' and measures relating to environmental conservation, among others (see generally Bartels 2015).

The interpretation and application of non-precluded measures provisions were central in more than thirty disputes arising out of the Argentine financial crisis of 2001. One of the few tribunals to accept Argentina's invocation of this provision was the tribunal in *LG&E*. It held that Argentina's deep financial crisis temporarily justified Argentina's non-compliance with investment treaty obligations. Most other tribunals rejected Argentina's attempt to invoke the non-precluded measures provision. Argentina's experience illustrates the challenges facing states that invoke non-precluded measures provisions to excuse breaches of investment treaties. Since the late 1990s, general exceptions in investment treaties have slowly become more common (Spears 2010), partly drawing on long-standing exceptions in the trade regime (Kurtz 2016, ch. 5).[45] To date, the application and interpretation of the general exceptions provisions of these treaties have not been significant issues in investment treaty arbitration. It remains to be seen how these exceptions apply in the investment context.

STANDARD OF REVIEW

The *standard of review* refers to the degree of deference that investment treaty tribunals show to the host state's factual, scientific, and policy judgements. It is a cross-cutting issue that is particularly relevant in the application of FET and indirect expropriation. With respect to MFN and NT, the primary relevance of the standard of review is in cases where a state asserts a policy justification for measures that would otherwise amount to *de facto* discrimination.

Guzman (2009) distinguishes between three standards of review in order of increasing deference: (i) *de novo* review—that is, full reconsideration of all the facts and evidence by the arbitral tribunal; (ii) intermediate review—a standard that recognizes that host states' primary decision-makers have a legitimate

---

[43] For example, Article 7 (4), US Model BIT 2012.
[44] For example, Article XI, Argentina-US BIT 1991.
[45] For example, Article 17, ASEAN Comprehensive Investment Agreement; Article 22.1, Australia–Korea FTA 2014.

degree of discretion in deciding contested factual and policy questions, and reviews whether that discretion was exercised erroneously; and (iii) rational basis review—that is, review of whether there was *any* rational basis for the decision. A fourth, still more deferential, standard of review is where a state is entitled to 'self-judge' whether certain factual or policy criteria are satisfied, in which case the only role for an arbitral tribunal is to confirm that the host state's judgement was made in good faith—that is, that it was not a sham. The standard of review associated with the application of any treaty standard has important practical implications for the way that investment treaty regime allocates decision-making authority between agencies of host states and arbitral tribunals (Henckels 2013).

Questions about the standard of review have arisen in investment disputes concerning the environment (Viñuales 2012) and public health (Vadi 2012). For example, Philip Morris argued that Uruguay's prohibition of tobacco companies from marketing multiple variants of the same brand of cigarettes breached the FET standard on account of being arbitrary. In response, Uruguay argued that this so-called 'single presentation requirement' addressed consumer misperceptions that brand variants previously marketed as 'light' or 'low-tar' were less harmful to health. The majority of the tribunal held that 'investment tribunals should pay great deference to governmental judgments of national needs in matters such as the protection of public health' (*Philip Morris v. Uruguay* 2016a, para. 399). On this basis, the majority declined to come to its own view about whether the single presentation requirement would be effective in achieving its public health objectives. For the majority, the fact that the measure was a genuine attempt to address a serious public health concern meant that it was not arbitrary and not a breach of FET. In contrast, the dissenting arbitrator argued that application of the FET standard required the tribunal to engage in 'at least some measure of objective consideration of the extent to which the [single presentation] requirement achieves, or is calculated to achieve, [its] objective' (*Philip Morris v. Uruguay* 2016b, para. 150)—adopting a less deferential standard of review. Because Uruguay's adoption of the single presentation requirement was not based on any evidence that the measure would be effective in achieving its public health objectives, he concluded that it was arbitrary and a breach of the FET standard.

The applicable standard of review was also contentious in a series of disputes arising out of the Argentine financial crisis of 2001–2002. As noted in the previous section, Argentina attempted to invoke a defence covering measures 'necessary' to protect its 'essential security interests'. Argentina argued that this defence was self-judging—that is, that arbitral tribunals could only review whether it had invoked the defence in good faith (Burke-White and von Staden 2010, 290). The great majority of arbitral tribunals rejected Argentina's necessity argument, but disagreed on the applicable standard of review. Some applied a standard akin to *de novo* review, while others applied a more deferent standard of review (Burke-White and von Staden 2010, 298; Henckels 2013, 209). In a coda to these disputes, new US investment treaties negotiated since 2004 expressly clarify that this defence can be invoked for any measure that the host state 'considers necessary' to protect its essential security interests. This new formulation gives states the power to self-judge the application of the non-precluded measures clause (Alvarez and Brink 2011, 360). The Argentina financial crisis cases—and subsequent changes in US treaty practice—highlight that questions relating to the standard of review are context-specific. The applicable standard depends on the substantive obligation or defence at issue, and the conduct of which state organ is under scrutiny.

Compensation and damages for breach of investment treaties

Although some scholars argue that investment treaty tribunals do have the power to order states to change their laws and regulations, the only remedy used in practically all cases is monetary compensation. As discussed in Chapter 3, this contrasts with other international regimes, such as the international trade regime, and domestic legal systems, in which non-monetary remedies are commonly used. The large amounts of compensation that tribunals occasionally award to foreign investors have led to particular controversy (see Chapter 1).

With the notable exception of expropriation clauses, however, investment treaties almost never contain provisions expressly specifying the appropriate remedy if the host state breaches the treaty's other substantive provisions. Investors that succeed in an investment treaty claim are awarded the value of the investment that was expropriated (in the case of expropriation), or damages equal to the loss caused by the host state's breach of the investment treaty (in the case of all other substantive protections). We consider the two in turn.

COMPENSATION FOR EXPROPRIATION

Throughout the twentieth century, the principles of customary international law governing compensation for expropriation were disputed between developed and developing countries. As described in Chapter 1, US Secretary of State Cordell Hull famously articulated the view of developed countries following the 1938 Mexican oil nationalizations—namely, that expropriation requires 'prompt, adequate, and effective' compensation. This formulation requires compensation equal to the investment's fair market value—that is, the price that a willing buyer would pay a willing seller for the investment in an arm's length transaction (Reisman and Sloane 2004, 138; *CMS v. Argentina* 2005, para. 402). In contrast, during the post-colonial period, many developing countries argued for the lower standard of 'appropriate' compensation (Charter of Economic Rights and Duties of States 1974, Article 2(c)). Against the background of mass expropriations at the time, such an equity-based standard of compensation, taking into account the burden on the public purse, could have considerably reduced the payouts to foreign investors.

One of the functions of investment treaties was to resolve this debate in favour of the Hull standard, which almost all investment treaties adopt. Where investment treaties use phrases other than 'prompt, adequate and effective', such as compensation equal to an investment's 'actual value' or 'true value', these have been interpreted as identical to the fair market value standard indicated by the Hull formula (Ripinsky and Williams 2008, 79). Notably, this means that investment treaties include a compensation standard which goes beyond that in some national constitutions. An example is the South African Constitution, where the amount of compensation must be 'just and equitable, reflecting an equitable balance between the public interest and the interests of those affected', having regard to, among other factors, 'the history of the acquisition and use of the property' (so as to address the economic inequalities resulting from Apartheid).[46] By contrast, South African investment treaties negotiated at the same time its Constitution was drafted relied on the Hull formula (Poulsen 2014).

DAMAGES FOR BREACH OF INVESTMENT TREATIES OTHER THAN EXPROPRIATION

Investment treaties do not explicitly address the principles governing quantification of damages for breaches of investment treaties other than expropriation. As a result, arbitral tribunals have applied customary international law,[47] which requires that states make a 'full reparation' for any injury caused by their breach (International Law Commission (ILC) Articles on State Responsibility, Article 31(1)). To apply this standard, tribunals must determine the position that the investor would be in 'but for' the breach of the investment treaty, and calculate damages so as to restore the investor to that position (Marboe 2009, 83). As such, the central issue is quantifying the extent of loss to the investor, which was *caused* by the treaty breach (*LG&E v. Argentina* 2007, para. 45).

---

[46] 1996 South African Constitution, Article 25(3).
[47] For example, *SD Myers v. Canada* (2000, para. 310); *ADC v. Hungary* (2006, paras. 483–9).

In theory, the principles governing damages for breach of an investment treaty differ from those governing compensation for an expropriation. Specifically, an investor that is awarded damages for breach of an investment treaty is, in principle, entitled to recover a wider array of consequential losses. For example, if a host state's breach of an investment treaty causes a foreign investor to breach a contract to supply its products to a third party, then the investor's losses resulting from its financial liability to the third party are recoverable from the host state. In contrast, an expropriation carried out in accordance with an investment treaty entitles an investor only to the fair market value of the expropriated investment itself, excluding recovery of other consequential losses resulting from the expropriation. However, notwithstanding these differences in theory, the application of both sets of principles normally leads to similar results in practice (e.g. S*iag and Vecchi v. Egypt* 2009, para. 542).

VALUATION OF COMPENSATION AND DAMAGES IN PRACTICE

Regardless of what legal principles investment arbitral tribunals apply, they need to use one or more valuation techniques to quantify the value of expropriated investments or the losses resulting from interference with investments. The great majority of investment treaties say nothing about appropriate valuation techniques. As such, the choice of valuation technique is left to arbitral tribunals, who in turn use three different valuation techniques individually or in combination: (i) income-based approaches; (ii) market-based approaches; and (iii) asset-based approaches (Marboe 2009, 186).

As the name suggests, income-based valuation techniques are based on an investment's past or predicted future income. The most popular income-based valuation technique is discounted cash flow (DCF). It values an investment as the sum of its predicted future net cash flows—that is, its future profits—discounted to the present at an appropriate rate. DCF valuation relies on a forecast of an investment's future net cash flows over its lifespan under certain assumptions (e.g. that the host state had not breached the investment treaty.) The discount rate applied to these forecast cash flows reflects both the time value of money—that is, US$1 profit earned 10 years in the future is worth less than US$1 profit in the present—and various risk adjustments to allow for uncertainty about whether the forecast cash flows will materialize (Ripinsky and Williams 2008, 197). Importantly, the amount that an investor has invested in an investment project plays no role in DCF valuation. As such, DCF valuation can lead to an investment being valued significantly higher or significantly lower than the amount of money that an investor has spent on establishing or acquiring the investment in question. For example, in *Gold Reserve v. Venezuela* (2014), the tribunal awarded the investor over US$700 million based on projections of lost profits, notwithstanding that the investor incurred expenditures of less than half this amount.[48]

DCF is the most widely used technique for valuing going concerns in commercial practice and in private law litigation in domestic courts. It has also become increasingly common in investment treaty arbitration. However, forecasting an investment's likely revenues 10 or 20 years into the future involves a degree of speculation. Minor differences in assumptions about the rate of future revenue growth or about the appropriate discount rate can lead to widely different valuations, because these rates compound over the lifespan of the investment. For these reasons, DCF is seldom used to value investments which do not have a consistent record of profitable operation that can provide the basis for reliable future projections.

Second, market-based techniques refer to the use of comparable transaction data to value an investment. In principle, the price paid for an investment in an arm's length transaction on or around the valuation date provides the best evidence of that investment's fair market value. However, in practice, such evidence is unavailable unless the investment changed hands on the open market immediately prior to an unanticipated expropriation or other treaty breach. Other contemporaneous transaction data—for example, the sale of shares in the investment in question—could shed some light on an investment's value (e.g. *BG Group v. Argentina* 2007, para. 440). Difficulties in finding relevant arm's length transactions mean that market-based valuation techniques play only a minor role in arbitral practice.

Third, asset-based approaches individually value the assets and liabilities of which the investment is comprised. Examples of asset valuation techniques are those based on the liquidation value, replacement value, or book value of the assets in question (Damodaran 2002; Kantor 2008). Book value, the most common asset-based valuation technique, is an accounting concept derived from each asset's purchase price, adjusted for inflation and depreciation. Tribunals have used asset-based valuation techniques to value investments without a reliable record of profitable operation (e.g. *Wena Hotels v. Egypt* 2000, paras. 124–5). For example, in *Metalclad v. Mexico* (2000), which we encountered earlier in this chapter, the tribunal rejected the investor's arguments that it should be awarded of US$90 million based on projections of the future revenue of the investment. Instead, it ruled that the investor should only recover its invested capital, given the early stages the project was at. Metalclad argued that it invested US$20–25 million, whereas Mexico claimed Metalclad's actual outlays were limited to US$3–4 million. The tribunal concluded based on

---

[48] Because the tribunal used DCF valuation to determine compensation, it did not quantify the amount that the investor expended on the project. But the investor appears to have conceded that its investment in the project was, at most, US$ 300 million (*Gold Reserve v. Venezuela*, para. 279).

the investor's tax filing that the invested capital was around US$11 million, plus almost US$6 million in compound interest of 6 per cent a year.

Conclusion

This chapter introduced the substantive standards that govern the protection of foreign investment, and the liberalization of the entry of foreign investment into host states. Two overarching conclusions emerge. First, the substantive standards of investment treaties go significantly beyond constraints on discrimination and outright expropriation. Provisions such as FET and the umbrella clause implicate a wide range of state conduct that affects foreign investment in disputes where there has been no expropriation, discrimination, or denial of justice. Second, substantial disagreement and uncertainty remains concerning the interpretation and application of key treaty clauses. Taken together, these conclusions suggest that states and investors may often struggle to know the precise contours of their rights and obligations under investment treaties.

By considering carve-outs, defences, and the standard of review, we gained a fuller picture of how investment treaties impact upon host states' ability to regulate foreign investment. Some investment treaties carve out sectors or types of government measures altogether (e.g. taxation), though the scope of these carve-outs is traditionally narrow. In the absence of carve-outs, investment treaties apply to all state conduct that affects foreign investors. A small, but growing, minority of investment treaties contain general or specific exceptions that justify breaches of substantive investment obligation based on, say, public health or national security grounds. Finally, the standard of review that tribunals employ determines the leeway that investment tribunals accord national decision-makers, and thereby shapes the way that various provisions of investment treaties apply in practice.

The final section of this chapter considered the principles governing compensation for expropriation and damages for breach of investment treaties' other provisions. These principles are hugely important in practice. Although much of the policy debate about investment treaties focuses on whether particular state actions breach investment treaties, the compensation awarded in cases where the foreign investor is successful is a central practical consideration for both investors and states.

5 The Microeconomics of Investment Treaties

Introduction

The following two chapters address the economics of investment treaties. The focus of this chapter is on the impact of investment treaties on decision-making at the firm[1] and government[2] level—that is, the microeconomics of investment treaties. These questions have received little attention from academics, particularly by comparison to the extensive and sophisticated literature on trade treaties. The aggregate economic effects of investment treaties, which depend largely on the cumulative impact of decisions of individual firms and states, are discussed in Chapter 6.

Our starting point for this chapter is the simplifying assumption that all actors, including firms and governments, act rationally to maximize their self-interest. Under this assumption, investment treaties can affect the decisions of firms and governments by altering the expected pay-offs associated with a given course of action for the actor in question—for example, a foreign investor's expected profit from proceeding with an investment project, or a state's expected benefit from expropriating a foreign investment. The assumption that actors rationally advance their self-interest is not necessarily a good predictor of how firms and states decide, but models based on this assumption provide an important stepping stone towards theories based on more complex accounts of decision-making.

---

[1] The terms 'firm' and 'investor' refer to all parts of a business organization, which consists of multiple internal actors (e.g. management, legal counsel, operations, shareholders) that may make decisions in different and potentially inconsistent ways. As a simplifying analytical assumption, we regard the firm as a unitary actor in the following chapters. Whether different parts of firms consider and respond differently to the investment treaty regime is an important question for further research for scholars in the field of international business.

[2] The term 'government' in Chapters 5 and 6 refers to the executive and the legislature, as well as state agencies. We use this term to highlight that, at the domestic level, there are multiple state actors, which may make decisions in different ways and which do not necessarily act consistently with one another. As this chapter shows, understanding the way that different parts of the government make decisions is central to the microeconomics of investment treaties. In the remainder of the book, we use the term 'host state' to refer to the action of all arms of government and all state organs. This is consistent with the fact that, under an investment treaty, the host state is responsible for the action of all arms of government and all state organs.

A central question in this chapter is whether investment treaties' influence on firms' and states' decisions leads to improvements in efficiency. *Efficiency* (or, more precisely, Hicks–Kaldor efficiency) refers to the net economic benefit or cost associated with a policy or a decision, regardless of to whom those costs and benefits accrue. The chapter is divided into three sections, each of which examines a different 'problem' that investment treaties could solve, thereby potentially increasing efficiency. The first section of this chapter examines the 'hold-up' problem, which provides the most influential and coherent microeconomic justification for the inclusion of investment protection provisions in investment treaties. The second section explores the problem of 'fiscal illusion' in host state decision-making, which could result in 'over-regulation' of foreign investment in the absence of an investment treaty.[3] The third section considers whether investment treaties solve problems of discrimination against foreign investors, as well as the possibility that investment treaties lead to discrimination in favour of foreign investors. Although the primary focus throughout is on questions of efficiency, each section also considers how the benefits and costs associated with investment treaties are distributed among different actors.

Investment treaties as a solution to hold-up problems

The most influential microeconomic justification for investment treaties is the argument that they solve hold-up problems (e.g. Markusen 2001; van Aaken 2009). A simple model of the hold-up problem is shown in Figure 5.1. The model involves a two-stage game. In the first stage, the investor decides whether to proceed with the investment, at which point it will incur the sunk costs associated with the project. Costs are sunk when they cannot be recovered once incurred—for example, the cost of building a mine to a mining company. At the second stage of the game, the host state decides whether to allow the investment to continue to operate or, alternatively, whether to expropriate the investment.

Suppose that the investment involves a sunk cost of US$50 million and that the investment, over its lifespan, promises to generate a return that covers the investor's sunk costs and leave an additional surplus of US$100 million. For simplicity, we assume that the investor and the host state have agreed to share the surplus equally between them. In ascribing values to the pay-offs, we also

---

[3] We follow Aisbett (2013) in distinguishing between hold-up problems and problems of over-regulation.

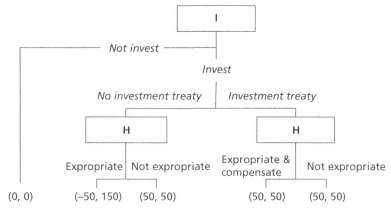

PAYOFFS: (Investor, Host)

Figure 5.1 Investment treaties as a solution to the hold-up problem

assume that, if the state expropriates the investment, it is able to operate the project as efficiently as the foreign investor.[4] The presence of an investment treaty affects the pay-offs of both the investor and the host state by requiring the host state to pay full market value compensation[5] in the event that it expropriates the investment at the second stage.

Figure 5.1 shows that, in the absence of an investment treaty, it is in the host state's interest to expropriate the investment once the investor has incurred the initial sunk costs. A rational investor will be aware of this and will, therefore, decline to make the investment in the first stage of the game. The presence of an investment treaty changes the pay-offs associated with expropriation at the second stage, which means that a rational investor will choose to invest. As such, the presence of an investment treaty leads to an outcome that benefits *both* the investor and the host state.

Hold-up problems are not specific to the risk of outright expropriation. They can also arise in any situation in which the most efficient outcome is for the investment to proceed; but (i) once the investment is made, the host state can appropriate a greater share of the benefits of the project; and (ii) the

---

[4] If the investor possesses technology or organizational capabilities that the state is unable to fully capture when it seizes control of the project, it is unlikely that the investment would operate as efficiently under government control. However, none of the basic features of the model would be altered if we assumed instead that the project would operate less efficiently under government control.

[5] As explained in Chapter 4, the full market value of an investment refers to the price that a willing buyer would pay a willing seller to purchase the investment in an arm's length transaction. This price reflects the expected profitability of the investment.

rational, self-interested decision for the host state at the second stage of the game would result in a negative pay-off for the investor.

One example of a situation in which the preceding criteria can be met is the case of the 'obsolescing bargain'. In an influential account of the relationship between foreign investors and host states in the extractives sector, Vernon (1971) argued that the bargaining power of the foreign investor is greater prior to making the investment. At that time, the investor possesses technology, finance, and organizational skills that the host state lacks. Any agreement made at this point to share the proceeds of the investment will reflect the investor's relatively strong bargaining position. However, once the investor has incurred the initial sunk costs, it cannot abandon the project without suffering heavy losses. At this point, the bargaining power shifts to the host state, which has an incentive to renege on the original agreement.[6] This could be done in several ways, including by increasing the tax rate on the investment. While it may not be in the interest of the host state to expropriate the investment outright—perhaps because the host state knows that the investor can operate the investment more efficiently—the risk of the host state reneging on the original bargain will lead to a hold-up problem if the rational decision for the host state at the second stage leaves the investor with a negative pay-off (Markusen 2001).

Shifts in bargaining power over time that cause investor–state agreements to 'obsolesce' do not *necessarily* lead to hold-up problems. Consider a modification to Figure 5.1 in which the host state is subject to constraints that prevent it from expropriating the investment or from increasing the tax rate to such an extent that the investor's pay-offs become negative.[7] In these circumstances, which Figure 5.2 depicts, no hold-up problem arises. Absent an investment treaty, the investor will still proceed with the project, despite knowing that the state is likely to demand a greater share of the project's proceeds once the investor has incurred the initial sunk costs. If an investment treaty applies that requires the host state to compensate for any increase in the contractually agreed rate of taxation (a question that depends on the legal content of the treaty but which could be the case if the treaty contains an umbrella clause; see Chapter 4), it would affect the ultimate *distribution* of the proceeds of the project, but it would not change the investor's decision to proceed with the project, nor affect the *efficiency* of the outcome.

At this point, it is useful to note two simplifications implicit in Figure 5.2 that would affect the implications of the model if they were relaxed. First,

---

[6] The term 'obsolescing bargain' refers to the prediction that the host state will see the relatively unfavourable terms of the original agreement as obsolete once the investment is made and its bargaining power has increased.

[7] There are several reasons why some states are constrained in this way, even absent investment treaties. These reasons are discussed in subsequent sub-sections.

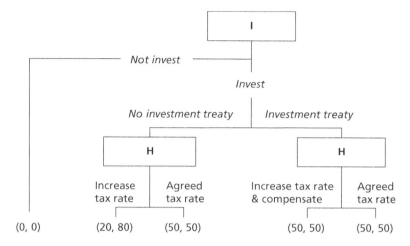

PAYOFFS: (Investor, Host).

Figure 5.2 The distributive impact of an investment treaty in the absence of a hold-up problem

Figure 5.2 depicts a single investment project in isolation. In practice, many different investors are likely to be considering many different projects in the host state's territory with different sets of pay-offs. Even relatively minor shifts in bargaining power may cause hold-up problems for marginal projects. However, the potential gains in efficiency that arise from solving hold-up problems for marginal projects are also lower.[8] Second, Figure 5.2 assumes that the investor is considering a single investment project, the returns to which can be predicted with certainty in advance. In contrast, in sectors such as oil and gas, a company may pursue several investment projects at the same time, knowing that some will succeed, some will fail, and that the revenue from projects that ultimately prove successful will have to cover losses from projects that fail. In these circumstances, the risk that a host state might renege on the agreed share of revenues for successful projects can lead to a hold-up a problem, even if the investor's pay-off for each successful project remains positive when considered individually.

Notwithstanding these simplifications, Figure 5.2 demonstrates two important points about the economic effects of investment treaties in situations where the bargain between the investor and the host state obsolesces over

---

[8] To illustrate this point, consider a situation in which an investment would involve US$50 million in sunk costs and generate a surplus of US$2 million, which the investor and the host state have agreed to share equally. Here, the potential for minor shifts in bargaining power could lead to a hold-up problem, but the gain from solving the hold-up problem—that is, the surplus—is also smaller.

time. First, for investment projects that would go ahead even in the absence of an investment treaty, the primary impact of the treaty is to alter the ultimate distribution of the investment's proceeds between the investor and the host state to the benefit of the investor. Second, the prevalence of hold-up problems in practice, as well as the magnitude of efficiency gains that result from an investment treaty's ability to solve them, depend on the extent to which other constraints make it costly for the host state to expropriate or renege on its initial bargain with the investor. We now examine this second issue in greater detail.

HOW PREVALENT ARE HOLD-UP PROBLEMS IN PRACTICE?

Whether foreign investors actually suffer from hold-up problems in the absence of investment treaties is an empirical question, the answer to which is likely to vary between countries and industries. In this section, we consider four reasons why hold-up problems might be less endemic than Figure 5.1 suggests. The first reason concerns the varied nature of investments across different industries. In particular, investments that involve a low ratio of sunk costs to overall costs of production are less susceptible to hold-up problems. This is because the investor stands to lose less in the event that the host state expropriates the investment. There are some challenges in measuring the ratio of sunk costs to overall costs associated with investments in particular sectors (e.g. Bresnahan and Reiss 1994). Nevertheless, relative sunk costs are much lower in, for example, garment manufacturing than in offshore oil production or large-scale infrastructure projects. As a result, it is likely that the prevalence of hold-up problems varies across *industries.*

Other differences between industries are also likely to affect the extent to which the balance of bargaining power between the investor and the host state 'obsolesces' over time. For example, Kobrin (1987) showed that ongoing technological and managerial improvements associated with foreign investment in many manufacturing industries help maintain the investor's bargaining position over time. In such situations, hold-up problems are unlikely to arise: the additional benefits that the foreign investor brings throughout the life of the investment mean that it is in the host state's self-interest to honour the terms of the original bargain with the investor.

A second reason why hold-up problems are less prevalent than Figure 5.1 suggests concerns the role of investment structuring (Ramamurti 2003). Figure 5.1 depicts a prospective investor faced with only two options—to invest or not to invest. In practice, an investor is likely to have a range of possible means of investing, some of which may reduce the cost to the investor of the host state reneging on their initial agreement. Such options could include: sequencing an investment differently, so that sunk costs are incurred later in the project's life span (Thomas and Worrall 1994); 'taking hostages'—for example, demanding that the host state post a bond or, perhaps more realistically, supply infrastructure at its own cost that is specific to the project (Williamson 1983); and partnering with local firms in the host state (Henisz 2000). Empirical work by Johns and Wellhausen (2016) suggests that foreign investors can also reduce hold-up problems by building other links with the host economy—notably, supply chains involving local firms. This is because host states realize that interference with such foreign investments results in indirect harm to domestic firms. The feasibility of each of these options is likely to vary by industry and by country. While they may be less efficient than the investment originally envisaged, they all reduce the likelihood of hold-up problems in practice.

A third reason concerns the role of reputation effects in repeated inter-actions.[9] Figure 5.1 depicts a single investment in isolation. However, in reality, states deal with a flow of new investments over time. As such, a rational state considering whether to expropriate a particular investment will take into account the impact of its decision on other investors contemplating new investments. Assuming that the game depicted in Figure 5.1 is played indefinitely and that all investors have full knowledge of whether the host state chooses to honour its commitments on each occasion, the host state's rational strategy would be to honour all its agreements with investors, unless the state's discount rate[10] is very high—that is, unless the state is highly myopic in the present value it ascribes to the potential gains from future investments (Markusen 2001).[11] However, this result is sensitive to variations in the simplifying assumptions, including the assumption of perfect information (Sasse 2011).

Several scholars have argued that reputation effects do play an important role in practice, in restraining opportunistic host state actions against foreign investors (e.g. Kolo and Wälde 2000; Yackee 2008a). A Multilateral Investment Guarantee Agency (MIGA) (2011) survey, which found that foreign investors perceive uncompensated expropriation of another investment to be the most significant indicator of risk associated with new investment in a host state, supports this view. Studies illustrating the importance of reputation effects in the context of sovereign lending (e.g. Tomz 2007) and diplomatic relations (e.g. Guisinger and Smith 2002) are also consistent with this proposition, as is the fact that many states make considerable efforts to advertise

---

[9] The properties of reputation effects have been examined in detail in game theory (e.g. Klein and Leffler 1981).

[10] The discount rate is the rate used in net present value calculations to convert future money into current money.

[11] The present value to the state of choosing to honour its agreements in every iteration of an indefinitely repeated game is the state's pay-off from honouring its agreement divided by the discount rate. So long as this value exceeds the one-off pay-off from defecting in the first iteration of the game, the rational strategy for the state is to honour its agreements.

themselves as attractive destinations for foreign investment (e.g. Harding and Javorcik 2011).

A fourth and final reason why hold-up problems are less endemic than Figure 5.1 suggests concerns the various legal constraints to which the host state is subject, aside from investment treaties. If a state possesses an independent and functioning judicial system, its own laws and constitution may already place sufficient constraints on the executive and legislature of that state to prevent hold-up problems from arising (North and Weingast 1989; Weingast 1993). In most Western countries, this situation prevails. For example, the Fifth Amendment to the US constitution prevents the US government from expropriating property without paying compensation. These legal protections apply equally to local and foreign investment in the United States. They significantly reduce the prevalence of hold-up problems for foreign investment in the United States. In contrast, in some developing countries, court systems are overloaded and dysfunctional. Even if the laws of such countries require the state to pay compensation for the expropriation of foreign investment, such legal guarantees may be difficult to enforce through local courts (see further in Chapter 3). As such, the prevalence of hold-up problems likely varies between *countries* as well as between *industries*.

That said, even if the laws and courts of the host state do not adequately solve hold-up problems, foreign investors could, individually, negotiate contracts with the host state that include the same combination of legal protection and access to investor–state arbitration that an investment treaty provides (Yackee 2008a). In practice, contractual protections are not equally accessible to all investors—investors making small investments in particular may face high transaction costs in negotiating such protections.[12] This is because the cost of the legal and technical advice required to negotiate sophisticated contracts is likely to be high, relative to the value of the investment. However, for investors that would, in any case, be negotiating a contractual relationship with the host state, incorporating additional protections into the contract is less likely to entail significant transaction costs. For such investors, additional contractual protection may be at least as effective as an investment treaty in solving hold-up problems (Bonnitcha 2014a).

Lawyers sometimes argue that small- and medium-sized investors lack the bargaining power necessary to negotiate contractual investment protection as a substitute for the protection of an investment treaty (e.g. Brower and Schill 2009). This argument confuses the hold-up problem identified in Figure 5.1 with the distributive impact of investment treaties identified in Figure 5.2. If there is a hold-up problem, *both* the investor and the host state benefit from the investment going ahead. A rational state with very strong bargaining

---

[12] See Chapter 3.

power will still offer contractual investment protection if such protection is necessary for a mutually beneficial investment to proceed. The situation is different for investments that would proceed regardless of whether the host state offers contractual investment protection. In such cases, the balance of bargaining power between the parties affects whether the state will offer contractual investment protection. However, such negotiation dynamics affect only the distribution of project benefits, and not whether the project proceeds, or the efficiency of the outcome.

Taken together, these four observations suggest that:

1. In practice, hold-up problems are not always present in investor–host state relationships;
2. Insofar as hold-up problems do exist in practice, there is a significant variation in their prevalence between states and between industries.

These conclusions are important for the microeconomics of investment treaties. They suggest that investment treaties are likely to have different impacts in different states, and that any analysis of the microeconomic impact of investment treaties cannot be divorced from a more fine-grained analysis of the situation within the states that sign them.

HOW WELL DESIGNED ARE EXISTING INVESTMENT TREATIES FOR SOLVING HOLD-UP PROBLEMS?

Assuming that foreign investors in some industries do suffer from hold-up problems in some countries, a key question is whether investment treaties are effective in resolving such problems. One way to answer this question empirically is to examine the impact of investment treaties on the decision-making of foreign investors and on the magnitude of investment flows between countries that enter into them. Although evidence that the presence of an investment treaty increases inward foreign investment is insufficient to prove that investment treaties solve hold-up problems,[13] it would be consistent with investment treaties having this effect. Chapter 6 reviews the evidence of how investment treaties affect investment flows, and shows that the extent of the impact remains unclear. In the absence of clear empirical evidence, we examine whether investment treaties meet the requirements for solving hold-up problems in theory.

---

[13] Subsequent sections of this chapter show that there could be other explanations for a positive impact of investment treaties on foreign investment flows. For example, if investment treaties institute a system of positive discrimination in favour of foreign investors, one would expect to see a positive causal relationship between investment treaties and foreign investment flows. Such an increase in foreign investment would not necessarily be associated with any increase in efficiency.

For a legal mechanism to solve the hold-up problem depicted in Figure 5.1, it should have three characteristics. First, it needs to impose an obligation on the host state to pay compensation if it expropriates an investment or reneges on an agreement relating to the investment. Second, this obligation needs to be enforceable in practice. Third, the compensation paid if the host state breaches the obligation needs to be calculated by reference to the loss suffered by the investor. (If the third condition is not satisfied, an investor might successfully demand compensation for expropriation of its investment, but still be left worse off than if it had not made the investment.)

Investment treaties generally satisfy the latter two conditions. Chapter 4 showed that, while there is always some uncertainty in the quantification of compensation in practice, the relevant legal principles seek to restore the investor to the position it would be in 'but for' the host state's interference with the investment. Investment treaties also satisfy the second condition through their enforceable dispute settlement provisions, particularly the majority of treaties allowing for investor–state arbitration. Chapter 3 explained how this mechanism allows foreign investors to pursue an arbitration against a host state and obtain a binding and enforceable monetary award.[14]

The first condition, which concerns the situations in which a host state is obliged to compensate the foreign investor, raises the most complex issues. In some respects, the substantive provisions of investment treaties correspond well with the types of legal rules that are necessary to solve hold-up problems. For example, almost all investment treaties require a state to pay compensation if it expropriates a foreign investment, and the risk of outright expropriation is a major cause of hold-up problems (see Chapter 4). However, the question of whether a host state is required to pay compensation if it reneges on an agreement on the sharing of the benefits of an investment project is less clear. As described in Chapter 4, some investment treaties contain 'umbrella clauses', which are normally interpreted to require the host state to pay compensation for any action by the host state that overrides a specific agreement with a foreign investor—for example, the terms of an investment contract between the investor and the host state. These strict obligations are likely to be effective in solving hold-up problems that arise from the risk of the state reneging on commitments made to foreign investors. However, in requiring a host state to compensate regardless of whether its actions were motivated by an attempt to capture a greater share of the benefits of the project, umbrella clauses provide protection to investors beyond what is

---

[14] In Chapter 3, we discussed some of the challenges associated with enforcing an award against an uncooperative state. However, in practice, states normally comply with awards made against them. The infrequency of state–state claims under investment treaties imply that foreign investors are not always able to rely on their home state to invoke state-to-state arbitration on their behalf. For this reason, the state-to-state enforcement mechanism contained in investment treaties may not, by itself, be sufficient to resolve hold-up problems (Yackee 2008b; see further Chapters 3 and 9).

necessary to resolve hold-up problems. Subsequent sections of this chapter show that strict requirements of this sort can reduce efficiency (similarly van Aaken 2009). In addition, the obligations under umbrella clauses (see Chapter 4) are likely to alter the balance of bargaining power between the investor and the host state, giving rise to the distributive effects in favour of the investor depicted in Figure 5.2.

Investment treaties also often contain national treatment provisions, which prohibit discrimination against foreign investors vis-à-vis domestic investors. Although these provisions are not directed toward state conduct that reneges on an agreement with investors per se, some scholars have argued that limits on discriminatory conduct can help prevent hold-up problems (van Aaken 2014a).[15] The argument is that measures that apply to all investors, regardless of nationality, are less likely to be disguised attempts to appropriate larger shares of benefits from existing investment projects than measures that single out, or discriminate against, particular foreign investments.

The FET provision is also potentially relevant. While Chapter 4 shows that jurisprudence on this provision is complex and occasionally inconsistent, the focus under many interpretations is on whether conduct of the host state was contrary to the investor's 'legitimate expectations' and whether, in the opinion of the tribunal, the conduct of the host state was reasonable or proportionate. These interpretations encourage tribunals to examine the strength of the policy justifications for state conduct and to review whether the host state struck an appropriate balance between competing interests. Under such interpretations, a host state can be required to compensate an investor even if the conduct under challenge did not benefit the host state. Such interpretations are poorly designed to solve hold-up problems, because they do not seek to identify situations in which the host state has attempted to capture a greater share of the proceeds of an investment (Bonnitcha 2014a).

Investment treaties as tools to induce efficient state decisions

Beyond the literature on investment treaties, a wider body of scholarship examines the economic effect of legal rules that require a state to pay compensation to property owners in the event that the state interferes with their property. Much of this scholarship is focused on the Fifth Amendment to the US Constitution, but the underlying economic analysis is relevant to any legal system that requires a state to pay compensation for interference with

---

[15] Kohler and Stähler (2016) formalize a version of this argument.

privately owned property, including the investment treaty regime. Rather than hold-up problems, this literature is concerned primarily with the (presumed) problem of 'fiscal illusion' within a state.

Fiscal illusion refers to the theory that, when a government makes decisions, it is primarily concerned with maximizing the benefits (and minimizing the costs) to government itself and, therefore, that it gives insufficient weight to the consequences of its actions for other actors (Blume, Rubinfeld, and Shapiro 1984). In the context of investment treaties, the more specific concern is that host states may fail to give sufficient weight to the harm that actions under consideration may inflict upon foreign investors (Aisbett, Karp, and McAusland 2010a). Fiscal illusion can lead to inefficient government decisions—for example, a government that suffers from fiscal illusion would be more likely to impose new regulations on foreign investments without considering whether the benefits of such regulations outweigh the harm to foreign investors. In theory, a legal requirement for the government to pay compensation for interference with investments can assist in redressing fiscal illusion by forcing public decision-makers to internalize the costs that measures under consideration would impose on affected investors, and factor these costs into the overall evaluation of those measures (Blume and Rubinfeld 1984).

In contrast to the model of the hold-up problem considered in Figure 5.1, where the state can appropriate the sunk costs of the investment, basic models of fiscal illusion often assume that such costs are lost if a government decides to interfere with an investment (e.g. Blume, Rubinfeld, and Shapiro 1984; Miceli and Segerson 1994; Aisbett, Karp, and McAusland 2010a). One example consistent with this assumption is the case of *Tecmed v Mexico*, which concerned a Spanish investor that owned a hazardous waste disposal facility in Mexico. The investor built the facility on the outskirts of a city; but, over time, the city expanded, and many more people came to be living close to the facility. Following pollution leaks, community opposition to the facility began to grow. In response, the Mexican environmental agency refused to renew the facility's operating permit, forcing the investment to close, with the result that sunk costs were lost (the Mexican government did not seize the facility). The investor then brought a successful claim for compensation against Mexico under the Spain–Mexico BIT.

The potential role of investment treaties in addressing fiscal illusion is illustrated in Figure 5.3, which is adapted and simplified from Aisbett, Karp, and McAusland (2010a). As with Figure 5.1, we assume that the investment requires the investor to incur a sunk cost of US$50 million. We also assume that the project will generate a surplus of US$100 million that the investor and the host have agreed to share equally. In addition, the project will have a negative external impact E that is borne by actors within the host state (e.g. the affected communities in *Tecmed*), and this impact is fully internalized in the host state's decision-making. The host state learns the value of E once

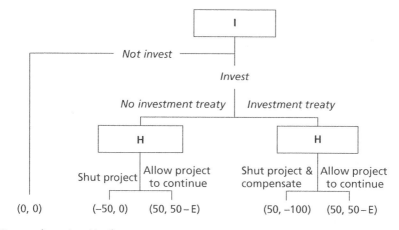

PAYOFFS: (Investor, Host).

Figure 5.3 Investment treaties and the problem of fiscal illusion

the investment begins operating. At this point, the host state decides whether to shut the project down. We assume that all sunk costs and potential surplus are lost if the host makes a decision to shut the investment project down. (This is because the interference involves shutting the project down, rather than the state seizing ownership of the project and continuing to operate it under government control.) To simplify, we further assume that an investment treaty always requires the host to pay compensation if it shuts the investment project down, regardless of the strength of the environmental justification for doing so.[16] Consistent with the standard approach of investment treaty tribunals, we assume that compensation for a breach of the investment treaty is awarded so as to put the investor in the position it would be 'but for' the breach of the treaty—in this case, the decision to shut the project down.

Figure 5.3 shows that, regardless of whether an investment treaty is in place, the most efficient outcome is for the investor to invest if the value of total project benefits (i.e. the aggregate benefits for the host state and the investor) exceeds the negative external impact—that is, if $E < 100$—and for the investor not to invest if the value of total project benefits is less than the negative external impact—that is, if $E > 100$.

Figure 5.3 also illustrates two potential sources of inefficiency. First, if an investment treaty is not in place, a government that suffers from fiscal illusion

---

[16] This is not an accurate characterization of the legal effect of investment treaties. In subsequent sections, we consider the implications of relaxing this simplifying assumption.

shuts down the investment if the negative external impact exceeds the government's share of project benefits—that is, if $E > 50$. However, for values of E between 50 and 100, the project's net pay-off remains positive, meaning that the most efficient outcome would have been for the project to continue to operate rather than being shut down. We term this type of inefficiency as 'over-regulation'. In theory, an investment treaty solves the problem of over-regulation by requiring the host to compensate the investor if it shuts a project down. Figure 5.3 also shows that all the benefits from redressing over-regulation accrue to the investor, as there is no benefit to the host state of preventing inefficiency due to over-regulation under the simplifying assumptions of the model (Aisbett 2013).

Importantly, however, a second source of inefficiency arises from the presence of the treaty. If the investment treaty depicted in Figure 5.3 is in place, the investor's pay-off from investing is *always* positive, regardless of the value of E. This induces the investor to proceed with investments with values of $E > 100$—that is, investments with negative net pay-offs. We term this type of inefficiency as 'over-investment', which refers to *misallocation* of capital to projects with net negative pay-offs. This possibility of investment in projects with negative payoffs is consistent with the evidence of the impact of foreign investment reviewed in Chapter 2. This evidence suggests that, while foreign investment is usually beneficial for host states, this is not necessarily the case for all foreign investments in all circumstances. The possibility that investment treaties might promote inefficient foreign investment is often overlooked in academic and policy debates.

Figure 5.3 also illustrates the related problem of 'under-regulation', also called 'regulatory chill' (Tienhaara 2011). If E is larger than 100 but smaller than 150, and there is an investment treaty, a rational government does not shut down the project, because the cost of having to compensate the investor (-100) is larger than the cost of allowing the inefficient and harmful project to continue to operate $(50 - E)$.[17] We return to this issue in the following text, and also in Chapter 9. Figure 5.3 also shows that all the costs associated with both over-investment and under-regulation are borne by the host state.[18]

The simplified model presented in Figure 5.3 can be extended to inefficient regulatory measures that merely interfere with an investment while allowing it to continue to operate (unlike in *Tecmed*), which is important in practice as the majority of regulatory measures that impose costs on foreign investors do

---

[17] In the simple model presented in Figure 5.3, under-regulation is not an *additional* source of inefficiency. Rather, under-regulation is the host state's best possible response to the inefficiency resulting from over-investment. However, under more complex models of government decision-making, under-regulation can be an additional source of inefficiency.

[18] Namely, the cost of paying compensation to shut the project down, which the host state will do when $E > 150$, and the impact of E if the host state does not shut the project down, which will occur when $150 > E > 100$.

not result in the actual shutting down of their projects. In theory, investment treaties could solve such problems of over-regulation. Similarly, Figure 5.3 depicts a simplified situation where the only decision of the investor is whether or not to proceed with an investment. However, in practice, proceeding with any given project requires an investor to decide on the project structure and production techniques that should be adopted. If an investment treaty guarantees an investor compensation for all new regulatory measures that interfere with the operation of the investment, a rational and self-interested investor would be less likely to avoid project structures or production techniques with high values of E—for example, investment projects with social or environmental costs for local communities (Bonnitcha and Aisbett 2013). Thus, in theory, an investment treaty could also lead to 'over-investment'—that is, inefficient misallocation of capital—in a wide range of investment-related decisions by foreign investors.

CAN INVESTMENT TREATIES INDUCE EFFICIENT GOVERNMENT DECISIONS IN THEORY?

The law and economics literature has extensively examined the tension between these two sources of inefficiency—over-regulation and over-investment. One theoretically elegant solution is to ensure that investment treaties require a host state to pay full compensation to the investor only if the host state's decision to interfere with an investment is inefficient *ex post* (Miceli and Segerson 1994).[19] In the example depicted in Figure 5.3, this is akin to requiring an arbitral tribunal to determine whether $E > 100$. When $E < 100$, the tribunal requires the host state to pay full compensation if it decides to shut the investment project down. This requirement dissuades a state from over-regulating. When $E > 100$, no compensation is required, as payment of compensation in these circumstances would induce over-investment (Miceli 2011).

However, the ability of an investment treaty to solve problems of over-regulation without inducing over-investment is highly sensitive to variation in the simplifying assumptions of Figure 5.3 (Been and Beauvais 2003; Aisbett, Karp, and McAusland 2010a). Two important assumptions on which the model rests are:

i Aside from the costs that its action imposes on foreign investors, the host government fully internalizes all the costs and benefits associated with its actions on itself and other actors—notably, the value of E in Figure 5.3 and

---

[19] Other solutions that are optimal in theory—for example, the *ex ante* rules discussed in Blume, Rubinfeld, and Shapiro (1984) and Miceli and Segerson (1994)—are less relevant in the context of investment treaties because they do not involve evaluation of the host state's conduct.

the cost of any compensation that must be paid to the investor if the host state breaches an investment treaty; and

ii The government has perfect information about the value of all the costs and benefits associated with any given regulatory action.

If one relaxes these two assumptions, an investment treaty that contains a provision requiring compensation only for inefficient measures will not necessarily improve efficiency, and could well make things worse. This is because, in the absence of perfect information about the value of E, a government decision-maker in Figure 5.3 needs to estimate the value of E and the corresponding probability that a decision to shut the project down will trigger a requirement to pay compensation.[20] Faced with uncertainty, a decision-maker who does not fully internalize the value of E would be more concerned with avoiding the risk of having to pay compensation in an investment treaty arbitration than the risk of failing to regulate in cases where the value of E turns out to be large enough to justify regulation. In conditions of uncertainty and less than full internalization of E, an investment treaty that contains a provision requiring compensation only for inefficient measures is likely to cause 'regulatory chill'. In these conditions, even carefully calibrated investment treaty provisions will not necessarily improve efficiency.[21]

IS THE MODEL OF FISCAL ILLUSION AN ACCURATE REFLECTION OF GOVERNMENT DECISION-MAKING?

The previous section suggests that, under certain simplifying assumptions, carefully calibrated investment protection provisions of investment treaties could improve efficiency by solving problems of over-regulation arising from fiscal illusion in government decision-making. It also suggested that the ability of investment treaties to generate these benefits is sensitive to variation in the underlying assumptions on which Figure 5.3 is based. As such, an important question is whether these simplifying assumptions are descriptively accurate. This section considers four reasons why the assumptions that underpin the model of fiscal illusion might turn out to be inaccurate.

Consider first the assumption that host government decision-makers undervalue the costs that their actions entail for foreign investors relative to the other social costs and benefits associated with their actions. Little empirical work has been done to test this assumption. However, an extensive literature

---

[20] Here, we are considering uncertainty on the part of the government and the investor. For models considering the implications of uncertainty for arbitral tribunals, see Sasse (2011) and Aisbett, Karp, and McAusland (2010a).

[21] We are grateful to Emma Aisbett for this point. Miceli (2011, 98) makes a similar argument, using different variations in the underlying assumptions.

argues that government decision-makers tend to undervalue diffuse costs that are spread thinly across a wide range of actors as compared to costs that are concentrated on small, relatively homogenous minorities (Olson 1965; Stigler 1971; Grossman and Helpman 1994). Their greater ability to organize opposition gives strongly affected minorities more influence over government decision-making than marginally affected majorities. Cases like Australia's decision to introduce tobacco plain packaging (*Philip Morris v. Australia*), Canada's decision not to approve a quarry in Nova Scotia (*Bilcon v. Canada*), and Germany's decision to phase-out nuclear power (*Vattenfall v. Germany II*) illustrate that disputes under investment treaties often arise in situations in which the benefits of the measure under challenge are spread across a large number of individuals and where the costs are concentrated on a handful of (foreign) investors.

A second issue is that the model of fiscal illusion assumes that all government decision-making conforms to the same assumptions. However, investment treaties apply to a wide range of government conduct across countries with very different systems of government—from new laws passed by parliaments, to the decisions of courts, the actions of specialized regulatory agencies, and the decrees of dictators. Again, there is little evidence of the way that different agencies of different governments value the costs that their actions impose on foreign investors. However, scholars considering the practical effect of legal rules protecting private property from government interference in a national context have argued that a single simplified decision-making theory cannot account for decision-making by different government entities (Levinson 2000).[22] For instance, some government actors may be prone to under-regulation of foreign investors (e.g. investment promotion agencies), whereas others may be prone to over-regulation of the same investor (e.g. taxation agencies).

A third issue is that the model of fiscal illusion assumes perfect information on the part of the government, not only of the value of externalities associated with foreign investments, but also of the content and effects of investment treaties. Aside from a handful of case studies, which are discussed in Chapter 6, little research has been done to assess the level of knowledge of investment treaties among government decision-makers. However, insofar as such evidence exists, it suggests that even those agencies that are responsible for *negotiating* investment treaties have not always been fully informed of their legal consequences—at least until recently (e.g. Poulsen 2015).[23] This suggests an even lower level of knowledge of investment treaties among government

---

[22] We are not suggesting that the 'unitary actor' theory of the state is an inappropriate simplifying assumption in all contexts. Our point is that, in seeking to understand the effects of investment treaties on government decision-making, this assumption may not be appropriate.

[23] We return to these findings in detail in Chapters 7 and 8.

decision-makers who have not been involved in treaty negotiations. Although some governments have instituted internal processes to share information between various arms and agencies about the state's obligations under investment treaties (UNCTAD 2010), these are the exception, not the rule.

Even if all government decision-makers were aware of investment treaty obligations, a fourth issue is that they may not *themselves* bear the costs of non-compliance. The model of fiscal illusion assumes that the constraints of investment treaties are fully internalized by the government decision-makers who are responsible for decisions that affect foreign investors. In reality, investment treaties bind states at the national level in relation to the conduct of *all* government entities—including specialized agencies and sub-national levels of government. For example, the dispute in *Metalclad v. Mexico* concerned a decree issued by the governor of San Luis Potosi three days before the end of his term in office. Three years later, an arbitral tribunal concluded that the decree expropriated Metalclad's investment, and that Mexico was required to compensate the investor. Legal constraints on the central government only solve problems of fiscal illusion in other government entities if an internal accountability or loss-allocation regime is in place—one that ensures that the costs of breaching an investment treaty are ultimately borne by the decision-maker responsible for the breach (Sattorova 2014). For this reason, some scholars argue that the legal constraints of investment treaties are unlikely to be fully internalized by the entities within government that actually make decisions in relation to foreign investment (Been and Beauvais 2003). The result could be more investment treaty claims without an associated reduction in inefficient over-regulation.

THE MODEL OF FISCAL ILLUSION AND INVESTOR DECISION-MAKING

A distinct question is whether the simple model of fiscal illusion presented in Figure 5.3 is based on accurate assumptions concerning the decision-making of *foreign investors*. Here, two issues arise. The first is that the simplified model of fiscal illusion assumes that investors are fully informed about the legal content of investment treaties *before* investing.[24] If this assumption is correct, treaties that protect investors from future regulatory change could encourage investors to proceed with projects with negative net pay-offs (over-investment). However, Chapter 6 raises questions about whether foreign investors do, in fact, carefully scrutinize investment treaties before investing. In this way, the extent to which investment treaties cause problems of over-investment also

---

[24] We leave aside here questions about the behaviour among different actors *within* firms; see footnote 1.

depends on a range of empirical questions that the existing scholarly literature, for the most part, has yet to address.

A second complication arises from the possibility that foreign investors are risk-averse (similarly, Blume, Rubinfeld, and Shapiro 1984; Kaplow 1986). *Risk aversion* refers to a preference for more certain to less certain outcomes. For example, risk-averse investors would prefer a certain loss of 10 per cent of the value of their investment to a 10 per cent chance of the loss of the entire value of their investment. A risk-neutral investor would be indifferent between these two options. Where investors face uncertainty—for example, if the value of E in Figure 5.3 is uncertain at the time of investment—risk aversion can deter investors from proceeding with projects that would otherwise be mutually beneficial for both the investor and the host state, given the *ex ante* probability distribution for the value of E.[25] Under-investment will occur even if the government is presumed to act efficiently—that is, even if the investor knows that the host will only shut the investment project down if it turns out that $E > 100$. In other contexts, concerns that risk aversion among investors may lead to under-investment have prompted scholars to propose legal rules requiring governments to pay compensation whenever they take *any* measure that significantly interferes with private property (Blume and Rubinfeld 1984).[26]

The extent to which foreign investors are risk-averse is an empirical question. Some studies support the view that foreign investors are indeed risk-averse in some contexts (Goldberg and Kolstad 1995). Yet, this does not necessarily provide an additional justification for investment treaties, as the most efficient solution to address risk-aversion is for investors to purchase insurance. Assuming that it is actuarially fair, political risk insurance provides a way for investors to reduce the risk to which they are exposed without changing the balance of incentives affecting the investment decision (Kaplow 1986). This is because the risks against which the investor insures are priced into the cost of the insurance policy. Insurance thereby solves the problem of under-investment due to risk aversion, without inducing the investor to proceed with projects that have negative net pay-offs. In practice, well-developed private insurance markets sell political risk insurance to foreign investors (Peinhardt and Allee 2016).

While investment insurance can address under-investment attributable to risk aversion among foreign investors, market-based investment insurance cannot solve hold-up problems. This is for two reasons. First, unlike the

---

[25] The 'probability distribution' of E refers to the range of likely values for E and the probability of E having various values within that range.

[26] Blume and Rubinfeld also argue that compensation for government interference should be calculated according to a lower standard than is applied under investment treaties, so as to avoid inducing over-investment.

provisions of an investment treaty, insurance purchased by an investor does not alter the pay-offs for the host government. In the absence of an investment treaty, the rational strategy for the government in Figure 5.1 is still to expropriate the investment, even if the investment is insured (Sasse 2011). Second, if the insurance is actuarially fair, the risk of expropriation will simply be priced into the cost of the insurance. As such, for an investor at the first stage of the game depicted in Figure 5.1, the risk of expropriation has the same impact on the expected value of the investment regardless of whether the investor insures against the risk. For example, if the risk of expropriation is 25 per cent and expropriation would result in total loss of the value of the investment, actuarially fair insurance would cost 25 per cent of the total value of the investment.

FISCAL ILLUSION AND THE LEGAL CONTENT OF INVESTMENT TREATIES

Thus far in this section, we have examined a basic model of fiscal illusion among government decision-makers. We have argued that designing legal requirements that improve efficiency in such circumstances requires consideration of two different problems—over-regulation by the host-state and over-investment on the part of the investor. We have seen that it is possible to design legal rules that solve both problems simultaneously and, thereby, maximize efficiency, but only so long as the process of government decision-making is consistent with highly restrictive simplifying assumptions—namely, the assumption of perfect information, and the assumption that government decision-makers fully internalize all costs and benefits associated with their actions aside from those that accrue to foreign investors. Thus, questions relating to the microeconomic implications of various investment treaty provisions cannot be divorced from underlying empirical questions.

Insofar as government decision-making conforms to the assumptions of Figure 5.3, the principle that compensation should be required for inefficient conduct (but not efficient conduct) that interferes with foreign investments remains an important touchstone for understanding the economic implications of investment treaties (Bonnitcha and Aisbett 2013). This principle provides a potential justification for some legal features of investment treaties. For example, many recent investment treaties clarify that tribunals should identify situations of indirect expropriation (for which compensation must be paid) by weighing a challenged measure's impact on a foreign investor against other characteristics of the measure, including whether it pursues a legitimate policy objective (see Chapter 4). While such provisions do not explicitly instruct tribunals to distinguish between inefficient and efficient measures, they recognize that there are circumstances in which the need to prevent harm to other actors justifies government interference with foreign investment without compensation. Such provisions are more efficient than the 'sole effects' interpretation of expropriation provisions (Aisbett, Karp, and McAusland 2010a; 2010b), which requires compensation to be paid for *any* measure that results in total, or near-total, loss of the value of an investment. For similar reasons, the exceptions provisions contained in some investment treaties are also likely to increase efficiency (van Aaken 2009; see also Chapter 4).

A recent trend in the interpretation of FET provisions in investment treaties has been for tribunals to balance the impact on the foreign investor of the challenge measure against the host state's ability to pursue other policy objectives. For example, in *Saluka v. Czech Republic*, the tribunal explained that, in determining whether compensation was required for interference with an investor's expectations, it would consider whether the conduct of the host state was:

reasonably justifiable by public policies and [whether] such conduct does not violate the requirements of consistency, transparency, even-handedness and non-discrimination (para. 307).

According to such an interpretation, compensation is only required if the harm to the investor is unreasonable or disproportionate. This does not explicitly focus on whether the conduct of the host state is inefficient, but it does encourage tribunals to weigh the costs of a measure for the investor in light of the measure's other benefits. Insofar as government decision-making conforms to the assumptions of Figure 5.3, such provisions could also increase efficiency by discouraging governments from over-regulating. Insofar as government decision-making does not conform to the assumptions of Figure 5.3, such provisions may be ineffective in discouraging over-regulation, and may also risk reducing efficiency by inducing over-investment and under-regulation. This is owing to the reasons previously explained in the discussion of whether the models' assumptions are accurate.

Finally, it is important to recall that any economic benefit derived from using investment treaties to solve problems of over-regulation accrues to foreign investors (Aisbett 2013). And, if investment treaties cause problems of over-investment and under-regulation, these costs fall on the host state. In a treaty between two countries where bilateral investment flows are roughly balanced, the benefit to each countries' investors operating abroad from solving problems of over-regulation could, in theory, leave both countries better off. However, it is unclear whether the inclusion of provisions in investment treaties that seek to redress over-regulation is in the interests of countries that are primarily recipients of foreign investment. This is an important point of contrast to hold-up problems. Insofar as investment treaties solve hold-up problems, they benefit both foreign investors and host states.

Investment treaties as tools to redress discrimination against foreign investors

A third way in which investment treaties could affect economic efficiency is by altering the competitive relationship between firms of different nationalities that operate, or are considering operating, in the host state. This contrasts with the models of hold-up and fiscal illusion examined in previous sections, both of which concern the relationship between foreign investors and the host state. Policy-makers regularly cite the objective of preventing discrimination against foreign investors as a justification for investment treaties. For example, the European Commission offers three core justifications for including invest-ment protection provisions in TTIP, one of which is 'to level the playing field for EU investment in the US' (European Commission 2015c; similarly, US Trade Representative 2015). Despite the role that discrimination-based arguments play in policy debates about investment treaties and how common non-discrimination provisions are in investment treaties (see Chapter 4), questions of discrimination have received surprisingly little attention from economists and political scientists studying the investment treaty regime.

THE ECONOMIC BENEFITS OF NON-DISCRIMINATION

The basic economic argument for treating investors of different nationalities equally is straightforward. Laws and policies that favour firms of one nation-ality over those of other nationalities protect favoured firms from displacement by more efficient competitors. Equal treatment allows more efficient firms to establish new investments, win contracts, and expand production at the expense of less efficient competitors. The result is a more efficient organization of production overall. Under common simplifying assumptions,[27] eliminating nationality-based discrimination among investors benefits the host state, even if it leads to the displacement of domestic firms by foreign firms. This is what economists call a 'static' benefit, in the sense that the benefits arise from a reallocation of resources following a one-off policy change (i.e. removing discriminatory laws and policies). In addition to these static benefits, econo-mists have long argued that competition has the 'dynamic' benefit of increasing the rate of productivity growth over time (e.g. Smith 1776). This theory suggests that discriminatory policies that insulate favoured firms from competition

---

[27]   Notably, the assumption that there are no increasing returns to scale and the assumption that any short-term monopoly rents are dissipated through competition.

reduce the rate of productivity growth over time (for empirical evidence, see e.g. Nickell 1996).[28]

At this point, it is important to recall the distinction from Chapter 1 between restrictions on new foreign investment and the treatment of foreign investments that a host state has already allowed in its territory. Historically, investment treaties have focused on the latter set of 'post-establishment' issues (see Chapter 4). The microeconomic analysis of post-establishment discrimination overlaps with the examination of hold-up and over-regulation problems in the previous sections. For example, the possibility that a host state will impose a new discriminatory tax on a foreign investment after the investor has incurred sunk costs can lead to a hold-up problem. The risk of hold-up problems provides a clear rationale for host states to agree to binding post-establishment national treatment provisions in investment treaties, rather than simply legislating to guarantee post-establishment national treatment through their own laws.

Conditions and restrictions on *new* foreign investment in a host state that do not apply equally to new domestic investment—that is, pre-establishment discrimination—raises different issues. Prior to making an investment, an investor has not committed capital or incurred sunk costs. As such, the possibility of pre-establishment discrimination does not create a risk of hold-up problems. Basic microeconomics suggests that the most efficient policy is for a government to allow new investment on a non-discriminatory basis.[29] A government concerned with maximizing the welfare of its citizens would maintain such policies out of self-interest, and could rely on its treaty partners to do the same. In the absence of hold-up problems, any potential benefit to 'locking in' such non-discriminatory policies through an investment treaty will be based on signalling or political economy considerations. Chapter 6 examines these issues, as well as the economic arguments against including such provisions in investment treaties. The remainder of this section focuses on post-establishment discrimination.

DO FOREIGN INVESTORS SUFFER FROM DISCRIMINATION IN PRACTICE?

The extent to which foreign investors and their investments suffer from discrimination at the hands of host states in the absence of investment treaties is an empirical question. This question is important for two reasons. First, the

[28] Some scholars have argued that discriminatory policies can also have positive dynamic effects, in that they allow favoured firms to earn additional monopoly profits. These additional profits can then be reinvested, accelerating the rate of productivity growth among favoured firms. This is the essence of the 'infant industry' argument for protection, which is considered in Chapter 6.

[29] Additional complications arising from market imperfections are considered in Chapter 6.

magnitude of economic benefits generated by treaty guarantees of non-discriminatory treatment depends, in part, on the extent to which foreign investors actually suffer from discrimination in practice. Second, and more importantly, investment treaties provide a suite of substantive and procedural rights to foreign investors that are not available to domestic investors. The extent to which these preferential rights are justified depends, in part, on the extent to which they redress discrimination that foreign investors are otherwise subject to.

Despite the central role that the objective of preventing discrimination plays in policy debates about investment treaties, there is little empirical work comparing the treatment of domestic and foreign firms by host states. There is a significant body of scholarship within the discipline of management studies on the 'liability of foreignness' (e.g. Zaheer 1995). This literature identifies a range of obstacles to foreign firms that seek to establish and expand investments in new markets. These obstacles include: lack of knowledge of the new market; lack of access to business networks; differences in cultural norms concerning the appropriate conduct of business; and higher transaction costs associated with coordinating economic activity across large distances (Sethi and Judge 2009). All of these obstacles stem from characteristics of foreign firms that make them less efficient than their local competitors in the market in which they seek to operate. However, such factors differ fundamentally from discriminatory laws and policies by host states whose effect is to put foreign firms at a disadvantage compared to equally efficient domestic competitors. It is this latter question that requires much more empirical scrutiny.

In Chapter 3, we noted the short supply of empirical evidence on the relative treatment of foreign investors in courts of host states (see also the following text). Insofar as evidence is available about treatment by the executive and legislative branches, it casts doubt on the view that host states treat foreign firms less favourably than their domestic competitors. For example, based on the World Bank's business environment survey covering 48 developing countries, Desbordes and Vauday (2007) conclude that foreign and domestic firms have similar levels of political influence over host states and, if anything, that foreign investors benefit from more generous regulatory concessions and lower tax rates. They also observe that the treatment of foreign investors does not appear to 'obsolesce'—that is, deteriorate—during the lifespan of their investment (see also Aisbett and McAusland 2013). Analysis of more recent World Bank data finds that foreign investors often tend to be treated the same, or better, than domestic firms, even after robustly controlling for size, sector, and other relevant factors that may distinguish foreign firms (Aisbett and Poulsen 2016). These studies provide important insights, but the literature remains in its infancy. Also, existing studies do not distinguish between the treatment of foreign investments covered by investment treaties and the treatment of those that are not. As such, it is not possible to determine whether the existence of investment treaties is one of the reasons why these aggregate studies suggest that foreign investors do not suffer from post-establishment discrimination.

NON-DISCRIMINATION PROVISIONS IN INVESTMENT TREATIES

As explained in Chapter 4, investment treaties commonly contain two provisions dealing with post-establishment discrimination: national treatment and MFN. Both provisions prohibit formal discrimination—for example, the intro-duction of new regulations that apply only to foreign investments (*de jure dis-crimination*)—as well as *de facto* discrimination—for example, discriminatory administrative practices that are not authorized by law. In countries where states would otherwise treat foreign firms worse than their domestic competitors, these provisions are likely to improve efficiency by ensuring competitive equality between firms of different nationalities (Stiglitz 2007).

As noted in Chapter 4, difficult questions arise when determining whether differences in treatment constitute *de facto* discrimination in practice. Recall again the case of *Occidental v. Ecuador I*, described in Chapter 4. In that case, the decisive legal question was whether Ecuadorian mining, seafood, and cut flowers companies were relevant comparators in determining whether a foreign oil company had been the victim of discrimination. The tribunal held that the foreign investor and these Ecuadorian companies were indeed in 'like situations' because they were all involved in production for export. On this basis, the tribunal concluded that Ecuador had breached the national treatment provision of the BIT. This decision has been criticized (e.g. Kurtz 2009), and most tribunals have taken a different approach. For instance, in assessing whether two differently treated firms were in 'like circumstances',[30] the tribunal in *SD Myers v. Canada* considered the extent to which the firms were competitors with one another.[31] The *SD Myers* tribunal also held that the assessment of 'like circumstances' should 'take into account circumstances that would justify governmental regulations that treat [the two firms] differently in order to protect the public interest'. It identified firms' environmental impacts as an example of a factor that could justify a conclusion that two firms were not in 'like circumstances', notwithstanding their competitive relationship.

The analysis of this section supports the *SD Myers* tribunal's interpretation. The microeconomic rationale for treaty-based guarantees of non-discrimination is to ensure competitive equality between firms. This rationale is inapplicable to firms that are not competitors, or potential competitors. Moreover, from an

---

[30] The national treatment provision of NAFTA uses the term 'like circumstances', in contrast to the term 'like situations', in the US–Ecuador BIT, although the legal issue is the same.
[31] This reasoning is different to the approach of the *Occidental v. Ecuador I* tribunal. A US oil company operating in Ecuador is not a competitor of an Ecuadorian-owned seafood company.

economic perspective, differences in treatment are justified if they reflect different patterns of externalities associated with the activities of different firms. Consistent with the interpretation of the tribunal in *SD Myers*, the analysis of this section suggests that states should be entitled to impose restrictions or taxes in response to such externalities, even if the burden of those measures falls more heavily on foreign-owned firms.

PREFERENTIAL PROCEDURAL AND SUBSTANTIVE RIGHTS IN INVESTMENT TREATIES: THE QUESTION OF REVERSE DISCRIMINATION

Notwithstanding their non-discrimination provisions, investment treaties are fundamentally preferential instruments. Only covered investors benefit from the substantive and procedural protections of an investment treaty. Domestic investors, as well as foreign investors not covered by any investment treaty, have no rights under investment treaties (subject to the caveat of corporate nationality planning, as explained in Chapter 2). Moreover, the 'absolute' substantive protections of investment treaties grant rights to covered foreign investors that are not defined by reference to the way that other investors are treated (see Chapter 4), raising the possibility that these substantive rights are more generous than those available to other investors under the domestic law of the host state.

All other things being equal, granting preferential rights to foreign investors of particular nationalities—'reverse discrimination'—reduces efficiency (Stiglitz 2007; similarly Bhagwati 2004).[32] This is because preferential rights confer an advantage on preferred foreign firms over domestic and foreign competitors—for example, the advantage of being entitled to compensation for future regulatory measures that destroy the viability of an investment; or the advantage of being able to invest without being subject to performance requirements that apply to other firms in the same sector. In theory, these advantages allow preferred firms to earn higher profits and to expand at the expense of more efficient competitors. If investment treaties have these effects in practice, which is an empirical question, we would expect to see increased foreign investment in a state from those other states with which it has investment treaties. However, this increase in investment would be a result of 'investment diversion' from domestic and foreign investors not covered by an investment treaty to foreign investors covered by an investment treaty

---

[32] This chapter focuses on the economic concerns relating to the preferential treatment of foreign investment. According to some critics, the conferral of greater rights to foreign as compared to domestic investors also affects the legitimacy of the investment treaty regime (e.g. Warren 2014). We return to the legitimacy critiques in Chapter 9.

(see Chapter 6), and would not entail any benefit to either party in its capacity as host state, or any net benefit to the treaty parties considered jointly.

Assessing whether investment treaties confer substantive rights on foreign investors that are more generous than those to which they would otherwise be entitled under national law is challenging. This is partly because investment treaties apply to any government conduct that affects foreign investors. In national legal systems, there is no single body of law that regulates all government conduct affecting investors. Instead, in national legal systems, different principles of constitutional law, environmental law, tort law, corporate law, contract law, tax law, and administrative law, among others, govern different aspects of the relationship between governments and investors. This makes comparison of the substantive rights conferred by investment treaties with those provided under national law difficult.

In a detailed study, Parvanov and Kantor (2012) review several areas of US law and conclude that investment treaties generally do not confer greater substantive rights on foreign investors than US law. In contrast, Johnson and Volkov (2013) argue that the fair and equitable treatment provisions of investment treaties do provide foreign investors with greater substantive rights than US law. Kleinheisterkamp (2014) has also argued that investment treaties provide more generous entitlements to compensation than EU law. These debates are particularly controversial because both the US Congress (Bipartisan Trade Promotion Authority Act, sec 2102(b)(3)) and the European Parliament (Resolution, 8 July 2015, sec 2(d)(xv)) have issued directives to their countries' treaty negotiators stating that investment treaties should not provide greater substantive rights than are available under their respective national laws (see Chapter 1). Such directives reflect economic concerns about reverse discrimination. However, because relatively little research has been done comparing the substantive rights in investment treaties with those available under domestic law, it is unclear whether the directives are being followed in practice.

In contrast, there is no doubt that investment treaties grant preferential procedural rights to foreign investors. Chapter 3 shows how investment treaties give advance consent to arbitration of disputes with foreign investors of particular nationalities. This procedural right is not available to domestic investors and foreign investors of nationalities not covered by investment treaties.[33]

Some commentators have argued that this preferential procedural right is justified in circumstances in which foreign investors are discriminated against

---

[33] No home country has ever granted to its own investors a general right to take investor–state disputes to international arbitration. It is rare, although not unprecedented, for a host country to grant this procedural right to all foreign investors regardless of nationality—for example, through advance consent to arbitration in a national investment law. We discuss this in Chapter 7.

in the host state's court system (Wälde and Weiler 2004). This argument implicitly invokes the economic theorem of the second best, which establishes that, when there is a market distortion, additional corrective distortions can increase efficiency (Lipsey and Lancaster 1956). Applied to the investment treaty context, the theorem suggests that, if foreign investors do suffer from discrimination in domestic courts, discriminating in favour of foreign investors by granting them a preferential procedural right to resolve disputes through arbitration could increase efficiency. For this reason, an important empirical question is whether foreign investors are, indeed, treated more poorly than domestic investors in domestic courts. While we have strong anecdotal evidence of the poor treatment of foreign investors in the courts of some countries, other countries—for example, Nigeria—have instituted preferential procedures for foreign investors in domestic courts. Using World Bank survey data, Aisbett and Poulsen (2016) find that foreign firms are *more* likely than comparable domestic investors to find that courts in the host state are fair, impartial, and uncorrupt, and that foreign firms are no more or less likely than comparable domestic firms to find that domestic courts are an obstacle to their operations. However, with a few exceptions, little systematic empirical work has been done on the relative treatment of foreign and domestic investors in host state courts. This is an important area for further research.

Conclusion

This chapter has examined the microeconomics of investment treaties. It showed how investment treaties could, in theory, increase efficiency by resolving hold-up problems, by preventing over-regulation due to fiscal illusion in government decision-making, and by redressing discrimination against foreign investors. It also showed how investment treaties could decrease efficiency by inducing over-investment, under-regulation (regulatory chill), and by granting preferential substantive and procedural rights to foreign investors. The balance of these effects depends on the answers to a range of empirical questions identified during the analysis. One important conclusion of this chapter is that the microeconomic analysis of investment treaties cannot be divorced from the underlying empirical questions about the legal systems and government decision-making in the states that are bound by them. Empirical questions about firms' decision-making are also an important consideration.

6   Investment Treaties, Foreign Investment, and Development

Introduction

This chapter examines the aggregate economic effects of investment treaties, focusing on their impact on investment flows and on economic development. The first section reviews studies of investment treaties' investment protection provisions on foreign investment. This subject has received a disproportionate share of attention in empirical work on the investment treaty regime. The second section examines the impact of investment treaties on governance in the countries that are bound by them, which in turn could have macroeconomic effects. Both these sections outline the findings of existing empirical studies, assess the relevance of these findings, and discuss methodological and measurement challenges that make it difficult to draw strong conclusions from the existing literature. The third section examines the impact of the investment liberalization provisions of investment treaties on foreign investment and development. As described in previous chapters, liberalization provisions were historically rare in BITs, but are increasingly common in new investment treaties, particularly plurilateral investment treaties and investment chapters of preferential trade agreements (PTAs). Such provision could have important—and thus far largely unexplored—macroeconomic effects.

The impact of investment treaties on foreign investment

Empirical work on the macroeconomic effects of investment treaties focuses primarily on the question of *whether* entering into an investment treaty increases inward FDI for developing countries. This focus reflects the common view that the purpose of investment treaties is to promote new foreign investment, on the assumption that increased inward investment leads to economic development (van Aaken 2011). The impact of investment treaties on foreign investment is an important question for policy-makers, as developing countries typically signed these treaties in the expectation that it would help them attract foreign investment (see Chapter 8). Nevertheless, three important caveats should be borne in mind when evaluating these studies.

First, both the review of evidence on the economic implications of foreign investment in Chapter 2 and the microeconomic analysis in Chapter 5 suggest that the economic effects of foreign investment vary depending on the reasons for the investment, the industry in question, and the economic and institutional conditions of the host state. As such, any rigorous analysis of the macroeconomic effects of investment treaties needs to go beyond the question of *whether* investment treaties affect FDI flows and also consider *how* and *why* investment treaties affect foreign investment. More recent studies have begun to probe some of these questions, but the question of *whether* investment treaties affect FDI continues to receive disproportionate attention.

Even if investment treaties increase inward FDI in states that sign them, policy-makers need to consider whether these increases are the result of a net increase in investment ('investment creation') or whether they come at the expense of other investment ('investment diversion'). The pool of capital available for FDI at any given time is not fixed.[1] Investment treaties may *create* new opportunities for direct investment and thereby increase the global direct investment stock—for example, by solving hold-up problems. On the other hand, investment treaties could also *divert* investment between states via three different mechanisms. The first is that, by providing protections for investment in one host state that are not available for investment in other host states, investment treaties could divert foreign investment from one host state to another. That would result in a classic collective action problem, whereby it may be individually rational for developing countries to sign treaties to increase their share of global FDI, but collectively irrational for developing countries as a group to sign investment treaties (Elkins, Guzman, and Simmons 2006).[2] While parallel considerations about diversion and creation of international trade resulting from preferential agreements have been widely discussed since the 1950s (Viner 1950), the issue has received little attention in empirical work on the macroeconomics of investment. Second, since investment treaties give foreign investors rights that domestic investors do not have, they could provide foreign investors with an 'ownership' advantage over their domestic competitors in host states (see Chapter 2). The result could be that investment treaties divert productive investment opportunities away from

---

[1] Capital is invested in many ways aside from direct investment, including real property, and gold, as well as through portfolio investment in debt and minority shareholdings (Feldstein 1995). Changes in the allocation of capital between direct investment and other forms of investment can increase or decrease the value of direct investment globally. The amount of capital available for direct investment can also change as a result of shifts in the allocation of current income between investment and consumption—for example, decisions by firms to retain and reinvest earnings rather than distribute dividends to shareholders, or decisions by consumers to save more.

[2] We return to the competition among developing countries for capital in Chapter 8.

domestic investors, as discussed in Chapter 5. A third form of investment diversion relates to the home state: investment treaties may encourage companies to route investments that they would have made in any event through a corporate intermediary in a third country in order to take advantage of an investment treaty between the third country and the host country (see Chapter 2).[3] All three scenarios would show up as 'positive' effects of investment treaties on investment in quantitative studies, but not because of actual investment 'creation'.

Finally, recall from Chapter 2 that most investment treaties cover not only FDI but also many forms of portfolio investment, such as minority shareholdings, debt, and financial derivatives. We noted in Chapter 2 that economists are more sanguine about the benefits of portfolio investment than FDI, both due to the greater volatility of portfolio investment flows and because portfolio investment does not normally entail positive spillovers for the host state such as technology transfer or human capital development. A comprehensive macroeconomic assessment of investment treaties would need to consider investment treaties' impact on the investment decisions of bankers and fund managers, as well as on states' ability to regulate portfolio flows.[4] However, at the time of writing, neither the impact of investment treaties on portfolio investment flows, nor the impact of investment treaties on governments' ability to regulate those flows, has been subject to significant theoretical and empirical scrutiny.

CAUSAL MECHANISMS

An important question in quantitative studies of how investment treaties affect FDI is whether to try to isolate the impact of an investment treaty on FDI between the partner countries or, alternatively, whether to assess the impact of entering into an investment treaty on total inflows of FDI to a country, including inflows from foreign countries that are *not* covered by the treaty. Choosing the appropriate approach depends on theories of which foreign investors are influenced by the existence of an investment treaty. There are two, potentially complementary, theories in the existing literature of how the investment protection provisions of investment treaties could affect

---

[3] There is evidence of cases in which this has occurred (*Mobil v. Venezuela* 2010, para. 204). Similarly, Petrobras is reported to have invested abroad via third countries to secure BIT protections because Brazil has no ratified BITs (Poulsen 2015, 7, ftn 28). That said, no study has suggested that this practice is sufficiently common to explain an observed impact of investment treaties on investment flows between treaty partners.

[4] Recall from Chapter 4 that the broad free transfer of funds provisions included in many investment treaties—for example, those contained in US BITs—place legal limits on the ability of states to impose capital controls, even when necessary to respond to financial crises (Waibel 2010b; Gallagher and Stanley 2013).

FDI. The first is *commitment theory*: the theory that the protection that investment treaties provide is directly relevant to the investment decisions of investors who are covered by the treaty. As discussed in Chapter 5, this could be, among other reasons, because they help such investors solve hold-up problems, or because they provide covered investors with legal rights that are not available to competitors of other nationalities. But the central premise of commitment theory is that only those investors who are covered by the treaty directly benefit from the protection provided by the treaty.

The second is *signalling theory*: the theory that, when a country enters into an investment treaty, it sends a signal to investors from all foreign countries, including those not covered by investment treaties, that it has laws and policies in place that protect foreign investment. The theoretical underpinnings of signalling theory have been examined in economics (e.g. Spence 1973). Investment treaties must satisfy two conditions to operate as signals. First, foreign investors must lack information about the investment climate in the country in question. If there were no such information asymmetries, investors could rely on their own (correct and fully informed) assessment of the investment climate in the host state because the existence of an investment treaty would not communicate any additional information. Second, it must be less costly for states that provide sufficient protection to foreign investment to become and remain parties to investment treaties than it is for states with bad investment climates. If that were not the case, all states would be equally likely to ratify investment treaties, and the existence of a treaty would not convey any meaningful information about the quality of the investment climate. Tobin and Rose-Ackerman (2011) contend that investment treaties meet the second condition because the risk of liability in investment treaty claims is greater for states with bad investment climates. On this basis, they argue that investment treaties act as signals of a good investment climate.[5]

QUANTITATIVE STUDIES OF THE IMPACT OF INVESTMENT TREATIES ON FDI: A SUMMARY

An Appendix to this chapter lists thirty-five published quantitative studies of how investment treaties affect FDI (Table A.6.1). The majority focus specifically on the impact of *bilateral* investment treaties on FDI in developing or middle-income countries. We are not aware of studies that have tested the

---

[5] Kerner (2009) proposes a different variation of signalling, according to which civil society actors' opposition to investment treaties means that the act of signing the treaty entails a political cost to a government, and the willingness of a government to incur that costs sends a signal that it will protect foreign investment. For a critique, see Bonnitcha (2014a).

investment impact of FCN treaties or the impact of investment treaties among developed countries, such as the ECT.

The studies' results are mixed. A majority find that investment treaties have a positive and statistically significant impact on inward FDI in at least some circumstances. Among these, the scale of the impact varies remarkably, with some reporting strong effects and others finding positive but only small effects. Among the studies reporting a positive effect of BITs on investment flows, some also come to apparently contradictory findings.[6] Finally, a sizeable minority of studies find that there is no statistically significant effect of BIT adoption on FDI flows. Studies examining signalling effects—that is, the impact of entering into investment treaties on total inflows of FDI to a country, including inflows from foreign countries that are *not* covered by the treaty—seem more likely to find that investment treaties have a positive impact on inward FDI than those examining commitment effects.

ESTIMATION CHALLENGES

The literature faces several challenges. It needs to account for theoretically relevant differences between (i) investment treaties; (ii) host states; and (iii) investors. Moreover, significant challenges arise from (iv) endogeneity. In this section, we examine each of these four challenges in turn, which will make clear that existing studies are not of equal quality. The quality of future studies in the field should also be assessed by examining the way in which they deal with these challenges.

The first challenge relates to the way in which investment treaties are coded by quantitative researchers. Several early studies treated the existence of a signed investment treaty as the independent variable. In doing so, these studies failed to distinguish between investment treaties that subsequently entered into force and those that were never ratified and thus never entered into force. Yet, in theory, only ratified treaties that become legally effective can act as a credible commitment and/or a costly pro-investor signal. For the most part, more recent studies have addressed this problem (see e.g. Haftel 2010).

Early studies also failed to distinguish between investment treaties that contained provisions allowing for enforcement through investment treaty arbitration and those that did not, a characteristic that is crucial to investment treaties' ability to function as commitment or signalling devices. For instance, Yackee (2009) showed that results indicating a strong impact of BITs on FDI (e.g. Neumayer and Spess 2005) are no longer significant once investment treaties are recoded to distinguish between those that allow for enforcement

---

[6] For example, one concludes that only US BITs increase co-signatories' FDI (Salacuse and Sullivan 2005), and another that most BITs increase FDI but US BITs do not increase co-signatories' FDI from the United States (Gallagher and Birch 2006).

through investment treaty arbitration. Three more recent studies have examined variation in the impact of investment treaties that provide advance consent to investment treaty arbitration and those that do not. These studies find that investment treaties that provide advance consent to arbitration are no more effective in attracting FDI than those that do not (Berger et al. 2011; 2013; Peinhardt and Allee 2012b). These finding are the opposite of what both commitment and signalling theories predict, and raise questions about whether more general findings that investment treaties increase FDI are, themselves, reliable.

Some contributions have tried to disaggregate investment treaties even further—for instance, by constructing indexes of treaty 'strength' (e.g. Haslam 2007; Dixon and Haslam 2015). If done carefully, such studies could allow researchers to test the importance of legally relevant features of investment treaties. However, studies that rely on a single index of treaty 'strength' come with their own challenges. While it may be possible to rank certain features of a treaty—for example, progressively wider definitions of the range of 'investments' covered by different treaties[7]—aggregating these aspects into a single index of treaty 'strength' involves a set of essentially arbitrary decisions about the relative importance of various features of the treaty. Moreover, aggregating different parts of treaties to create a single measure of treaty 'strength' ignores the interaction between different provisions—most importantly through the MFN clause (Poulsen and Yackee 2016; see also the following text). These challenges are further augmented in the context of investment chapters that form part of broader trade agreements, where there may be interaction effects between investment and non-investment provisions.

A second challenge is that investment treaties could have different effects in different host states. If investment treaties attract FDI by solving hold-up problems, they are likely to be most effective in countries that are poorly governed. In contrast, if investment treaties attract FDI through signalling effects, they are likely to be most effective in states that have recently improved their internal governance. As such, a core question is whether investment treaties are more effective in attracting FDI to countries that are poorly governed or to countries whose governance has improved. Findings of studies on this point are mixed. Some find that investment treaties are more effective in attracting FDI to countries with relatively strong domestic institutions (Desbordes and Vicard 2009; Tobin and Rose-Ackerman 2011), whereas others come to the opposite conclusion (Neumayer and Spess 2005). One possible explanation for these different results is the difficulty in capturing intangible domestic political and institutional characteristics within a metric of 'governance quality'. We return to this issue in the following text.

---

[7] See Chapter 2 for a discussion of the range of 'investments' that investment treaties typically cover.

A third challenge is that investment treaties could be more effective in promoting some types of investment than others. For example, Chapter 5 suggested that investment treaties are likely to be more effective in promoting investment in sectors that involve high sunk costs, such as natural resources and utilities.[8] Whether this hypothesis is correct is an important empirical question for policy-makers, as Chapter 2 showed that foreign investment in different sectors is associated with different patterns of costs and benefits for the host state.

The difficulty in obtaining good data on foreign investment disaggregated by sector makes it difficult to test the impact of investment treaties on investment in different sectors. Thus far, only a few studies have examined the impact of investment treaties on FDI disaggregated by sector. Colen and Guariso (2013) find that investment treaties have a significant positive impact on FDI in the mining sector but not on FDI in any other sector. These findings are consistent with those of Busse, Königer, and Nunnenkamp (2010), who find that investment treaties are more effective at attracting FDI to resource-rich countries. Similarly, Danzman (2016) finds that investment treaties have a positive impact on investment in infrastructure projects, but no impact on aggregate FDI.[9] Further support for the view that investment treaties are more effective in promoting investment that entails high sunk costs comes from Kerner and Lawrence (2014). Rather than disaggregating FDI by sector, they use annual data supplied by US companies operating across all sectors on the value of their foreign affiliates' assets, which is disaggregated into fixed and liquid capital. Fixed capital includes plants, equipment, and concession rights; liquid capital includes cash and inventories. They find that US investment treaties—including free trade agreements with investment chapters—have a positive, but small, impact on investment in fixed capital but no impact on the value of firms' holdings of liquid capital. Disaggregating foreign investments by capital intensity, Colen, Persyn, and Guariso (2016) find similar results for foreign investment in 13 countries in the former Soviet Union and Central and Eastern Europe.

The fourth and, perhaps, greatest challenge is the problem of endogeneity. In particular, studies should account for the fact that many states adopted laws and policies that might have an independent impact on FDI around the same time that they entered into investment treaties (omitted variable bias), and the possibility that growth in FDI between a given pair of countries could be a

---

[8] Another issue that may be relevant is the size of the investor and the investment, given that the costs of investor–state arbitration make it uneconomic for investments below a certain value. See Chapter 3 for a discussion on the costs of investor–state arbitration.

[9] Danzman uses the broad World Bank classification of 'infrastructure' investment as including: oil, gas, and mining; electric power and other energy; water sanitation and flood protection; transportation and roads; and information and communication. All these sectors are associated with high ratios of sunk costs to total investment value.

reason why those states decided to negotiate an investment treaty (reverse causality).[10] For instance, both Neumayer and Spess (2005) and Salacuse and Sullivan (2005) suggest a causal link between investment treaties and FDI, but their results are not robust once endogeneity is taken into account (Aisbett 2009). Omitted variable bias is a particularly serious concern with studies of the signalling effect of investment treaties. As Chapter 8 shows, many developing countries signed investment treaties around the same time that they amended national laws and policies governing FDI. Signalling theory predicts that investment treaties affect inward FDI from all countries, as is likely to be the case with national reforms. Because it is difficult to construct metrics that capture relevant national reforms (see the following text), the relative importance of the two factors is difficult to disentangle.

THE DEPENDENT VARIABLE

Another issue that has received less attention is the quality and relevance of the measure of foreign investment used as the dependent variable. The vast majority of quantitative studies use data on FDI flows or, less frequently, FDI stocks. There are three main limitations associated with these measures. First, there are problems of overall *data quality* of FDI. Second, there is a mismatch between the *investments* covered by investment treaties and what FDI statistics measure. Third and finally, there is a mismatch between the *investors* covered by investment treaties and what FDI statistics measure.

First, the quality of FDI stock data is poor. In 2007, only about 100 economies reported inward FDI stock data, and among those the method of evaluation differed significantly (Fujita 2008, 115). Outward FDI stock data is even more patchy. This lack of stock data is the reason the majority of quantitative studies use data on FDI flows, which is generally more reliable. That said, there are also problems with FDI flow data (Fujita 2008, 107). These problems could also bias results if errors in FDI data were correlated with host country characteristics— for example, if underestimation of FDI flows correlated with low quality of government institutions and bureaucracy.

The second issue arises because FDI flow is a measure of the cross-border movement of capital. FDI flows comprise loans, equity, and reinvested earnings contributed by the investor to a foreign entity in which the investor has a shareholding of 10 per cent or more.[11] FDI flow data does not include the

---

[10] One possible explanation for reverse causality could be that investors that have invested in a given host country have an incentive to lobby their home country to enter into an investment treaty. We return to this issue in Chapter 7.

[11] We have already noted that investment treaties cover portfolio investment, which is not counted in FDI statistics. In this section, we do not engage in further discussion of this dimension of mismatch between what is covered and what is measured.

value of investments in a host country that are owned by foreigners but financed by loans or capital raised in the host country (Beugelsdijk et al. 2010). In contrast, whether an investment falls within the protection of an investment treaty depends on whether it is foreign-owned, not on whether it is financed by foreign capital.[12] FDI flow data may still be useful as a proxy for changes in the value of foreign-owned investment covered by an investment treaty. However, the mismatch between the two could also be a source of bias—for example, if the quality of local institutions in the host state influences the extent to which foreign investors rely on local financing.

In principle, the use of FDI stock data could partially resolve these problems. FDI stock data is intended to measure the value of foreign-owned assets and, therefore, corresponds more closely with the value of 'investments' covered by an investment treaty. However, FDI stock data is often calculated by aggregating FDI flows over time, rather than through direct measures of the market value of foreign-owned assets (Kerner 2014).[13] FDI stock data calculated in this way suffers from the same basic mismatch between what is measured and what is covered by an investment treaty as FDI flow data.

A third limitation is the mismatch between the *investors* covered by an investment treaty and what FDI statistics measure. Many investment treaties cover both directly and indirectly owned foreign investments. For example, an investment in Ecuador that is owned by a Cayman Islands subsidiary of a US parent company qualifies for protection under the Ecuador–US BIT.[14] In contrast, FDI data measures only the immediate source and destination of investment. The previous example would show up twice in FDI data—once as US investment in the Cayman Island and again as Cayman Islands investment in Ecuador—but would not show up in FDI data on US investment in Ecuador. This is major issue in practice because roughly 27 per cent of global FDI flows through tax havens and jurisdictions offering special purpose entities that facilitate transit investments (UNCTAD 2015a, ch. 5).[15] This mismatch between what is measured and what is covered by investment

---

[12] Moreover, from an economic policy perspective, the more important question for a host state is whether foreign investment is foreign-owned, not whether it is foreign-financed. This is because positive spillovers associated with foreign investment—such as technology transfer, skills, and improved management (see Chapter 2 for discussion)—arise from foreign ownership or control of an investment, rather than from foreign financing of an investment.

[13] Historical cost-based US outward FDI stock is defined by the Bureau of Economic Analysis as 'net book value of U.S. parents' equity in, and net outstanding loans to, their foreign affiliates. The position may be viewed as the U.S. parents' contributions to the total assets of their foreign affiliates or as the financing provided in the form of equity or debt by *U.S. parents* to their foreign affiliates' (italics added) (BEA 2004, M-21).

[14] Article 1(a) of the Ecuador–US BIT 1993 states that the treaty covers 'every kind of investment in the territory of one Party owned or controlled directly or indirectly by nationals or companies of the other Party'.

[15] For example, in 2014, the Netherlands was the largest recipient of US outward FDI, and Luxembourg, Ireland, the British Caribbean Islands, and Bermuda were all in the top ten.

treaties is an especially serious problem for empirical testing of commitment theory. Using FDI data to test commitment theory depends on the problematic assumption that the immediate source of foreign investment is a satisfactory proxy for whether that investment is covered by an investment treaty.

Partly for these reasons, some quantitative studies have begun to test the impact of investment treaties using different dependent variables as proxies for the value of foreign investment stocks and flows. Egger and Merlo (2012) find that the presence of a German BIT is correlated with an increase in the number of German multinational firms that are active in the partner country and the volume of investment made by such firms. Provided the result is not due to endogeneity, which from the study is unclear, questions arise as to whether this result is generalizable to other countries or may be driven by the close link between German investment treaties and the provision of German investment insurance (see Chapter 7). Jandhyala and Weiner (2014) find that the coverage of an investment treaty significantly increases the price that international companies pay for foreign petroleum assets in market transactions. This finding suggests that investors in that sector value the protection provided by investment treaties, and that the presence of an investment treaty is likely to lead to additional investment in that sector. These studies are useful additions to a literature largely relying on highly aggregated FDI flows.

QUALITATIVE STUDIES

In light of the methodological challenges and mixed findings of econometric studies, other scholars have employed different methodologies to examine the relationship between foreign investment and investment treaties. One alternative is directly surveying those responsible for firms' investment decisions to see whether they regard investment treaties as a relevant factor in their decision-making. In the early 1990s, a series of surveys of British, German, Swedish, and US investors by the World Bank indicated that, at that time, Western investors were rarely aware of investment treaties: only '[p]rofessional advisors, such as accountants or merchant bankers, would be people to concern themselves with such minutia, only after detailed project planning was already underway' (MIGA PAS 1991a, 92). They considered other parts of the investment regime complex, such as DTTs, to be far more important.

Investors are now likely to be more aware of investment treaties due to the rise of investment treaty arbitration over the last two decades (see Chapter 1). However, some more recent surveys are broadly consistent with the World Bank's findings. Yackee (2009, 429) surveyed in-house general counsel of seventy-five Fortune 500 companies. The responses 'indicate a low level of familiarity with BITs, a pessimistic view of their ability to protect against adverse host state actions, and a low level of influence over FDI decisions'.

Equally, Copenhagen Economics found that European investors in China were rarely familiar with relevant BITs and, even when they were, that the treaties were only relevant for actual investment decisions in a small number of cases (Copenhagen Economics 2012).

Other surveys point to a greater awareness and relevance of investment treaties. In an *Economist* survey of 602 corporate executives, 19 per cent of respondents indicated that the existence of an investment treaty influenced their investment decisions 'to a very great extent' (Shinkman 2007). Although Sachs (2009) raised doubts about the reliability of Shinkman's results, it does suggest that investment treaties play at least some role in influencing the destination and volume of foreign investment in some countries. In a more recent survey, Hogan Lovells, the Bingham Centre for the Rule of Law, and the British Institute of International and Comparative Law (BIICL) (2015) received responses from 301 senior decision-makers at Fortune 2000 companies. The responses suggest a high level of familiarity with investment treaties, and that senior decision-makers regard investment treaties as an important consideration when making decisions about foreign investment. However, other responses to the survey cast doubt on the reliability of these results. For example, in many cases, the respondent's company had, in fact, invested in countries in which the respondent said the company would not invest due to the absence of an investment treaty (Hogan Lovells, Bingham Centre for the Rule of Law, and BIICL 2015). This highlights one major methodological challenge with surveys in general: responses of investors do not necessarily match their behaviour in practice.

A second approach has been to focus on the impact of investment treaties on the availability and pricing of political risk insurance. The political risk insurance industry is important for two related reasons. First, because political risk insurers take on the financial risk of failure of investments, they have a strong self-interest in being fully informed about the effectiveness of legal arrangements that can mitigate those risks. Second, if the presence of investment treaties affects the pricing of political risk insurance, it would give investors who purchase insurance a financial incentive to invest more in countries covered by investment treaties. In a detailed series of interviews with private and government-sponsored political risk insurers, Poulsen (2010) found that the existence of an investment treaty covering a proposed investment had little impact on the coverage and pricing of political risk insurance. There were exceptions, such as the German investment insurance program (see Chapter 7), but the vast majority of private and public providers did not report investment treaties to have a significant impact on their decision-making (cf. also Yackee 2011). It is an open question, whether these results would be different today, now that the potency—but also unpredictability—of investment treaty arbitration has become more apparent to investors and their advisors.

Finally, one study has assessed whether investment promotion agencies use investment treaties when marketing their country to foreign investors (Yackee 2015). If investment treaties operate as signals of an attractive domestic climate, we would expect rational states to actively publicize information about the existence of their investment treaties. Yet, Yackee finds that hardly any states do so. This could be because the agencies fail to act in their own interest—or that of their government—or because the agencies have made an accurate judgment that the treaties are not a significant factor for foreign investors considering whether to invest in the host state.

At the time of writing, academic scholarship has yet to produce detailed case studies focusing on the role of investment treaties in individual investment decisions. Nor has business literature assessed the importance of the treaties for different actors *within* firms. If carefully constructed, such studies could give us greater micro-level insights on how investment treaties influence foreign investment decisions, which in turn can have macro-level impacts. We know of at least a couple of cases where investment treaties are reported to have had a decisive impact on foreign investment decisions,[16] but when and under what circumstances investment treaties influence the destination and volume of individual investments remain open questions.

All in all, there is a large and growing literature seeking to assess the extent to which investment treaties influence foreign investment decisions. Most of this literature uses econometric techniques to measure the impact of investment treaties on FDI flows, which involve significant challenges in terms of data availability and econometric specification, but some recent studies have begun to use other methods and more fine-grained measures of investment. The results are mixed. Taken together, the literature suggests that investment treaties do have some impact on *some* investment decisions in *some* circumstances, but that they are unlikely to have a large effect on the majority of foreign investment decisions. When considering the macroeconomic implications of these conclusions, it is also important to recall the caveats noted at the beginning of this section: any evaluation of the investment treaties' economic impact depends not only on *whether* investment treaties increase aggregate inward foreign investment, but also on *how* and *why* investment treaties affect different types of investment.

---

[16] As an example, in discussions with his colleagues, the Dutch ambassador to Venezuela reported that the investment treaty arbitration provision in the 1993 Netherlands–Venezuela BIT was instrumental for Royal Dutch Shell's participation in a large natural gas project (Poulsen 2015, 8, ftn 29). It is unclear from the report whether an investor–state arbitration provision in a contract would have been an adequate substitute for Shell, nor is it clear whether the treaty's arbitration provision was required for Shell to acquire political risk insurance.

Macroeconomic effects through changes in government decision-making

We turn now to a second macroeconomic effect of investment treaties that has received significantly less attention in empirical literature: the impact of the treaties on government decision-making. As explained in Chapter 4, several protections that investment treaties provide to foreign investors concern the *process*, as opposed to the outcome, of government decision-making. For example, arbitral tribunals have interpreted FET provisions as requiring host states to provide due process in administrative decision-making. Decision-making processes that affect foreign investors and that are fundamentally biased or that completely ignore relevant evidence are likely to breach FET provisions (Dolzer and Schreuer 2012, 130–59). In theory, investment treaties should encourage governments to ensure that decision-making processes conform to these procedural standards, as breaching them runs the risk of costly investment treaty arbitrations by foreign investors (Echandi 2011). On this basis, several legal scholars have argued that investment treaties encourage 'good governance' and respect for 'the rule of law' in countries that sign them (e.g. Dolzer 2006; Schill 2010; Vandevelde 2010). These effects on government decision-making processes could contribute to economic development, both through the direct benefit of 'better' government decisions and by encouraging both foreign and domestic investment.[17] If investment treaties promote better investment governance for *all* investors, this should be of particular interest to small- and medium-sized domestic firms without privileged access and influence over domestic policy-makers (on the joint interest of foreign firms and smaller domestic firms in replacing cronyism with property right protections, see e.g. Markus 2012).

There are three core assumptions underlying the hypothesis that investment treaties improve government decision-making. The first is that the constraints that investment treaties place on host state conduct correspond with underlying concepts of 'good governance' and 'the rule of law'. We do not address this question here, save to note that this assumption is the subject of significant disagreement, and that 'good governance' and 'the rule of law' are, themselves, contested concepts.[18] Instead, we focus on the second assumption, namely that the constraints imposed by investment treaties are internalized in

---

[17] For example, Dolzer (2006, 953–4) contends that investment treaties reduce 'the space for unprincipled and arbitrary actions of the host state and thus contribute to good governance, which is a necessary condition for the achievement of economic progress in the host state'.

[18] For the argument that the provisions of investment treaties align with these concepts, see Vandevelde (2010) and Schill (2010). For critiques, see Van Harten (2007) and Calamita (2015). These issues are central to debates among legal academics about how vague substantive provisions of investment treaties should be interpreted and applied. Those debates are discussed in Chapter 4.

national administrative practices and judicial systems.[19] Legal scholars generally assume that 'the monetary sanctions [that investment treaty tribunals] can impose exert considerable pressure on States to bring their domestic legal orders into conformity with the investment treaty obligations' (Schill 2012, 137). However, as we will see, this empirical proposition remains largely untested and, to the extent that evidence exists, it raises serious doubts about whether this second assumption is correct. A third assumption is that 'good governance' and 'the rule of law' contribute to economic development. We do not address this assumption here, save to note that it is the least controversial of the three, and that it is the subject of its own highly sophisticated empirical literature.[20]

IMPACT OF INVESTMENT TREATIES ON ADMINISTRATIVE AND JUDICIAL DECISION-MAKING

One way in which states could seek to ensure that they internalize the constraints of investment treaties in national administrative practices is by establishing processes to share information about investment treaties between different parts of government. There is no direct evidence of any state establishing such mechanisms prior to the early 2000s.[21] The absence of institutional arrangements to ensure compliance with investment treaties is consistent with the fact that few developing country governments expected investment treaties to 'bite' in practice (see Chapter 8). This may have changed as states became more aware of investment treaty arbitration. Chapter 5 notes that some countries have now implemented internal processes of information sharing among agencies that deal with foreign investment in an attempt to ensure compliance (UNCTAD 2010). The spread of such institutions and the ways in which they influence administrative decision-making in practice are two important questions for further research.[22]

---

[19] We do not examine the impact of investment treaties on national legislators, as there has been no published research on this question.

[20] On the role of governance in economic performance, see, for example, North (1990) and Rodrik, Subramanian, and Trebbi (2004); on the rule of law and economic growth, see, for example, Haggard and Tiede (2011).

[21] Of course, the absence of evidence does not prove that such mechanisms did not exist. Nor does the absence of an institution with the express mandate of ensuring compliance with investment treaties rule out the possibility that legal agencies within some states are aware of investment treaties and play a role in vetting policy proposals in light of a range of legal risks, including the legal risk of claims under investment treaties (e.g. Van Harten and Scott 2016). Moreover, even if states do not have institutions or practices in place to ensure compliance with investment treaties across government, this does not rule out the possibility that investment treaties influence government decision-making in specific cases—for example, cases in which foreign investors themselves invoke the existence of an investment treaty when bargaining with government. We discuss this in more detail in Chapters 5 and 9.

[22] Note that another way in which investment treaties may have indirectly influenced the development of national law in some countries is through the World Bank Guidelines on the Treatment of Foreign Direct Investment. These guidelines were inspired by BIT obligations and, throughout the 1990s, the World Bank encouraged governments of developing countries to incorporate them into their

Qualitative studies have started to shed more light on the impact of investment treaties in particular countries. Following surveys and interviews with government officials, Côté (2014) concludes that officials with responsibility for health, safety, and environment regulation in Canada's national government and officials with responsibility for tobacco control in a selection of developing countries had low levels of awareness of the content of investment treaties and of the risk of claims by foreign investors under such treaties. Her conclusion that Canadian officials were largely unaware of their investment treaty obligations is significant as, at the time her research was conducted, Canada had already been the subject of over a dozen investment treaty arbitrations over a period of a decade. Interviews conducted by Van Harten and Scott (2016) with government officials in the Canadian province of Ontario paint a very different picture.[23] They find that the Ontario trade ministry played an important role in reviewing policy proposals of various environmental agencies for compliance with Canada's obligations under investment treaties. They also find significant, albeit variable, levels of knowledge of investment treaties among government officials.

In a third study, Sattorova, Omiunu, and Erkan (2016) examined the impact of investment treaties on administrative decision-making in Nigeria, Turkey, and Uzbekistan through a series of interviews with government officials. Although they interviewed only twenty-eight officials across these three countries, their findings suggest a relatively low awareness of investment treaties in each of the three countries, even after their first experience of investment treaty arbitrations. They also suggest that none of the three countries had established an institutional mechanism to ensure that administrative decision-making was consistent with the provisions of investment treaties.

The divergent findings of these studies suggest that an important question for further research is whether investment treaties have different impacts on domestic governance in different states and on different actors within a government in the same state. One concern noted by Sattorova, Omiunu, and Erkan (2016) is that:

> ... the high costs of putting in place dispute prevention and management mechanisms also highlight the fact that the ability of host governments to actively prevent their exposure to international liability by changing domestic governance practices can be severely circumscribed by the very weaknesses in the domestic legal and bureaucratic culture which international investment law allegedly aims to improve.

---

own legal systems (Shihata 1993; Poulsen 2015, Ch. 4). The World Bank and the IFC continue to encourage developing countries to include provisions inspired by BIT obligations in their national investment laws—see, for example, Appendix 6 to the World Bank's Investment Law Reform Handbook (2010), which provides the basis for the IFC's advisory work on investment law reform to developing countries.

[23] We return to possible explanations for the different conclusions of these two studies in the subsection on methodological issues, in the following text.

In addition, it remains an open question whether the extent to which a state internalizes the constraints of investment treaties is related to that state's form of government—that is, democratic, authoritarian, etc. There is a wider body of scholarship which suggests that compliance with international law varies with regime type (Slaughter 1995; see also Alter 2014, Chs. 2 and 9), although this literature largely relates to compliance with obligations of international law that are not backed by an enforcement mechanism akin to investment treaty arbitration.

Apart from the impact of investment treaties on administrative decision-making, a related issue is the impact of investment treaties on domestic courts and legal institutions. As explained in Chapter 4, investment treaties place obligations on states to ensure that foreign investors receive a basic level of procedural fairness in domestic court proceedings. If these treaty obligations encourage states to reform their judicial systems, they could lead to greater conformity with the principle of 'the rule of law'—for example, by encouraging a state to introduce reforms that give the judiciary greater independence from the executive branch of government. Testing this hypothesis raises similar empirical questions to hypotheses concerning the impact of investment treaties on administrative decision-making—that is, to what extent are investment treaty provisions internalized within institutions of the host state? Moreover, there is a further mechanism by which investment treaties could affect domestic judicial institutions. This mechanism rests on the premise that foreign investors have an interest in a functioning court system in the states in which they invest. By giving foreign investors the possibility to resolve disputes with the host state through investment treaty arbitration, investment treaties could *reduce* the incentive of foreign investors to lobby for improvements in judicial quality (Ginsburg 2005; see also Mazumder 2016). If this hypothesis is correct, investment treaties that provide for investment treaty arbitration could have a negative impact on the quality of judicial institutions.

These hypotheses about the potential impact of investment treaties on judicial institutions give us three empirical propositions, outlined in Figure 6.1. The first two are mutually exclusive, whereas the third may be correct regardless of whether either of the first two is correct.

Relatively little empirical research has been done to test these hypotheses. Ginsburg (2005) examines the impact of signing a BIT on changes in the quality of governance in developing countries over subsequent years, as rated by the World Bank's Worldwide Governance Indicators (WGIs). He concludes that signing a BIT does not have a positive impact on governance and has a minor negative impact on the 'rule of law' indicator. This is consistent with the hypothesis that investment treaties reduce investors' incentive to advocate for improvements in the legal system of the host state by giving them access to an alternative system to resolve disputes. Aranguri (2010) reports that the number of BITs a country signs leads to improvement in

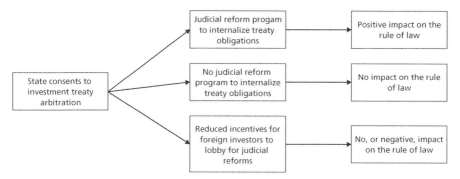

Figure 6.1 Investment treaties and judicial institutions: three options

the country's rating on the WGI 'regulatory quality' indicator but none in the 'rule of law' indicator. He interprets these findings as consistent with the hypothesis that investment treaties improve the quality of administrative decision-making but do not improve the quality of judicial institutions.[24] Sasse (2011) examines the impact of the number of BITs a country ratifies on the WGIs. He finds that the number of BITs a country ratifies has a negative association with 'regulatory quality' and the 'rule of law' indicators but that these correlations are not statistically significant. This is an important area for future research.

METHODOLOGICAL CHALLENGES

Quantitative studies of the impact of investment treaties on government decision-making face similar methodological challenges to those faced by studies examining the relationship between investment treaties and FDI. Foremost among these is endogeneity. As mentioned, many developing countries adopted investment treaties at the same time that they implemented reforms of their domestic investment regimes (see further discussion in Chapter 8). As such, investment treaties may be correlated with improvements in governance and the rule of law, but not because the former had any causal impact on the latter.

Measuring the quality of 'governance' or 'the rule of law' also raises difficult issues. Existing quantitative studies generally use the WGIs. However, the WGIs aggregate data from a wide range of variables. For example, the WGI rule of law index includes some sub-components that are relevant for the study of investment treaties, such as expropriation risk and other property

---

[24] He also finds that adverse arbitral awards in investment treaty arbitrations under BITs lead to decreases in regulatory quality and the rule of law in developing countries. It is not immediately obvious why this should be the case. Bearing in mind that the World Bank's indicators are based on survey respondents' perceptions of governance, one possible explanation is that adverse awards influence perceptions of governance.

right measures, but it also includes others that are not, such as tax evasion, trust in the police, and human trafficking. Moreover, the WGIs are based largely on survey responses and, therefore, reflect the perceptions of respondents. A large share of respondents to the WGI surveys are either business people or commercial risk-rating agencies, and perceptions among these groups—for example, perceptions of problems with 'burdensome' taxes or rules—do not necessarily correspond to the 'quality' of governance as perceived by other groups (Kurtz and Schrank 2007a).[25] This problem highlights the underlying challenges arising from the contested character of 'good governance' and 'the rule of law' as concepts.

Qualitative studies face a range of different challenges. Foremost among these is that investment treaties potentially implicate a vast array of host state conduct. As such, it is difficult to draw strong conclusions from interviews with officials within any one agency of government. For example, Côté (2014) and Van Harten and Scott (2016) paint very different pictures of the level of awareness of investment treaties among government officials in Canada. One possible explanation for these divergent findings is simply that different arms of the Canadian government have different levels of knowledge of investment treaties and different institutional practices. A second challenge is that government lawyers with direct knowledge of the impact of investment treaties of government decision-making are often unable to speak about their experiences due to confidentiality constraints (Van Harten and Scott 2016). There are no easy solutions to these challenges.

At the time of writing, there is insufficient evidence either to confirm or to reject claims about the impact of investment treaties on host government decision-making processes. However, the evidence that is available raises serious questions about the assumption that states regularly and reliably internalize the constraints that investment treaties place on administrative and judicial action within their domestic systems. Until more research is available, claims that investment treaties promote 'good governance' or 'the rule of law' should be treated with caution.

Macroeconomics of investment liberalization provisions

As outlined in Chapter 4, a small but growing minority of investment treaties contain provisions governing the admission and establishment of new foreign

---

[25] Citizen surveys are also included in the indicators, but only from Africa and Latin America, and even there they play a comparatively smaller role to that of corporate entities, and their responses differ in important ways from that of business people (Kurtz and Schrank 2007b). For a response to these criticisms, see Kaufmann, Kraay, and Mastruzzi (2007).

investment. There are two main types of these 'pre-establishment' provisions—namely, MFN and NT provisions. Both prohibit discrimination between investors and investments on the grounds of nationality in the admission and establishment of new investments. Pre-establishment NT is the more powerful obligation, as it gives foreign investors the right to establish new investments in a host state on the same terms as those applicable to domestic investors. As such, this section focuses on the macroeconomic implications of pre-establishment NT.

Investment liberalization provisions are a central concern for policy-makers and treaty negotiators in practice. For example, both the European Commission and the Office of the US Trade Representative (USTR) cite investment liberalization as a main negotiating objective for the investment chapter of TTIP (USTR 2014; European Commission 2015d), and disagreements between the United States and China about the inclusion of pre-establishment national treatment stymied the negotiation of a prospective US–China BIT from 2008 to 2013 (Weijia 2015). However, to date, the theoretical and empirical implications of the investment liberalization provisions of investment treaties have received relatively little academic attention.

THE ECONOMICS OF INVESTMENT LIBERALIZATION

Chapter 2 examined the underpinnings of arguments in favour of a state voluntarily providing pre-establishment national treatment to foreign investors as a matter of domestic law and policy. To summarize: simplified theoretical models of the international economy, such as the Heckscher–Ohlin model, imply that a non-discriminatory regime for new cross-border investment benefits both capital-importing and capital-exporting countries. Moreover, evidence of positive spillovers associated with inward FDI provides a further reason not to discriminate against foreign investment. To be sure, these two observations do not imply that host states should not regulate investment. Rather, they suggest that any restrictions or conditions on new investment—for example, prohibition of activities that cause unacceptable environmental impacts or restrictions on mergers that lead to monopolies—should be applied equally to both domestic and foreign investors.

The economic case *against* pre-establishment national treatment rests on arguments similar to those made in support of 'infant industry' protection in international trade. In its simplest form, the argument is that new domestic companies require protection from foreign competition in order to grow to the size and level of sophistication required to compete with foreign-owned firms. Although favouring inefficient domestic firms is costly in the short-term, such policies could benefit a state in the long-term if they accelerate productivity growth for domestic firms and allow them to realize economies of scale (Melitz 2005). Such arguments depend on the presence of externalities, asymmetric information, monopoly rents, or other market imperfections (e.g. Rodrik 2008; World Bank 2009).

Historically, many countries placed discriminatory restrictions on the entry of new foreign investment. For example, China has encouraged FDI in many manufacturing sectors, while requiring that investment in sectors such as consumer electronics be made by way of joint ventures with local partners (for a positive account, see e.g. Rodrik 2006). These policies go some way to explaining why, at the time of writing, China has not ratified any investment treaty providing for pre-establishment national treatment.

As described in Chapters 1 and 2, countries have progressively lifted restrictions on FDI since the 1990s. Outright prohibitions on FDI are much rarer than they once were. And, in many sectors and countries, governments discriminate *in favour* of foreign investors, offering special tax breaks or incentives that are not available to domestic investors (Tavares-Lehmann et al. 2016). Nevertheless, all countries impose discriminatory conditions on the entry of FDI in at least some sectors (OECD 2015b). Such restrictions are imposed for a variety of reasons. Countries restrict foreign investment in the arms sector for strategic reasons; foreign investment in print and broadcast media is often limited for reasons relating to media independence and plurality; and foreign investment in utilities is often subject to conditions because such industries are expected to provide broad public access to services. Decisions about whether to admit foreign investment—and, if so, on what terms—continue to raise a range of competing policy considerations.

A large body of scholarship debates the merits of government policies that actively seek to direct a state's economic development, compared to laissez-faire policies that emphasize the importance of non-discriminatory treatment of foreign investment (e.g. Pack and Saggi 2006). Rather than reviewing these debates in detail, our purpose here is to assess their relevance for investment liberalization provisions of investment treaties. This is because, even if the economic arguments in favour of unilaterally implementing a *policy* of pre-establishment national treatment are correct, a central question is whether there is any economic benefit to a host state from entering into *binding commitments* in an investment treaty to grant pre-establishment national treatment.

THE ECONOMICS OF INVESTMENT LIBERALIZATION COMMITMENTS IN INVESTMENT TREATIES

The first section of this chapter highlighted two different causal mechanisms by which the investment protection provisions of investment treaties could affect foreign investors' investment decisions. The first of these is commitment theory. In the case of the post-establishment treatment of foreign investment, the putative need for an internationally binding commitment arises because the investor has sunk capital in the project, which is then at risk from policy reversals by the host state (Guzman 1998). In contrast, foreign investors' capital is not at risk from policy reversals by the host state that change the conditions governing the entry of *new* foreign investment. Due to this fundamental point of difference, commitment theory does not provide an economic rationale for a host state to enter into pre-establishment national treatment obligations in investment treaties.[26] A state that wished to adopt a policy of pre-establishment national treatment could achieve the same benefits by unilaterally implementing such a policy through its national law,[27] while still retaining the flexibility to reimpose restrictions on new foreign investment in the future.

The second causal mechanism by which the investment protection provisions of investment treaties could affect foreign investors' investment decisions is *signalling theory*. Via this logic, the inclusion of pre-establishment national treatment provisions in investment treaties could send a signal to foreign investors that the country in question has laws and policies in place that are conducive to new foreign investment. For a signal to convey any information, it must be costly. Binding pre-establishment NT provisions in an investment treaty satisfy this requirement, because such provisions make it costly for the state in question to abandon policies liberalizing the entry of new foreign investment in the future. However, the ability of investment liberalization provisions to have macroeconomic effects in practice via signalling depends on a range of further empirical assumptions—for example, the assumption that prospective foreign investors are able to distinguish between investment treaties that guarantee pre-establishment NT and those that do not. Empirical studies have yet to test these assumptions directly.[28]

Some empirical studies do speak to these questions indirectly. In one quantitative study, Lesher and Miroudot (2006) find that PTAs with 'stronger' investment provisions lead to a greater increases in FDI. In a similar study, Dixon and Haslam (2015) find that only 'strong' investment treaties increase inward FDI for Latin American countries. Both studies use indexes for the 'strength' of a treaty's investment provisions, which include an assessment of

---

[26] Similarly, Chapter 5 shows that the 'hold-up' problem and the problem of 'over-regulation' stem from the sunk costs that a foreign investor incurs when it makes an investment in the host state. In the absence of sunk costs, these problems do not arise.

[27] This is analogous to the situation in simplified theoretical models of international trade, which predict that it is efficient for a country to liberalize unilaterally, unless the country is large enough that its tariffs induce terms-of-trade effects (Krugman, Obstfeld, and Melitz 2014).

[28] Several studies have examined the impact of preferential trade agreements on FDI. Many recent preferential trade agreements (PTAs) contain investment chapters, and such investment chapters often contain pre-establishment national treatment and MFN provisions. However, studies of the impact of PTAs on FDI do not normally distinguish among PTAs on the grounds of whether they contain such chapters or provisions (e.g. Medvedev 2012).

whether the treaty includes pre-establishment liberalization commitments, among other factors. However, neither study allows the effect of investment liberalization provisions, if any, to be isolated. As noted in the first section of this chapter, there are also significant methodological difficulties associated with indexes of treaty 'strength'.

Berger et al. (2013) seek to isolate the impact of pre-establishment liberalization provisions more directly. They conclude that the inclusion of such provisions in BITs does not have any additional impact on FDI, but that the inclusion of identical provisions in PTAs does result in significant additional FDI. The authors suggest that this apparently anomalous result could be explained by the limited public attention that BIT negotiations receive, and hypothesize that investors are unaware of the actual legal content of investment treaties. If so, this would be consistent with the view that, insofar as they have any impact, investment treaties' liberalization provisions influence FDI flows through signalling effects. That said, it is worth reiterating that very little research has been conducted on this question. For studies of the impact of investment treaties' liberalization provisions, disentangling the role of treaty commitments and national-level reforms raises particular difficulties. Given the caveats about methodology noted in the first section of this chapter, claims about the impact of liberalization provisions in investment treaties on FDI should be treated with caution.

THE POLITICAL ECONOMY OF INVESTMENT LIBERALIZATION COMMITMENTS

Insofar as scholars have considered the economics of investment treaties' investment liberalization provisions, they have generally focused on benefits arising from the political economy of investment liberalization (e.g. Vandevelde 2000). Allowing foreign investment in a sector that was previously closed or restricted to foreign investors creates both winners and losers within host countries. The most obvious losers are inefficient domestic firms in the liberalized sector, which may find their profit margins squeezed by more efficient foreign competitors. The obvious winners are workers in the liberalized sector in the host state, although consumers and suppliers also potentially benefit (Pandya 2014).[29] Even if the benefits to the winners significantly outweigh the costs to the losers, the political influence of protected domestic firms may make it difficult for host governments to open their economies to foreign investment (Grossman and Helpman 1996). There is a substantial literature in the political economy of trade policy showing how small and well-organized industry

---

[29] These distributive effects of foreign investment are consistent with the predictions of the Heckscher–Ohlin model, which is introduced in Chapter 2.

lobbies with an interest in protection can influence national trade policy (e.g. Grossman and Helpman 1994; see also Chapter 5).

In theory, the negotiation of binding and reciprocal liberalization commitments in investment treaties could encourage the formation of broader political coalitions in favour of investment liberalization. For example, in the context of investment liberalization negotiations, workers in the host state and firms with an interest in investing abroad could be mobilized in support of the treaty as a counter-balance to firms campaigning for protection at home. This could allow states to bind themselves to a package of binding and reciprocal commitments that would be politically difficult to maintain if implemented solely through national law.

In Chapter 8, we discuss the extent to which developing countries saw investment treaties—for instance, those with liberalization provisions—as devices to 'tie in' or promote liberalizing reforms. However, to date, there has been little empirical research into whether investment treaties alter political economy dynamics in a way that allow host states to enact or maintain liberalizing reforms. If investment treaties do have political economy effects, one would expect the inclusion of investment liberalization provisions in investment treaties to lead to the 'opening' of new sectors to foreign investment on a national treatment basis. In contrast, if binding investment liberalization commitments are primarily intended to operate as signals, we would expect such commitments to reflect prior domestic reforms—that is, for host states to enter into binding commitments only in relation to sectors in which foreign investment is already allowed on a national treatment basis as a matter of domestic law. These are important questions for future research.

Different political economy considerations arise in relation to the practicalities of the negotiation of liberalization commitments. All investment treaties that contain pre-establishment NT provisions also contain reservations to those provisions. Developed states generally have greater capacity within government to foresee situations in which pre-establishment NT obligations could conflict with future political priorities. Stiglitz (2007) suggests that they are also more likely to have industry lobbies that understand the implications of treaty negotiations for their interests, although this proposition has not yet been subject to empirical testing. This imbalance in information, expertise, and negotiating capacity may go some way to explaining why, in BITs between developed and developing countries, the developed country often has the more extensive list of reservations to pre-establishment national treatment (Cotula 2014).[30]

Manger (2009) argues that political economy dynamics in home states also play a central role in explaining the inclusion of investment liberalization

---

[30] We see a similar effect in relation to the negotiation of service liberalization commitments in PTAs between developed and developing countries (VanGrasstek 2011).

provisions in the investment chapters of PTAs. Drawing on case studies that include EU, Japanese, and US PTA negotiations with Chile and Mexico, he argues that home state firms lobbied for the inclusion of investment liberalization provisions with a view to establishing export platforms in the host country to supply the home state market. The inclusion of preferential investment liberalization and tariff reduction provisions in the same PTA was important, as they gave home state firms mutually reinforcing advantages over firms from other developed countries seeking to use the host state as an export platform from which to supply the home state's market. Manger's thesis is provocative in that it suggests that the protectionist objectives of home states at least partly drove the inclusion of investment liberalization provisions in investment treaties. Whether the same is true for the investment liberalization provisions of bilateral and multilateral investment treaties is an important question for further research. Manger's thesis also draws attention to possible interactions between the investment liberalization provisions and non-investment provisions of PTAs—particularly, in relation to their impact on FDI. This, too, is an important question for further research.

Conclusion

This chapter has examined the macroeconomics of investment treaties. Most of the empirical literature on investment treaties remains narrowly focused on the question of whether investment treaties promote inward FDI. Much of this work suggests that the investment protection provisions of investment treaties do have some positive effects on FDI, although these findings should be interpreted in light of the significant methodological challenges facing econometric studies. Qualitative studies suggest that investment treaties influence some investors' investment decisions, but that such effects are uncommon.

As we know relatively little about *how* and *why* investment treaties affect different types of investments in different types of host states, strong claims about the macroeconomic effects of investment protection provisions in investment treaties should be treated with caution. Investment treaties may change the legal structure of foreign investments, for instance, rather than their destination and volume. Equally, even if investment treaties increase investment flows to some countries, recall from Chapter 2 that not all foreign investment necessarily promotes economic development. Similarly, recall from Chapter 5 that investment treaties could, in theory, promote 'overinvestment' by encouraging investors to proceed with investment projects that have negative externalities (knowing that states may have to pay compensation if they implement future measures to reduce such externalities).

The second and third sections of this chapter examined the impact of investment treaties on the quality of governance in the countries bound by them and the implications of investment liberalization provisions, respectively. Both sections also highlighted the gaps in our understanding of the macroeconomic effects of investment treaties. Although some legal scholars make bold claims about the ability of investment treaties to promote 'good governance' or 'the rule of law' in the countries bound by them, such claims have been subject to little empirical scrutiny. Equally, few studies have considered the macroeconomic impact of liberalization provisions, and we therefore know little about their impact on investment flows or political economy dynamics within host states. This is particularly important for North–North investment treaties. Assuming that they lead to reciprocal investment liberalization at the domestic level, liberalization provisions are the most plausible way such agreements can promote investment among developed countries.

▨ APPENDIX

Table A.6.1 Quantitative studies examining the impact of investment treaties on FDI

Author and date	Causal mechanism	Main reported finding of the study
Aisbett (2009)	Commitment and signalling effects	BITs with OECD countries do not increase FDI to developing countries either through commitment or signalling effects
Banga (2008)	Signalling effects	BITs with developed countries increase FDI to Asian developing countries through signalling effects
Berger et al. (2011)	Commitment effects	BITs with full advance consent to investment treaty arbitration have no greater impact on FDI than other BITs, suggesting that BITs do not increase FDI through commitment effects
Berger et al. (2013)	Commitment effects	BITs and regional trade agreements with full advance consent to investment treaty arbitration have no greater impact on FDI than other investment treaties, suggesting that investment treaties do not increase FDI through commitment effects
Blanton and Blanton (2012)	Commitment effects	US BITs decrease US outward FDI stock in partner countries
Busse, Königer, and Nunnenkamp (2010)	Commitment effects	BITs increase FDI flows to developing countries through commitment effects
Büthe and Milner (2009)	Signalling effects	BITs increase FDI to developing countries through signalling effects
Büthe and Milner (2014)	Signalling effects	PTAs with investment protection provisions akin to those found in BITs increase FDI to developing countries through signalling effects
Colen and Guariso (2013)	Signalling effects	BITs increase FDI in the mining sector in Central and Eastern European countries through signalling effects
Colen, Persyn, and Guariso (2016)	Signalling effects	BITs increase FDI in sectors with high sunk costs in Central and Eastern European countries through signalling effects
Coupé, Orlova, and Skiba (2009)	Commitment effects	BITs with developed countries increase FDI to transition countries
Desbordes and Vicard (2009)	Commitment effects	BITs increase OECD countries' outward FDI stock in partner countries (i.e. commitment effect)

(*continued*)

Table A.6.1 Continued

Author and date	Causal mechanism	Main reported finding of the study
Danzman (2016)	Signalling effects	BITs with developed countries increase FDI inflows to infrastructure investment in developing countries, but do not increase total FDI inflows
Egger and Merlo (2007)	Commitment effects	BITs increase OECD countries' outward FDI stock in partner countries (i.e. commitment effect)
Dixon and Haslam (2015)	Commitment and signalling effects	BITs do not increase FDI through signalling effects; 'strong' investor provisions in ratified BITs among Latin American states increase FDI through commitment effects in the context of, or combined with, trade agreements
Egger and Pfaffermayr (2004)	Commitment effects	BITs increase OECD countries' outward FDI stock in partner countries (i.e. commitment effect)
Gallagher and Birch (2006)	Commitment and signalling effects	BITs with the United States do not increase FDI in Latin American countries from the United States. But the number of BITs signed increases total FDI through signalling effects
Grosse and Trevino (2009)	Signalling effects	BITs increase FDI to Central and Eastern European countries through signalling effects
Haftel (2010)	Commitment effects	Ratified US BITs increase FDI from the United States (i.e. commitment effect)
Hallward-Driemer (2003)	Commitment effects	BITs with OECD countries do not increase FDI to developing countries
Kerner (2009)	Commitment and signalling effects	BITs with OECD countries increase FDI to developing countries through both commitment and signalling effects
Kerner and Lawrence (2014)	Commitment effects	US BITs increase investment in fixed capital by US firms in partner countries
Lesher and Miroudot (2006)	Commitment effects	BITs do not increase FDI through commitment effects; investment provisions in PTAs do increase FDI through commitment effects
Neumayer and Spess (2005)	Signalling effects	BITs increase FDI to developing countries through signalling effects
Peinhardt and Allee (2012a)	Commitment effects	BITs with the United States do not generally increase FDI
Peinhardt and Allee (2012b)	Commitment effects	BITs with OECD countries increase FDI from partner countries, but there is no difference between the effect of BITs with and without investment treaty arbitration
Salacuse and Sullivan (2005)	Signalling effects	US BITs increase FDI to developing countries from all sources (i.e. signalling effect); other OECD BITs have no significant signalling effect
Sokchea (2007)	Signalling effects	BITs with OECD countries increase FDI to Asian countries through signalling effects
Swenson (2005)	Signalling effects	BITs increase FDI to developing countries through signalling effects
Tobin and Rose-Ackerman (2005)	Commitment and signalling effects	BITs with the United States do not increase FDI to developing countries from the United States; in general, BITs do not increase FDI through signalling effects
Tobin and Rose-Ackerman (2011)	Signalling effects	BITs with OECD countries increase FDI to developing countries through signalling effects; these effects are greater for host countries with stronger domestic political institutions
UNCTAD (2009a)	Commitment effects	BITs have only a 'minor and secondary' impact on FDI
Yackee (2009)	Signalling effects	BITs do not increase FDI to developing countries through signalling effects
Yackee (2016a)	Commitment effects	French BITs do not increase partner countries' share of outward French FDI flows
Zeng and Lu (2016)	Commitment effects	Chinese BITs increase partner countries' FDI in China, with 'stronger' BITs having stronger effects

7 Politics of Investment Treaties in Developed Countries

Introduction

The following two chapters address the politics of investment treaties in developed and developing countries. With over 3000 existing treaties, it is impossible to assess why every single country has signed every single agreement. The aim, therefore, is to focus on the main factors driving investment treaty policy-making. This can only be done based on an understanding of the changing socio-economic environment for foreign investments, and the two chapters therefore provide significant historical context to the law and economics of the investment treaty regime discussed in the previous chapters.

This chapter focuses on the politics of investment treaties in developed countries, a surprisingly understudied area of the investment treaty regime. It evaluates four potential explanations for why and how developed countries adopted investment treaties. These are: (i) the promotion of business interests; (ii) de-politicizing investment disputes; (iii) building customary international law; and (iv) using investment treaties for diplomatic and symbolic reasons. The chapter concludes by examining recent developments. These include the rise of investment treaty arbitration against developed country states themselves, which has prompted unprecedented political debate about investment treaties.

Business interests

A first, intuitively plausible explanation for the spread of investment treaties is that the interests and lobbying of private corporations in developed countries shaped the investment treaty regime (e.g. Swenson 2005; Neumayer 2006; Van Harten 2007, 38; Allee and Peinhardt 2010). Foreign investors typically have substantial financial resources and are well organized, allowing them to assert potentially significant political pressure on home states. For instance, private firms whose assets are expropriated or otherwise mistreated abroad have often managed to obtain a strong response from their home governments (Krasner 1978; Lipson 1985; Maurer 2013; see the following text). Corporate lobbying may equally have been responsible for developed states pursuing investment treaty negotiations.

If true, it would not be the first time that corporate interests shaped international law. Anghie (2004) and Cutler (2003) describe the close relationship between corporate power and the development of international economic law. International investment law also has roots in the colonial era, where private trading companies played crucial roles in promoting legal doctrines for the protection of their interests (Miles 2013). More broadly, the role of business actors is regularly invoked to understand the behavior of Western states in the international system. In addition to Marxist conceptions of the international order (Lenin 1917; Cox 1987), countless studies on comparative political economy, business–state relations, and inter-state bargaining also integrate corporate interests in their models in order to understand the behavior of Western governments (e.g. Milner 1988; Rugman and Verbeke 1990; Odell 2000; Hall and Soskice 2001). Trade policy in advanced economies is often tied to industry and producer interests (e.g. Grossman and Helpman 1994; Rodrik 1995; Hiscox 2001), and corporate influence is a key factor in studies of preferential trade agreements (Milner 1997; Chase 2003; 2005; Manger 2009) and WTO negotiations (Sell 2000; Woll 2008).

This section assesses the extent to which private commercial interests influenced the creation and design of the investment treaty regime. In doing so, we trace the role of corporate lobbying from the beginning of the regime after the Second World War, when the United States and Europe together established the institutional frameworks that govern world trade and investment.

THE ITO AND THE US FCN PROGRAMME

After the Second World War, threats of the use of force and 'gunboat diplomacy' to protect investments abroad were not only practically infeasible in many parts of the world, they were also inconsistent with the prevailing liberal ideas of the time, not to mention the UN Charter. This posed a challenge for the governance of foreign investment, as developing countries were increasingly sceptical towards the foreign investment protection norms developed during the colonial era (see Chapter 1).

Committed to constructing an open international economy through multilateral means, the United States proposed an International Trade Organization (ITO), introduced in Chapter 1, which would have enshrined international minimum standards of treatment for foreign investors, including the Hull standard of compensation for expropriation. US businesses were pleased and offered significant input on the drafting of ITO's investment rules (Vandevelde 2012).[1] Resistance from capital-importing states, however, meant that the

---

[1] Initially, the US Chamber of Commerce and the National Association of Manufacturers (NAM) suggested going even further by establishing an international organization exclusively devoted to

drafters relaxed the investment protection provisions during negotiations, which turned US businesses against the agreement. The National Foreign Trade Council complained that the final compromise text, 'not only affords no protection for foreign investments of the United States but it would leave them with less protection than they now enjoy' (quoted in Diebold 1952, 18). An advisory group consisting of representatives from Bank of America, Chase National Bank, John Deere, US Steel, and Westinghouse also noted in 1949 that 'ratification of the ITO Charter would render foreign investment impossible because of the investment provisions it contains' (quoted in Vandevelde 2012, 247). Since other trading partners were not particularly keen on the Charter either, the Truman Administration never submitted it to the US Congress (Jupille, Mattli, and Snidal 2013, ch. 3).

Following the failure of the ITO, the less ambitious GATT remained as the primary governing instrument for international trade in the post-war era. As GATT lacked rules on foreign investment, the ICC prepared an International Code for Fair Treatment of Foreign Investments in 1949. It included protections against discrimination, expropriation and restrictions on impeding the transfer of funds, and suggested that investors should have direct recourse to international arbitration. States were wary of such a broad convention, however, and never adopted the proposal (Nwogugu 1965, 143–4).

The absence of a multilateral convention on investment protection was not a major concern for US foreign investors, who continued to rely on US power to secure their investments abroad (Maurer 2013; see the following text).[2] The ITO discussions did, however, institutionalize talks between US business groups and the US government about investment treaties. The US government gave consideration to drafting a stand-alone BIT, which would have been the first of its kind. But it decided ultimately that US Friendship, Commerce, and Navigation (FCN) agreements should be re-focused to deal primarily with investment treatment and protection. And although US business groups did not convince the government to coerce developing countries into signing FCN treaties, for instance by withholding foreign aid, they still played important roles for both the strategy and design of this first US investment treaty program (Vandevelde 2012; see the following text).

THE GERMAN BANKER

On the other side of the Atlantic, European investors no longer had imperial regimes to back them when investment disputes flared up abroad. Although

---

investment to complement the rules and work of the ITO (trade), the IMF (monetary), and the World Bank (long-term lending) (Vandevelde 2012, 171–2).

[2] This paragraph is based on Vandevelde (2012).

European states did occasionally intervene on behalf of their foreign investors after the Second World War, such as the joint British–French military intervention after the nationalization of the Suez Canal in 1956, such forays were increasingly difficult. With growing amounts of capital ready to invest outside of Europe combined with growing scepticism towards multinationals in the developing world, this posed a challenge.

Both the Swiss government and a parliamentary group in the United Kingdom suggested international investment conventions during the 1950s. But it was a simultaneous German initiative that proved particularly influential. After the Second World War, German investors had lost almost all their assets overseas as part of the reparation strategies pursued by allied powers to make Germany pay for the war-time conduct of the Nazi regime (US Department of State 1960, 1485–7). So when economic recovery began in the 1950s and German firms were once again looking to invest abroad, protections against confiscation and expropriation were high on their agenda. Under the leadership of then chairman of Deutsche Bank—Hermann Abs—the German Society to Advance the Protection of Foreign Investment suggested what Abs called a 'Magna Carta' for foreign investment—a treaty to defend private investors from mistreatment by host states. The proposal codified an international minimum standard of treatment of foreign investment, and it was backed by investor–state arbitration freely available to foreign investors without a requirement to first exhaust local remedies. National courts would be required to give full effect to the decisions of arbitral tribunals. In addition, the draft granted foreign investors a right to make new investments on a national treatment basis and imposed a 30-year prohibition on expropriation except during serious emergencies.

Abs suggested his ideas to the European Economic Community (EEC), which in his view lacked a proper external investment protection policy. Along with a joint European investment treaty program, he proposed withholding financial aid from countries not willing to grant European investment sufficient investment protections (ELEC 1958). Although there was little political appetite for either suggestion, Abs' views on the need for investment protection treaties gained traction in some parts of Europe. Lord Hartley Shawcross led a group of British and continental lawyers who worked on a parallel initiative, which included similar protections—though not an investor–state arbitration provision. Shawcross had a long career in public service behind him, most notably as Attorney General of the United Kingdom and Chief UK Prosecutor at the Nuremberg Trials, but by the 1950s he had entered the world of business. One of his positions was as a director of Shell, where he became concerned about the protection of foreign private capital in the developing world (Shawcross 1995, 306). Shawcross had also been part of several post-war oil arbitrations (St John 2017, ch. 3). When Shawcross and Abs learned about each other's proposals, they decided to merge the two and establish the Association for the Promotion and Protection of Private Foreign Investment in Geneva. A small group of major European companies funded the group. In 1958, it published the draft Abs–Shawcross Draft Convention.

Although the draft was a compromise between Abs' far-reaching proposals and the more conservative proposals of Shawcross—for instance by making investor–state arbitration optional—some commentators at the time criticized it as 'a statement of banker's terms sought to be elevated to the dignity of law' (Proehl 1960, 362). While the Convention never left the drafting stage, it played a major role in shaping subsequent treaty practice, as we describe in the following text. Along with international lawyers, senior officers at two of the largest European corporate players—Deutsche Bank and Shell—were thereby instrumental in drafting and promoting one of the 'founding documents' of the modern investment treaty regime.

THE ICSID CONVENTION

The OECD proposed a revised version of the Abs–Shawcross Convention in 1962, which did not extend national treatment to the pre-establishment phase and had significant constraints on investors' ability to file arbitrations, much to the frustration of business groups (Katzenstein 2013, 85–6). Yet, even this watered-down convention failed to gather support (St John 2017, ch. 3). The US wanted developing countries on-board and Britain was concerned about outward flows of investments (due to it's balance of payments difficulties) and the potential that it might become liable for future nationalizations. Greece and Turkey were wary due their role as capital importers. Instead, OECD members tried to encourage the World Bank to pursue a multilateral investment protection treaty. Given the North–South divide on investment protection norms at the time, the Bank declined (Parra 2012). As an alternative, however, it proposed a convention dealing solely with investment dispute resolution—the International Centre for Settlement of Investment Disputes (ICSID).

Unlike the Abs–Shawcross Convention, international investors and their lobbyists were largely silent during the preparation of the ICSID Convention. In the two detailed account of the process, there is no indication that private companies or international business organizations paid much attention to the genesis of the ICSID Convention (St John 2017). It cannot be ruled out, of course, that investment lobbyists deliberately stayed clear of the drafting and negotiation of the ICSID Convention to avoid giving the impression this was an agreement pushed by big capital—the United States did not lead the way on the ICSID Convention for that reason (Meeker, n.d.)—but there is no publicly available information indicating such a strategy.

Given the crucial role played by the ICSID Convention today, the lack of business interest may appear surprising. It is important to recall, however, that, unlike the Abs–Shawcross Convention and later investment treaties, the ICSID Convention does not contain any substantive rules concerning the protection of foreign investment. As Chapter 3 explains, resolution of investment disputes through investor–state arbitration under the ICSID Convention is only possible if a state party to the Convention has expressly consented to the resolution of investment disputes through ICSID arbitration under investment treaties, laws, or contracts. Absent such consent, the ICSID Convention is of little use. Moreover, ICSID dealt solely with a particular class of disputes—those between investors and host states. By contrast, the 1958 New York Convention on the Recognition and Enforcement of Arbitral Awards addressed the much larger universe of commercial disputes as well and was therefore considered crucially important for the international business community (Hale 2015).[3] On the other hand, investors regarded ICSID as unimportant during the 1960s (St John 2017).

EARLY EUROPEAN BIT PROGRAMS: THE IMPORTANCE OF SUBROGATION

Although the OECD draft convention failed to materialize—and the World Bank refused to pursue it multilaterally—it became the main inspiration for the German BIT program. Both the 1959 Germany–Pakistan BIT and later German BITs were modelled directly on the OECD draft, which, in turn, provided the inspiration for other European BIT models.[4]

In parallel with its new investment treaty program, Germany developed a federal guarantee program to benefit German companies concerned about expropriation, restrictions on currency convertibility, politically motivated violence, and other political risks that investors faced when operating abroad. To ensure the ability to recover compensation paid out to insured firms, a condition for a federal guarantee was that the host state protected German firms according to international minimum standards and agreed to state–state arbitration. Most European countries and the United States recognized and

---

[3] To establish a stronger system of recognition and enforcement of arbitral awards, the ICC suggested a treaty in 1951. The ICC drafted a proposal and submitted it to the UN's Economic and Social Council, which set up the United Nations Conference on International Commercial Arbitration (UNCITRAL) to finalize a convention. At the Conference, the ICC was represented alongside the American Foreign Insurance Association, the Inter-American Council of Commerce and Production, as well as a number of legal NGOs. The US Chamber of Commerce strongly supported the project as well, and in the end the 1958 New York Convention closely followed the ICC draft, although with greater emphasis on domestic judicial oversight of arbitral awards (Hale 2015).

[4] It is perhaps for this reason that European states traditionally refrained from including liberalization provisions in their investment treaties—unlike the United States, where FCN agreements provided important inspiration for later BITs. This question has yet to be subject to empirical scrutiny. As Chapter 4 showed, the focus on investment protection as opposed to investment liberalization continues to characterize the great majority of European investment treaties. On the 'anchoring' to template agreements in investment treaty negotiations, see Poulsen (2015).

adhered to the former standards. In developing countries, however, the absence of former colonial links left German investors in an even weaker position than French and British companies (Burkhardt 1986, 99–104), and Germany therefore required an international commitment in riskier jurisdictions. Inspired by Abs' campaign, this commitment took the form of a treaty. Similar to the vast majority of BITs since then, the 1959 German–Pakistan BIT consequently included a clause allowing Germany to pursue claims against the host state on behalf of German investors in the event that it had paid out compensation to the investors in question under an investment guarantee or insurance program. The insurer stepping into the shoes of the insured in this way is known as *subrogation*.

By linking investment treaties to the provision of federal investment guarantees, German corporations had a direct stake in the conclusion of BITs from the very beginning. For instance, companies such as Daimler-Benz, Liebherr, Man, Quelle-Versand, Siemens, and Wella wanted to form joint ventures with Chinese partners and therefore lobbied for a German BIT with China, negotiations for which were initiated in 1979 and concluded four years later. The companies even offered specific assistance and expertise in the negotiations.[5] In other countries, German companies had less interest in new investments but individual firms still lobbied successfully for concluding a BIT to protect their existing assets. This was the case in Zambia, for instance, where the German embassy pushed for a BIT to protect the Germany company Behrens from what it saw as overly strict currency regulations on the company.[6]

One of the European countries that emulated Germany's approach was the Netherlands. Partly motivated by nationalization of Dutch properties in Indonesia in the late 1950s, the Dutch investment protection program began in 1963 (Schrijver and Prislan 2013). Six years later, the Netherlands initiated a government-backed investment insurance scheme. The Investment Re-Insurance Act stipulated that the existence of an investment treaty was one way in which Dutch investments in a given developing country could qualify for investment insurance. This became a main motivation for the Netherlands to enter into the treaties at the time.[7] In fact, given the prominence of investment treaty arbitration, it would probably surprise most observers of the investment treaty regime today that, when given a choice, Dutch negotiators occasionally considered the inclusion of subrogation clauses in investment treaties to be even more important than investment treaty arbitration.[8]

Apart from their role in facilitating insurance, some Dutch investors were, as with German investors, interested in investment treaties as instruments to obtain additional protection for already existing investments. A particularly active company at the time was Shell, which regularly found itself affected by the wave of

---

[5] PA AA, Zwischenarchiv, 12136.
[6] PA AA, Zwischenarchiv, 121366.
[7] Dutch national archive, 2.05.313-7602. See also 2.05.216-59.
[8] Dutch national archive, 2.06.107-1202.

post-colonial resentment towards multinationals in the 1960s. As mentioned earlier, one of Shell's directors at the time was Lord Shawcross, who had been agitating for investment treaties since the 1950s. It was probably no coincidence, therefore, that this particular company made strong representations to both the British and Dutch governments about the need for investment treaties to protect its overseas interests (Poulsen 2015). Shell also provided detailed comments on the UK model investment treaty,[9] as well as the drafts of specific treaties under negotiation—for instance, on the first Dutch BIT with Tunisia.[10]

In European countries where investment treaties and investment insurance were not directly linked, investor interest in BITs was less widespread. For instance, in the early years, the British BIT program was largely driven by the government—rather than by businesses. Both the British BIT program and government insurance program began in the early 1970s with inspiration from other European countries (Denza and Brooks 1987). Yet, coverage and pricing of investment insurance was not made contingent on treaty protections, which made BITs considerably less important for investors in practice (Poulsen 2015). However, business still played a minor role in shaping early UK BITs. The Confederation of British Industry (CBI) was involved in the development of the BIT programme, and some British firms occasionally provided direct input to the process. In the early 1970s, for instance, British–American Tobacco convinced Whitehall to initiate BIT negotiations with Zaire and Nigeria, where the company had operations (Poulsen 2015). However, overall, Whitehall realized that it was 'probably unrealistic to expect an individual investor to be greatly concerned about [BITs]' (quoted in Poulsen 2015, 68).[11] The reason was simple. When not linked to insurance, BITs did not have any immediate implications for companies' 'bottom-line'.[12] And, unlike trade agreements, they did not open up new areas for economic activity as early European BITs only covered post-establishment issues. Although the treaties could be used by home governments to remind host states of their international legal obligations, they had limited teeth without the possibility of recourse to investor-state arbitration. The German experiences made this clear: while some BITs were used to resolve disputes by providing a focal point for host states' international legal obligations when engaging in diplomatic consultations, the treaties were of little use if the host state refused to comply with the standards of investment protection that developed countries promoted (Poulsen 2015; 2017). We return to this in the following text. For now, it suffices to say that when there was no link to insurance, foreign investors did not pay much attention to investment treaties.

---

[9] Foreign and Commonwealth Office (FCO), 59/698.
[10] Dutch national archives, 2.05.118-10510; 2.05.118-10864.
[11] This, of course, was not the message British negotiators gave to developing-country negotiating partners, as we show in the next chapter.
[12] For this reason, Western companies were much more concerned with the negotiation of double taxation treaties than investment treaties.

EUROPEAN BIT PROGRAMS IN THE 1980s–1990s

From the mid-1980s onwards, Western European countries began to reliably include advance consent to investment treaty arbitration in their BITs. Government archival material from this period remains classified in many countries, but there is little evidence that private investors became more active in lobbying their home states for investment treaties. We noted in the previous chapter, for instance, how a 1991 MIGA survey of Western companies concluded that BITs were 'relatively unknown', and that only '[p]rofessional advisors, such as accountants or merchant bankers, would be people to concern themselves with such minutia' (MIGA PAS 1991a, 92). According to MIGA's survey, British investors, for instance, hardly ever took BITs into account when deciding where, and how much, to invest. Nor did US investors.

European BIT negotiators also report that private firms only rarely encouraged them to initiate negotiations. For instance, as an official in charge of the Spanish program during the 1990s noted: 'During the 1990s at least, Spanish firms were not very interested. I did not receive any visit from Spanish firms asking [for] information about the treaties or telling me to take care of certain clauses or points. Not at all'.[13] Similarly, Reinisch notes that the early Austrian BIT programme 'was clearly government driven. Even up to the present, it seems that business is more interested in double taxation treaties than in BITs' (Reinisch 2013, 15). An Austrian BIT negotiator confirms this: 'There was hardly any interest in 1990s from companies.... The real sea change began in 2003–2004, when the cases got media attention'.[14] A former Danish negotiator similarly noted as late as 2009 that 'apart from a couple of lawyers, I seem to be the only one who knows about BITs here in Denmark'.[15]

There were, of course, exceptions. For instance, after having gone through a series of conflicts with Chilean regulators during the 1990s, the Spanish telecommunications company Telefónica used the European Services Forum and European Telecommunications Network Operators' Association to lobby the European Commission to include BIT-like protections into the EU–Chile FTA (Manger 2008). The attempt was unsuccessful. Similarly, while the Danish BIT program was more government than business driven, the Confederation of Danish Industries made submissions to the government on the countries with which Denmark should initiate negotiations, and the shipping giant Maersk was routinely in touch with the Foreign Ministry about the program.[16] More examples of this sort will undoubtedly emerge once archives from the 1990s are

---

[13] Interview with former Spanish negotiator, November 2012.
[14] Interview with former Austrian negotiator, November 2012.
[15] Interview with former Danish negotiator, June 2009.
[16] Danish Ministry of Foreign Affairs archive, UM 400.E.15-15; UM 400.E.13.Bolivia.12; 400.E.15-5; 400.E.13.Venezuela.12; 400.E.18.Nordkorea.12.

opened in European capitals. However, records available to date indicate that the majority of European outward investors showed little, if any, interest in investment treaties until recently—particularly when compared with preferential trade agreements and double taxation treaties.

THE US BIT PROGRAM

In the United States, the 1974 Trade Act formalized business influence on US trade and investment policy by establishing an advisory system where the private sector could help ensure that US trade policy reflected US commercial interests (Walter 2001, 54). After the US FCN program came to a halt, business groups were partly responsible for the initiation of the US BIT program in the 1980s. In light of dissatisfaction with the lack of progress on services and investment in GATT, the 1984 Trade and Tariff Act authorized the US executive to increase its focus on preferential agreements for trade and investment liberalization (Manger 2008, 66). The US BIT program grew out of the resulting shift to bilateralism. Although later versions of the US model BIT came to include binding investment liberalization commitments, the original justification among business groups was the demand for similar legal *protections* for *existing* US-owned investments as European BITs provided to European-owned investments (Vandevelde 1988, 208–9, ftn. 67; St John 2017, ch. 7). The program was thus a defensive reaction to the European BIT programs.

In contrast to Western European countries, the US investment insurance program—the Overseas Private Investment Corporation (OPIC)—had its own set of agreements providing for subrogation, which meant that investment treaties were less important in the establishment phase for US investors than, say, German firms. The treaties thus attracted far less attention among US businesses than negotiations over trade preferences. In the words of one of the architects of the program, it was 'an initiative proposed by international legal specialists within the US Government . . . originally endowed with primarily legal policy concerns' (Gudgeon 1986, 111). With respect to the choice of BIT partners, Chilton (2016) also finds that investor lobbying played little role.

In the 1990s, US firms and business groups did give considerable inputs to the NAFTA negotiations (Chase 2003). During the Senate hearings, Senator Hollings strongly supported Chapter 11—NAFTA's investment chapter—arguing that the absence of an 'insurance policy of binding arbitration' was why US 'businesses have not gone down [to Mexico]'.[17] This claim seems overstated, because the inclusion of investment *protection* and investor–state arbitration provisions in NAFTA was not the priority for US businesses

---

[17] Hearing before the Committee on Finance, US Senate 130 Cong, 1st sess, September 15, 21, and 28, 1993.

during the negotiations. The primary consideration among US companies was greater investment liberalization in Mexico. In particular, firms in service industries—such as banking and telecommunications—sought strong pre-establishment obligations on Mexico to reduce obstacles to new foreign investment, whereas manufacturing firms in the auto and textiles industries were concerned about competitive European and Japanese firms using Mexico as a backdoor to the US market, and therefore pushed for a strict 'rules of origin' regime (Manger 2009, ch. 3). Negotiations over investment protections remained a largely technical affair. They were concerned, primarily, with how the terms of the US model BIT could be included in Chapter 11 without being too explicit about the fact that it contradicted the Mexican constitution (which included a Calvo clause) and re-introduced the Hull rule of compensation, which Mexico had objected to during the 1938 expropriations (Cameron and Tomlin 2000, 100–2, 112–13).[18] To our knowledge, no evidence suggests that there was significant corporate involvement in the negotiation of NAFTA's investment chapter.

THE MULTILATERAL AGREEMENT ON INVESTMENT

Another indication that investment protection treaties were not very high on the Western corporate agenda at the time involves the Multilateral Agreement on Investment (MAI). The OECD launched negotiations for the MAI in 1995 after a series of failed proposals for multilateral and regional investment protection rules. The United States had tried to include substantive protections in the Tokyo and Uruguay rounds of GATT negotiations (Price and Christy 1996), and Germany and France tried to include protection provisions in the MIGA Convention and the World Bank Guidelines on the Treatment of Foreign Direct Investment (Shihata 1993). All failed.

In fact, before the MAI negotiations, OECD countries could not even agree to a binding national treatment instrument among themselves (Graham 2000). European companies had begun to own considerable assets in the United States and wanted to ensure treatment on an equal footing as US investors. Yet, the national treatment instrument failed, partly because Washington did not want to guarantee post-establishment national treatment by subnational levels of government within the United States (agreements binding states would require Congress to legislate). Unable to reach an agreement on this limited set of issues, OECD countries decided to open negotiations for a more ambitious broader investment agreement that included BIT-like investment protections, investment treaty arbitration, and, importantly, investment

---

[18] 18 March is still 'Oil Expropriation Day' in Mexico—a national holiday spent celebrating the expropriations of 1938.

liberalization. Although European governments tried to shift the talks to the WTO, US business groups—most notably the US Council for International Business—encouraged the US government to push for a comprehensive agreement within the OECD along the lines of NAFTA's Chapter 11. They thought that significant progress would be easier among like-minded developed countries.

Yet, three factors undermined the MAI negotiations (Graham 2000). First, in 1996, the US company Ethyl lodged a controversial NAFTA claim against Canada. It asked Canada for more than US$250 million in compensation for an environmental measure that banned interprovincial trade of a fuel additive. Canada settled the case by reversing the ban, paying Ethyl US$13 million and issuing a statement that there was no scientific evidence that the fuel additive harmed the environment (see further Chapter 9). This and other early NAFTA cases mobilized civil society and labour union opposition against the MAI. Second, whereas there was initial corporate support for the agreement, this was based on prospective liberalization of European and US services markets. But when OECD states tabled no substantial liberalization commitments, business interest waned. Although they were initially favourably inclined towards the agreement (see e.g. Keidenren 1997), the perception within corporate groups was that, absent significant liberalization commitments, the deal would not add much compared to the status quo. A case in point is Denmark, where archival files show a government repeatedly attacked in detailed letters from civil society groups, whereas private business groups rarely lobbied the government and, when they did, made only brief and generic statements of support for the project.[19] Finally, and importantly, mid-level bureaucrats conceived and negotiated the MAI with little attention and support from the top leaderships among the participating states. Hence, with rising societal pressures to stop negotiations and limited corporate support to continue, government leaders failed to join forces to save the MAI.

SUMMARY

Overall, little historical work has been done on developed country investment treaty programs. Nevertheless, it seems that, while employer organizations and international business groups promoted investment treaties and individual firms played some role—particularly in the early years of the investment treaty regime—corporate interests were not the main drivers of the investment treaty movement during the twentieth century. This is in contrast with the trade regime, where a former director of the WTO Service Division, for instance, has

[19] Danish Ministry of Foreign Affairs archive, UM 95.K.10 M/1 'MAI Forhandlingerne I OECD Regi'.

said that 'without the enormous pressure generated by the US financial services sector, particularly companies like American Express and CitiCorp, there would have been no services agreement' (quoted in Woll 2008, 50). This 'enormous pressure' has been absent for the vast majority of investment treaty negotiations, which made it difficult for policy-makers to finalize controversial multilateral agreements such as the MAI. As we will describe in the following text, similar challenges have plagued ambitious investment treaty negotiations among developed states in recent years, including the TPP and TTIP, despite a greater focus on investment treaties among business groups.

De-politicization

A second potential explanation for developed countries' decisions to sign investment treaties relates specifically to the institution of investment treaty arbitration. Abbott and Snidal note that one of the benefits of legalized international dispute settlement is that it allows states to 'minimize political conflict in relations with other states or in particular issue areas' (Abbott and Snidal 2000, 433). In theory, this effect should be particularly strong in a system that gives private investors direct access to international dispute settlement, and in which the investor's home state plays no role (on the politicization of trade disputes, see e.g. Davis 2012). Accordingly, one of the main justifications for investor–state arbitration among the founders of the ICSID Convention was that it could 'de-politicize' investment disputes. The idea was that providing foreign investors recourse to an enforceable international arbitration mechanism meant that investment disputes would no longer evolve into disputes between home and host states on the inter-state level. Lowenfeld is worth quoting at length:

[T]he essential feature of investor–[s]tate arbitration, as it has developed since the ICSID Convention... is that controversies between foreign investors and host states are insulated from political and diplomatic relations between states. In return for agreeing to independent international arbitration, the host state is assured that the state of the investor's nationality (as defined) will not espouse the investor's claim or otherwise intervene in the controversy between an investor and a host state, for instance by denying foreign assistance or attempting to pressure the host state into some kind of settlement. Correspondingly, the state of the investor's nationality is relieved of the pressure of having its relations with the host state disturbed or distorted by a controversy between its national and the host state.... The paradigm in investor–[s]tates disputes... is a dispute between the first party (nearly always the investor) as plaintiff, and the second party (nearly always the host state or state agency) as respondent. There is no third party (*Corn Products v. Mexico* 2008, paras. 1–4).

This justification draws from Western countries' experience of international investment disputes prior to investment treaties. One example is particularly illustrative. In the famous 1938 oil expropriations in Mexico alluded to previously, a labour dispute between Mexican unions and foreign oil companies threatened the collapse of the country's most important industry.[20] In response, Mexican president Cárdenas nationalized the companies and placed their assets under the control of Pemex, the state-owned oil company. Initially, US president Franklin Roosevelt did not react. The Good Neighbour policy towards Latin America combined with his sympathies towards the labour movement and state control of natural resources meant that he was not instinctively supportive of US corporate oil giants such as Jersey Standard. Several members of the administration shared his ambivalence towards the companies. They feared that US intervention risked pushing Mexico either towards an alliance with the Axis powers or towards communism. However, the oil companies managed to influence the secretary of state, Cordell Hull, who demanded payment of compensation for the expropriations that was 'prompt, adequate, and effective' (on this Hull-standard of compensation, see Chapter 4). In the United States, Hull played an important role as well. Backed by Congress' support for an aggressive stance towards Mexico, Hull pressured the White House towards lowering the price of silver imports from Mexico, which in turn forced a settlement highly favourable for Jersey Standard.

This example illustrates a common dynamic in the relationship between US companies investing abroad, the US executive, and the US legislature throughout the nineteenth and twentieth centuries (Maurer 2013). During the Cold War, the State Department and CIA feared that sanctions could push host states into the hands of the Soviet Union or China. Congress was far more responsive to corporate lobbying, however, which meant investors regularly used their influence over Congress to pressure the US executive to intervene on their behalf. For instance, in 1962, the US Congress passed the Hickenlooper Amendment to the Foreign Assistance Act in response to President Kennedy's refusal to cut off foreign aid after Brazil expropriated US companies. The amendment required the executive to end all foreign assistance to states expropriating US capital without compensation. Although US presidents rarely invoke it formally, it compelled them to sanction expropriating states. An example is Indonesia, where Sukarno's mass nationalization in 1964 led the US Congress to aggressively invoke the Hickenlooper Amendment. The Johnson administration was hesitant, but it faced severe domestic policy costs if it refused to intervene. As Maurer notes, 'when Indonesia nationalized US property, Lyndon Johnson said, "If we cut off all assistance, Sukarno will probably turn to the Russians"—and then proceeded to cut off assistance and

----

[20] This paragraph is based on Maurer (2013, Ch. 7).

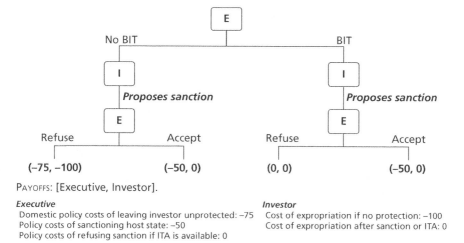

PAYOFFS: [Executive, Investor].

Executive	*Investor*
Domestic policy costs of leaving investor unprotected: −75	Cost of expropriation if no protection: −100
Policy costs of sanctioning host state: −50	Cost of expropriation after sanction or ITA: 0
Policy costs of refusing sanction if ITA is available: 0	

Figure 7.1 Investment treaties as an instrument for the home state executive to insulate foreign policy from interference by outward investors

watch Sukarno turn to the Russians' (Maurer 2013, 21). Contrary to Krasner's (1978) argument that the United States' strategic interests always prevailed over the interests of US corporations, Maurer shows it was often the other way around.

Maurer's account is illustrated graphically in Figure 7.1. Here, expropriation prompts an investor (I) to ask the executive of its home state (E) to impose sanctions against the expropriating state. These could be trade sanctions, reduction in aid flows, or even military intervention. The executive would prefer not to impose sanctions, as to do so would conflict with broader foreign policy goals vis-à-vis the host state, and because voters rarely support expensive international action to protect the interests of big businesses. Yet, the executive is faced with greater domestic costs if it refuses to intervene, due to pressure by the legislature more attuned to corporate interests. Foreign investors are a privileged and well-organized special interest group that captures legislators, who in turn value short-term interests (re-election) over longer-term goals (foreign policy gains). Investment treaty arbitration is a response to this domestic problem, in that it compartmentalizes 'lowly' conflicts over money, thereby avoiding escalation into broader diplomatic clashes (Puig 2014).[21] By providing an alternative dispute resolution mechanism to the formal espousal of claims by the home state—i.e. 'diplomatic protection'—or other forms of diplomatic involvement, the executive is able to justify a policy of non-involvement in investment disputes to domestic constituencies.

In addition to these dynamics between outward foreign investors and the executive of their home state, the availability of investment treaty arbitration

---

[21] For a useful conceptual critique of the de-politicization argument, see Paparinskis (2010). We use the term in the way the drafters of ICSID promoted it.

could also benefit host states, by ending the practice of aggressive diplomatic protection by Western powers (this is not shown in Figure 7.1). In this way, 'modern' investment treaties can be seen as a solution for a game of chicken:[22] neither home nor host state want to escalate an investment dispute into a diplomatic conflict, but the home state would like the dispute resolved in favour of the investor, whereas the host state would prefer the dispute resolved in its own favour. If both insist on their own strategy, however, it can ultimately result in diplomatic conflicts to the detriment of both states. Investment treaty arbitration allows governments to avoid this worst-case scenario.

This account raises two questions. First, has investment treaty arbitration actually de-politicized investment disputes? We know surprisingly little about the extent to which the investment treaty regime has achieved this purported benefit. On one hand, Maurer posits that, along with the increasing availability of investment insurance, the availability of investment treaty arbitration explains why the United States government has been far less involved in investment disputes over the last two decades (Maurer 2013, 428–33). In the absence of investment treaty protections, the Brazilian government has resorted to 'old-fashioned' foreign policy tools such as diplomatic intervention to defend Brazilian investors in neighbouring states (Maurer 2013, ch. 11). This may be accurate. On the other hand, Gertz, Jandhyala, and Poulsen (2016) use leaked US diplomatic cables to show that the availability of investment treaty arbitration to US investors has had no significant effect on whether, or the extent to which, the US government raises the issue of the treatment of US investors at the inter-governmental level. They show that the US government routinely intervenes in investment disputes to promote broader foreign policy agendas—such as 'good governance' reforms—and suggest that the United States is not an exceptional case in this regard. This is an important area for further research, as it questions an often-made justification for investment treaty arbitration.

A second question pertains not to the function of investment treaty arbitration but to the intent of the architects of the regime. Was de-politicization the main reason the United States, and other developed countries, crafted and signed up to the investment treaty regime in the first place? This is not clear either. In his extensive writings on the US BIT program, former BIT negotiator Kenneth Vandevelde identifies de-politicization as one among several policy objectives of the architects of the US investment treaty program (Vandevelde 1992a; 2009; 2012). While the US government still cites de-politicization in investment treaty negotiations as a reason for other states to sign BITs with the United States (Gertz, Jandhyala, and Poulsen 2016), other factors have been equally, if not more, important in shaping the US investment treaty program,

---

[22] A 'chicken game' is when two parties are in a conflict, or potential conflict, and both parties stand to lose if they yield to the other (they prefer not to be a 'chicken'). Yet, if neither party yields, it will result in the worst possible outcome for both. The game is also known as the Hawk-Dove game.

as we shall see in below. And with respect to the ICSID Convention, de-politicization played only a minor role in the ratification hearings in Washington. Senator Morse made a brief statement that the Convention could reduce inter-state tension as a result of investment disputes, but the vast majority of comments were about the ability of the Convention to promote and protect US capital (St John 2017, ch. 5).

The objective of de-politicizing investment disputes played next to no role in the initiation and development of European BIT programmes either.[23] A case in point is the United Kingdom, which during the Cold War used sanctions as a foreign policy tool in a few investment disputes. Among others, it imposed sanctions on Egypt after the Suez crisis, Libya after the BP nationalization, and Sudan after the 1970 nationalization. The cancellation of Anglo-Iranian Oil Company's concession also played a key role in the overthrow of the Iranian government under Prime Minister Mohammad Mosaddegh, in which MI6 was deeply involved. Yet, aside from these high-profile disputes, Whitehall rarely subordinated foreign policy interests to the interests of private firms.[24] The foreign office thus repeatedly refused to use aid flows as a lever in investment disputes, much to the dissatisfaction of British investors and a handful of members in Parliament. In this context, the architects of the UK BIT program never mentioned de-politicization as a benefit accruing from the treaties. British discussions about the ICSID Convention did not highlight its potential to de-politicize investment disputes either,[25] and negotiators of early British investment treaties do not recall it being an important issue.[26]

In Germany, the objective of de-politicizing investment disputes was not crucial either. In fact, one of the reasons why the initial German model BIT did not include recourse to investment treaty arbitration—against the wishes of Hermann Abs—was the fear that it 'could turn every case of expropriation into an international litigation with political relevance' (quoted in Poulsen 2015, 52–3). The German government was concerned that providing German investors with a private remedy would lead to increased international litigation, drawing the government into disputes that it would rather ignore. This was not an unreasonable expectation. Levy and Srinivasan (1996) use a simple model to show that private standing in international dispute settlement can result in net costs for the home state if it prefers for such disputes to be resolved without international litigation. Alter similarly notes that private standing increases the likelihood of litigation that states themselves would have considered too politically 'hot' (Alter 2006, 24). While not phrased in

---

[23] Except if otherwise noted, this paragraph is based on Poulsen (2015).
[24] More broadly, empirical work casts doubt whether 'gunboat diplomacy' was in fact a particularly important enforcement mechanism in international economic governance during the nineteenth and early twentieth centuries (Tomz 2007, ch. 6).
[25] FCO 59/969; FCO 59/633.
[26] Interview with former UK negotiator, February 2012.

these terms, this also appears to have been the logic of Germany's initial hesitation to give investors direct recourse to international arbitration.

While de-politicization was clearly on the minds of the architects of ICSID, it played a limited role in the development of the investment treaty programs of Western countries. A more important driver of early Western BIT programs was the perceived need to respond to resolutions of the UN General Assembly that had been sponsored by developing countries. This rationale is the subject of the following section.

Investment treaties as a response to the New International Economic Order

As described in Chapter 1, nationalist economic policies in many developing countries culminated in large-scale expropriations of foreign investment with either little or no compensation during the 1960s and 1970s. The policies were justified in the General Assembly of the UN, where developing countries sought to challenge the view of developed countries that customary international law required full compensation for the expropriation of foreign-owned property and, more broadly, that foreign investors should be protected by international minimum standards. Recall that customary international law is established by the existence of state practice, accompanied by the belief that those practices are legally required by international law (*opinio juris*). The combination of developing countries' statements in the UN with the wave of expropriations of foreign-owned property without full compensation raised questions at the time whether state practice and *opinio juris* did in fact support the norms of customary international law asserted by developed countries. In the words of the United States Supreme Court in 1964, '[t]here are few if any issues in international law today on which opinion seems to be so divided as the limitations on a state's power to expropriate the property of aliens' (*US v. Sabbatino* 1964, 428).

In this context, preferential investment treaties were potentially useful to developed countries in two ways. First, insofar as developing countries believed that they were in a 'competition for capital' among themselves, developed countries could exploit a 'prisoners' dilemma' and negotiate protections for their investors on a bilateral basis that developing countries, as a group, rejected in multilateral forums such as the UN General Assembly (Guzman 1998). Chapter 8 examines the extent to which this dynamic shaped the development of the investment treaty regime. Second, developed countries could use investment treaties to strengthen Western arguments about the content of customary international law—for example, by endorsing the Hull standard of full compensation for expropriation. If investment treaties were able to influence the development of customary international law, they would have implications for all states, including states that did not sign investment treaties and which disputed Western conceptions of customary international law. Even developing countries that rejected the Hull standard of compensation might then be compelled to observe it, either because of rational cost–benefit considerations (see generally Keohane 1984; Guzman 2008, ch. 5), or because of normative considerations about wanting to be perceived as a 'law-abiding' state (Franck 1990; 2006; Koh 1997; Zangl 2008).

The objective of reinforcing Western views about customary international law was influential among State Department lawyers in the United States. It explains why Washington only signed investment treaties with countries willing to accept the US-model BIT without any significant modifications (Vandevelde 1988; 1992b). Although more limited investment treaties could have benefited US investors and, potentially, insulated the executive from politicization of disputes, the State Department took the view that no treaty should be signed which could call into question the US view on the proper protection of foreign investment under customary international law. It was partly for this reason that the United States had difficulties expanding its investment treaty network as compared to European states, which at least during the 1970s and 1980s were far more flexible when it came to deviating from their models (Poulsen 2015). In Europe, investment treaties were also regularly justified by their ability to support a particular view of customary international law. In the United Kingdom, for instance, this argument was regularly invoked when the investment treaty program was initiated (Denza and Brooks 1987; Poulsen 2015). As an example, one of the architects of the British program noted to the Aid Department in 1972 that the model investment treaty 'very largely seeks to restate the principles of international law to which we attach importance regarding expropriation'.[27]

Were the United States and other developed countries successful in bolstering the customary international law on investment through preferential agreements? This is a legal question. Some scholars take the view that none of the provisions of investment treaties establish customary international law (Guzman 1998, 684–6; Sornarajah 2010, 232–3). According to this view, investment treaties are tailored and separate bargains entered into between particular countries who have a strategic *quid pro quo* arrangement in mind, and not an attempt to codify norms that both parties agree would be binding even in the treaty's absence. In other words, there is no evidence of *opinio juris*. Moreover, investment treaties differ in their substantive and procedural

---

[27] FCO 59/699.

provisions. Around 60 per cent include national treatment provisions, for instance, and only around 5 per cent include explicit prohibitions on performance requirements.[28] And even 'standard' clauses, such as fair and equitable treatment, are often worded differently, which has implications for their scope. Such variation arguably fails to satisfy the requirements of consistent state practice necessary for the generation of customary international law.

Other commentators suggest that investment treaties have in fact generated customary international law from the bottom up (Lowenfeld 2003; Schwebel 2004; Alvarez 2009). They contend that the treaties are highly similar in their terms and that practically every state has signed at least one, indicating agreement among states to a common core of provisions found in almost all investment treaties. Those who make this argument acknowledge that some provisions of investment treaties have a much stronger claim to the status of custom than others. For instance, while investment treaties have strengthened the view that customary international law requires compensation for expropriation according to the Hull standard (e.g. *AIG v. Kazakhstan* section 12.1), there is widespread consensus that customary international law does not require host states to provide national treatment to foreign investment.[29] Some tribunals have also suggested that the ability of shareholders to pursue independent claims against states for harm caused to a company in which they hold shares has been elevated to a general rule.[30]

In summary, the objective of Western investment treaty programs was not just to protect individual investors but also to develop customary international law on foreign investment, which is binding on all countries, including those without investment treaties. The extent to which investment treaties have succeeded in shaping customary international law is a contentious issue, about which lawyers disagree. And whether the strategy of developed countries has increased compliance with particular standards that they regard as part of customary international law—such as the Hull rule on compensation for expropriation—is a further question that has not been subject to any serious scrutiny and is therefore an important subject for future research.

---

[28] See Table 4.1.

[29] There is a complex, ongoing debate concerning the relationship between FET provisions of investment treaties and the minimum standard of treatment of foreign investment under customary international law (see e.g. Vasciannie 1999; Paparinskis 2013). See also Chapter 4.

[30] *CMS v. Argentina* (2003, para. 48). Seven years after this decision, the International Court of Justice (ICJ)—the world court—considered the same issue and held that customary international law continued to prevent shareholders from pursuing claims independently from a company in which they hold shares (*Diallo* 2010, para. 115). The ICJ's view is consistent with the basic principles of corporate law shared by most national legal systems (Gaukrodger 2014b).

Investment treaties and diplomacy

We turn now to a fourth and final driver of investment treaties pursued by developed countries: the promotion of foreign-policy agendas. Just as negotiations for trade agreements are often initiated as part of broader diplomatic strategies (e.g. Gowa and Mansfield 1993; Feinberg 2003; Ravenhill 2008), quantitative work shows that military aid and diplomatic links between states are causally related to BIT adoption (Neumayer 2006; Poulsen and Aisbett 2016). States that align diplomatically are also more likely to adopt investment treaties.

The United States is the most obvious case in point. The first US investment treaties—post-war FCN agreements—were not just commercial agreements for US businesses to secure their capital abroad. Rather, Vandevelde (2012) has shown that the Truman administration used the agreements to promote its post-war economic strategy: signing treaties that promoted US investment would earn host states foreign exchange to import US goods, which in turn would promote economic development abroad and thus help contain communism. Commercial and diplomatic incentives were aligned.

Moreover, US BITs were consciously used as diplomatic symbols. Following the end of the Cold War, the United States used the treaties to signify that developing countries now subscribed to Western principles of open markets and property rights. For instance, the United States concluded a BIT with Argentina in the early 1990s to provide a strong symbol that the Argentine government had abandoned the Calvo doctrine and joined the Washington Consensus (Vandevelde 1992b). Press reports at the time also noted that the treaty '... signals US satisfaction with Argentina's remarkable economic progress and a recognition of Menem's new political stature in the international community' (Priest 1991). In Eastern Europe and Central Asia, as well, several BITs were justified as signals that former communist states now adhered to Western capitalist principles. The treaties were useful, a former US negotiator states, 'because they symbolize a commitment to economic liberalism' (Vandevelde 1998, 628).

In other cases, the treaties were linked to broader foreign policy and security interests. President Bush justified the US BIT with Poland, for example, on the grounds that the United States wanted to 'welcome Poland as a full partner in the community of nations' (Devroy and Kamen 1990). This, of course, was not the only reason the United States initiated the BIT, and the fact that Poland could be a frontrunner for reforms in the region did play a role (St John 2017). Similarly, in the case of Kazakhstan, President H.W. Bush signed a BIT as part of a broader public display of support for the country's independence. In connection with talks about a nuclear arms deal, Bush joined President Nazarbayev for signing of the BIT in what the *Washington Post* described as a 'symbolic show of US regard for Kazakhstan' (Oberdorfer 1992). On the occasion, Bush noted that '[t]he United States supports your independence...We believe your security, Kazakhstan's security, is important for stability in Europe and in Asia'. The United States agreed on similar 'package' deals with other former communist countries.[31] As a former Dutch negotiator noted, 'geopolitically speaking, some countries want to connect with the Western world and this can be an argument for a BIT'.[32]

We discuss this important driver of the investment treaty movement further in Chapter 8. For now, the chapter concludes with more recent developments in developed countries' investment treaty programs.

Recent developments

The politics of investment treaties changed drastically in developed countries following the rise to prominence of investment treaty arbitration since the 2000s. The interest in investment treaty negotiations is greater among many foreign investors today than during any previous period. At the same time, investment treaty arbitrations have revealed to developed country governments and civil society groups that the regime can be both uncertain and costly. Whereas early investment treaty negotiations were considered mostly as a 'one-way street', developed countries today negotiate in the knowledge that investors are likely to bring arbitrations against them as well.[33]

The early NAFTA cases against the United States, for instance, took US policy-makers by surprise (see e.g. Edwards 2016, 65–6). In 2002, Senator John Kerry noted that 'not a single word was uttered in discussing Chapter 11 [of NAFTA, ed.]. Why? Because we didn't know how this provision would play out. No one really knew just how high the stakes would get' (quoted in Moyers 2002). In Europe too, some of the recent arbitrations against 'old'

---

[31] See, for example, 'Joint Statement on Development of US–Ukrainian Friendship and Cooperation', *Ukrainian Weekly*, No. 23, Vol. LXIII, 13 March 1994.

[32] Interview with former Dutch negotiator, April 2009.

[33] That said, it is not an entirely new phenomenon for Western states to see themselves not just as home but also host states in investment treaty negotiations. European states routinely sought FCN agreements with the United States in the 1950s so as to attract more US investment. For instance, promotion of US investment was a core driver for Belgium, Italy, and Ireland when negotiating FCN agreements with the US government (Vandevelde 2012, 284, 315–16, 340–3). Similarly, as already described earlier, one of the reasons why OECD could not agree to a joint investment treaty in the 1950s was because members with few outward investments—such as Greece, Portugal, and Turkey—thought it was weighed too heavily in favour of foreign investors at the expense of host states (Sinclair 2004, 432).

members of the EU have been met with surprise. For instance, recall from the Preface how German policy-makers were taken aback when Vattenfall used the ECT to challenge the country's environmental policies.

The arbitrations against developed countries have prompted some to update their investment treaty models by more carefully clarifying and restricting core terms (Manger and Peinhardt 2017; see Chapter 4). More generally, they have changed the politics of the treaties—particularly with respect to agreements *among* developed states. An illustrative case is the TTIP negotiations, the status of which was uncertain at the time of writing. Negotiations of the TTIP were initiated partly for geo-political reasons: an 'Economic NATO' that would ensure the primacy of the West in writing global trade and investment rules (Hamilton and Pelkmans 2015).[34] Within Europe, it was also a crucial agreement for the European Commission, which with the 2007 Lisbon Treaty had secured the legal competence to enter into EU-wide investment protection agreements. European and US business groups vocally supported a strong investment protection chapter in the agreement as well. Not only would it give them recourse to investment treaty arbitration in the EU and the United States, but also set a precedent for future negotiations with developing countries.[35]

The negotiations prompted heated discussions in Europe, where concerns were raised about the risks of allowing US investors to bypass domestic courts in Europe. Civil society groups organized successful campaigns throughout Europe, mobilizing large numbers of citizens and newspaper editorials against including investment arbitration in TTIP. Groups of European judges also complained about the proposal.[36] Similarly, in the United States, 220 economics and law professors, including Laurence Tribe and Joseph Stiglitz, signed a public letter urging the US government not to include investment treaty arbitration in TTIP or the TPP (Tribe, Stiglitz, and Sachs 2016). Moreover, unlike previous decades when Western labour groups showed little to no interest in investment treaties (with the notable exceptions of NAFTA and the MAI), some groups strongly opposed the investment rules in TTIP (see e.g. submissions to House of Lords 2015). This is broadly what we would expect from the political economy of foreign investment outlined in Chapter 2, where labour in developed countries can lose out because of outward FDI.[37]

[34] The US-initiated Trans-Pacific Partnership agreement (TPP), signed in 2015, reflects similar geopolitical dynamics. While the United States has been negotiating a BIT with China for more than a decade, Beijing was not invited to be a part of TPP.
[35] See, for exampl, US Chamber of Commerce (2013); Fleming (2014). See also discussion between Poulsen, Bonnitcha, and Yackee (2015) and Baetens (2015).
[36] Deutscher Richterbund (2016).
[37] The Heckscher–Ohlin model predicts that outward foreign investment will leave workers in capital-exporting countries worse off. See further Chapter 5.

The dividing lines were not clear-cut, however. In Scandinavia, for instance, labour unions did *not* oppose a strong investment protection chapter (e.g. Danish Union of Metalworkers and Confederation of Danish Industries 2014), and levels of enthusiasm varied within the business community as well. As described in Chapter 1, the European Commission received 150,000 responses when it held a public hearing in 2014 on the investment chapter in TTIP.[38] Yet, only 60 companies thought the issue was important enough to submit individual responses beyond those submitted by collective associations purporting to represent the business community. Also, the German Association for Small and Medium Sized Enterprises argued *against* investment treaty arbitration in TTIP, as the high litigation costs favoured large multinationals. This submission contrasts with the position of larger companies such as Chevron, which argued that the investment chapter would deter unwanted regulation (Neslen 2016). Finally, the TTIP debate highlighted that the community of investment arbitrators occasionally have—or seek—political agency as well. Much of their influence is bound to take place behind closed doors, something that is difficult to assess in empirical studies,[39] but the TTIP debate prompted several major law firms to establish an NGO—the European Federation for Investment Law and Arbitration (EFILA)—to support the investment treaty regime in Europe.

Australia presents another illuminating case of the politics of investment treaties in the twenty-first century. The 2004 Australia–US FTA included an investment chapter that did not provide for investment treaty arbitration. There was little business opposition to the omission of investment treaty arbitration in either country. During a subsequent government inquiry, hardly any Australian multinational made submissions in favour of the inclusion of investor–state arbitration clauses in investment treaties (Productivity Commission 2010; Tienhaara and Ranald 2011). Partly as a result, the Labour-led government decided in 2011 to exclude such provisions from future Australian investment treaties, and further decided that it would oppose provisions 'that would confer greater legal rights on foreign business than those available to domestic businesses' (Australian Department of Foreign Affairs and Trade 2011, 14; see generally Chapter 5). This policy shift gained public attention only two months later, when Philip Morris challenged Australia's tobacco plain packaging laws under the Hong Kong–Australia BIT. Publicity around the arbitration resulted in a public campaign by unions and civil society groups against investment treaties, but Australian business organizations fought back and now began to lobby for the inclusion of investor–state arbitration provisions in future investment treaties (Kurtz 2012).

---

[38] The high volume of responses was due largely to an organized campaign by various NGOs opposing the inclusion of ISDS in the investment chapter of the TTIP.

[39] On the role of investment lawyers in advising *developing* countries, see Poulsen (2015, Ch. 4).

Following a change of government in 2013, Australia reversed its short-lived opposition to investment treaty arbitration. The new government announced that it would consider the inclusion of investor–state arbitration provisions in new investment treaties on a case-by-case basis. Australia thus agreed to the inclusion of investor–state arbitration provisions in the TPP, signed in February 2016 with eleven other countries including the United States. In response to concerns from the opposition, the then trade minister—Andrew Robb—expressed confidence that Australia would not be subject to investment treaty arbitrations pursuant to TPP.[40]

These are examples of how the rise of investment treaty arbitration has politicized the negotiation of investment treaties to an extent never seen before in Western capitals—or at least for *some* negotiations in *some* capitals. Negotiations with developing countries are still seen as largely uncontroversial at the time this book goes to press. It also seems that many civil society groups and labour unions remain much more concerned with implications of the regime for their own country than how investors have used the regime against other countries. The EU, for instance, has recently negotiated deals with Singapore and Vietnam without much public attention, at least in Europe. Equally, the prospect of consenting to investment treaty arbitration in agreements with the United States has become controversial among developed countries in Europe (in the context of TTIP) and parts of Asia (in the context of the TPP), yet some North–North agreements have been negotiated with much less scrutiny and concern.[41] Understanding the sources for such variation is an important subject for future research (for a recent contribution, see Brutger and Strezhnev 2017).

Conclusion

Research on the politics of developed countries' investment treaty programs remains in its infancy. We have hardly any detailed case studies on European investment treaty programs, for instance. We know little about how developed countries have coordinated their programs vis-à-vis developing countries—for instance, in the OECD or the World Bank. We know hardly anything about how, or if, developed country policy-makers have considered the interactions between the investment treaty regime and other parts of the investment regime complex. And we have only basic information about the role of

---

[40] 'TPP gives no ground for legal disputes: Robb', *Skynews.com.au*, 4 February 2016. As mentioned in Chapter 1, President Trump withdrew the United States as a signatory to the TPP in 2017, but it is unclear at the time of writing whether other member states will pursue the agreement without the United States.
[41] See, for example, the discussion on Japan in Hamamoto (2016, 8–11).

non-state actors—such as investors, arbitration lawyers, and labour unions—in influencing developed countries' treaty programs, most of which comes from the 2010s. These are important subjects for future research.

Yet, the existing evidence indicates that developed countries largely promoted investment treaties for bureaucratic and political reasons, and not as a response to lobbying by their own outward investors. In some cases, the treaties may have been useful to avoid diplomatic entanglements in investment conflicts abroad. However, at least in the early years, Western states primarily initiated investment treaty programs as a response to challenges to customary international law on investment by repeated UN General Assembly resolutions. During the 1980s and 1990s, the political drivers behind the investment treaty regime evolved, with investment treaties becoming increasingly important as political statements. Except for large agreements, such as the MAI and NAFTA, investment treaties were often the product of mid-level bureaucrats working more or less in isolation, and the investment treaty regime was not a subject of extensive political debate. This is no longer the case. As governments and societal actors have become more aware of the potency and scope of investment treaty arbitration, the regime has become increasingly controversial—particularly when treaties are negotiated between developed countries.

8 Politics of Investment Treaties in Developing Countries

Introduction

As we have seen in Chapter 7, the politics of investment treaties in developed countries has some surprising features. It is an even greater puzzle, however, why developing countries so enthusiastically embraced investment treaties, particularly in the 1990s—the subject of this chapter. For while investment treaties are formally reciprocal, foreign investment between developed and developing countries has traditionally flowed primarily from the former to the latter. As such, the obligations in investment treaties to protect inward foreign investment fell primarily on developing countries in their capacity as host states. This raises the question of why developing countries agreed to treaties that exposed them to potentially expensive arbitrations and restricted their ability to exercise state powers inside their own borders.

This question is the subject of a larger literature than the politics of the investment treaty regime in developed countries. On the basis of this literature, this chapter evaluates three potential explanations for why developing countries adopted the treaties—(i) investment promotion; (ii) promoting or tying in domestic reforms; and (iii) diplomatic and symbolic reasons (unlike the previous chapter, this chapter subsumes 'de-politicization' under this third category). We then examine an important cross-cutting issue—the role of expertise. Regardless, of the objectives that developing countries sought to achieve by adopting investment treaties, this is an important issue as many failed to appreciate the risks and implications of the treaties (Poulsen 2015). The chapter concludes by briefly examining recent developments in the politics of the investment treaty regime in developing countries—including the newfound role of some developing countries as seeking rights for 'their' investors abroad.

Investment promotion

The first and most important reason why developing countries entered into investment treaties was the belief that it would help them attract foreign investment. North–South BITs were originally premised on a 'grand bargain':

'a *promise* of protection of capital in return for the *prospect* of more capital in the future' (Salacuse and Sullivan 2005, 77). Take the example of Zimbabwe. After opening up to foreign investment in 1989, Zimbabwe signed its first BIT in 1990 and joined ICSID in 1991. Robert Mugabe—the president of Zimbabwe and a former Marxist—noted in his opening address to the Zimbabwean Parliament in 1990 that:

The Government has now stepped up its efforts to increase investment, especially in the productive sectors. In addition to the protection of investment embedded in our Constitution, the Government will enter into multilateral and bilateral investment agreements with those countries whose nationals are willing to invest in Zimbabwe. These agreements should go a long way towards attracting investment into Zimbabwe.[1]

This set off a busy negotiation schedule for the Zimbabwean negotiator: 'we were negotiating treaties to promote investment', he recalled, because 'we wanted to be the most competitive investment destination' (quoted in Poulsen 2015, 107).

This is but one example of how investment promotion was the primary justification for adopting investment treaties in developing countries (Poulsen 2015). Insofar as developing countries considered the *reasons* why investment treaties would promote foreign investment, most appear to have believed that investment treaties provided a 'credible commitment' necessary to solve hold-up problems,[2] and/or that entering into such treaties provided a positive 'signal' to foreign investors.[3] As an example of the former, a previous Czech negotiator notes that BITs were seen as necessary to attract foreign investment, as 'investors want guarantees for long-term investments that they will not be expropriated' (quoted in Poulsen 2015, 103). As an example of the latter, a former South African negotiator saw the treaties as instruments that could 'prove to foreign investors . . . that South Africa was an investor friendly country' (quoted in Poulsen 2014, 8). Some developing countries also expected that investment treaties would have an indirect impact on investment flows by facilitating and lowering the price on investment insurance. For instance, when Chile ratified the ICSID Convention in 1991, the president of Chile noted lower insurance premiums as a primary reason not just to become a member of ICSID but also to negotiate BITs, on the basis that they would:

. . . permit foreign investors to obtain lower insurance premiums than those actually obtained in the normal situation [without a BIT]. Therefore, the accession of Chile to

---

[1] Quoted in Foreign Broadcasting Information Service, Sub-Saharan Africa, Daily Report, FBIS-AFR-90–125, 28 June 1990.
[2] For investment treaties as a solution to hold-up problems, see Chapter 5.
[3] For investment treaties as signals of a safe investment climate, see Chapter 6.

this type of treaties would permit the country to keep an advantaged position in order to attract foreign investment (quoted in Montt 2009, 115).

We raised questions in Chapter 6 about whether these expectations have proven correct. Nevertheless, at the time of signing, it was not always unreasonable for developing countries to believe that investment treaties would help them attract more foreign investment.

When initiating negotiations with developing countries, developed countries often asserted that investment treaties were necessary to attract foreign investment. Germany, for example, used the link between investment treaties and federal investment guarantees as a selling point to initiate negotiations (see Chapter 7). Other developed countries used the same argument as a bargaining tactic. Recall from Chapter 7, for instance, that Whitehall acknowledged internally that investment treaties were unimportant for British investors seeking to commit capital abroad. Yet, when the British Foreign and Commonwealth Office initiated negotiations in the early years of its BIT program, it introduced the treaty by noting that:

British industry and British investors have represented to the British Government that, in their view, bilateral investment protection agreements could assist significantly in the creation of a climate of confidence, which would encourage further substantial investment in the Third World. . . . we wish to reinforce success and to encourage our investors to play an even larger part in the strengthening of your economy. It is our hope that the conclusion of agreements of this kind will play a part in promoting a greater flow of resources from developed countries to the developing Third World within a framework of law . . . [4]

In negotiations, US officials also regularly stated that an investment treaty would help the other party attract more investment (Poulsen 2015, ch. 4, ftn. 77).[5] International organizations, too, promoted the idea that investment treaties were important for developing countries if they wanted to attract foreign investment. The World Bank played a particularly important role in generating support for investment treaty arbitration, as did UNCTAD during the late 1990s and early 2000s.[6] Finally, Western legal advisors occasionally played an important role in spreading the idea that the treaties were critical to promote foreign investment (Poulsen 2015, ch. 4).

---

[4] FCO 59/701.
[5] Formal US policy documents do not repeat this assertion, as it risked inflaming opposition from organized labour unions in the United States concerned about the loss of US jobs (Vandevelde 1992a, 32).
[6] The IMF does not appear to have played a significant role, partly because transfer provisions in many investment treaties conflicted with member state obligations under Article VI Sec 1 of the IMF Articles of Agreement by failing to include exceptions allowing for restrictions on transfers of funds to be imposed in the event of serious balance of payments difficulties (Siegel 2013).

The views expressed by developed countries, international organisations and 'experts' in international investment law provide a partial explanation for how and why developing countries came to believe that entering into investment treaties would help them attract foreign investment. The question of how these beliefs became so widespread notwithstanding the limited empirical evidence to support them (see Chapter 6) remains an important question for further research. But the basic contention that most developing countries adopted the investment treaties due to some vague sense that they would promote foreign capital is uncontroversial. Consistent with this rationale, Betz and Kerner (2015) find that developing countries were most likely to enter into the treaties when they needed foreign capital.[7]

BITS AND THE PRISONER'S DILEMMA

Some scholars have taken the idea that investment treaties were signed to attract foreign investment further and attempted to model negotiation dynamics for developing countries competing for capital. An influential account comes from Guzman (1998). His starting point is a puzzle: why did developing countries oppose Western notions of investment protection in the UN General Assembly, while at the same time signing up to those very same obligations in bilateral treaties with Western countries? Guzman's answer is that developing countries, as a group, would have preferred to offer less generous protections to foreign investors, but had an individual incentive to break the 'cartel' and sign up to bilateral agreements with Western states (Guzman 1998, 643). They were in a prisoner's dilemma.

Figure 8.1 illustrates this dynamic. Two homogeneous developing countries compete for a fixed pool of capital.[8] Foreign investors divide their capital between countries A and B in the absence of BIT protections. Both A and B would be able to extract more value from these investments in the absence of investment treaties, and they would therefore be jointly better off if they did not sign any BITs. Yet, if A signs a BIT and B does not, foreign investment shifts from B to A. While the presence of a BIT would reduce the value that A is able to extract per unit of foreign capital invested,[9] A would still be better off if the treaty leads to significant relocation of foreign investment from B to A. Anticipating this dynamic, B will sign a BIT as well, so as to remove A's competitive advantage. The end result is an outcome in which each developing country is worse off compared to the no-BIT scenario.

---

[7] This finding is also important because it is difficult to reconcile with other theories of why developing countries adopted investment treaties. For example, it has been suggested to the authors by investment arbitration practitioners that developing countries may have adopted the treaties out of enthusiasm for international law and tribunals. However, although attitudes towards international law during the 1990s undoubtedly provide important context for the investment treaty movement (see Chapter 1), there is little direct evidence that the treaties were used by developing countries primarily to embrace legal internationalism.

[8] For extensions, see Engel (2008). In Chapter 6, we argued that the assumption of a fixed pool of capital available for FDI in developing countries is unhelpful.

[9] See Figure 5.2.

	B		
		No BIT	*BIT*
A	*No BIT*	100, 100	40, 140
	BIT	140, 40	80, 80

PAYOFFS: (State A, State B)

Figure 8.1 Investment treaty adoption as a prisoner's dilemma

Although elegant in its simplicity, a major difficulty with Guzman's model is that it suggests that developing countries would have avoided signing investment treaties if they had only been able to act as a group. Alvarez (2009) correctly points out that this is inconsistent with observed patterns in developing countries' BIT negotiations. During the 1960s and 1970s, when developing countries perceived foreign investment as a continuation of colonial control and as contrary to their import-substitution strategies for industrialization, European states struggled to persuade key investment partners to sign up to investment treaties, and were mostly left with countries of minor commercial importance. In a meeting with the German negotiating team in 1976, for instance, one British official lamented that BITs 'could be made only where they were not necessary, because where they were necessary they could not be negotiated' (quoted in Poulsen 2015, 54). As described in Chapter 1, the network of BITs at the time was limited primarily to Africa. Accordingly, it is inaccurate to suggest that many developing countries were, individually, undermining their collective support for a New International Economic Order at the UN General Assembly, when in fact very few BITs were signed during this period.

Instead, the spread of modern investment treaties went hand in hand with liberalization of domestic investment regimes during the 1980s and, particularly, the 1990s, due to the changing investment policy principles (see Chapter 1). At the time, developing countries implemented similar standards of protection to those found in investment treaties in their domestic legal regimes (Alvarez 2009), and a few even consented to investor–state arbitration in domestic investment laws (see Chapter 3).[10] The fact that developing countries adopted investment treaties in parallel to changes in domestic laws and policies illustrates the importance of shifts in prevailing ideas about the benefits of foreign investment in explaining the spread of BITs. Typically, developing countries began looking to sign investment treaties abroad only once they had opened the door to FDI at home. By the time the investment treaty movement took off, many developing countries had thus already

---

[10] By 1981, 13 domestic laws gave advance consent to ICSID–often prompted by the ICSID secretariat (St John 2017, ch. 6).

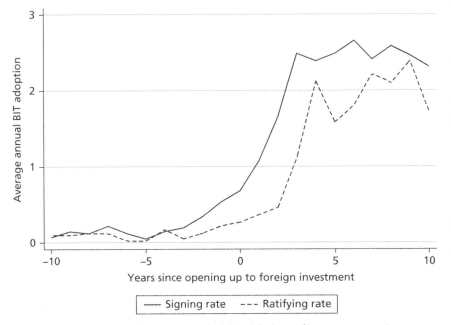

Figure 8.2 Domestic liberalization preceded the global era of investment treaties

Notes: Figure shows the average rate of signing and ratifying BITs among 47 developing countries against the year in which the same countries initiated considerable reforms to attract foreign investment. *Source*: Poulsen (2015).

accepted the basic standards enshrined in the agreements (Figure 8.2).[11] In short, developing countries *did* sign investment treaties to attract capital, but not due to the dynamics suggested by the prisoner's dilemma.

Take the example of India.[12] While pursuing import substitution policies during the 1960s and 1970s, India discouraged FDI except in a few sectors. At the time, New Delhi was a strong proponent of the NIEO and accordingly refused Western invitations to sign BITs. After opening up its economy during the 1990s, however, India began adopting BITs with the primary aim of attracting foreign investment. In fact, during investment talks in the WTO in the 2000s—a multilateral forum where developing countries could negotiate as a group—India resisted with the argument that BITs better served India's interests. India's WTO representative noted in 2001 that BITs 'were favoured by countries like India because they did not require countries to make fundamental changes to their FDI policies, required countries to grant national treatment only in the post-establishment phase and made it possible

---

[11] For an extension of this claim, see Poulsen (2015, chs. 7–8).
[12] Unless otherwise stated, this paragraph is based on Poulsen (2015, 130–1).

to vary the definition of investment in light of the particular needs of the parties to such treaties'.[13]

NETWORK EFFECTS

Bubb and Rose-Ackerman (2007) and Montt (2009) pose two different challenges to Guzman's account. In their models, developing countries also compete for capital, and BITs are credible commitment devices that affect investors' willingness to invest in host states. In Bubb and Rose-Ackerman's account, as in that of Guzman's, BITs promote FDI, and the marginal benefit of individual treaties decreases as the global network of treaties expands. However, according to their view, the decision of developing countries to accept the Hull rule in bilateral negotiations did not leave them worse off as a group.[14] On the contrary, once developing countries had reaped the windfall from expropriating investments made during the colonial period, they were prepared to commit to protect *future* investments in order to attract new FDI. In their account, this strategic timing explains both the very limited adoption of BITs in the early years following decolonization, and their rapid spread from the late 1980s onwards.

Montt (2009) also contests Guzman's model of prisoner's dilemma. His starting point is opposite to that of Bubb and Rose-Ackerman. In his view, rather than decreasing in value as the number of BITs go up, investment treaties have *increasing* returns to scale (network effects). Once boilerplate treaties became readily available, it became 'cheaper' to draft and negotiate treaties—negotiators simply had to jump onto the BIT 'bandwagon'. Moreover, with a critical mass of similarly worded treaties already in place by the 1990s, developing countries could reasonably expect a predictable and efficient (quasi) jurisprudence to evolve. While the standards may have been broad and open-ended—and thus offer little predictability—developing-country negotiators expected that tribunals would operationalize them through interpretation, and thereby reduce the uncertainty of their scope and implications (Montt 2009, 113). Rather than spending considerable time and costs on agreeing to specific investment rules, negotiators anticipated that arbitrators would interpret common open-ended clauses in investment treaties in a way that gave greater precision to their legal content while bearing in mind developing countries' interests (Montt 2009, 157). This process of arbitrators increasing the precision in the legal effect of investment treaties[15] is also in

---

[13] World Trade Organization, Report on the Meeting of 7 and 8 March 2001, note by the secretariat, WT/WGTI/M/14.

[14] On the Hull rule, see Chapter 4.

[15] Greater precision by decisions of arbitrators differs fundamentally from the trend in the 2010s, discussed in Chapters 4 and 9, towards greater precision in investment treaty *drafting* by states.

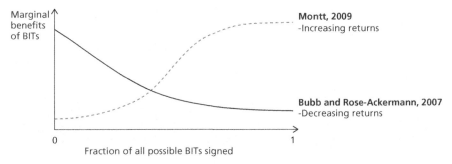

Figure 8.3 Investment treaty adoption with network effects

investors' interests as they could now assess the value of the treaties, and would therefore increasingly factor them into their FDI decisions. Once a critical mass of countries had adopted the treaties by the early 1990s to attract investment, the costs for other developing countries staying out of the regime increased considerably. This was because investors and other market actors now perceived a country with no BITs as a riskier jurisdiction (Montt 2009, 114–15, 122). Montt argues that this dynamic explains the s-shaped diffusion pattern of BITs—slow at first in the 1970s and 1980s, then spreading like wildfire in the 1990s.

Figure 8.3 contrasts the two accounts. In the two models, the size of the global BIT network has opposite effects on the marginal benefits of individual BITs. Montt's model results in an s-shaped curve, whereas the model of Bubb and Rose-Ackerman results in a concave curve. Crucially, however, both models accept Guzman's premises that:

1. Investment treaties provide unique credible commitment instruments for developing countries seeking to attract foreign investment (see particularly Montt 2009, 128; Bubb and Rose-Ackermann 2007, 300); and
2. Developing countries adopted investment treaties as the results of fully rational decisions.

We raised questions about the first premise in Chapters 5 and 6: investment treaties were never *unique* credible commitment devices, but rather complements to a range of other instruments addressing political risks, such as investment contracts and investment insurance (Yackee 2007; Alvarez 2011a, ch. 2). Perhaps for this reason, evidence of investment treaties' effectiveness in increasing FDI is mixed. However, even if investment treaties were not as effective in attracting foreign investment as anticipated, the second premise could still be correct. It would still have been rational for states to enter into investment treaties if developing countries had good reasons to *believe* the treaties were important to attract investment at the time they entered into them (Peinhardt and Allee 2012a, 777; Montt 2009, 122). This scaled-down assumption underpins Guzman's later work with Elkins and Simmons, to which we now turn.

A CAREFUL AND STRATEGIC COMPETITION FOR CAPITAL?

In the widely quoted account of Elkins, Guzman, and Simmons (2006), investment treaties matter in particular for footloose investors—that is, investors with low relocation costs. Light manufacturing plants, for instance, can more easily move from one country to another than large energy or mining investments with considerable sunk costs. They argue that developing countries *believe* that they are in a competition for such investment, and that investment treaties are highly relevant to the investment location decisions of such investors. One testable proposition that follows from this theory is that countries that depend on, and compete for, light manufacturing investments are most likely to adopt investment treaties, and they find evidence to sustain this view. Whether developing countries saw BITs as credible commitments or signals to imperfectly informed investors, Elkins, Guzman, and Simmons argue that they were engaged in a strategic race to attract capital—as in Guzman's original model.[16]

This argument is difficult to reconcile with theories of *how* investment treaties promote foreign investment. Chapter 5 suggests that footloose investors should be the *least* interested in investment treaty protections because their exit from host states in case of mistreatment is less costly. Only a small minority of registered ICSID cases have involved claimants of the type that Elkins, Guzman, and Simmons consider to be most important in driving the adoption of investment treaties. By contrast, more than 40 per cent have been in industries typically characterized by large sunk costs (energy, mining, and utilities) (ICSID 2017). Moreover, Elkins, Guzman, and Simmons do not provide any direct evidence that developing-country policy-makers in fact believed that investment treaties were particularly important for footloose manufacturing firms. Perhaps it is for these reasons that their econometric results do not appear robust when making small, but justified, changes to their statistical model (Poulsen and Aisbett 2013).

Furthermore, if developing countries signed investment treaties as part of a rational competition for capital in line with this account, we would also expect this competition to manifest itself in the content of the treaties. Yet, very few countries tried to progressively 'upgrade' their BITs to become more 'competitive'—for instance, by including increasingly higher levels of protection for foreign investment (Poulsen 2015). Instead, investment treaties have remained remarkably similar, 'anchoring' to template agreements rather than including

---

[16] Swenson (2005) presents a related account. She argues that foreign investors who have *already* invested abroad use a tacit threat of exit to lobby host states to sign BITs.

ever more investor-friendly provisions. Finally, extensive qualitative evidence shows that very few developing-country governments investigated whether the treaties actually worked as intended—through simple investor surveys or otherwise—and hardly any host state reacted strategically to the BIT adoption of 'competitor' countries (Poulsen 2015; see also Chalamish 2010, ftn. 89). So, although most developing countries *did* enter into investment treaties to attract investment, they were rarely as strategic and careful in their approach as the model of Elkins, Guzman, and Simmons suggests.

Investment treaties and domestic reforms

Apart from investment promotion, some developing countries also adopted investment treaties to 'lock in' domestic policies by preventing successors from scaling back reforms of their domestic investment regimes. This type of strategic behaviour is the subject of a long tradition in political science scholarship, including work on how governments use international agreements to play 'two-level games'[17] (Putnam 1988)—for instance, in the fields of human rights (Moravcsik 2000), European integration (Moravcsik 1998), and trade (e.g. Mansfield and Milner 2012).

The role of investment treaties for domestic policy-making has not been subject to considerable research to date. The interaction between investment treaty obligations and domestic reforms is bound to vary significantly depending on whether the treaties only include post-establishment protections or are among the small minority that also include binding liberalization obligations, such as US BITs and the investment chapters of preferential trade agreements (PTAs) (e.g. NAFTA). The latter are the most likely to have an immediate impact on the domestic regulatory environment in host states (cf. the comments by India's WTO representative earlier), so we address these first.

LIBERALIZATION

By including obligations to provide pre-establishment national treatment in investment treaties, the contracting parties agree not to impose any conditions

---

[17] The nature of a two-level game is that a government is assumed to be involved in two different 'games' at any given point in time. It is trying to achieve certain objectives at the international level through its interactions with other states; at the same time, it is also trying to achieve certain domestic policy objectives within its own territory. Two-level games emphasize the ways in which actions taken by players of the game at one 'level' can affect the options, pay-offs, and incentives of players in the game at the other level.

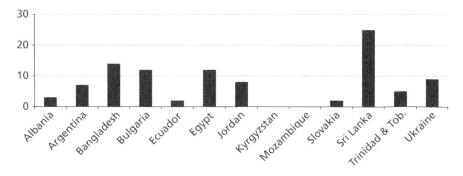

Figure 8.4 Exceptions to pre-establishment national treatment in selected US investment treaties

Note: Figure counts the number of sectors or matters, where the countries reserve the right to make or maintain exceptions to pre-establishment national treatment in their BITs with the United States. The figure does not necessarily represent the scope of the exceptions, which will depend on the exact formulation as well as the importance of the relevant sector or matter.

Source: Compiled by the authors.

or restrictions on new foreign investment beyond those that apply to new domestic investment. Typically, these obligations are subject to reservations enumerated through a 'negative list' (see Chapter 4), where the parties specify the sectors and areas of activity excluded from the scope of the pre-establishment national treatment obligation. If none are listed, the country allows foreign investors of the other party to invest in all sectors of the economy on the same terms and conditions that apply to domestic investors. And indeed, some US BIT partners have included no, or very few, exceptions to their liberalization schedules (Figure 8.4).

To the extent that these obligations reflected pre-existing domestic regulation, they have the effect of increasing the cost to a future government of imposing new restrictions or conditions on inward US investment. Mexico's accession to the NAFTA is the classic example. After its spiralling debt crisis in the 1980s, Mexico agreed to an IMF-designed austerity program, part of which entailed opening up the Mexican economy to foreign trade and investment. Mexico subsequently joined GATT (in 1986) and opened up most of the economy to majority foreign ownership. In 1990, President Salinas initiated talks with Canada and the United States to join their PTA, the Canada–US FTA (CUSFTA), partly to attract capital but primarily to lock in his liberalizing reforms (Manger 2009). To 'stabilize the policy environment' against future 'backtracking' by the opposition at the time (Pastor and Wise 1994, 484), Salinas pushed not just for deep trade obligations but also strong disciplines on foreign investment (Cameron and Tomlin 2000, 101). The result was NAFTA's Chapter 11 and the subsequent initiation of Mexico's

BIT program.[18] Mexico is not the only example of such motivations. When discussing the US–Egypt trade and investment agreement, for instance, the former Egyptian finance minister noted that 'if anybody in the future wants to go backwards, they cannot' (quoted in Alden 2005).

To the extent that the liberalization provisions of investment treaties entail commitments to allowing foreign investment in sectors in which foreign investment was previously restricted, these obligations require a significant *change* in the domestic regulatory framework. In such cases, policy-makers may have used investment treaties to overcome pressure from domestic constituencies who oppose investment liberalization. For example, they may have agreed to liberalization commitments within a treaty that other domestic constituencies support for other reasons (for similar arguments in the trade regime, see e.g. Mansfield and Milner 2012).[19] This contrasts with the situation mentioned earlier where liberalization commitments in treaties are used to 'lock-in' *pre-existing* reforms. However, at the time of this writing, the authors are aware of no publicly available evidence of states using investment treaties as tools to facilitate *new* domestic reforms, although the growing number of investment treaties with liberalization provisions makes this an important subject for further research. Moreover, there may be important interaction effects between investment, trade, and other obligations in broader PTAs, as these more recent agreements allow governments to push forward a broader set of domestic reforms. This, too, has yet to be studied in empirical work.

POST-ESTABLISHMENT TREATMENT AND PROTECTION

A related issue is whether, and if so how, states have used post-establishment standards such as national treatment and FET to tie in domestic reforms (see e.g. Echandi 2011). Although it is possible for a country to enact similar protections to those contained in investment treaties through domestic laws, treaty obligations can be important complements as countries cannot unilaterally alter them. As Chapter 3 describes, survival clauses in investment treaties in some cases tie in treaty obligations for up to twenty years. So even if a future government did want to shield domestic investors from competition from established foreign firms already operating in the host country, enforceable treaty commitments preventing discrimination and mistreatment of foreign investors would, in principle, tie the hands of future governments. In

[18] See further Poulsen (2015, ch. 6).

[19] Note that this argument assumes that those negotiating investment treaties on behalf of developing countries fully understood the present and future implications of the investment liberalization obligations included in the treaties. See the following text.

turn, this should act as a deterrent from policy reversals, which would improve long-term predictability for foreign investors.

Some developing countries used this argument as a justification for adopting investment treaties. For instance, when Argentinean president Carlos Menem initiated wholesale privatizations in the early 1990s, the Argentine Congress passed an Economic Emergency Law that authorized the executive branch to adopt investment treaties. The treaties were useful instruments to attract investment in newly privatized industries, partly by making sure that future governments would not renationalize those assets or dismantle the regulatory framework established to govern the industries in question. The Argentinean foreign minister noted in 1990 that the reason the country had begun adopting BITs was ' . . . so that people from abroad know that Argentina offers the utmost in legal security. Not only under a domestic law, which might be amended by another one, but under bilateral agreements, which obviously can be altered only by mutual accord'.[20]

Poland is another example. St John (2017) describes how, in 1989, the communist leader Jaruzelski told the United States that the inexperience of the Solidarity movement meant that its imminent takeover of the Polish government would quickly bankrupt the country. The transition to a market economy had already begun, and the BIT was a useful tool to tie in future governments. In this context, President Jaruzelski explicitly told President HW Bush that 'pressure is needed from the outside to adopt the reforms' (quoted in St John 2017, 161). Poland quickly signed and ratified the agreement, such that commitments to protect foreign-owned private property would be locked in, even when Solidarity assumed power.[21] More broadly, US negotiators have noted that some investment treaty negotiations with Central and Eastern European countries proceeded in parallel to the revision of their national investment laws after the Cold War, and the treaties thereby served 'to anchor their economic reform efforts in these areas' (quoted in Poulsen 2015, 86).

Apart from *tying in* existing or ongoing reforms, 'traditional' BITs may also theoretically *push forward* reforms, provided treaty obligations go beyond domestic laws. As an example, many developing (and indeed developed) countries would have to initiate significant regulatory reforms if they were to live up to *Tecmed's* expansive understanding of fair and equitable treatment:

The foreign investor expects the host State to act in a consistent manner, free from ambiguity and totally transparent in its relations with the foreign investor, so that it

---

[20] Quoted and translated in Daily Report: Latin America, FBIS-LAT-91-012, 17 January 1991. See also Post (2014).

[21] Note that the US–Poland BIT includes national treatment for the pre-establishment phase, but the provision is subject to domestic laws and regulations, which significantly reduces the teeth of the obligation.

may know beforehand any and all rules and regulations that will govern its investments, as well as the goals of the relevant policies and administrative practices or
directives . . . (*Tecmed v. Mexico*, para. 154)

Although less far-reaching, a minority of treaties also explicitly includes treaty
language on transparency, requiring host states to make relevant regulations,
laws, and administrative rulings promptly available, and a few require relevant
foreign stakeholders to be consulted before implementing relevant measures
to the extent possible (UNCTAD 2012). The reforms that these interpretations
and innovations in treaty language require could theoretically *promote* domestic reforms.[22]

   In Chapter 6, however, we noted that, insofar as evidence is available, it
suggests that investment treaties have not triggered fundamental reform at the
domestic level.[23] Moreover, the evidence available again suggests that, when
post-establishment provisions of investment treaties were part of a 'two-level
game', they were primarily used by developing countries to tie in—rather than
push forward—domestic reforms (Poulsen 2015). The expected impact of the
treaties on domestic policies and policy-making therefore remains a critical
subject for future research.[24]

Investment treaties and diplomacy

The accounts in the preceding text are unable to explain a significant number
of investment treaties signed among countries that were not significant trading
or investment partners. In 1996, for instance, Vietnam signed BITs with
Algeria, Bulgaria, and Uzbekistan. And, in 1998, North Korea signed BITs
with countries such as the Czech Republic, Serbia, and Slovakia. In the absence
of foreign investment in either direction, these treaties have no practical
implications (except for their effect on other investment treaties through
MFN clauses, or in the event of significant future investment between
the countries). Yet, hundreds of such 'strange' investment treaties have been

---

[22] Such reforms could, in turn, benefit domestic investors and other domestic constituencies as well.
[23] A partial explanation may be that investors cannot typically directly invoke investment treaties
before domestic agencies and courts—unless they are given effect in domestic law. How treaties are
given effect in domestic law varies significantly across countries, and the literature has yet to take this
variation into account in evaluating the effect of investment treaties on domestic reforms.
[24] Some studies point to the theoretical possibility that authoritarian regimes may have used
investment treaties to increase leadership survival. On this basis, one study argues that the treaties
promote foreign investment into authoritarian regimes and thereby help political leaders to stay in
office (Arias, Hollyer, and Rosendorff 2015), whereas another argues that the treaties undermine
property right protections for small- and medium-sized domestic firms to the benefit of rent-seeking
business elites propping up authoritarian leaders (Mazumder 2015). It remains to be seen whether
qualitative evidence exists to back up these claims.

signed, which points to a third category of explanations on how developing countries used investment treaties to promote diplomatic agendas. Four arguments are particularly relevant: (i) de-politicization; (ii) foreign policy objectives; (iii) diplomatic symbolism; and (iv) investment treaties used as diplomatic 'perks'. These arguments are not necessarily inconsistent with the objectives of investment promotion and tying in domestic reforms. Indeed, the second, third, and fourth arguments all complement the two accounts considered in the preceding text.

As outlined in the previous chapter, a first explanation for the popularity of BITs among developing countries was the promise that investment treaty arbitration would 'de-politicize' investment disputes, and thereby avert the threat of home state intervention in one form or another (Shihata 1986). The founders of ICSID emphasized this argument at a time when major investment disputes threatened to undermine sensitive foreign policy and security goals. As such, investment treaty arbitration should make inter-state conflicts less likely, which should be a particular benefit for weak states.

Yet, de-politicization does not seem to have been a primary objective of investment treaty programs in developing countries (Poulsen 2015).[25] A partial exception is Costa Rica, where the primary impetus to ratify the ICSID Convention in 1993 was to stop pressure from the United States in an investment dispute.[26] Even Costa Rica, however, had initiated its BIT program in the 1980s, with the primary objective of promoting foreign investment rather than de-politicizing investment disputes (Poulsen 2015). Moreover, as Chapter 7 describes, it is unclear whether de-politicization even played a particularly crucial role in the BIT programs of developed countries. So while some of the early architects (particularly the founders of ICSID) of the investment treaty regime saw de-politicization as an important promise of investment treaty arbitration, other diplomatic factors were more important.

Second, a large literature in political science suggests that broader diplomatic strategies often drive international economic integration (e.g. Gowa and Mansfield 1993). As Chapter 7 mentioned, this was an important factor in some investment treaty negotiations of developed countries. And, in some developing countries, governments also used investment treaties to signal and reinforce friendly diplomatic relations. Diplomatic links between countries are a significant predictor of investment treaty adoption, and governments often justified BITs in the broader context of promoting and reinforcing diplomatic

---

[25] Collectively, the authors of this book have also advised several developing countries on their investment treaty programs and specific investment treaty negotiations. In their (admittedly anecdotal) experience, the authors have also not found de-politicization of investment disputes to be among the primary objectives of developing countries in negotiating investment treaties.

[26] *Compañia del Desarrollo de Santa Elena S.A. v. Costa Rica* (2000).

links (Poulsen and Aisbett 2016). In the case of Chile, for instance, a previous negotiator notes that BITs were signed during the early 1990s as part of a 'policy to put the name of Chile among the international community coming back from Dictatorship. We wanted to renew relationships with a lot of countries, where we did not have political relationships before. So BITs were part of that bigger picture' (quoted in Poulsen and Aisbett 2016, 86). During the 1990s, Chile signed BITs not just with important investment partners but also countries such as Croatia, Romania, and Tunisia. Equally, Vandevelde describes a telling case in point:

Just prior to a State visit to Washington in early 1990, the Congolese government notified the United States that it would be interested in concluding a BIT. Negotiations were complete during the State visit and an agreement signed at the conclusion of the visit. The final agreement was identical to the 1987 model negotiating text.... the almost unavoidable inference is that the value of the BITs as political symbols was an important factor in their negotiation (Vandevelde 1992b, 635–6).

Third, Jandhyala, Henisz, and Mansfield (2011) offer a complementary explanation for such behaviour. They argue that the adoption of BITs during the 1990s was often about 'keeping with accepted norms or standards' (2011, 1056). Political symbolism and transnational mimicry were the main drivers of many investment treaties rather than instrumental considerations relating to the legal content and the practical implications of the treaties. There is a degree of similarity here to human rights agreements, which states also increasingly ratified in the 1990s, not because they thought they entailed material benefits or they were coerced to ratify them, but merely because it was considered the *appropriate* thing to do (Lutz and Sikkink 2000; Wotipka and Ramirez 2007; Simmons, 2009; see generally, Axelrod 1986; March and Olsen 1998; Goodman and Jinks 2013).

Fourth, and finally, apart from diplomatic agendas and symbolism, individual bureaucrats and politicians sometimes used investment treaties for their own 'selfish' reasons.[27] This is in line with the public choice literature, which high-lights how personal interests of officials can shape broader public policies (e.g. Buchanan and Tullock 1962).[28] As one South African official notes:

South African politicians went all over Africa, and because politicians want to be seen doing something constructive, they would often suggest a BIT even if no investments were flowing between the countries (quoted in Poulsen 2015, 181).

Embassy and investment promotion officials have also typically supported investment treaties. For ambassadors, the treaties were occasionally used 'as an

---

[27] Unless otherwise stated, this paragraph is based on Poulsen and Aisbett (2016).
[28] For public choice perspectives on other international legal regimes, see Colombatto and Macey (1996) and Abbott (2008). See also Gray (2015) on the patronage functions of international organizations.

indicator of their performance', 'a possible achievement during their tenure', and the ability to finish their posting 'with a bang' (various developing-country officials quoted in Poulsen 2015, ch. 6). For officials at home, the process of negotiating BITs facilitated funded business trips to attractive locations—an important perk for officials in some of the poorest developing countries (see also Rose-Ackerman and Truex 2013). A previous Pakistani investment official recalls that whenever there was 'a proposal for an international agreement to be negotiated, everyone says "yes", because you get a free trip out of it' (quoted in Poulsen and Aisbett 2016, 89). Even if collectively irrational for the country as a whole, this can be rational for the individual bureaucrat. For, even if the treaty gives rise to arbitrations against the state in the future, those involved in negotiations would likely have moved on to other positions at the time. So, particularly during the early days of the investment treaty movement with few arbitrations, bureaucrats and politicians sometimes pursued the treaties primarily to advance their own careers.

The role of expertise

In Chapter 7, we suggested that developed countries have frequently been surprised by the way in which arbitral tribunals interpreted and applied certain provisions of investment treaties. This is not unexpected, as no one could have accurately predicted how tribunals would fill in the blanks of vaguely drafted provisions such as FET. In many developing countries, however, the failure to appreciate the implications of investment treaties was more fundamental. Many policy-makers and negotiators did not realize the basic point that the treaties were enforceable, and potentially costly, not just in principle but also in fact. As such, this was not just a problem of imperfect information resulting from the fact that investors had filed very few arbitrations before the 2000s. Many developing countries also suffered from imperfect processing of information that was publicly available due to a lack of expertise.[29]

At least until the end of the 1990s, developing countries normally entered into investment treaties without careful negotiations and with little consideration of the implications. Legal experts rarely negotiated investment treaties, as governments typically delegated the task to generalist bureaucrats, many of who mistook the emerging investment treaty regime for aspirational 'soft-law'.

---

[29] Unless otherwise stated, the following section is based on Poulsen (2015). Note that, in some cases, a fundamental lack of understanding hampered developed countries as well. The Israeli government, for instance, offered BITs to two Korean firms in 2005, which according to Chalamish reflects 'the confusion between a bilateral investment treaty between states and an Israeli governmental contract' (Chalamish 2010, ftn. 47). The authors are also aware of a couple of developed countries whose negotiators have been generalist bureaucrats rather than legal experts.

Numerous investment treaty negotiators, stakeholders, as well as archival records confirm this crucial point. In the case of South Africa, for instance, officials incorrectly assumed that the treaties contained only broad statements of policy principles and failed to realize that their provisions potentially gave foreign investors' protections over and beyond those enshrined in the South African constitution (Poulsen 2014; on compensation for expropriation in the South African constitution see Chapter 4). Similarly, in the Czech Republic, a former negotiator recalls that the staff involved: 'really didn't know that the treaties had any bite in practice ... They were neither aware of the costs or the fact that it could lead to arbitration' (quoted in Poulsen 2015, 141–2; cf. also Veselá 2009 and Fecák 2011). Mexico is representative of the 'strategies' that many developing countries adopted,

During the 1990s, BITs were a very different animal than FTAs, the WTO, and other globalization instruments ... Many here in Latin America thought it was harmless to sign these treaties, no one had an idea what they meant ... They just signed them off within a few days or hours ... There was no legal review, control, or scrutiny of the content ... No one cared until the dispute came (quoted in Poulsen 2015, 146).

Although future studies may reveal similar lack of expertise among some developed countries, previous negotiators from several major developed countries have suggested that their developing-country counterparts often failed to appreciate the meaning of even basic provisions. Arbitrators themselves have also noted this peculiar aspect of the investment treaty regime. Schreuer is one,

... many times, in fact in the majority of times, BITs are among clauses of treaties that are not properly negotiated. ... and I have heard several representatives who have actually been active in this Treaty-making process ... say that, 'We had no idea that this would have real consequences in the real world' (Schreuer quoted in *Wintershall v. Argentina* 2008, para. 85).

Similarly, Sands describes how one of his former students contacted him in the mid-1990s asking if he could assist with an arbitration against Albania, where the first hearing was scheduled only two weeks later:

... He was based in the legal adviser's office, and until shortly before our phone conversation had been denied access to a locked wooden cupboard. Inside he eventually discovered a bundle of discarded and mostly unopened Federal Express packages sent from the Secretary General of [ICSID]. .... ICSID's initial letters had received no response from Albania, perhaps because they were being treated as bills. ... Plainly, no one had taken the trouble to explain to Albania exactly what it was signing up to ... (Sands 2006, 117–18).[30]

---

[30] The arbitration was *Tradex v. Albania* (1999).

Partly because of the absence of any significant expertise going into the negotiations, investment treaty talks during the 1990s and early 2000s often proceeded as 'mock-negotiations', with template agreements of developed countries accepted as 'default rules' almost without question (on similar 'copy–pasting' in trade agreements, see Allee and Elsig 2016).[31] As a former South Korean official noted,

> ... until recently most Korean experts of international litigation ... were found only in the private sector and not in the government. ... negotiators were often unable to adequately address the complex procedural issues surrounding investor–State dispute resolution. As a result, they often resorted to using the same simple provisions as in previous investment agreements (Kim 2011, 68).

Berge and Stiansen (2016) confirm this link between expertise and acceptance of the other party's model BIT template. In addition, the failure of some developing countries to appreciate the potency of BITs also helps explain why they preferred bilateralism in the regime. When the potential inclusion of investment protection provisions was placed on the WTO agenda in the early 2000s, for instance, core South African officials objected in the belief that their existing BIT obligations did not exceed those relating to foreign investment in the WTO (Poulsen 2014). This, of course, was a mistake.[32]

There were exceptions to this lack of expertise going into negotiations. For idiosyncratic reasons, Costa Rica always appreciated the potency of investment treaties, and put experts on international law in charge of BIT negotiations. China has also pursued a careful and strategic investment treaty policy since the 1980s (Berger 2011; see the following text), and, during the late 1980s and early 1990s, legal bureaucrats in Thailand were hesitant to include investor–state arbitration clauses into investment treaties (Nottage and Thanitcul 2016). Similar examples are bound to emerge as more detailed case studies are conducted. But, overall, it is difficult to account for the popularity of BITs in many developing countries without appreciating the limited understanding of the implications of the treaties among negotiators and stakeholders at the time they were negotiated. This also explains why some developing countries adopted investment treaties in such a haphazard fashion. Since other agencies within governments failed to appreciate the potential liabilities involved, the individuals and agencies that were directly involved in treaty negotiations could conclude many

---

[31] This is in stark contrast to investment treaty negotiations during the 1960s and 1970s, when the underlying principles enshrined in the treaties were not shared among governments in most developing countries (on the principles of the investment treaty regime, see Chapter 1 and Poulsen 2015).
[32] The WTO agreements do not contain investment protections, aside from the narrowly drafted restrictions on the use of performance requirements contained in the TRIMs agreement.

agreements in a short period—possibly for selfish reasons—with few, if any, questions asked.

Recent developments

As with developed countries, the politics of investment treaties has changed significantly in recent years in many developing countries. This is primarily for three reasons: (i) the rise of investment treaty arbitration; (ii) the growing role of outward investment flows from developing countries; and (iii) the move towards integrating investment protection standards into broader trade and investment agreements.

RESPONDING TO INVESTMENT TREATY ARBITRATION

Developing countries have responded to the rise of investment treaty arbitration in different ways. As Chapter 1 describes, a few countries, such as Indonesia and South Africa, have attempted to terminate existing investment treaties. Yet, these are the exceptions, and many developing countries continue to sign investment treaties, though now typically as part of broader trade agreements and ordinarily with more caution than during the 'heyday' of the BIT movement. Developing countries typically began to slow down their rush to sign investment treaties after they themselves became subject to arbitrations, and the experience of such arbitrations has also resulted in clarifications and restrictions of the content of new investment treaties and, in some cases, led to calls for re-negotiations (Poulsen and Aisbett 2013; Poulsen 2014; 2015; Haftel and Thompson 2015; Henckels 2016). Organizations such as UNCTAD and the International Institute for Sustainable Development (IISD), an NGO, have been instrumental in assisting with these reforms.[33]

Latin America provides a useful illustration of the varied responses to the rise of investment treaty arbitration. While countries in the region rushed to adopt BITs during the late 1980s and the 1990s, some Latin American countries have now turned against the investment treaty regime. Bolivia, Ecuador, and Venezuela have begun to terminate some of their BITs and denounced the ICSID Convention (Waibel et al. 2010). Bolivia left ICSID in 2007, Ecuador in 2009, and Venezuela in 2012.[34] Questions arise as to what exactly denouncing ICSID and cancelling investment treaties imply in the short term, not least

---

[33] See for example UNCTAD's 2015 Investment Policy Framework for Sustainable Investment (UNCTAD 2015) and IISD's 2005 Model BIT (IISD 2005).

[34] Nicaragua has threatened to leave ICSID as well, but had yet to do so at the time of this writing.

given the survival clauses in the latter (UNCTAD 2010), but the development is undoubtedly important over the long term, politically as well as legally. The parallels to the 1960s and 1970s are clear, when many Latin American states refused to sign the ICSID Convention.

In the case of Ecuador, the government has faced several multi-billion-dollar claims by foreign energy companies. Having spent US$94 million in legal fees attempting to defend an arbitration by US oil company Occidental (Arauz 2013), the tribunal ordered Ecuador to pay US$2.3 billion in compensation to Occidental in 2012.[35] According to the minister of foreign affairs, the ICSID award was 'unjust, illegal, illegitimate and absurd' (quoted from Franck and Wylie 2015, 478). The resulting public anger in Ecuador prompted Ecuador to pull out of some investment treaties and ICSID. Leaving ICSID was necessary, said Ecuadorian president Rafael Correa, as the organization signified 'colonialism, slavery with respect to transnationals, with respect to Washington, with respect to the World Bank' (Bretton Woods Project 2009). As an alternative, Ecuador has proposed an arbitration centre under UNASUR—the Union of South American Nations—based in Latin America instead of Washington (Fiezzoni 2011). Although it is unclear whether the centre will materialize, the proposal is likely to include more comprehensive rules on transparency in investment treaty arbitration than ICSID and exclude party-appointed arbitrators (see also Chapter 9 on how similar features are included in EU's recent policy proposals, CETA, and the EU–Vietnam FTA).

In Venezuela and Bolivia, the turn against the regime has also had populist overtones, with ICSID and investment treaties regarded as part of a broader capitalist—and US—imperial project. '[W]e are not going to bow down to imperialism and its tentacles!', President Hugo Chavez said in a televised speech on ICSID in 2012 (quoted in Garcia 2012). In Bolivia, the denouncement of ICSID came after President Morales nationalized the entire hydrocarbon industry—one of his first initiatives as president. Even before the election of Morales, however, the investment treaty regime had become highly politicized in Bolivia after a foreign company brought an ICSID arbitration following a failed privatization of the water sector in the country (de Gramont 2006; Spronk and Crespo 2008). Morales was clear: '(We) emphatically reject the legal, media and diplomatic pressure of some multinationals that … resist the sovereign rulings of countries, making threats and initiating suits in international arbitration' (Investment Treaty News, May 9, 2008).

Importantly, however, the removal from the regime has remained only partial (Peinhardt and Wellhausen 2016). Bolivia has not terminated any of its investment treaties to date; Venezuela has only cancelled some, and has even signed others; and in Ecuador some investment treaties were also kept in

---

[35] This amount was subsequently reduced to just over US$1 billion in ICSID annulment proceedings (2015).

place—partly because the national assembly insisted and partly because of pressure from other states with significant investments in the country (such as China). This potentially leaves open the possibility for investors to restructure their operations to seek treaty protections through the remaining treaties. Recall also that, even for those few states that have withdrawn from ICSID, most investment treaties give foreign investors a choice of pursuing invest-ment treaty arbitration under several different sets of procedural rules, of which the ICSID Convention is only one (see Chapter 3).

In other Latin American countries, the reaction to investment treaties and the experience of defending arbitrations brought under such treaties has been different. In Peru, the government has gone to great lengths to distance itself from the resource nationalism of its neighbours, and instead reacted to the claims by setting up domestic institutional structures to manage invest-ment disputes (UNCTAD 2010). Other countries, such as Colombia, the Dominican Republic, and Guatemala, have considered similar initiatives. Chile and Mexico have continued their support for investment treaties and investment treaty arbitration, albeit with greater clarifications and restric-tions for the scope of key substantive provisions. Argentina too has yet to cancel any of its investment treaties despite having to defend itself in almost sixty arbitrations, most of which were filed after its 2001 financial crisis. Whether this is because Argentina remains dependent on FDI and expects a pull-out from the regime to have significant reputation costs,[36] or because it wants to distance itself from more populist regimes in the region, it is notable that the country subject to by far the largest number of investment treaty arbitrations remains a rank and file member of the regime (Haftel and Levi 2016).[37]

Finally, Brazil has recently decided to initiate an investment treaty program, yet with a radically different type of agreement. After conducting a survey of Brazilian companies, the government found that they sought different, and more practical, assistance from their government, rather than protections against political risks traditionally provided by investment treaties (Gomes 2013). In contrast to almost all other investment treaties, the resulting Brazilian model is focused on practical investment facilitation initiatives, such as visas and investment logistics. Its coverage is limited to FDI, and its investment protection provisions only require compensation for direct forms of expropri-ation. Investor obligations are included as well—again in contrast to traditional investment treaties—and disputes are to be settled through state-to-state

---

[36] Note that even if an investment treaty is not an effective positive signal to promote investment— partly because of the thousands of treaties already in place—cancelling an investment could still send a strong negative signal, and thus have significant reputation costs among foreign investors. This is an important subject for future research.
[37] Recall from Chapters 1 and 3, however, how Argentina dragged its feet in paying several awards.

procedures.[38] At the time of going to press, Brazil had already signed two new BITs based on its model treaty with Angola and Mozambique, respectively.

PROTECTING OUTWARD INVESTMENTS

Apart from the growth of investment treaty arbitrations, a second important recent development is the growth in outward investments from developing countries. During the 1990s, the number of investment treaties signed among developing countries themselves increased rapidly. By the second half of the 1990s, South–South BITs comprised more than half of all BITs (see generally Poulsen 2010). Although some of these treaties were simply 'photo-ops', others reflected a shift in policy priorities as developing countries gradually became capital exporters themselves and sought to use investment treaties to protect outward investment. Simultaneously, many OECD countries have gradually become significant importers of capital. In 1999, for instance, Austria signed a BIT with India as part of a broader campaign of marketing Austria as an investor-friendly entry-point into the EU for Indian investors.[39]

Over the last decade, the objective of protecting their own investors abroad has been increasingly reflected in the investment treaty practices of developing countries. A good illustration is China (Schill 2007; Gallagher and Shan 2009; Berger 2011). China began negotiating investment treaties in the early 1980s after Deng Xiaoping embraced foreign investment as part of his 'open door' policy. The first 'generation' of Chinese investment treaties were limited in scope. They excluded a broad consent to investment treaty arbitration and did not contain national treatment obligations. Only the amount of compensation for expropriation could be subject to investment treaty arbitration, not whether expropriation had actually occurred. This practice changed in parallel with domestic reforms in China through the 1990s. After adopting the 'going abroad' strategy in 1998, Chinese investment treaty policy began to focus more on protecting the rising stock of Chinese capital abroad. The growing role of Chinese companies in Africa, for instance, has been complemented by more than 25 BITs. Even when negotiating with the European Union and the United States, China is not just a capital importer with defensive interests but also a capital exporter attempting to ensure protections for Chinese outwards investors who are perceived to be subject to unfair restrictions in developed countries—not least when the investors in question are government owned or controlled (Berger 2011). In negotiations with some developed countries, notably Canada, China was even seen as the primary capital exporter (van Harten 2015). The changing objective of China's investment

---

[38] See Chapter 3.
[39] Kingshuk (1999).

treaty program is also reflected in the content of the treaties. New Chinese BITs now include most of the standard investment protections that were traditionally found in the BITs of developed countries, along with full advance consent to investment treaty arbitration.

China is not alone. Brazil's decision to negotiate some form of investment treaty (mentioned earlier) came after Brazilian companies called upon the Brazilian government to support their interests abroad (Whitsitt and Vis-Dunbar 2008; see the following text). To support the growth of Arab investments, countries such as Qatar, Saudi Arabia, and the United Arab Emirates have negotiated many investment treaties aimed at protecting capital abroad. Countries such as Thailand and Turkey also report that investment treaties are no longer solely used to attract investment but also to protect outgoing investors (Akpinar 2001; Mangklatanakul 2012). And, even after initiating the withdrawal from the investment treaty regime, South Africa still decided to sign a BIT with Zimbabwe to protect South African investments there (Poulsen 2014).

In short, as outward foreign investment from 'developing' countries such as China expands, the reciprocity of the investment treaty regime is no longer a legal fiction, and the traditional developed/developing country divide is becoming progressively less useful in explaining attitudes and policies towards investment treaties in different states.

FROM BITS TO BROADER TRADE AND INVESTMENT AGREEMENTS

Third, and finally, the politics of investment treaties has changed with the inclusion of investment protection rules in broader economic integration agreements. This remains too recent a phenomenon to have been subject to detailed scrutiny in the literature, but we can already now speculate about at least two potential drivers and effects of this development.

First, resistance to enforceable investment protection provisions could, in principle, be addressed through 'issue-linkages', where developing countries agree to accept such provisions in return for tariff reductions or other non-investment concessions. In some cases, the very participation in a major economic integration agreement such as the TPP can bring perceived diplomatic benefits—for instance, by aligning closer with the United States or countering the rise of China—which is a factor that developing countries may weigh against any concerns with the agreement's specific investment provisions.[40] The relationship between concerns about investment provisions

---

[40] For empirical studies showing how the investment chapter in TPP is based primarily on US investment treaties, rather than on those of its developing country partners, see Allee and Lugg (2016) and Alschner and Skougarevskiy (2016).

and the wider dynamics of PTA negotiations is an important area for further research.

Second, there is the question of whether these broader agreements will be more effective in promoting foreign investment than stand-alone BITs. Developing-country negotiators might believe that foreign investors are more likely to care about investment protection provisions, when they come as part of a package with trade and other investment-related provisions. UNCTAD, for instance, has used existing studies to suggest that this is the case (UNCTAD 2009c, 105–6), despite the difficulty of testing the value added by investment protection provisions in these agreements (see Chapter 6). Insofar as negotiators share this belief about the efficacy of investment provisions in PTAs, another important question for further research is whether those beliefs are derived from careful cost–benefit analyses, or 'gut feelings' similar to those prevailing for BITs during the 1990s.

Conclusion

The vast majority of developing countries entered into investment treaties to attract foreign investment, and, in some cases, the treaties were used to tie in domestic investment reforms. Occasionally, diplomatic considerations were also important, but the perceived need to de-politicize investment disputes was hardly ever a core driver of developing-country investment treaty programmes.

Unlike claims in much early scholarship on the investment treaty regime, developing countries rarely approached the negotiation process strategically or carefully. They often failed to assess whether the treaties in fact mattered for foreign investment flows into their country. More importantly, most entirely overlooked the potential costs of these agreements. This meant they were often negotiated and signed off in a rush, with little—if any—scrutiny. It is also partly for this reason that 'strange' developing-country pairs with few commercial links signed some BITs.

In the last decade, the politics of investment treaties has changed significantly in some developing countries. The rise of investment treaty arbitration has underscored the potential costs and binding nature of the agreements, which has led negotiators and other stakeholders to engage and scrutinize investment treaties more carefully. In a few cases, states have withdrawn from agreements because they entailed, in their view, significant risks without any associated economic benefits. The withdrawal has only been partial so far, however, and most other developing countries have decided to stay within the regime for now and instead pursue only incremental reforms to their investment treaty policies. For some, this is partly because of the changing nature of global investment flows, where companies from developing countries increasingly invest abroad. Finally, the move towards including investment protection in broader economic integration agreements may change the politics of the regime significantly as compared to the politics of stand-alone BITs.

9 Legitimacy and Governance Challenges

Introduction

The previous chapters showed that the rapid growth of investment treaty arbitrations in often sensitive policy areas has focused public attention on the investment treaty regime. Whereas the regime was little known just a few decades ago, it is now the subject of an often-heated debate. Supporters of the regime argue that it promotes the rule of law in international economic relations, and protects foreign investors from arbitrary state action (e.g. Schill 2016). Critics, however, label the regime a 'bill of rights for multinational corporations' (Klein 2001) that limits the ability of states to regulate in the public interest (Sornarajah 2015). They describe investment treaty tribunals as 'secret courts' (DePalma 2001) comprised of 'biased' arbitrators (Eberhardt and Olivet 2012) that empower corporations 'to bend countries to their will' (Hamby 2016a). The system, according to US senator Elizabeth Warren, is 'rigged' in favor of big capital and corporate lawyers (quoted in Hamby 2016d). Taken together, these criticisms are said to amount to a 'legitimacy crisis' of the investment treaty regime (Brower, Brower, and Sharpe 2003; Franck 2005), much like the legitimacy crisis of the international trade regime around the time of the World Trade Organization (WTO) Ministerial Conference in Seattle in 1999 (Keohane and Nye 2001; Esty 2002).

The use of the concept of 'legitimacy' to frame debates about investment treaties reflects the centrality of that concept in global governance literature over the past two decades (e.g. Keohane 2011). However, 'legitimacy' has multiple related meanings, creating potential for confusion (Crawford 2004; Koskenniemi 2009; Thomas 2014). For example, 'legitimacy' in a *normative* sense refers to the desirability or appropriateness of legal rules and institutions. 'Legitimacy' in a *descriptive* sense also refers to desirability or appropriateness but is focused on the beliefs of relevant actors (e.g. Brower and Schill 2009). While the two are related, the distinction is significant. Regardless of whether they are justified, the beliefs of governments are important— for example, in explaining patterns of compliance with international law (see generally Franck 1990; Brunnée and Toope 2010). Similarly, popular beliefs about the investment treaty regime matter, even if they are based on misunderstandings. Some critics argue that investors can win investment treaty arbitrations purely based on lost profits, for instance, which is a mischaracterization of the substantive rights in the treaties. And some proponents argue that investment treaty arbitration is primarily concerned with redressing expropriation and discrimination, which is equally misleading. Yet, even if incorrect, such beliefs can have important political ramifications for the regime, particularly when they diffuse to policy-makers and officials. Although this chapter refers to beliefs about the investment treaty regime, we are primarily interested in whether criticisms of the investment treaty regime are justified. Accordingly, we focus on debates about legitimacy in the normative sense.

The chapter draws together several strands of the book to focus on two central debates about the investment treaty regime. The first section considers the impact of investment treaties on national governance. In particular, it assesses criticisms that investment treaties unduly fetter democratic decision-making and discourage states from regulating in the public interest. The second section examines the legitimacy of investment treaty arbitration—the regime feature that has come under closest scrutiny over the last decade (e.g. Tribe, Stiglitz, and Sachs 2016). It assesses debates about transparency and consistency in investment treaty arbitration; its impact on the broader investment regime complex; the selection, identity, and alleged biases of arbitrators; as well as the lack of investor obligations.

The chapter does not examine every issue relevant to debates about the legitimacy of investment treaties. For example, questions of whether, and under what circumstances, investment insurance, investor–state contracts, domestic courts, or inter-state dispute settlement are alternatives to investment treaty arbitration are also central to debates about normative legitimacy. Analysis of the economic effect of investment treaties is also relevant, but we have already covered these (and several other) relevant debates elsewhere in the book (see Chapters 3, 5, and 6).

The investment treaty regime and national governance

One of the most powerful criticisms of the investment treaty regime focuses on its relationship to, and implications for, democracy. This criticism concerns the relationship between the investment treaty regime and political decision-making at the national level. A related criticism is that the regime interferes with the ability of states to regulate in the public interest by excessively constraining national policy autonomy—for example, with respect to measures intended to protect the environment or public health. This section examines each in turn.

DEMOCRACY

Subject to the limited carve-outs and defences discussed in Chapter 4, investment treaties apply to all state conduct affecting covered foreign investments. As such, investors can seek review in investment treaty arbitration of legislation enacted by democratically elected parliaments and of the exercise of administrative power that elected officials validly delegated to agencies. It is no defence for host states to argue that they enacted the measure in question according to a democratic process. According to some critics, this feature of the investment treaty regime unduly constrains majoritarian politics (e.g. Schneiderman 2008).

This argument must be qualified in three important respects. First, the description of investment treaties as constraints on majoritarian politics could apply equally to any regime of international law backed by binding dispute settlement, such as the European Convention on Human Rights (ECHR) or the WTO. This observation does not answer the substance of the criticism against investment treaties, but it does provide important context. Second, recall from Chapter 3 that, in practice, investment treaty tribunals invariably award compensation to foreign investors, rather than ordering states to abandon measures. Of course, the award of compensation may have the practical effect of precluding states from adopting or maintaining particular measures, but because states retain the *option* to maintain measures subject to challenge and pay compensation, investment treaties do not foreclose democratic decision-making as such. Third, the criticism only applies when investment treaties bind democracies and states transitioning to more democratic forms of government (Van Harten 2000; Bonnitcha 2014b). Yet, many states bound by investment treaties are not democratic, or are only partially so (Alvarez 2008).[1]

The extent to which legal rules should circumscribe democratic decision-making is the subject of a rich and sophisticated literature in other legal regimes.[2] Such questions are central to debates about whether national constitutions should

---

[1] An additional qualification is that states can exit the investment treaty regime altogether by terminating treaties. Yet, the effect of 'survival clauses' renders this a slow and potentially costly option (e.g. Voon and Mitchell 2016; see also Chapters 1 and 3). Even if all countries started to renegotiate all their investment treaties tomorrow, it would take up to twenty years to replace the existing stock of investment treaties.

[2] The architecture of other legal regimes also reflects concerns about the relationship between international legal constraints and democracy. For example, under the ECHR, member states are entitled to interfere with some human rights recognized in the Convention if such interference is 'necessary in a democratic society'; claimants are required to exhaust local remedies before bringing an international claim to the ECtHR; and the ECtHR affords a margin of appreciation to its member states (Letsas 2006; Legg 2012). Recall from Chapters 3 and 4 that the default rule in the investment treaty regime is that investors do not need to exhaust local remedies before commencing investment treaty arbitration, and that investment tribunals do not routinely afford a margin of appreciation to host states.

protect individual rights from the interference of majoritarian politics (e.g. Waldron 2006) and debates about the so-called 'democratic deficit' in the European Union (e.g. Majone 1998; Follesdal and Hix 2006). In these debates, most accept that there are at least some circumstances in which constraints on democratic decision-making are justified—for example, when international legal constraints are, themselves, adopted through democratic processes at the national level and are necessary to achieve the instrumental benefits arising from international cooperation (Kurtz 2014). Investment treaties to which democratic states have consented in accordance with their constitutional requirements meet the first condition of indirect democratic legitimation. Whether the second condition is met depends on the effect of investment treaties on investment flows or other expected benefits, such as the promotion of 'good governance' (see Chapter 6). Unlike literature on other legal regimes, however, questions about investment treaties and democracy have received little attention in scholarship on the investment treaty regime (but see Koskenniemi 2017).

One basic question that requires attention is whether challenges to certain types of state measures involve distinct legitimacy concerns. Some scholars have argued that investment treaty arbitrations challenging administrative and executive conduct do not raise the same legitimacy concerns as challenges to legislative measures (Tietje and Baetens 2014). This argument requires quali- fication. As mentioned, democratically elected legislatures often delegate powers to agencies. One example is environmental legislation that often confers powers on administrative agencies to determine whether individual investments meet legislative requirements. Investor challenges to such exer- cises of administrative authority also raise questions about the impact of the regime on democratic processes. Moreover, investment treaty arbitrations often relate to the combined effect of the conduct of several different domestic institutions. This factor not only complicates coding in empirical studies (see the following text), but also affects normative debates about whether certain types of measures raise particular legitimacy concerns.

With these caveats in mind, Figure 9.1 shows that the majority of investment treaty arbitrations arise from administrative or executive action, although legislative measures are the single most common source of known investment treaty arbitrations (Williams 2016).[3] Interestingly, arbitrations involving devel- oped countries are more likely to relate to legislative measures than those involving developing countries. Conversely, investment treaty arbitrations

---

[3] For an earlier attempt at coding the types of measures that give rise to investor–state arbitrations, see Caddel and Jensen (2014). Caddel and Jensen find that legislative measures account for a smaller percentage of disputes than Williams (2016). This could be due to differences in the way disputes are coded or due to Williams' more comprehensive data set. Her data is drawn from 568 disputes, compared to 163 disputes for Caddel and Jensen.

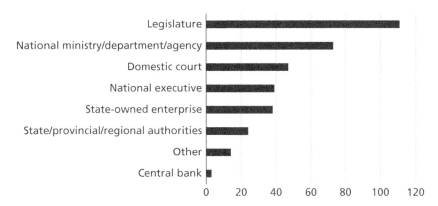

Figure 9.1 Domestic institutions involved in investment treaty disputes

Note: This figure has been modified from the original to include only investment treaty arbitrations (i.e. excluding arbitrations in which the host state consented by way of contract or domestic law). We thank Zoe Williams for providing the data.

Source: Williams (2016), Figure 2.6.

concerning the conduct of domestic courts are significantly more common against developing countries (Williams 2016).

Apart from the measures targeted in investment treaty arbitration, a related set of tensions between investment treaties and political decision-making arise when arbitrators examine the political motivations behind state measures against foreign investors (Schneiderman 2010; Van Harten 2013; Williams 2016). To illustrate the importance of this debate, consider the dispute in *Bilcon v. Canada* (2015). Recall that this dispute arose from the environmental impact assessment of a proposed gravel mine, in which a Canadian environmental review panel rejected the proposal of the investor. A majority of the tribunal held that the review panel gave too much weight to community opposition to the proposal, which the tribunal characterized as arbitrary behaviour by Canada that in turn breached NAFTA's FET provision. In contrast, the dissenting arbitrator argued that it was legitimate for the panel to take into account the affected 'community's own expression of its interests and values' (*Bilcon v. Canada,* Dissent, para. 49).

The disagreement between the majority and the dissenting arbitrator in *Bilcon* illustrates the differences in the way arbitral tribunals have evaluated state conduct motivated by public opinion, protests, or electoral appeal. Some arbitral tribunals see a role for investment treaties in protecting foreign investors from state conduct driven by 'political' considerations of this sort (e.g. *Tecmed v. Mexico* 2003, para. 127; *Biwater v. Tanzania* 2006, para. 698). Conversely, other tribunals have noted that the willingness of legislatures and executive agencies to consider public opinion is a normal feature of democratic societies, and is not inherently inconsistent with the protections that investment treaties grant to foreign investors (*AES v. Hungary* 2010, para. 10.3.24). This debate is crucial for growing concerns that investment treaty arbitration challenges democratic decision-making.

There are large unresolved questions about the relationship between democracy and the investment treaty regime that future research needs to address. Here, theoretical work might usefully draw on various bodies of literature to more explicitly consider whether the constraints that investment treaties place on democratic (and non-democratic) decision-making are justified. Empirical work on the extent to which investment treaties affect the deliberations of national and sub-national parliaments would also further our understanding of the impact of the regime on majoritarian politics. More broadly, it would be relevant to understand what role—if any—domestic regime type has for investment treaty arbitration. Williams (2016) finds that investors are more likely to target democracies with investment treaty arbitrations even after controlling for factors such as income levels. If this is the case, it raises questions as to why. Is it because democracies are less likely to settle claims informally due to domestic 'audience costs' (see a related argument in the trade regime by Davis 2012)? Or are democracies less prone to complying with investment treaties than authoritarian regimes (see generally Tomz 2002)?[4] Finally, further work examining systematic differences in the way arbitrators evaluate state conduct motivated by 'political' considerations (e.g. Van Harten 2013, ch. 3), and the drivers of such potential differences, would be useful—a subject we return to later in this chapter.

REGULATORY CHILL

A second criticism concerns the investment treaty regime's impact on the ability of states to adopt measures in the public interest. Here, criticisms are articulated in a range of different ways. Some invoke the basic prerogative of states to regulate activity within their own territory and criticize investment treaties for unduly restricting this so-called 'right to regulate' (see generally Shaw 2008, ch. 12; Crawford 2012, ch. 21). This framing focuses attention on *legal* questions of whether various types of state measures breach investment treaties (e.g. Titi 2014). Others focus specifically on the impact of investment treaties on the ability of states to enact particular categories of regulatory measures, such as those intended to protect the environment (Wälde and Kolo 2001; Moloo and Jacinto 2011) or human rights (Mann 2008; Simma 2011). This framing draws attention to possible tensions between the interests of

---

[4] This would contradict the results of Jensen (2008) but be consistent with earlier work on the political economy of some forms of authoritarianism (O'Donnell, Schmitter, and Whitehead 1986).

foreign investors and of individuals and groups *within* the host state, as opposed to the interests of the host state itself.

We adopt a different framing that encompasses both these issues—namely, the notion of *regulatory chill*. As we have seen in Chapter 5, *regulatory chill* refers to the possibility that investment treaties discourage states from adopting legitimate regulatory measures in practice (Tietje and Baetens 2014). Debates about regulatory chill are not unique to the investment treaty regime. For example, the WTO has known similar debates on the collision of private and public interests since its inception (e.g. Staiger 2003; Cass 2005). Yet, the extent to which investment treaties cause regulatory chill is one of the most controversial issues in contemporary debates about investment treaties (EFILA 2015; Schneiderman, Tienhaara, and Van Harten 2015).

Concerns that investment treaties might discourage legitimate regulatory measures—that is, what we refer to as *regulatory chill*—have been a significant driver of revisions in new investment treaties, particularly revisions responding to unexpectedly broad interpretations of existing investment treaties by arbitration tribunals (USTR 2015; Alschner 2016). Chapter 4 reviewed some of these reforms, including efforts to: (i) align investment treaty provisions with equivalent standards of national law; (ii) draft substantive provisions more precisely (e.g. FET); and (iii) include more carve-outs and exceptions, often modelled on those contained in the WTO. Concerns over regulatory chill have also prompted states to insert provisions in investment treaties that explicitly give states greater interpretative control over their treaties (Roberts 2010).[5]

Despite the centrality of regulatory chill to public debate and treaty practice, however, there is surprisingly little research on whether and to what extent concerns of regulatory chill are justified. This is partly because debates about regulatory chill raise a complex set of overlapping legal, normative, and empirical questions. We address some of the difficult legal and normative considerations before honing in on the challenges in empirical work on regulatory chill.

First, Chapters 3 and 4 examined the *law* of the investment treaty regime. Yet, the wide reach of investment treaties and investment treaty arbitration tells us little about whether the regime is a cause of regulatory chill, as several other legal institutions also constrain states. For example, if an investment treaty only precludes a state from adopting measures that are, in any event, unlawful under that state's own law, then the investment treaty is unlikely to cause regulatory chill. Conversely, if investment treaties require a state to compensate foreign investors for regulatory measures that are permissible as a matter of that state's domestic law, regulatory chill is more likely. Further research comparing the provisions of investment treaties and their interpretation by tribunals with the constraints of domestic law in various states would

---

[5] For example, US Model BIT 2012, Article 21(2).

be helpful to inform debates about this aspect of regulatory chill (Poulsen, Bonnitcha, and Yackee 2015).

Second, any assessment of the extent to which investment treaties discourage legitimate regulatory measures presupposes a *normative* theory that distinguishes between legitimate and illegitimate interferences with foreign investments. To illustrate why, consider a situation in which a state plans to seize a foreign investor's factory without compensation, but abandons this plan when the investor threatens investment treaty arbitration. In this example, the investment treaty influenced state decision-making—yet, few would consider it to be a case of regulatory chill as investment treaties are designed to protect foreign investors precisely against such forms of interference. This shows that one of the reasons why debates about regulatory chill remain so controversial is that different stakeholders have different, often unarticulated, normative theories of what constitutes illegitimate interference with foreign investment. Chapters 5 and 6 offered one possible basis for a normative theory of legitimate and illegitimate interferences with foreign investment based on the premise that legal rules and institutions should maximize societal welfare. Other scholars have argued that we should evaluate the constraints that investment treaties place on states in light of normative theories derived from 'the rule of law' (e.g. Schill 2010; Vandevelde 2010) or 'justice' (Kläger 2011)—both highly contested concepts.[6]

These legal and normative considerations are not only important in themselves, they also critical for the framing of *empirical* questions about the impact of investment treaties on host state decision-making. Such research raises distinct challenges on its own, which form the subject of the remainder of this section. As in the discussion about the impact of the regime on democracy, a first question is whether to focus on the interaction between investment treaties and particular types of state action. Critics of investment treaties are particularly concerned with the implications of investment treaties for measures of general application, such as tobacco control measures, environmental regulation, or the banning of products on public health grounds (e.g. Schneiderman 2008; Johnson and Volkov 2013). This concern reflects an implicit assumption that legitimate public policy objectives are more likely to be behind measures of general application than measures targeted at individual foreign investors.

According to one analysis, approximately one in three investment treaty arbitrations concern measures of general application (Williams 2016).[7] Yet, distinguishing 'general' from 'specific' measures is tricky, as the latter may be associated with broader policy changes. For instance, the cancellation of an

---

[6] For a critique of Kläger and an alternative normative framework, see Bonnitcha (2014a).

[7] Williams (2016) also includes sixteen arbitrations based on investor–state contracts and domestic laws, but the statistic does not change when excluding them from the sample (correspondence with Zoe Williams, on file with the authors).

individual mining permit may result from a *general* shift in state policy towards mining. Moreover, even conduct that is limited to a single investor may be motivated by a legitimate regulatory objective—for example, if an investor's permit to operate in a regulated industry is cancelled for persistent failure to comply with environmental conditions attached to that permit. Conversely, measures of general application include sector-wide takings of property that may fall outside most conceptions of legitimate public-interest regulation (Williams 2016).

A second critical question for empirical research relates to the underlying *causal mechanisms* that drive regulatory chill. Investment treaties can influence host state decision-making in two ways (Tienhaara 2011). First, various host state actors may internalize the constraints of investment treaties, in which case these constraints may influence state decision-making even in the absence of specific disputes with foreign investors. Second, a foreign investor's threat of an investment treaty arbitration in relation to a particular dispute may also influence host state decision-making by encouraging the host state to modify or abandon the measure in question. Recall from Chapter 6 that empirical evidence on the extent to which investment treaties influence state decision-making through internalization is very limited. In the following sections, we therefore focus on evidence of regulatory chill arising from threats of investment treaty arbitration.

Some arbitrators suggest that no evidence of regulatory chill exists (e.g. Paulsson in Hamby 2016b). And, indeed, many investment treaty disputes result from state decisions to maintain regulatory measures in the face of the *known* risk of investment treaty arbitration (Williams 2016). For example, South Africa maintained and applied its affirmative action policies in the mining sector, notwithstanding the decision of an Italian mining company to initiate investment treaty arbitration (*Foresti v. South Africa* 2010). Similarly, Canada and the United States went ahead with bans on chemicals harmful to human health in the face of investment treaty arbitrations (*Methanex v. US* 2005; *Chemtura v. Canada* 2010).

But while the risk of investment treaty arbitration does not *necessarily* lead to regulatory chill, we do have evidence that it has done so on at least some occasions. One example is when New Zealand delayed the implementation of tobacco plain packaging for several years while the investment treaty arbitration arising from Australia's tobacco plain packaging legislation remained pending (Turia 2013). Following Australia's successful defence against Philip Morris (2015), New Zealand proceeded with its plans[8], so the chilling effect in this case was only temporary.

---

[8] Smoke-free Environments (Tobacco Standardised Packaging) Amendment Act 2016, Act No. 2016, No. 43, 14 September 2016.

The more interesting and policy-relevant question is not whether regulatory chill has ever occurred—it has—but the extent to which regulatory chill occurs in practice. Surprisingly little empirical research exists on the extent to which states respond to threats of investment treaty arbitration by modifying or abandoning measures under consideration.[9] This is due, in part, to three significant challenges associated with such research. First, neither host states nor foreign investors have obvious incentives to publicize situations in which states responded to threats of arbitration by abandoning the measures under consideration. Attempts to determine the frequency with which such events occur through interviews with government lawyers or freedom of information requests regularly run up against confidentiality constraints (Van Harten and Scott 2016).

Even when evidence surfaces that a state abandoned or modified a proposed course of conduct following a threat of arbitration, a second challenge is to establish causality. For example, the *Ethyl v. Canada* (1998) case introduced in Chapter 7 arose out of Canada's ban on the import of a fuel additive on environmental grounds. Canada reversed the ban after Ethyl—a US investor—initiated arbitration under NAFTA's Chapter 11. While this suggests that the investment treaty arbitration resulted in the reversal of the ban, concurrent domestic legal proceedings played a role as well (Tienhaara 2009). Isolating the role of investment treaty arbitration, as in *Vattenfall v. Germany I* (2011) described in the Preface, raises a similar challenge. In that case, Germany relaxed the environmental requirements on a coal-fired power plant in exchange for the Swedish investor dropping an ICSID arbitration and proceedings in German courts.

In other cases, it is unclear whether the risk of investment treaty arbitration or the risk investor–state arbitration under a contractual consent to arbitration was responsible for a modification or abandonment of a measure. For example, in 2004, Indonesia decided to exempt foreign mining companies from a new environmental law for protected forestlands following investor threats of investor–state arbitration (Hamby 2016b). Yet, at the time of writing, it remains unclear whether the threats were based on investment treaties, investor–state contracts, or both. In addition, lobbying by an investor's home state could be a separate source of regulatory chill. In cases where a host state responds to diplomatic pressure from the home state, the risk of investment treaty arbitration might not play a significant role. In sum, the treaties could have complex, and as yet unstudied, effects in reducing some

---

[9] See Howse (2017) for a compilation of the terms of settlement in investment treaty arbitrations that settled prior to a final decision by the arbitral tribunal. Howse notes that 'Of the settlements for which public information was available, almost all appeared to involve either significant monetary relief for the investor (almost always in the multiple millions and in some cases reaching the billions); or significant adjustment of the regulatory framework to the benefit of the [investor].' This data provides an important point of reference in debates about regulatory chill, but does not cover situations in which a state responds to a threat of arbitration before the investor commences proceedings.

forms of regulatory chill (e.g. from diplomatic pressure by the investor's home state) while increasing others (e.g. from threats of investment treaty arbitration).

Apart from access to information and the difficulty of establishing causality, a third challenge arises because countries may respond differently to threats of investment treaty arbitration. This would limit our ability to draw generalizable conclusions from the study of one particular country. Country responses to threats of arbitration may differ for a range of reasons, including political priorities, internal legal constraints, and institutional capacity. In particular, some critics have argued that developing countries are more vulnerable to regulatory chill, both due to lower levels of capacity to evaluate the legal and financial risks associated with threats of arbitration (Tienhaara 2011) and due to the greater size of the amounts at stake relative to national budgets (Mann 2007).

These are plausible arguments, but they are difficult to assess, particularly in light of the first two challenges already noted. For example, Uruguay successfully defended its own tobacco control measures against Philip Morris (2016), but its ability to do so depended on millions of dollars of legal and technical support provided by Michael Bloomberg and the Gates Foundation (Council of Foreign Relations 2012).[10] This is relevant when considering that tobacco companies have threatened several other developing countries with investment treaty arbitration in response to proposals to introduce new tobacco control measures (e.g. Tavernise 2013; Puig 2016).[11]

The potential for regulatory chill and the public concerns surrounding it make it an important area for further research. This research agenda could be organized around four sets of questions. First, *legal* studies comparing the constraints arising from investment treaties with those arising from domestic regimes are few and far in between. Chapter 5 reviews the few studies that have attempted partial comparisons of this sort. This is an important, albeit difficult, area for further research as it requires analysis of the entire array of domestic laws, regulations, and principles that potentially apply in foreign investment disputes.

Second, as this section showed, more *empirical* research is required. Here, further detailed studies would be useful to assess when states respond to threats of investment treaty arbitration by amending or abandoning measures under challenge (e.g. Tienhaara 2009) and when they maintain measures notwithstanding the threat of arbitration (e.g. Williams 2016). Comparative studies could also consider whether the breakdown of general vs. specific

---

[10]   As we saw in Chapter 3, given the high average costs of arbitrations, third-party funding has been a growing trend in the investment treaty regime, particularly on the investor side.

[11]   The authors also have direct personal knowledge of further threats of investment treaty arbitration by tobacco companies against developing countries in cases that have not been publicly reported. Note that regulatory chill of future tobacco control measures may be less likely following Australia's and Uruguay's successful defenses of investment treaty arbitrations by Philip Morris. It is also unclear whether the tobacco industry is an outlier in its willingness to aggressively invoke investment treaties in regulatory disputes with developing countries.

measures in investment treaty arbitration is similar to disputes in which arbitration is only threatened.

Third, research into the institutional mechanisms by which states manage threats of arbitration could give a better picture of why regulatory chill does or does not occur in relation to particular types of threats of arbitration against particular states.[12] Government lawyers speak privately about the challenges of coordinating responses to threats of investment treaty arbitration across different arms of government. Institutional dynamics—such as the relationship between lawyers with whole-of-government responsibility and line ministries with the primary responsibility for measures under challenge—affect decisions about whether to amend challenged measures or to risk litigation in response to such threats. Unfortunately, these questions have received little attention to date.

Fourth and finally, research into investor–state contract negotiations, as well as contract renegotiations in response to changed circumstances, could give a better picture of how investment treaties affect investor–state bargaining.[13] We know from other areas that legal options for dispute resolution shape the way that parties bargain toward agreed settlements outside formal adjudication (e.g. Mnookin and Kornhauser 1979; Busch and Reinhardt 2001). Lawyers who act for foreign investors also privately confirm the importance of investment treaties in shaping investor–state bargaining—yet, there has again been little published academic work on such questions.

In sum, debates about the impact of the investment treaty regime on national governance have become heated in recent years. While some of the strong claims made on both sides of the debate are incorrect, the lack of scholarship on several important questions makes a more nuanced appraisal difficult. Further research into normative, legal, and empirical questions is required to better understand the impact of the regime on democracy and the adoption of legitimate regulatory measures.

Investment treaty arbitration as a system of dispute resolution

Apart from the impact of the regime on national governance, a second set of debates focuses on investment treaty arbitration as a way of resolving disputes

---

[12] Such institutional mechanisms include central, inter-departmental monitoring and warning systems (as in Peru) and a dedicated team of in-house investment lawyers (as in Argentina and Poland).

[13] See also Chapter 5 generally, and Figure 5.2 on the distributive impact of investment treaties specifically.

between states and foreign investors. This topic has become particularly pertinent after the EU proposed in September 2015 to replace the existing system of party-appointed arbitrators with standing investment tribunals, which in turn are meant to provide the template for a multilateral investment court (Council of the European Union 2016, para. 6:i). The EU's new PTAs with Canada and Vietnam reflect this new approach.[14] The European Commission justifies the new policy as a way to address what it sees as the 'fundamental lack of trust' by the public in the current investment treaty regime and to provide for dispute settlement 'in full accordance with the rule of law' (European Commission 2016). It launched a public consultation on its multilateral investment court project in December 2016. While the outlines of the investment court system are known, many details still need be worked out at the time of writing.

The new model for investment treaty dispute resolution seeks to address several of the criticisms of investment treaty arbitration that we review in this section. Specifically, the selection of arbitrators at random from a pool of salaried individuals appointed by the state parties is intended to address concerns about arbitrator selection, and the inclusion of an appellate mechanism is intended to ensure consistency across rulings. The EU has also followed the recent practice of other Western states, by insisting on transparency and a loser-pays-costs principle.

While proponents of investment treaty arbitration argue that a system of standing investment tribunals based on the EU's agreements with Canada and Vietnam would depart too far from the status quo (e.g. Brower and Blanchard 2014; EFILA 2015), some critics argue that it does not go far enough (e.g. Van Harten 2015). The prospects of a multilateral investment court are even more uncertain. Changes in the political context in the United States underway at the time this book went to press raise questions about the US's support for major trade and investment agreements, such as the multilateral investment court initiative. In early 2017, the US withdrew its signature to the TPP, stated its intention to re-negotiate NAFTA and froze negotiations of the TTIP. The Trump administration's policies seem to prioritize bilateral negotiations and show an aversion to international dispute settlement (United States 2017). As this book went to press, the EU's ambition for a multilateral investment court also lacked the public support of other key states, like China and India.

Yet, the very existence of this proposal from an actor such as the EU in response to a perceived lack of legitimacy of the status-quo highlights the relevance of ongoing legitimacy debates about investment treaty arbitration as a system of dispute resolution. Although not always articulated, the starting

---

[14] CETA, Article 8.28(1); EUVFTA, Articles 13 and 28. The European Parliament ratified CETA on 15 February 2017, but ratification by Canada and national parliaments of EU member states remain outstanding at the time of writing.

point for this debate is the question of how to conceptualize investment treaty arbitration in the first place. In particular, do arbitrators serve only the disputing parties, or do they also have law-making and governance roles? The answer has critical implications, and therefore needs to be addressed before turning to more specific criticisms of investment treaty arbitration as a dispute settlement mechanism.

THE FUNCTION OF INVESTMENT TREATY ARBITRATION

Arbitration—particularly commercial arbitration—is traditionally conceived as a form of *private* dispute settlement under the control of the disputing parties (see Chapter 3; Ware 1999; Cutler 2003; Lustig and Benvenisti 2014). According to this view, the mandate of party-appointed arbitrators is limited to settling one particular dispute. Some arbitrators continue to see their role in this way also in investment treaty arbitration (e.g. Born 2012, 872). This view implies that tribunals should not consider the governance implications of their decisions (including the interests of third parties) because the outcome of the dispute is only relevant to the disputing parties themselves. Second, for the same reason, transparency in dispute settlement has no particular value. Third, tribunals are limited to applying the law chosen by the disputing parties—that is, the investment treaty and, possibly, any related investment contract—even if the exclusive application of these sources of law rubs up against other domestic and international legal institutions.

Many of the criticisms against investment treaty arbitration flow from an alternative conception of investment treaty arbitration as being more than a mechanism to settle individual disputes. On this alternative view, foreign investors use investment treaty arbitration to challenge the improper exercise of public power by states. Whereas commercial parties traditionally established arbitral tribunals with only two functions in mind—to find facts and settle commercial disputes by applying the law—investment treaty tribunals have two additional functions: to develop the law and to engage in governance (see generally von Bogdandy and Venzke 2012; Alvarez 2014). Only the first two functions are concerned with the disputing parties. The third function, law-making, refers to the role of arbitrators in articulating and clarifying legal principles, which then affect the behaviour of the disputing parties and third parties *ex ante* (Kronstein 1944; Besson 2014; von Bogdandy and Venzke 2014; Schill 2015). The fourth function, governance, refers to their role in endorsing or reflecting certain normative values in the course of developing the law (Alvarez 2014).

In our view, investment treaty tribunals play a law-making role in that they articulate and clarify the meaning of core treaty standards such as FET.[15] The

---

[15] See Chapter 4.

frequency with which these tribunals use awards of other investment treaty tribunals when justifying their interpretation of treaty provisions also confirms this role (e.g. Fauchald 2008). Tribunal decisions also play a governance role, in that certain conceptions of the appropriate exercise of public power inform the way they develop and apply international investment law. As Chapter 4 shows, tribunals endorse and reflect certain normative values—for example, when they interpret core treaty standards such as FET in light of various understandings of 'arbitrariness' in the exercise of public power.

One implication of this broader conception of investment treaty arbitration is that the mechanism should be evaluated in light of norms of accountability, openness, coherence, and independence in adjudication that are central to how other institutions (e.g. domestic courts) review the exercise of public power (Van Harten 2007). Such values may be, but are not necessarily, in tension with other norms that are traditionally associated with the settlement of commercial disputes between private parties—notably, norms emphasizing the value of cheap, swift, predictable, and final resolution of the dispute in question (Alvarez 2016a). In particular, if investment treaty tribunals contribute to the development of international law and the governance of foreign investment, there are important implications for transparency and consistency—the subject of the following sections.

TRANSPARENCY

As Chapter 3 described, the degree of transparency in investment treaty arbitration varies somewhat, depending on the arbitration rules and the applicable investment treaty. Until recently, however, confidentiality was the norm. This was a remnant of the commercial arbitration paradigm from which investment treaty arbitration borrowed heavily in procedural terms (Roberts 2013). Given the flexibility of investment treaty arbitration, the disputing parties in investment treaty arbitration could in principle agree to a greater degree of transparency than required by the arbitral rules or the investment treaty. ICSID streamed parts of the Vattenfall II case against Germany online. Yet, this rarely happens. One of the disputing parties invariably has some individual interest in keeping the proceedings confidential—possibly to avoid embarrassment or external criticism, or to seek a tactical advantage. Consequently, the existence, content, and outcome of investment treaty arbitrations are sometimes hidden from the public—unlike domestic litigation.[16]

---

[16] However, as Chapter 3 explained, the degree of transparency of domestic civil proceedings also varies.

This precludes scholars and the wider public from debating and critically scrutinizing at least some awards. The lack of transparency in investment treaty arbitration has therefore been a major concern among critics since the early 2000s (DePalma 2001; The Economist 2009; Rowley 2013; Wallach and Beachy 2013; Hamby 2016a).

As a result of these criticisms, the level of transparency in investment treaty arbitrations is set to increase due to the UNCITRAL Transparency Rules and the Mauritius Transparency Convention. Although the application of these initiatives still remains severely limited in practice,[17] they have nevertheless significantly changed public debate about the regime. In contrast to the situation only a decade ago, lack of transparency in investment treaty arbitration is no longer among the main concerns that critics of investment treaties raise (e.g. Alliance for Justice 2015; Schneiderman, Tienhaara, and Van Harten 2015).

Despite the waning public attention towards transparency in the investment treaty regime, or perhaps exactly because of it, we need a more fine-grained understanding of how transparency under the main arbitral rules in investment treaty arbitration compares to transparency in civil proceedings across jurisdictions (which, as noted in Chapter 3, is not uniform). Some studies have begun to apply empirical methods to assess the circumstances under which tribunals rely on each other's rulings, with transparency being a precondition for such cross-fertilization (e.g. Commission 2007; Fauchald 2008). Others have looked into party preferences for opacity (Hafner-Burton, Steinert-Threkheld, and Victor 2016). Yet, important questions remain unanswered.

Two categories of questions arise. The first is about what drives transparency or opacity in investment treaties and arbitral rules. For instance, do states that include greater transparency provisions in their investment treaties have common characteristics? And with respect to arbitral rules, what role did the reputational concerns of arbitrators, law firms, and states play in the drafting and adoption of the UNCITRAL Transparency Rules and the Mauritius Transparency Convention? Equally, was the outcome of the UNCITRAL initiatives influenced by some states appointing investment arbitrators as their representatives in these negotiations?

A second set of questions relates to the impact of transparency on investment treaty arbitration. For instance, does public knowledge of the existence or the content of arbitrations threaten to embarrass or put pressure on the state and/or the investor, and if so, what are the implications for normative questions of whether transparency is desirable? Also, what is the impact of the recent partial turn towards transparency? Does it increase consistency of arbitral awards and spillovers, and, if so, how (see the following text)? Does it affect the cost and length of arbitrations? Relatedly, do arbitrators adopt

---

[17] See Chapter 3.

different (or more extensive) reasoning in their awards or respond otherwise to legitimacy concerns as a result of greater transparency (e.g. Langford and Behn 2016)? Finally, do transparency requirements in investment treaty arbitration result in greater use of ADR, including informal negotiations and settlement? These are all critical questions for future research.

CONSISTENCY

A related, and more persistent, criticism of investment treaty arbitration concerns the sometimes inconsistent decisions by tribunals (e.g. Franck 2007). The decentralized nature of the investment treaty regime gives rise to possibilities of forum shopping (Busch 2007; Pauwelyn and Salles 2009), parallel proceedings (McLachlan 2009), and the persistence of different interpretations of common treaty provisions (Dupuy and Viñuales 2014). This can result in inconsistent decisions. Following Reinisch (2010), we can distinguish three different types of inconsistency, which are potentially problematic from a regime perspective:

1. *Inconsistency in interpreting investment treaty provisions*: Different tribunals interpret identical or near-identical provisions of different treaties in different ways. Examples include divergent decisions on umbrella clauses and MFN provisions (see Chapter 4).
2. *Inconsistency in fact-finding*: Tribunals assess the same facts under the same legal standard differently. An example is when tribunals reached different conclusions on whether the response of Argentina to its financial crisis fell within the non-precluded measures clause of the US–Argentina BIT (see again Chapter 4).
3. *Inconsistency in outcomes*: Tribunals issue contradictory decisions in essentially the same dispute. This can happen when different entities within a single corporate chain bring arbitrations under different investment treaties containing near-identical provisions. An oft-cited example is the two arbitrations against the Czech Republic mentioned in Chapter 1, where a Dutch company brought a successful arbitration under the Czech–Netherlands BIT (*CME v. Czech Republic* 2001), even though the majority shareholder of the company had been unsuccessful in a separate arbitration under the Czech–US BIT in relation to the same facts (*Lauder v. Czech Republic* 2001).

The potential for all three types of inconsistency arises from the lack of an anchor organization or appellate body with the power to resolve inconsistency across disputes under more than 3000 investment treaties.

Commentators disagree as to how serious the problem of inconsistency is. First, conceptualizations of investment treaty arbitration differ, as we explained earlier. If investment treaty tribunals are solely charged with settling individual disputes—as some arbitrators argue—none of the three forms of inconsistencies would significantly undermine the legitimacy of the regime. However, if tribunals have law-making functions and contribute to governance in the investment treaty regime, as is our view, then inconsistency could be a cause for concern. In particular, the potential for all three types of inconsistency makes it more difficult for states to comply with their investment treaties *ex ante*.

Second, existing research leaves major gaps in our understanding of consistency in investment treaty arbitration. At a basic level, the very notion of consistency has not been subject to sufficient critical examination. More comparisons with domestic legal systems would be useful to understand the extent of the problem. Also helpful would be a clearer understanding of whether and why certain types of inconsistencies are more problematic than others. For instance, are inconsistent interpretations more problematic from a normative perspective than inconsistent outcomes? Equally, what is the relationship between inconsistency and regulatory chill? Greater consistency reduces uncertainty about the scope of investment treaties, which could, in turn, reduce regulatory chill if states are risk-averse. But greater consistency could also increase regulatory chill if tribunals' rulings are consistently constraining.

Third, and relatedly, what are the underlying causes of inconsistency? Here, two factors are particularly relevant: the role of arbitrators and the design of investment treaties. With respect to the first, one view is that inconsistency is less of a problem than is often suggested because the interpretation of common treaty provisions will converge over time due to a closely knit 'community' of investment law arbitrators (Schill 2011; cf. also Commission 2007; Fauchald 2008). We will return to this 'community' in more detail in the following text, but this proposition should be subject to empirical testing. Is it really the case that arbitral tribunals resolve inconsistencies over time, rather than exacerbate them? Or do patterns of convergence/divergence vary across provisions and issues? Another observable implication of this theory would be that tribunals with members within the 'core' of the investment law 'community' are more likely to produce consistent decisions than tribunals consisting of 'outsiders'.

Another view is that inconsistency will characterize the investment treaty regime as long as states include varying provisions in their investment treaties (Kaufmann-Kohler 2008; Banifatemi 2013; Schreuer 2013; Vadi 2015, 240). This, again, is an empirical proposition that scholars should scrutinize. The challenge, of course, is to identify arbitrations that are similar in relevant respects except for the design of the underlying treaties. These, too, are critical questions for future research so as to develop a better understanding of the drivers and effects of inconsistency in the investment treaty regime.

REGIME SPILLOVERS

In addition to consistency *within* the investment treaty regime, a related—but broader—set of issues concern the impact of investment treaty arbitration on the wider investment regime complex. As Chapter 1 described, this complex of regimes includes various codes of investor conduct, regional institutions, trade agreements, finance and debt agreements, double taxation treaties, international insurance, as well as human rights and environmental agreements, all of which relate to the governance of foreign investment. Arguments for consistency *between* regimes are arguably less compelling than those for consistency within a regime, because different regimes may impose different rules on different actors to achieve different purposes (e.g. Ratner 2008). However, not all regimes are equally effective in achieving their purposes. And because the investment treaty regime contains a powerful international mechanism for binding and enforceable dispute settlement, the regime is more likely to create spillovers to other parts of the investment regime complex.

In general terms, spillovers from one regime to another can be divided into synergies ('positive' spillovers) and conflicts ('negative' spillovers) (see generally Johnson and Urpelainen 2012; Gómez-Mera 2015). Synergies occur when the investment treaty regime promotes the goals of other parts of the investment regime complex (e.g. providing protections that fill some of the 'gaps' in political risk insurance). Conflicts occur when the regime impedes such goals (e.g. protecting tax haven investors may complicate international tax governance).[18] Yet, very little research has been undertaken on the extent of such spillovers from the investment treaty regime. To illustrate why this is a major gap, consider the following three examples.

The first is the human rights regime. If a foreign investor brings a successful investment treaty arbitration arising from interference with its human rights—for example, if the host state interfered with a foreign media company's right of free expression—there is a synergy between the investment treaty regime and the human rights regime. At the time of writing, Al Jazeera was pursuing such an arbitration against Egypt under the Egypt–Qatar BIT (Bollinger and Sauvant 2016). However, in mapping the spillovers between the investment treaty regime and the human rights regime, recall that investment treaties provide limited protection to the human rights of only one particular, and often powerful, group of actors—namely, foreign investors (Alvarez 1997). And when foreign investors use investment treaties to oppose or challenge host state measures intended to protect or promote the human rights of other actors, negative spillovers from the investment treaty to the

---

[18] Whether the goals are normatively desirable is irrelevant from this perspective; the focus is on the effectiveness of institutions, which is understood as their ability to reduce or solve the problems they were created to address. See, generally, Levy, Young, and Zürn (1995).

human rights regime can result. For example, foreign utility firms have relied on investment treaties to oppose universal access requirements designed to ensure the adequate supply of drinking water to poor or remote communities (Meshel 2015).

Second, the investment treaty regime partially supports the WTO's goal of establishing an international economic order underpinned by principles of non-discrimination. But it also conflicts with this goal by providing foreign investors with enforceable protections that go well beyond prohibitions on discrimination and that potentially limit the ability of states to impose non-discriminatory regulations on foreign investment (see Chapter 4 on FET and indirect expropriation; see generally Kurtz 2016; Puig 2015).

Third, arbitral tribunals have held that sovereign debt owed to foreign creditors qualifies as an 'investment' under investment treaties. Such protection of debt instruments could complement the international sovereign debt regime if increased creditor rights facilitate the ability of debtor states to raise money in international capital markets. Negative spillovers could also arise, however, if investment treaty arbitration allows foreign hold-out creditors to obtain full repayment of sovereign debt following a restructuring facilitated by the IMF and the Paris Club and agreed by a supermajority of creditors (Waibel 2007a).

The impact of investment treaty arbitration on the investment regime complex varies not only with treaty texts but potentially also with how arbitrators understand their own function. Arbitrators who see themselves as solely involved in settling disputes may be discouraged from considering other bodies of law that specify the rights and obligations of both investors and host states vis-à-vis third parties (recall that only investors have standing to bring arbitrations, and not host states). For example, in *Micula v. Romania* (2013), Romania's suspension of subsidies to a Swedish foreign investor breached an investment treaty, even though the EU Commission had required Romania to terminate the subsidies because they constituted illegal state aid under EU law. This could be characterized as a negative spillover effect from the investment treaty regime to the EU. By contrast, arbitrators attuned to their law-making and governance functions may be more inclined to consider their impact on the broader investment regime complex. Determining whether and under what circumstances investment treaty arbitrators should consider these impacts in their decisions raise a series of thorny and inter-twined legal and normative issues (see e.g. Alvarez 2016a).[19]

---

[19] A normative implication that follows from the law-making and governance functions of investment treaty arbitration is that arbitrators should consider the impact of their rulings on states, persons, or entities not directly represented in the case before them (Alvarez 2005, 528–9). Consistent with this view, investment treaties have begun to confer the power on arbitral tribunals to accept *amicus curiae* submissions from individuals or entities that are not parties to the dispute; for example, CAFTA 2004,

In short, the relationships between the investment treaty regime and the broader investment regime complex are important but understudied. Future research should consider not just (i) where and how legal institutions within the investment regime complex create synergies and conflicts with investment treaty texts and arbitral awards; but also (ii) why and how states and other actors facilitate spillovers from the investment treaty regime in the first place (see generally Benvenisti and Downs 2007; Helfer 2009; Gehring and Faude 2014; Ranganathan 2014); and (iii) how spillovers affect the distribution of benefits and impact different actors, institutions, and processes in domestic and international arenas across the investment regime complex (see generally Alter and Meunier 2009; Jinnah 2011b).

ARBITRATOR SELECTION

In addition to questions of transparency, consistency, and regime spillovers, normative debates about the legitimacy of the investment regime have in recent years focused on the backgrounds and beliefs of arbitrators themselves (Pauwelyn 2015; Venzke 2016). These debates are rooted in an underlying assumption that third-party adjudicators are not necessarily neutral and disinterested parties. And, indeed, a large literature shows that the personal motives and characteristics of adjudicators can shape the outcomes of legal disputes across a wide range of fields (e.g. Farhang and Wawro 2004; Sunstein et al. 2006; Voeten 2008).

Before reviewing criticisms of the status quo, let us first consider some of the arguments from supporters of the current system of party-appointed arbitrators. As in previous sections, many of these arguments follow from a particular conception of investment treaty arbitration. Defenders of party appointments often rely on the traditional conception of arbitration as a form of *private* dispute settlement in which the mandate of a tribunal is limited to settling a *particular* dispute. As Veeder (2013, 401) puts it, 'the right of each party to appoint an arbitrator makes the arbitration the *parties'* arbitration, deciding *their* dispute with *their* tribunal'. Defenders of party appointments also contend that each party's ability to appoint its 'own' arbitrator gives each party confidence that its arguments have had a fair hearing within the tribunal and, thus, increases the likelihood that the losing party complies with the tribunal's award (e.g. Posner and Yoo 2005; Shany 2008). This latter proposition is an empirical question, which has yet to be subject to rigorous scrutiny.[20]

Article 10.20(3). This is not the same, however, as suggesting that arbitrators should consider the impact of their rulings on other regimes.

[20] Moreover, this argument does not provide a reason for allowing an investor to appoint an arbitrator. Because only investors can initiate investment treaty arbitration, questions of compliance

A different argument in favour of party appointments is that it prevents all arbitrators from being dependent on states for their appointment. As alluded to earlier, this argument has become particularly pertinent after the European Commission (2015a) suggested a standing international investment court, where investors have no role in appointing tribunal members. According to supporters of the existing party-appointment model, such alternative arrangements 'may undermine the very foundations of arbitration (and of justice): the equality of arms between the parties' (EFILA 2015, 23). This normative argument has some uncomfortable implications, however. If one accepts that 'justice' and 'the equality of arms' require that states have no greater influence than plaintiffs over the choice of tenured judges, it seems to follow that courts such as the German Bundesverfassungsgericht and the US Supreme Court are not legitimate fora to resolve claims against states. Such views have little resonance outside debates about investment treaties, and are inconsistent with the ordinary role of courts in reviewing state conduct in democratic societies. Even if domestic courts lack independence, it does not follow that foreign investors themselves—as opposed to the home state of the investor—should be able to influence the composition of investment treaty tribunals.

That said, important arguments have been made in favour of the existing system of party-appointments in investment treaty arbitration—notably, those that draw attention to its simplicity and flexibility (American Bar Association 2016). It is therefore important to carefully scrutinize criticisms against the status quo. Here, we briefly address three criticisms relating to: (i) the dependence of arbitrators on the disputing party that appoints them; (ii) the career and financial incentives of arbitrators; and (iii) the link between arbitrator background and arbitration outcomes, including the exclusive 'community' of elite arbitrators. All are critical for legitimacy discussions about investment treaty arbitration.

The first line of criticism concerns arbitrator moral hazard—the idea that party-appointments for individual cases encourages each party to identify and appoint individuals who are (at least perceived to be) sympathetic to their position (Paulsson 2010). For instance, parties may favour arbitrators who share a similar legal or cultural background (Bishop and Reed 1998, 395; Blackaby and Partasides 2015, para 4.76). Accordingly, the interests of party-appointed arbitrators may be closely aligned with their appointing party, as was the case in inter-state arbitrations in the nineteenth century when arbitrators often assumed the mantle of advocates for their appointing parties (Alter 2008; Shany 2008).

---

with adverse awards arise mostly in relation to states. That said, tribunals sometimes order investors to pay costs.

Concerns with moral hazard run somewhat contrary to a second criticism, which focuses on the financial and career incentives of arbitrators considered as a group (Van Harten 2007, 152–3; Sornarajah 2008, 218; see generally Blanes i Vidal, Draca, and Fons-Rosen 2012). When interpreting and applying investment treaty provisions, full-time arbitrators who earn fees for each arbitration may have an incentive to expand the scope of the regime so as to facilitate more arbitrations and thus potential appointments for themselves (Drahozal 2004). Part-time arbitrators could have similar incentives as expansive interpretations not only mean future appointments but also an overall expansion of the field from which they derive income as lawyers and experts. A particular concern may arise when arbitrators wear 'multiple hats' in investment treaty arbitration by also representing investors. An analogous situation in domestic legal systems would be if a judge could also represent claimants against the state—or the state against claimants—in which case the neutrality of the judge may be in doubt.

Finally, a third, and broader, strand of criticism centres on the backgrounds and homogeneity of arbitrators. Sixty six per cent of ICSID arbitrators have been OECD nationals (Waibel and Wu 2012), 63 per cent have been practicing lawyers, and 26 per cent have been academics (Puig 2014, 405; Franck et al. 2015, 446). Other common traits of investment arbitrators include a high incidence of elite education, particularly for arbitrators from developing or transition countries.[21] The gender gap is wide: 93 per cent of arbitral appointments went to men, and two women account for three-quarters of all female appointments (Puig 2014, 405; see generally Grossman 2016). Arbitrators of Asian or African nationality are under-represented, despite significant inward and investment flows to and from Asia in particular, and associated investment treaty disputes. This homogeneity of investment arbitrators is all the more striking when compared with WTO panellists (Costa 2011; Pauwelyn 2015). Moreover, many arbitrators share similar professional backgrounds (Sornarajah 2006b, 341; Tienhaara 2009, 206). Of the 536 individuals appointed to ICSID tribunals at the time of writing, only 25 per cent have been public international lawyers; 11 per cent have been public lawyers, whereas the remaining arbitrators have mostly specialized in commercial law (Waibel and Wu 2012).[22]

---

[21] More than one-third of all ICSID arbitrators have degrees from only five universities (Cambridge, Harvard, Oxford, Stanford, and Yale) (Waibel and Wu 2012).

[22] The percentage of public international lawyers has not increased over time. Of the 50 arbitrators appointed to ICSID tribunals for the first time over the period 2008–2016, only 18 per cent have been specialists in international law, and only 6 per cent have been public lawyers. Yet, of the 21 elite arbitrators in Table 1.4, 38 per cent are specialists in public international law, and 70 per cent have been in full-time private practice before becoming—for the most part—full-time arbitrators (Waibel and Wu 2012).

These characteristics could matter when arbitrators look for answers to difficult and new questions, particularly when interpreting and applying open-ended standards of treatment such as indirect expropriation or FET. For instance, a background in commercial law might render some arbitrators less sympathetic to interests outside their traditional domains, such as human rights law, or less willing to consider the impact of their awards on other parts of the investment regime complex. More broadly, critics contend that the homogeneity among arbitrators could create—in appearance or in reality—a pro-investor bias in investment treaty arbitration and undermine the objective of a neutral forum for dispute resolution (Franck et al. 2015).

In addition to shared professional backgrounds, many arbitrators are arguably part of a closely knit network characterized by shared values and frequent and overlapping personal connections (Borgen 2007; Puig 2014). This is particularly important when considering the remarkably high re-appointment rate within the investment treaty regime, where a small group of individuals decide a very large share of all investment treaty arbitrations (see Table 1.4).[23] That states have delegated law-making and governance functions to such a small group of lawyers, most of who are in commercial practice, is an ongoing source of controversy.

Some of the arguments by proponents and critics of the system of party appointments have begun to be subject to empirical testing (e.g. Franck 2007; 2009; Kapeliuk 2010; 2012; Van Harten 2012; Puig and Strezhnev 2016a; 2016b; Tucker 2016). Yet, we still know very little about three core questions. First, the track record of appointments and awards suggest that at least some arbitrators position themselves as pro-investor or pro-host state arbitrators, whereas others position themselves as 'neutrals' (Puig 2014; Abi-Saab 2015; Dupuy and Maupin 2015; Waibel and Wu 2012).[24] However, we know little at present about the role of financial and career incentives for arbitrators, and how they relate to outcomes. Recent experimental research lends some initial weight to the hypothesis that arbitrators are influenced by who appointed them (Puig and Strezhnev 2016a). Yet, any explanatory theory of the balance of career and professional incentives facing the tribunal as a whole needs to also consider the incentives of arbitrators marketing themselves as 'neutral'—particularly those who are regularly appointed as presiding arbitrators. (Recall that tribunals decide by majority. In the event of disagreement between the arbitrator appointed by the investor and the arbitrator appointed by the host state, the views of the presiding arbitrator are likely to be decisive.) In a recent

---

[23] Between 1972 and 2011, 372 individuals sat as ICSID arbitrators, yet only 37 of these arbitrators accounted for 50 per cent of all appointments (Puig 2014, 407).

[24] 'Neutral' here is used in a very narrow sense, as between the disputing parties in relation to a particular dispute at the time of appointment. It does not imply neutrality in a wider sense—for example, 'neutral' as between the interests of the disputing parties and the interests of those who are not parties to the dispute.

empirical contribution, Donaubauer, Neumayer and Nunnenkamp (2017) suggest that the previous experience and 'bias' of the presiding arbitrator have a significant impact on the outcome of investment treaty arbitrations. Future studies could also consider the relevance of the policies and practices of the default appointing authority that appoints the presiding arbitrator when the disputing parties cannot reach an agreement (see Chapter 3).

Second, there is little systematic evidence on whether, and to what extent, arbitrator backgrounds and social interactions have an impact on investment treaty arbitration. Assessing these questions will be riddled with methodological challenges. What is bias, and how do we measure it? For instance, does statistical analysis of only those cases that result in final awards allow us to meaningfully assess bias, given that parties that expect to lose are more likely to settle (Strezhnev 2016)? Also, what are the relevant arbitrator characteristics to consider? Is it really relevant where an arbitrator was born (as Franck 2009 tested), or are their education, socio-economic backgrounds, and social interactions more important? How can researchers account for dynamics between tribunal members, and to what extent can outsiders assess bias from awards when many of the deciding facts of the case may not be made public. These are but some of the thorny questions about the role of arbitrator backgrounds and interactions that a combination of qualitative, quantitative, and experimental research has yet to address.

Finally, even in the absence of actual bias, critics argue that party-appointed arbitrators risk being *perceived* as biased, thereby undermining perceptions that the investment treaty regime as a whole is neutral and legitimate, which in turn may risk compliance (Van Harten 2007; Paulsson 2010; Smit 2010; van den Berg 2011). Just like the opposite proposition by defenders of party appointments—that is, that legitimacy and compliance are promoted through party appointments—this has yet to be subjected to empirical testing. Here, the EU's standing investment court could provide a counter-factual if it materializes.

INVESTOR OBLIGATIONS

Finally, we turn to another influential criticism of the investment treaty regime: that it lacks binding investor obligations. In some limited circumstances, host states can raise investor misconduct as a bar to a tribunal hearing a case—for example, if the investor acquired the investment by corrupt means or, possibly, in breach of domestic law. The investment treaty regime thereby complements efforts to promote responsible investment in the minimal sense that investors who wish to ensure they retain their option to initiate investment treaty arbitration must avoid such forms of misconduct. However, investor treaties do not create investor obligations that can be enforced by host states acting on their own initiative.[25] Almost since their inception in the mid-twentieth century, critics have contended that this exclusive focus on investor rights in investment treaties makes them 'unbalanced' instruments (e.g. UNCTC 1984, 8; Stiglitz 2007, 536–40; Miles 2013, 348–72). As with the criticisms described earlier, this raises important questions that have yet to be assessed in detail.

First, is it in fact necessary to give states the right to file arbitrations under investment treaties to achieve 'balance'? As Chapter 3 notes, host states are generally able to bring proceedings in their own courts against foreign investors present in their territory.[26] Critics are sometimes unclear why this avenue is inadequate. One possible answer is that, if the foreign investor lacks assets in the territory of the host state,[27] the host government may need to enforce any decision against the foreign investor outside its own jurisdiction. In these circumstances, it may be easier for a host state to enforce the ruling of a 'neutral' international tribunal abroad than one of a 'politicized' domestic court (Toral and Schultz 2010).

Even if a normative case can be made for including investor obligations in investment treaties, such proposals raise legal difficulties. The ICSID Convention does not rule out state claims against investors, for instance, but they are only possible if both parties have consented to the arbitration of such claims. As Chapter 3 describes, investors consent to states' 'standing offer' to investment treaty arbitration by initiating the arbitration. For states to be able to initiate arbitrations against investors, the consent of investors to such arbitration claims would need be obtained by other means. Although this is possible in principle—for instance, by drafting investment treaties in a way that requires foreign investors to give advance consent to arbitration at the point of admission of their investment in order to be covered by the protection of the investment treaty—such a system would create additional administrative burdens for host states.

Even if a system were established to secure investors' advance consent to arbitration, further questions arise as to the types of investor obligations that should be included. A first option could be a 'reverse umbrella clause', where an investor's alleged breach of contract, and possibly even an investor's alleged breach of obligations under national law, could be the basis for a treaty claim (Laborde 2010). Yet, this route would be fraught with difficulties, particularly

---

[25] Host states can formulate so-called counterclaims in limited circumstances in investment treaty arbitrations initiated by investors.

[26] Moreover, in some very narrowly defined situations, investors may also be subject to proceedings initiated by non-state plaintiffs in home state courts for their extraterritorial activities—examples include claims under the US Alien Torts Claims Act and tort claims in a range of common law jurisdictions alleging liability for extraterritorial harm resulting from decisions made by business executives within the territory of the home state.

[27] A related issue is that the investor may be a limited liability company incorporated in a jurisdiction different from its ultimate parent.

in light of the concerns about 'ordinary' umbrella clauses that Chapter 4 reviewed. A second option is to include binding investor obligations in investment treaties that are derived from other parts of the investment regime complex—for instance, obligations defined by reference to the UN Guiding Principles on Business and Human Rights or the OECD's Guidelines for Multinational Enterprises (see e.g. IISD 2005).[28] A third possibility is for investment treaties to endorse such instruments in investment treaties, without attempting to render them enforceable through arbitration. Although significantly less ambitious, such an approach might still be useful in establishing a focal point in investment treaties for social expectations about responsible business conduct, which in theory could strengthen non-legal forms of accountability for corporate misconduct.

Future research could usefully inform debate about these questions. First, it would be helpful to investigate why hardly any of the over 3000 existing investment treaties include binding investor obligations.[29] Second, is it possible to assess the impact of those few investment treaties that do include investor obligations?[30] Even without formal treaty claims brought against investors, we know from the human rights regime that non-legal channels of accountability can be important to ensure treaty compliance (Simmons 2009). Third, in line with the observations about arbitrator characteristics in the preceding text, is it possible to identify systematic differences in the extent to which arbitrators consider instruments from other parts of the investment regime complex pertaining to investor obligations? Fourth, and finally, does the exclusive focus of investment treaties on the rights of foreign investors have implications for efforts to promote international standards of responsible investor conduct through initiatives? In other words, does the 'unbalanced' nature of investment treaties have negative spillovers to initiatives such as the UN Guiding Principles on Business and Human Rights and the UN Global Compact?

All in all, debates about investment treaty arbitration as a dispute settlement mechanism are as heated as they are complex. Some criticisms may be misguided, whereas others warrant serious attention. As with discussions about the impact of investment treaties on national governance, it is critical

---

[28] The Guiding Principles cover only human rights while the OECD Guidelines cover a wide range of corporate misconduct. In addition, in July 2014, the Human Rights Council established a working group to come up with a binding instrument on MNCs and human rights. The outcome of this initiative is difficult to predict, but there has been some discussion on whether human rights should have 'primacy' over international investment treaties.

[29] For instance, India scrapped plans to include binding investor obligations in the 2015 Indian Model BIT after a critical review by the Indian Law Commission (Law Commission of India 2015).

[30] For example, the plurilateral investment treaty among member states of the Islamic Conference (Article 9), and particularly the South African Development Community (SADC) Model BIT (Articles 10, 15, and 17).

that further research be conducted into the normative, legal, and empirical effects of this potent but controversial dispute settlement mechanism.

Conclusion

Competing forces are at work in the investment treaty regime. On the one hand, the intensifying criticism of the regime even in Europe, where the regime was created, and in the United States, reminds us that it is a fragile construct. There may be thousands of treaties in place, but many of them are due for renewal in the coming years. The 'modern' investment treaty regime is also young; it was only from the 1980s that investment treaties began to commonly include investor–state arbitration provisions, and the number of investment treaty arbitrations has grown rapidly only since the early 2000s. If the controversy intensifies, the regime could unravel just as quickly as it was established.

On the other hand, recent European proposals remind us that, despite the heated debates about the regime, most reforms have remained partial and incremental to date. Hardly any country has begun to revisit whether foreign investors should in fact have substantive treaty protections that go beyond guarantees of non-discrimination. The majority of states continue to favour a dispute settlement system that gives foreign investors direct standing to bring arbitrations against host states without investors having to exhaust local remedies. Equally, states have not, on the whole, attempted to 'rebalance' the regime to focus more on legally binding investor obligations. Only very few states have begun to terminate their agreements outright. Whether such path dependency is a boon or a threat to the governance of the investment treaty regime remains to be seen, but outside observers could be forgiven for considering ongoing reforms as little more than tinkering at the margins.

Whatever the future holds for the investment treaty regime, any assessment of the status quo and its alternatives requires scholars and stakeholders to appreciate both the law and the political economy of the regime. Lawyers need to understand the economics and politics of both foreign investment and investment treaties, and those without a legal background need to be familiar with the basic legal features of the regime. Our aim in this book has been to fill some of the gaps in understanding among members of both groups. In addition, our mapping and synthesis of the existing academic literature shows that many important questions about the regime remain unanswered, particularly those relating to its political and economic implications. In doing so, we hope to have contributed to a more informed debate about the past, present, and future of this crucial regime underwriting economic globalization.

BIBLIOGRAPHY

2016. 'TPP gives no ground for legal disputes: Robb', http://www.skynews.com.au/news/top-stories/2016/02/04/robb-says-australia-won-t-be-sued-under-tpp.html (4 February), last accessed 10 March 2017.

1995. 'Pakistan, Kyrgyzstan sign pact on reciprocal protection of investment', *Business Recorder*, 27 August.

Abbott, Kenneth W. and Duncan Snidal. 2000. 'Hard and soft law in international governance', *International Organization* 54, 421–56.

Abbott, Kenneth W. 2008. 'Enriching rational choice institutionalism for the study of international law', *University of Illinois Law Review* 5, 5–46.

Abbott, Kenneth W., Robert O. Keohane, Andrew Moravcsik, Anne-Marie Slaughter, and Duncan Snidal. 2000. 'The concept of legalization', *International Organization* 54, 401–19.

Abdelal, Rawi. 2007. *Capital Rules: The Construction of Global Finance*, Cambridge: Harvard University Press.

Abi-Saab, Georges. 2015. 'The Third World intellectual in praxis: confrontation, participation or operation behind enemy lines?', keynote address at the American University in Cairo, Third World Approaches to International Law on Praxis and the Intellectual, 21–24 February. On file with the authors.

Ahlquist, John S. and Aseem Prakash. 2010. 'FDI and the costs of contract enforcement in developing countries', *Policy Sciences* 43, 181–200.

Aisbett, Emma. 2009. 'Bilateral investment treaties and foreign direct investment: correlation versus causation' in Karl Sauvant and Lisa Sachs (eds.), *The Effect of Treaties on Foreign Direct Investment: Bilateral Investment Treaties, Double Taxation Treaties and Investment Flows*. Oxford University Press.

Aisbett, Emma. 2013. ISDS Through the Lens of Welfare Economics. Conference paper given at 21st Investment Treaty Forum Public Meeting: The Economic and Financial Aspects of Investor-State Arbitration, British Institute of International and Comparative Law, 24 October. On file with the authors.

Aisbett, Emma, Larry Karp, and Carol McAusland. 2010a. 'Police powers, regulatory taking and the efficient compensation of domestic and foreign investors', *The Economic Record* 86, 367–83.

Aisbett, Emma, Larry Karp, and Carol McAusland. 2010b. 'Compensation for regulatory taking in international investment agreements: implications of national treatment and rights to invest', *Journal of Globalization and Development* 1, 1–33.

Aisbett, Emma and Lauge Poulsen. 2016. 'Are aliens mistreated'. On file with the authors.

Aisbett, Emma and Carol McAusland. 2013. 'Firm characteristics and influence on government rule-making: theory and evidence', *European Journal of Political Economy* 29, 214–35.

Aitken, Brian and Ann Harrison. 1999. 'Do domestic firms benefit from direct foreign investment? Evidence from Venezuela', *The American Economic Review* 89, 605–18.

Aitken, Brian, Ann Harrison, and Robert E. Lipsey. 1996. 'Wages and foreign ownership. A comparative study of Mexico, Venezuela, and the United States', *Journal of International Economics* 40, 345–71.

Aizenman, Joshua, Yothin Jinjarak, and Donghyun Park. 2013. 'Capital flows and economic growth in the era of financial integration and crisis, 1990–2010', *Open Economies Review* 24, 371–96.

Akpinar, Hasan. 2001. 'Turkey's experience with bilateral investment treaties', paper presented at the OECD Investment Compact Regional Roundtable, 28–29 May, Dubrovnik. On file with the authors.

Al-Sadig, Ali. 2013. 'Outward foreign direct investment and domestic investment: the case of developing countries', *Working Paper WP/13/52*, Washington, DC: International Monetary Fund.

Albuquerque, Rui. 2003. 'The composition of international capital flows: risk sharing through foreign direct investment', *Journal of International Economics* 61, 353–83.

Alden, Edward. 2005. 'US faces tough talks with Egypt in its push for regional trade accords', *The Financial Post*, 29 September.

Alessi, Christopher and Beina Xu. 2015. 'China in Africa', Council on Foreign Relations Backgrounders. Available at http://www.cfr.org/china/china-africa/p9557.

Alfaro, Laura. 2014. 'Foreign direct investment: effects, complementarities, and promotion', *Harvard Business School Working Paper* 15-006.

Alfaro, Laura and Andrew Charlton. 2007. 'International financial integration and entrepreneurial firm activity', *Harvard Business School Working Paper* 07-012.

Alfaro, Laura and Andrew Charlton. 2013. 'Growth and the quality of foreign direct investment: is all FDI equal?' in Joseph Stiglitz and Justin Lin Yifu (eds.), *The Industrial Policy Revolution I: The Role of Government Beyond Ideology*. London, New York: Palgrave Macmillan.

Alfaro, Laura, Areendam Chanda, Sebnem Kalemli-Ozcan, and Selin Sayek. 2010. 'Does foreign direct investment promote growth? Exploring the role of financial markets on linkages', *Journal of Development Economics* 91, 242–56.

Alfaro, Laura and Maggie X. Chen. 2015. 'Market reallocation and knowledge spillover: the gains from multinational production', *Harvard Business School BGIE Unit Working Paper No. 12*.

Alfaro, Laura, Sebnem Kalemli-Ozcan, and Vadym Volosovych. 2008. 'Why doesn't capital flow from rich to poor countries? An empirical investigation', *The Review of Economics and Statistics* 90, 347–68.

Allee, Todd and Manfred Elsig. 2015. 'Dispute settlement provisions in PTAs' in Andreas Dür and Manfred Elsig (eds.), *Trade Cooperation: The Purpose, Design and Effects of Preferential Trade Agreements*. Cambridge University Press.

Allee, Todd and Paul K. Huth. 2006. 'Legitimizing dispute settlement: international legal rulings as domestic political cover', *American Political Science Review* 100, 219–34.

Allee, Todd and Andrew Lugg. 2016. 'Who wrote the rules for the Trans-Pacific Partnership?', *Research & Politics* 3, 1–9.

Allee, Todd and Clint Peinhardt. 2010. 'Delegating differences: bilateral investment treaties and bargaining over dispute resolution provisions', *International Studies Quarterly* 54, 1–26.

Allee, Todd and Clint Peinhardt. 2011. 'Contingent credibility: the impact of investment treaty violations on foreign direct investment', *International Organization* 65, 401–32.

Allee, Todd and Manfred Elsig. 2016. 'Are the contents of international treaties copied-and-pasted? Evidence from preferential trade agreements', *Working Paper*, August 2016. On file with the authors.

Allen, Tom. 2000. *The Right to Property in Commonwealth Constitutions*. Cambridge University Press.

Allende, Salvador. 1972. Address of the President of the Republic of Chile, UN General Assembly, Twenty-Seventh Session, 4 December, UN Doc A/PV.2096.

Alliance for Justice. 2015. 'Letter from law professors to congressional leaders regarding the opposition to inclusion of ISDS provisions in TTP and TTIP', 11 March. Available at http://www.afj.org/wp-content/uploads/2015/03/ISDS-Letter-3.11.pdf.

Alschner, Wolfgang. 2013. 'Americanization of the BIT universe: the influence of friendship, commerce and navigation (FCN) treaties on modern investment treaty law', *Goettingen Journal of International Law* 5, 455–86.

Alschner, Wolfgang. 2016. 'The impact of investment arbitration on investment treaty design: myth versus reality', *Yale Journal of International Law*, forthcoming.

Alschner, Wolfgang and Dmitriy Skougarevskiy. 2015. 'Consistency and legal innovation in the BIT universe', *Stanford Public Law Working Paper No.* 2595288.

Alschner, Wolfgang and Dmitriy Skougarevskiy. 2016. 'The new gold standard? Empirically situating the TPP in the investment treaty universe', *Journal of World Investment and Trade* 17, 339–73.

Alter, Karen J. 1998. 'Who are the "masters of the treaty"? European governments and the European Court of Justice.' *International Organization* 52, 121–47.

Alter, Karen J. 2006. 'Private litigants and the new international courts', *Comparative Political Studies* 39, 22–49.

Alter, Karen J. 2008. 'Agents or trustees? International courts in their political context', *European Journal of International Relations* 14, 33–63.

Alter, Karen J. 2014. *The New Terrain of International Law: Courts, Politics, Rights*. Princeton University Press.

Alter, Karen J. and Laurence R. Helfer. 2014. *International Legal Transplants: the Law and Politics of the Andean Tribunal of Justice*. Oxford University Press.

Alter, Karen J. and Sophie Meunier. 2009. 'The politics of international regime complexity', *Perspectives on Politics* 7, 13–24.

Altwicker-Hamori, Szilvia, Tilmann Altwicker, and Anne Peters. 2016. 'Measuring violations of human rights: an empirical analysis of awards in respect of non-pecuniary damage under the European convention on human rights', *Zeitschrift für ausländisches öffentliches Recht und Völkerrecht* 76, 1–52.

Alvarez, José E. 1997. 'Critical theory and the North American Free Trade Agreement's Chapter Eleven', *University of Miami Inter-American Law Review* 28, 303–12.

Alvarez, José E. 2005. *International Organizations as Law-Makers*. Oxford University Press.

Alvarez, José E. 2008. 'Review: investment treaty arbitration and public law by Gus van Harten', *The American Journal of International Law* 102, 909–15.

Alvarez, José E. 2009. 'A BIT on custom', *New York University Journal of International Law and Policy* 42, 17–80.

Alvarez, José E. 2010. 'The once and future foreign investment regime' in Mahnoush Arsanjani, Jacob Katz Cogan, Robert Sloane, and Siegfried Wiessner (eds.), *Looking to the Future: Essays on International Law in Honor of W. Michael Reisman*. Boston, Leiden: Brill.

Alvarez, José E. 2011a. *The Public International Law Regime Governing International Investment*. Boston, Leiden: Brill Nijhoff.

Alvarez, José E. 2011b. 'Are corporations "subjects" of International Law?', *Santa Clara Journal of International Law* 9, 1–36.

Alvarez, José E. 2012a. 'Sovereign concerns and the international investment regime' in Karl P. Sauvant, Lisa E. Sachs, and Wouter P.F. Schmit Jongbloed (eds.), *Sovereign Investment: Concerns and Policy Reactions*. Oxford University Press.

Alvarez, José E. 2012b. 'The return of the State', *Minnesota Journal of International Law* 20, 223–64.

Alvarez, José E. 2014. 'What are international judges for? The main functions of international adjudication' in Cesare P.R. Romano, Karen J. Alter, and Yuval Shany (eds.), *The Oxford Handbook of International Adjudication*. Oxford University Press.

Alvarez, José E. 2016a. '"Beware: boundary crossings"—a critical appraisal of public law approaches to international investment law', *The Journal of World Investment & Trade* 17, 171–228.

Alvarez, José E. 2016b. 'Is investor-state arbitration "public"?', *Journal of International Dispute Settlement* 7, 534–76.

Alvarez, José E. and Brink Tegan. 2011. 'Revisiting the necessity defense: *Continental Casualty v. Argentina*' in Karl P. Sauvant (ed.), *Yearbook on International Investment Law and Policy 2010–2011*. Oxford University Press.

Alvarez, José E., Karl P. Sauvant, Gerard Ahmed Kamil, and Gabriela P. Vizcaîno. 2011. *The Evolving International Investment Regime: Expectations, Realities, Options*. Oxford University Press.

American Bar Association. 2016. 'Task force report on the investment court system proposal,' *Investment Treaty Working Group, Initial Task Force Discussion Paper*, 14 October.

Anghie, Anthony. 2004. *Imperialism, Sovereignty, and the Making of International Law*. Cambridge University Press.

Aranguri, Cesar. 2010. 'The effect of BITs on regulatory quality and the rule of law in developing countries'. On file with the authors.

Arauz, Andres. 2013. Ecuador's Experience with International Investment Arbitration. Presentation at 7th Annual IISD Forum of Developing Country Investment Negotiators, Jakarta, 5 November. On file with the authors.

Arias, Eric, James R. Hollyer, and Peter B. Rosendorff. 2015. 'Leader survival, regime type and bilateral investment treaties'. On file with the authors.

Arndt, Christian, Claudia Buch, and Monika Schnitzer. 2010. 'FDI and domestic investment: an industry-level view', *The B.E. Journal of Economic Analysis & Policy* 10 Article 69.

Arrow, Kenneth J. and Gerard Debreu. 1954. 'Existence of an equilibrium for a competitive economy', *Econometrica* 22, 265–90.

Australian Department of Foreign Affairs and Trade. 2011. *Gillard Government Trade Policy Statement: Trading Our Way to More Jobs and Prosperity*, April.

Axelrod, Robert. 1986. 'An evolutionary approach to norms', *American Political Science Review* 80, 1095–111.

Baetens, Freya. 2015. 'Transatlantic investment treaty protection–a response to Poulsen, Bonnitcha and Yackee' in Jacques Pelkmans and Daniel Hamilton (eds.), *Rule-Makers or Rule-Takers? Exploring the Transatlantic Trade and Investment Partnership*. London: Rowman & Littlefield.

Bagwell, Kyle and Robert W. Staiger. 2002. 'Economic theory and the interpretation of GATT/WTO', *The American Economist* 46, 3–19.

Bagwell, Kyle and Robert W. Staiger. 2002. *The Economics of the World Trading System*. Cambridge: MIT Press.

Balasubramanyam, Venkataraman N., Mohammed Salisu, and David Sapsford. 1996. 'Foreign direct investment and growth in EP and IS countries', *The Economic Journal* 106, 92–105.

Balcerzak, Filip and Jarrod Hepburn. 2015. 'Publication of investment treaty awards: the qualified potential of domestic access to information laws', *Groningen Journal of International Law* 3, 147–70.

Banga, Rashmi. 2008. 'Government policies and FDI inflows of Asian developing countries: empirical evidence' in José María Fanelli and Lyn Squire (eds.), *Economic Reform in Developing Countries Reach, Range, Reason.* Cheltenham, Northampton: Edward Elgar.

Banifatemi, Yas. 2009. 'The emerging jurisprudence on the most-favoured-nation provision in investment arbitration' in Andrea K. Bjorklund, Ian A. Laird, and Sergey K. Ripinsky (eds.), *Investment Treaty Law, Current Issues III.* London: British Institute of International and Comparative Law.

Banifatemi, Yas. 2013. 'Consistency in the interpretation of substantive investment rules: is it achievable?' in Roberto Echandi and Pierre Sauvé (eds.), *Prospects in International Investment Law and Policy.* Cambridge University Press.

Barrell, Ray and Nigel Pain. 1997. 'Foreign direct investment, technological change, and economic growth within Europe', *The Economic Journal* 107, 1770–86.

Bartels, Lorand. 2015. 'The chapeau of the general exceptions in the WTO GATT and GATS agreements: a reconstruction', *The American Journal of International Law* 109, 95–125.

Been, Vicki and Joel C. Beauvais. 2003. 'Global fifth amendment—NAFTA's investment protections and the misguided quest for an international regulatory takings doctrine', *New York University Law Review* 78, 30–143.

Belderbos, Rene A. 1997. 'Antidumping and tariff jumping: Japanese firms' DFI in the European Union and the United States', *Weltwirtschaftliches Archiv* 133, 419–57.

Bell, John. 2006. 'Comparative administrative law' in Mathias Reimann and Reinhard Zimmermann (eds.), *The Oxford Handbook of Comparative Law.* Oxford University Press.

Benfratello, Luigi and Alessandro Sembenelli. 2002. 'Research joint ventures and firm level performance', *Research Policy* 31, 493–507.

Bengoa, Marta and Blanca Sanchez-Robles. 2003. 'Foreign direct investment, economic freedom and growth: new evidence from Latin America', *European Journal of Political Economy* 19, 529–45.

Benvenisti, Eyal and George W. Downs. 2007. 'The empire's new clothes: political economy and the fragmentation of international law', *Stanford Law Review* 60, 595–632.

Berge, Tarald and Øyvind Stiansen. 2016. 'Negotiating BITs with models: the power of expertise', *Working Paper*, 12 October. On file with the authors.

Berger, Axel. 2011. 'The politics of China's investment treaty-making program' in Tomer Broude, Marc L. Busch, and Amelia Porges (eds.), *The Politics of International Economic Law.* Cambridge University Press.

Berger, Axel, Matthias Busse, Peter Nunnenkamp, and Martin Roy. 2011. 'More stringent BITs, less ambiguous effects on FDI? Not a BIT!', *Economics Letters* 112, 270–2.

Berger, Axel, Matthias Busse, Peter Nunnenkamp, and Martin Roy. 2013. 'Do trade and investment agreements lead to more FDI? Accounting for key provisions inside the Black Box', *International Economics and Economic Policy* 10, 247–75.

Bergsten, C. Fred. 1974. 'Coming investment wars?', *Foreign Affairs* 53, 135–52.

Bergstrand, Jeffrey and Peter Egger. 2007. 'A knowledge-and-physical-capital model of international trade flows, foreign direct investment', *Journal of International Economics* 73, 278–308.

Bernstein, Steven and Benjamin Cashore. 2012. 'Complex global governance and domestic policies: four pathways of influence', *International Affairs* 88, 585–604.

Besson, Samantha. 2014. 'Legal philosophical issues of international adjudication: getting over the amour impossible between international law and adjudication' in Cesare P.R. Romano, Karen J. Alter, and Yuval Shany (eds.), *The Oxford Handbook of International Adjudication*. Oxford University Press.

Betz, Tim and Andrew Kerner. 2016. 'The influence of interest: real US interest rates and bilateral investment treaties', *The Review of International Organizations* 11, 419–48.

Beugelsdijk, Sjoerd, Jean-François Hennart, Arjen Slangen, and Roger Smeets. 2010. 'Why and how FDI stocks are a biased measure of MNE affiliate activity', *Journal of International Business Studies* 41, 1444–59.

Bhagwati, Jagdish N. 2004. *In Defense of Globalization*. New York: Oxford University Press.

Bhagwati, Jagdish N. 2008. *Termites in The Trading System: How Preferential Agreements Undermine Free Trade*. Oxford University Press.

Bhala, Raj. 2014. 'Trans-Pacific partnership or trampling poor partners? A tentative critical review', *Manchester Journal of International Economic* Law 11, 2–59.

Bhattacharya, Utpal, Neal Galpin, and Bruce Haslem. 2007. 'The home court advantage in international corporate litigation', *The Journal of Law and Economics* 50, 625–60.

Bishop, R. Doak, James Crawford, and W. Michael Reisman. 2014. *Foreign Investment Disputes: Cases, Materials, and Commentary*, 2nd edn. The Hague: Kluwer Law International.

Bishop, R. Doak and Lucy Reed. 1998. 'Practical guidelines for interviewing, selecting and challenging party-appointed arbitrators in international commercial arbitration', *Arbitration International* 14, 395–430.

Bjorklund, Andrea. 2008. 'Emergency exceptions: state of necessity and force majeure' in Peter Muchlinski, Federico Ortino, and Christoph Schreuer (eds.), *The Oxford Handbook of International Investment Law*. Oxford University Press.

Bjorklund, Andrea. 2010. 'The national treatment obligation' in Catherine Yannaca-Small (ed.), *Arbitration Under International Investment Agreements: A Guide to Key Issues*. Oxford University Press.

Bjorklund, Andrea. 2013. 'The role of counterclaims in rebalancing investment law', *Lewis & Clark Law Review* 17, 461–80.

Blanton, Robert and Shannon Blanton. 2012. 'Rights, institutions, and foreign direct investment: an empirical assessment', *Foreign Policy Analysis* 8, 431–52.

Blomström, Magnus and Ari Kokko. 1997. 'Regional integration and foreign direct investment', *NBER Working Paper No.* 6019. Cambridge: National Bureau of Economic Research.

Blomström, Magnus and Ari Kokko. 2003. 'Human capital and inward FDI', *CEPR Discussion Paper No.* 3762, London: Center for Economic Policy Research.

Blonigen, Bruce A. 2002. 'Tariff-jumping antidumping duties', *Journal of International Economics* 57, 31–49.

Blonigen, Bruce A. 2005. 'A review of the empirical literature on FDI determinants,' *Atlantic Economic Journal* 33, 383–403.

Blackaby, Nigel and Sylvia Noury. 2006. 'International arbitration in Latin America', *World Arbitration and Mediation Review* 3.

Blackaby, Nigel and Constantine Partasides. 2015. *Redfern and Hunter on International Arbitration*, 6th edn. Oxford University Press.

Blackwood, Elizabeth and Stephen McBride. 2006. 'Investment as the achilles heel of globalisation?', *Policy and Society* 25, 43–67.

Blanes i Vidal, Jordi, Mirko Draca, and Christian Fons-Rosen. 2012. 'Revolving door lobbyists', *The American Economic Review* 102, 3731–48.

Blume, Lawrence and Daniel Rubinfeld. 1984. 'Compensation for takings: an economic analysis', *California Law Review* 72, 569.

Blume, Lawrence, Daniel L. Rubinfeld, and Helen Shapiro. 1984. 'The taking of land: when should compensation be paid?', *Quarterly Journal of Economics* 109, 71–92.

Bodenheimer, Susanne. 1971. 'Dependency and imperialism: the roots of Latin American underdevelopment' in K.T. Fann and Donald Hodges (eds.), *Readings in U.S. Imperialism.* Boston: Porter Sargent.

Bollinger, Lee C. and Karl P. Sauvant. 2016. 'How investment agreements can protect free media', *Project Syndicate*, 11 July.

Bonnitcha, Jonathan. 2014a. *Substantive Protection under Investment Treaties: A Legal and Economic Analysis.* Cambridge University Press.

Bonnitcha, Jonathan. 2014b. 'Investment treaties and transition from authoritarian rule', *Journal of World Investment and Trade* 15, 965–1011.

Bonnitcha, Jonathan. 2016. 'Foreign investment, development and governance: what international investment law can learn from the empirical literature on investment', *Journal of International Dispute Settlement* 7, 31–54.

Bonnitcha, Jonathan and Emma Aisbett. 2010. 'Submission regarding the merits of including post-establishment protection for foreign investment in Australian FTAs', *Productivity Commission 2010, Bilateral and Regional Trade Agreements, Research Report.* Canberra, Melbourne.

Bonnitcha, Jonathan and Emma Aisbett. 2013. 'An economic analysis of the substantive protections provided by investment treaties' in Karl P. Sauvant (ed.), *Yearbook on International Investment Law & Policy 2011–2012.* Oxford University Press.

Borensztein, Eduardo, José De Gregorio, and Jong-Wha Lee. 1998. 'How does foreign direct investment affect economic growth?', *Journal of International Economics* 45, 115–35.

Borgen, Christopher J. 2007. 'Transnational tribunals and the transmission of norms: the hegemony of process', *George Washington International Law Review* 39, 685–764.

Born, Gary. 2009. *International Commercial Arbitration*, 3rd edn. Alphen aan den Rijn: Kluwer Law International.

Born, Gary. 2012. *International Arbitration: Law and Practice.* Alphen aan den Rijn: Kluwer Law International.

Brainard, S Lael. 1997. 'An empirical assessment of the proximity-concentration trade-off between multinational sales and trade', *American Economic Review* 87, 520–44.

Braithwaite, John and Peter Drahos. 2000. *Global Business Regulation.* Cambridge University Press.

Bresnahan, Timoth and Peter Reiss. 1994. 'Measuring the importance of sunk costs', *Annales d'Économie et de Statistique* 34, 181–217.

Bretton Woods Project. 2009. 'ICSID in Crisis: Straight-Jacked or Investment Protection?' 10 July. Available at www.brettonwoodsproject.org/2009/07/art-564878/.

Brewer, Antony. 2002. *Marxist Theories of Imperialism: A Critical Survey.* London: Routledge.

Brewer, Thomas L. and Stephen Young. 1997. 'Investment incentives and the international agenda', *The World Economy* 20, 175–98.

Brewer, Thomas L. and Stephen Young. 2000. *The Multilateral Investment System and Multinational Enterprises.* Oxford University Press.

Brewster, Rachel and Adam S. Chilton. 2014. 'Supplying compliance: why and when the United States complies with WTO rulings', *Yale Journal of International Law* 39, 201–46.

Broches, Aaron. 1980. 'Foreign investment and the settlement of disputes with particular reference to ICSID' in Aaron Broches (1995), *Selected Essays: World Bank, ICSID, and Other Subjects of Public and Private International Law*. London: Martinus Nijhoff.

Broner, Fernando and Ventura Jaume. 2016. 'Rethinking the effects of financial globalization', *The Quarterly Journal of Economics* 131, 1497–542.

Brosig, Malte. 2013. 'Introduction: the African security regime complex—exploring converging actors and policies', *African Security* 6, 171–90.

Broude, Tomer. 2015. 'Behavioral international law', *University of Pennsylvania Law Review* 164, 1099–157.

Brower, Charles H. and Sadie Blanchard. 2014. 'What's in a meme? The Truth about investor-state arbitration: why it need not, and must not, be repossessed by states', *Columbia Journal of Transnational Law* 52, 689–777.

Brower, Charles H., Charles H. Brower II, and Jeremy K. Sharpe. 2003. 'The coming crisis in the global adjudication', *Arbitration International* 19, 415–40.

Brower, Charles H. and Charles B. Rosenberg. 2013. 'The death of the two-headed nightingale: Why the Paulsson-van den Berg presumption that party-appointed arbitrators are untrustworthy is wrongheaded', *Arbitration International* 23, 7–44.

Brower, Charles N. and Stephan W. Schill. 2009. 'Is arbitration a threat or a boon to the legitimacy of international investment law?', *Chicago Journal of International Law* 9, 471–98.

Brown, Chester. 2013. *Commentaries on Selected Model Investment Treaties*. Oxford University Press.

Brown, Drusilla K., Alan Deardorff, and Robert M. Stern. 2004. 'The effects of multinational production on wages and working conditions in developing countries' in Robert E. Baldwin and L. Alan Winters (eds.), *Challenges to Globalization: Analyzing the Economics*. University of Chicago Press.

Brunnée, Jutta and Toope Stephen J. 2010. *Legitimacy and Legality in International Law: An Interactional Account*. Cambridge University Press.

Brunnermeier, Smita B. and Arik Levinson. 2004. 'Examining the evidence on environmental regulations and industry location', *The Journal of Environment & Development* 13, 6–41.

Bruno, Randolph and Nauro Campos. 2011. 'Foreign direct investment and economic performance: a systematic review of the evidence uncovers a new paradox', *Final Report for the Department for International Development Systematic Reviews Programme*. On file with the authors.

Ryan Brutger and Anton Strezhnev. 2017. 'International Disputes, Media Coverage, and Support for Economic Engagement.' Working paper, available at wp.peio.me/wp-content/uploads/2016/12/PEIO10_paper_103.pdf.

Bubb, Ryan and Susan Rose-Ackerman. 2007. 'BITs and bargains: strategic aspects of bilateral and multilateral regulation of foreign investment', *International Review of Law and Economics* 27, 291–311.

Buchanan, James and Gordon Tullock. 1962. *The Calculus of Consent*. Ann Arbor: University of Michigan Press.

Buckley, Peter J. and Mark Casson. 1976. The *Future of the Multinational Enterprise*. London: Macmillan.

Buckley, Peter J. and Mark Casson. 1981. 'The optimal timing of a foreign direct investment', *The Economic Journal* 91, 75–87.

Buckley, Peter J., Jeremy Clegg, and Chengqi Wang. 2007. 'Is the relationship between inward FDI and spillover effects linear? An empirical examination of the case of China', *Journal of International Business Studies* 38, 447–59.

Bureau of Economic Analysis. 2004. *Benchmark Survey of US Direct Investment Abroad.* Washington, DC: Bureau of Economic Analysis.

Burford. 2014. 'Burford capital receives $26 million from innovative corporate debt facility backed by arbitration claim', 3 June, http://www.burfordcapital.com/wp-content/uploads/2014/11/2014-06-03-BUR-Rurelec-press-release-Final.pdf.

Burke-White, William W. and Andreas von Staden. 2010. 'Private litigation in a public law sphere: the standard of review in investor-state arbitrations', *The Yale Journal of International Law* 35, 283–346.

Burke-White, William W. 2010. 'The Argentine financial crisis: state liability under BITs and the legitimacy of the ICSID system' in Michael Waibel, Asha Kaushal, Kwo-Hwa Liz Chung, and Claire Balchin (eds.), *The Backlash against Investment Arbitration: Perceptions and Reality.* Alphen aan den Rijn: Kluwer Law International.

Burkhardt, Hans-Martin. 1986. 'Investment protection treaties: recent trends and prospects', *Aussenwirtschaft: Schweizerische Zeitschrift für Internationale Wirtschaftsbeziehungen* 41, 99–104.

Burley, Anne-Marie and Walter Mattli. 1993. 'Europe before the Court: a political theory of legal integration', *International Organization* 47, 41–76.

Busch, Marc L. 2007. 'Overlapping institutions, forum shopping, and dispute settlement in international trade', *International Organization* 61, 735–61.

Busch, Marc L. and Eric Reinhardt. 2001. 'Bargaining in the shadow of the law: early settlement in GATT/WTO disputes', *Fordham International Law Journal* 24, 158–72.

Busse, Matthias, Jens Königer, and Peter Nunnenkamp. 2010. 'FDI promotion through bilateral investment treaties: more than a BIT?', *Review of World Economics* 146, 147–77.

Busse, Matthias, Peter Nunnenkamp, and Mariana Spatareanu. 2011. 'Foreign direct investment and labour rights: a panel analysis of bilateral FDI flows', *Applied Economics Letters* 18, 149–52.

Büthe, Tim and Helen Milner. 2009. 'Bilateral investment treaties and foreign direct investment: a political analysis' in Karl Sauvant and Lisa Sachs (eds.), *The Effect of Treaties on Foreign Direct Investment: Bilateral Investment Treaties, Double Taxation Treaties and Investment Flows.* Oxford University Press.

Büthe, Tim and Helen Milner. 2014. 'Foreign direct investment and institutional diversity in trade agreements: credibility, commitment, and economic flows in the developing world, 1971–2007', *World Politics* 66, 88–122.

Caddell, Jeremy and Nathan M. Jensen. 2014. 'Which host country government actors are most involved in disputes with foreign investors?', *Columbia FDI Perspectives* No. 120, 28 April, New York: Columbia University Vale Columbia Center on Sustainable International Investment.

Calabresi, Guido and A. Douglas Melamed. 1972. 'Property rules, liability rules, and inalienability: one view of the cathedral', *Harvard Law Review* 85, 1089–128.

Calamita, Jansen. 2015. 'The rule of law, investment treaties, and economic growth: mapping normative and empirical questions' in Jeffrey Jowell, Chris Thomas, and Jan van Zyl Smit (eds.), *The Importance of the Rule of Law in Promoting Development.* Singapore Academy of Law.

Calderón, César, Norman Loayza, and Luis Servén. 2004. 'Greenfield foreign direct investment and mergers and acquisitions: feedback and macroeconomic effects', *World Bank Policy Research Working Paper* No. 3192. Washington, DC: World Bank.

Colombatto, Enrico and Jonathan R. Macey. 1996. 'Public choice model of international economic cooperation and the decline of the nation state', *Cardozo Law Review* 18, 925–56.

Calvo, Carlos. 1868. *Derecho internacional teórico y práctico de Europa y América*. Paris: D'Amyot.

Cameron, Maxwell A. and Brian W. Tomlin. 2000. *The making of NAFTA: how the deal was done*. Ithaca: Cornell University Press.

Campello, Daniela and Leany Lemos. 2015. 'The non-ratification of bilateral investment treaties in Brazil: a story of conflict in a land of cooperation', *Review of International Political Economy* 22, 1055–86.

Capobianco, Antonio and Hans Christiansen. 2011. 'Competitive neutrality and state-owned enterprises: challenges and policy options', *OECD Corporate Governance Working Papers* No. 1. Paris: Organisation for Economic Cooperation and Development.

Caputo, Luis A., Secretary of Finance, Argentina. 2016. *Notice to Bondholders Participating in the Abaclat Case*, 24 February.

Carkovic, Maria and Ross Levine. 2005. 'Does foreign direct investment accelerate economic growth?' in Theodore H. Moran, Edward M. Graham, and Magnus Blomström (eds.), *Does Foreign Direct Investment Promote Development?* Washington, DC: Peterson Institute for International Economics.

Caron, David D. and Shirlow Esmé. 2015. 'Most favoured nation treatment—substantive protection in investment law' in Kinnear Meg and others (eds.), *Building International Investment Law: The First 50 Years of ICSID*. Alphen aan den Rijn: Wolters Kluwer.

Carr, David L., James R. Markusen, and Keith E. Maskus. 2001. 'Estimating the knowledge-capital model of the multinational enterprise', *The American Economic Review* 91, 693–708.

Carrubba, Clifford J., Matthew Gabel, and Charles Hankla. 2008. 'Judicial behavior under political constraints: evidence from the European Court of Justice', *American Political Science Review* 102, 435–52.

Cass, Deborah Z. 2005. *The Constitutionalization of the World Trade Organization: Legitimacy, Democracy, and Community in the International Trading System*. Oxford University Press.

Cavalcante, Pedro Mendonça. 2015. 'The investment cooperation and facilitation agreement—a new approach to investment treaties', *Columbia/Oxford Series on New Thinking on Investment Treaties*. Available at youtube.com/watch?v=cV7SYzSS3-E.

Caves, Richard E. 1996. *Multinational Enterprise and Economic Analysis*. Cambridge University Press.

Caves, Richard E. 1971. 'International corporations: the industrial economics of foreign investment', *Economica* 38, 1–27.

Chakrabarti, Avik. 2001. 'The determinants of foreign direct investments: sensitivity analyses of cross-country regressions', *Kyklos* 54, 89–114.

Chalamish, Efraim. 2010. 'An oasis in the desert: the emergency of Israeli investment treaties in the global economy', *Loyola of Los Angeles International and Comparative Law Review* 32, 123–208.

Chalmers, Damian, Gareth T. Davies, and Giorgio Monti. 2010. *European Union Law: Cases and Materials*, 2nd edn., Cambridge University Press.

Chase, Kerry A. 2003. 'Economic interests and regional trading arrangements: the case of NAFTA', *International Organization* 57, 137–74.

Chase, Kerry A. 2005. *Trading Blocs: States, Firms, and Regions in the World Economy*. Ann Arbor: University of Michigan Press.

Chaudhuri, Amrita Ray and Hassan Benchekroun. 2013. 'The costs and benefits of IIAS to developing countries: an economic country perspective' in Armand De Mestral and Céline Lévesque (eds.), *Improving International Investment Agreements*. Abingdon, New York: Routledge.

Chew Ging, Lee. 2010. 'Outward foreign direct investment and economic growth: evidence from Japan', *Global Economic Review* 39, 317–26.

Chilton, Adam S. 2016. 'The political motivations of the United States' bilateral investment treaty program', *Review of International Political Economy* 23, 614–42.

Choi, Seung-Whan. 2009. 'The effect of outliers on regression analysis: regime type and foreign direct investment', *Quarterly Journal of Political Science* 4, 153–65.

Choudhury, Barnali. 2008. 'Recapturing public power: is investment arbitration's engagement of the public interest contributing to the democratic deficit?', *Vanderbilt Journal of International Law* 41, 775–832.

Chowdury, Abdur and George Mavrotas. 2006. 'FDI and growth: what causes what?', *The World Economy* 29, 9–19.

Cleeve, Emmanuel. 2008. 'How effective are fiscal incentives to attract FDI to Sub-Saharan Africa?', *The Journal of Developing Areas* 42, 135–53.

Clermont, Kevin M. and Theodore Eisenberg. 1996. 'Xenophilia in American courts', *Harvard Law Review* 109, 1120–43.

Coase, Ronald H. 1937. 'The nature of the firm', *Economica* 4, 386–405.

Clodfelter, Mark A. 2009. 'The adaptation of states to the changing world of investment protection through model BITs', *ICSID Review* 24, 165–75.

Coe, Jack Jr. 2005. 'Toward a complementary use of conciliation in investor-state disputes-a preliminary sketch', *University of California, Davis Law Review* 12, 7–46.

Coe, Jack Jr. and Noah D. Rubins. 2005. 'Regulatory expropriation and the Tecmed: context and contributions' in Todd Weiler (ed.), *International Investment Law and Arbitration—Leading Cases from the ICSID, NAFTA, Bilateral Treaties and Customary International Law*. London: Cameron May.

Cohn, Richard, Wilbur Lewellen, Ronald Lease, and Gary Schlarbaum. 1975. 'Individual investor risk aversion and investment portfolio composition', *The Journal of Finance* 30, 605–20.

Cohn, Theodore. 2011. *Global Political Economy*. London: Routledge.

Colen, Liesbeth and Andrea Guariso. 2013. 'What type of FDI is attracted by BITs' in Olivier de Schutter, Johan Swinnen, and Jan Wouters (eds.), *Foreign Direct Investment and Human Development: the Law and Economics of International Investment Agreements*. New York: Routledge.

Colen, Liesbeth, Miet Maertens, and Johan Swinnen. 2013. 'Foreign direct investment as an engine of economic growth and human development' in Olivier de Schutter, Johan Swinnen, and Jan Wouters (eds.), *Foreign Direct Investment and Human Development: the Law and Economics of International Investment Agreements*. New York: Routledge.

Colen, Liesbeth, Damiaan Persyn, and Andrea Guariso. 2016. 'Bilateral investment treaties and FDI: does the sector matter?, *World Development* 83, 193–206.

Commission, Jeffery P. 2007. 'Precedent in investment treaty arbitration: a citation analysis of a developing jurisprudence', *Journal of International Arbitration* 24, 129–58.

Conyon, Martin J., Sourafel Girma, Steve Thompson, and Peter W. Wright. 2002. 'The productivity and wage effects of foreign acquisition in the United Kingdom', *The Journal of Industrial Economics* 50, 85–102.

Copeland, Brian R. and M. Scott Taylor. 2004. 'Trade, growth, and the environment', *Journal of Economic Literature* 42, 7–71.

Copenhagen Economics. 2012. 'EU-China Investment Study'. *Report for European Commission.* Copenhagen: Copenhagen Economics.

Costa, José Augusto Fontura. 2011. 'Comparing WTO panelists and ICSID arbitrators: the creation of international legal fields', *Oñati Socio-Legal Series* 1, 1–24.

Côté, Christine. 2014. 'A chilling effect? The impact of international investment agreements on national regulatory autonomy in the areas of health, safety and the environment', PhD thesis, London School of Economics and Political Science. Available at http://etheses.lse.ac.uk/897/.

Cotterill, Joseph. 2013. 'Argentina tries to settle with holdouts: not those ones though', *Financial Times Alphaville*, 11 October.

Cotula, Lorenzo. 2014. 'Investment treaties and sustainable development: investment liberalisation', *International Institute for Environment and Development Briefing Paper.*

Council of the European Union. 2016. 'Joint Interpretative Instrument on the Comprehensive Economic and Trade Agreement (CETA) between Canada and the European Union and its Member States', Document No 13541/16, 27 October 2016.

Council of Foreign Relations. 2012. 'The tobacco wars: international trade disputes and tobacco control'. Available at http://www.cfr.org/united-states/tobacco-wars-international-trade-disputes-tobacco-control/p35293.

Coupé, Tom, Irina Orlova, and Alexandre Skiba. 2009. 'The effect of tax and investment treaties on bilateral FDI flows to transition economies' in Karl Sauvant and Lisa Sachs (eds.), *The Effect of Treaties on Foreign Direct Investment: Bilateral Investment Treaties, Double Taxation Treaties and Investment Flows.* Oxford University Press.

Cowell, Frank. 2006. *Microeconomics: Principles and Analysis.* Oxford University Press.

Cox, Robert W. 1987. *Production, Power, and World Order: Social Forces in the Making of History.* Columbia University Press.

Crawford, James. 2004. 'The problems of legitimacy-speak', *ASIL Proceedings* 98, 271–3.

Crawford, James. 2008. 'Treaty and contract in investment arbitration', *Arbitration International* 24, 351–74.

Crawford, James. 2012. *Brownlie's Principles of Public International Law*, 8th edn. Oxford University Press.

Criscuolo, Chiara and Ralf Martin. 2003. 'Multinationals, foreign ownership and US productivity leadership: evidence from the UK', in *Royal Economic Society Annual Conference* No 50.

Criscuolo, Chiara and Ralf Martin. 2009. 'Multinationals and U.S. productivity leadership: evidence from Great Britain', *The Review of Economics and Statistics* 91, 263–81.

Cui, Lin, Klaus E. Meyer, and Helen Wei Hu. 2014. 'What drives firms' intent to seek strategic assets by foreign direct investment? A study of emerging economy firms', *Journal of World Business* 49, 488–501.

Cutler, A. Claire. 2003. *Private Power and Global Authority: Transnational Merchant Law in the Global Political Economy.* Cambridge University Press.

Damodaran, Aswath. 2002. *Investment Valuation: Tools and Techniques for Determining the Value of Any Asset*, 2nd edn. New York: Wiley.

Danish Union of Metalworkers and Confederation of Danish Industries. 2014. 'We Danes remain committed to TTIP', *Financial Times*, 13 July.

Danzman, Sarah. 2016. 'Contracting with whom? The differential effects of investment treaties on FDI', *International Interactions: Empirical and Theoretical Research in International Relations* 42, 452–78.

Davey, William J. 2007. 'Dispute settlement in the WTO and RTAs: a comment' in Bartels Lorand and Ortino Federico (eds.), *Regional Trade Agreements and the WTO Legal System*. Oxford University Press.

Davey, William J. 2009. 'Compliance problems in WTO dispute settlement', *Cornell International Law Journal* 42, 119–28.

Davis, Christina L. 2012. *Why adjudicate? Enforcing trade rules in the WTO*. Princeton University Press.

de Gramont, Alexandre. 2006. 'After the water war: the battle for jurisdiction in Aguas Del Tunari, S.A. v. Republic of Bolivia', *Transnational Dispute Management* 3(5).

De Mooij, Ruud A. and Sjef Ederveen. 2003. 'Taxation and foreign direct investment: a synthesis of empirical research.' *International Tax and Public Finance* 10, 673–93.

Delaney, Joachim and Daniel Barstow Magraw. 2008. 'Procedural transparency' in Peter Muchlinski, Federico Ortino, and Christoph Schreuer (eds.), *The Oxford Handbook of International Investment Law*. Oxford University Press.

Denza, Eileen and Shelagh Brooks. 1987. 'Investment protection treaties: the British experience', *International and Comparative Law Quarterly* 36, 908–23.

DePalma, Anthony. 2001. 'NAFTA's powerful little secret, obscure tribunals settle disputes, but go too far, critics say', *The New York Times*, March 11.

Desai, Mihir C., C. Fritz Foley, and James R. Hines Jr. 2005. 'Foreign direct investment and the domestic capital stock', *NBER Working Paper* No. 11075. Cambridge: National Bureau of Economic Research.

Desai, Mihir C., C. Fritz Foley, and James R. Hines Jr. 2006. 'The demand for tax haven operations', *Journal of Public Economics* 90, 513–31.

Desbordes, Rodolphe and Julien Vauday. 2007. 'The political influence of foreign firms in developing countries', *Economics & Politics* 19, 421–51.

Desbordes, Rodolphe and Vincent Vicard. 2009. 'Foreign direct investment and bilateral investment treaties: an international political perspective', *Journal of Comparative Economics* 37, 372–86.

Deutscher Richterbund. 2016. 'Stellungnahme zur Errichtung eines Investitionsgerichts für TTIP – Vorschlag der Europäischen Kommission vom 16.09.2015 und 12.11.2015', February. Available at http://www.drb.de/fileadmin/docs/Stellungnahmen/2016/DRB_160201_Stn_Nr_04_Europaeisches_Investitionsgericht.pdf.

de Vita, Glauco and Khine Kyaw. 2009. 'Growth effects of FDI and portfolio investment flows to developing countries: a disaggregated analysis by income levels', *Applied Economics Letters* 16, 277–83.

Devroy, Ann and Al Kamen. 1990. 'Bush says "Poland must have a voice"', *The Washington Post*, March 22.

Dezalay, Yves and Bryant G. Garth. 1996. *Dealing in Virtue: International Commercial Arbitration and the Construction of a Transnational Legal Order*. University of Chicago Press.

Diebold, William Jr. 1952. 'The End of the I.T.O', *Princeton Essays in International Finance* No. 16, October.

DiMascio, Nicholas and Joost Pauwelyn. 2008. 'Nondiscrimination in trade and investment treaties: worlds apart or two sides of the same coin?', *The American Journal of International Law* 102, 48–89.

Dixit, Avinash. 1987. 'Issues of strategic trade policy for small countries', *Scandinavian Journal of Economics* 89, 349–67.

Dixon, Jay and Paul Alexander Haslam. 2015. 'Does the quality of investment protection affect FDI flows to developing countries? Evidence from Latin America', *The World Economy* 39, 1080.

Dixon, Jay and Haslam Paul Alexander. 2016. 'Does the quality of investment protection affect FDI flows to developing countries? Evidence from Latin America', *The World Economy* 39, 1080–108.

Dollar, David. 2001. 'Globalization, inequality, and poverty since 1980', *World Bank Policy Research Working Paper* No. 3333, June 2004. Washington, DC: World Bank.

Dolzer, Rudolf. 2006. 'The impact of international investment treaties on domestic administrative law', *International Law and Politics* 37, 953–72.

Dolzer, Rudolf and Christoph Schreuer. 2012. *Principles of International Investment Law*, 2nd ed. Oxford University Press.

Doms, Mark E. and J. Bradford Jensen. 1998. 'Comparing wages, skills, and productivity between domestically and foreign-owned manufacturing establishments in the United States' in Robert E. Baldwin, Robert E. Lipsey, and J. David Richards (eds.), *Geography and Ownership as Bases for Economic Accounting*. University of Chicago Press.

Donaubauer, Julian, Eric Neumayer, and Peter Nunnenkamp. 2017. 'Winning or losing in investor-to-state dispute resolution: The role of arbitrator bias and experience' Kiel Working Paper, No, 2074. available at http://hdl.handle.net/10419/156236.

Donaldson, Megan. 2016. 'Secrecy and publicity in the international order, 1919–45', JSD Thesis, NYU School of Law. On file with the authors.

Donnan, Shawn. 2015. 'EU calls for global investment court', *Financial Times*, 5 May.

Douglas, Zachary. 2003. 'The hybrid foundations of investment treaty arbitration', *British Yearbook of International Law* 74, 152–284.

Douglas, Zachary. 2009. *The International Law of Investment Claims*. Cambridge University Press.

Douglas, Zachary. 2010. 'The ICSID regime of state responsibility' in James Crawford, Alain Pellet, and Simon Olleson (eds.), *The Law of International Responsibility*. Oxford University Press.

Drahozal, Christopher R. 2004. 'A behavioral analysis of private judging', *Law and Contemporary Problems* 67, 105–32.

Drake, William J. and Kalypso Nicolaïdis. 1992. 'Ideas, interests, and institutionalization: "trade in services" and the Uruguay Round', *International Organization* 46, 37–100.

Dumberry, Patrick and Gabrielle Dumas-Aubin. 2013. 'How to impose human rights obligations on corporations under investment Treaties? Pragmatic guidelines for the amendment of BITs' in Karl P. Sauvant (ed.), *Yearbook on International Investment Law & Policy 2011–2012*. Oxford University Press.

Dunning, John. 1980. 'Toward an eclectic theory of international production: some empirical tests', *Journal of International Business Studies* 11, 9–31.

Dunning, John. 1988. 'The eclectic paradigm of international production: a restatement and some possible extensions', *Journal of International Business Studies* 19, 1–31.

Dunning, John. 2001. 'The eclectic (OLI) paradigm of international production: past, present and future', *International Journal of the Economics of Business* 8, 173–90.

Dunning, John, and Sarianna Lundan. 2008. *Multinational Enterprises and the Global Economy*, 2nd edn. Cheltenham, Northampton: Edward Elgar.

Dupont, Cédric, Thomas Schultz, Melanie Wahl, and Merih Angin. 2015. 'Types of political risk leading to investment arbitrations in the oil & gas sector', *Journal of World Energy Law & Business* 8, 337–61.

Dupuy, Pierre-Marie and Jorge E. Viñuales. 2014. 'The challenge of "proliferation": an anatomy of the debate' in Cesare P.R. Romano, Karen J. Alter, and Yuval Shany (eds.), *The Oxford Handbook of International Adjudication*. Oxford University Press.

Dupuy, Pierre-Marie and Julie A. Maupin. 2015. 'Of wit, wisdom and balance: reflections on the Tokyo Resolution of the Institut de Droit International' in David D. Caron, Stephan W. Schill, Abby Cohen Smutny, and Epaminontas E. Triantafilou (eds.), *Practising Virtue: Inside International Arbitration*. Oxford University Press.

Durham, J. Benson. 2003. 'Foreign portfolio investment, foreign bank lending, and economic growth', *Board of Governors of the Federal Reserve System International Finance Discussion Papers No. 757*. Washington, DC: Federal Reserve Board.

E15 Task Force on Investment Policy. 2016. 'The evolving international investment law and policy regime: ways forward', *Policy Options Paper*. Geneva: International Centre for Trade and Sustainable Development (ICTSD) and World Economic Forum.

Eberhardt, Pia and Cecilia Olivet. 2012. *Profiting from Injustice: How Law Firms, Arbitrators and Financiers Are Fuelling an Investment Arbitration Boom*. Amsterdam, Brussels: Corporate Europe Observatory and Transnational Institute.

Echandi, Roberto. 2011. 'What do developing countries expect from the international investment regime' in José Alvarez, Karl Sauvant, Kamil Ahmed, and Gabriela Vizcaino (eds.), *The Evolving International Investment Regime*. Oxford University Press.

Echandi, Roberto and Priyanka Kher. 2013. 'Can international investor-state disputes be prevented? Empirical evidence from settlements in ICSID arbitration', *ICSID Review* 29, 41–65.

Edwards, Haley Sweetland. 2016. *Shadow Courts: The Tribunals That Rule Global Trade*. New York: Columbia Global Reports.

Egger, Peter and Valeria Merlo. 2007. 'The impact of bilateral investment treaties on FDI dynamics', *The World Economy* 30, 1536–49.

Egger, Peter and Valeria Merlo. 2012. 'BITs bite: an anatomy of the impact of bilateral investment treaties on multinational firms', *Scandinavian Journal of Economics* 114, 1240–66.

Egger, Peter and Michael Pfaffermayr. 2004. 'The impact of bilateral investment treaties on foreign direct investment', *Journal of Comparative Economics* 32, 788–804.

Eichengreen, Barry. 1998. *Capital Account Liberalization: Theoretical and Practical Aspects*, Washington, DC: International Monetary Fund.

Ekholm, Karolina, Rikard Forslid, and James R. Markusen. 2007. 'Export-platform foreign direct investment', *Journal of the European Economic Association* 5, 776–95.

Elkins, Zachary, Andrew Guzman, and Beth Simmons. 2006. 'Competing for capital: the diffusion of bilateral investment treaties, 1960–2000', *International Organization* 60, 811–46.

Elliott, Mark, Jack Beatson, and Martin H. Matthews. 2010. *Beatson, Matthews and Elliot's Administrative Law: Text and Materials*, 4th edn. Oxford University Press.

Ely, John Hart. 1980. *Democracy and Distrust: A Theory of Judicial Review*. Cambridge: Harvard University Press.

Encarnation, Dennis J. and Louis T. Wells. 1985. 'Sovereignty en garde: negotiating with foreign investors', *International Organization* 39, 47–78.

Engel, Christoph. 2008. 'Governments in dilemma: a game theoretic model for the conclusion of bilateral investment treaties—a comment on competing for capital', *University of Illinois Law Review* 2008, 305–18.

Esdaile, Chris. 2016. 'While we wait for a treaty: court endorses UN Guiding Principles'. Available at www.leighday.co.uk/Blog/March-2016/Whilst-we-wait-for-a-binding-treaty,-Court-endorse.

Esty, Daniel C. 2002. 'The World Trade Organization's legitimacy crisis', *World Trade Review* 1, 7–22.

Esty, Daniel C. 2006. 'Good governance at the supranational scale: globalizing administrative law', *The Yale Law Journal* 115, 1490–562.

European Commission. 2015a. 'Commission proposes new investment court system for TTIP and other EU trade and investment negotiations', Press release, 16 September. Available at http://europa.eu/rapid/press-release_IP-15-5651_en.htm.

European Commission. 2015b. 'Transatlantic Trade and Investment Partnership—trade in services, investment and e-commerce', Commission Draft. Available at http://trade.ec.europa.eu/doclib/docs/2015/september/tradoc_153807.pdf.

European Commission. 2015c. 'Investment protection in TTIP: attracting US investors while protecting EU governments' rights'. Available at http://trade.ec.europa.eu/doclib/docs/2015/january/tradoc_153018.5%20Inv%20Prot%20and%20ISDS.pdf.

European Commission. 2015d. 'Factsheet on investment'. Available at http://trade.ec.europa.eu/doclib/docs/2015/january/tradoc_153018.5%20Investment.pdf.

European Commission. 2016. 'CETA: EU and Canada agree on new approach on investment in trade agreement', Press release, 29 February. Available at http://europa.eu/rapid/press-release_IP-16-399_en.htm.

European Federation for Investment Law and Arbitration (EFILA). 2014. 'TTIP Consultation Submission', 12 July, Brussels. Available at http://efila.org/wp-content/uploads/2014/07/EFILA_TTIP_final_submission.pdf.

European Federation for Investment Law and Arbitration (EFILA). 2015. 'A response to the criticism against ISDS', 17 May, Brussels. Available at http://efila.org/wp-content/uploads/2015/05/EFILA_in_response_to_the-criticism_of_ISDS_final_draft.pdf.

European League for Economic Cooperation (ELEC). 1958. *Common Protection for Private International Investments*. Brussels: ELEC.

European Union Committee. 2014. *The Transatlantic Trade and Investment Partnership*. London: House of Lords.

Faeth, Isabel. 2009. 'Determinants of foreign direct investment—a tale of nine theoretical models', *Journal of Economic Surveys* 23, 165–96.

Farhang, Sean and Gregory Wawro. 2004. 'Institutional dynamics on the U.S. Court of Appeals: minority representation under panel decision making', *Journal of Law, Economics and Organization* 20, 299–330.

Fatouros, Arghyrios A. 1961. 'An international code to protect private investment: proposals and perspectives', *University of Toronto Law Journal* 14, 77–102.

Fauchald, Ole Kristian. 2008. 'The legal reasoning of ICSID Tribunals—an empirical analysis', *European Journal of International Law* 19, 301–64.

Fecák, Tomáš. 2011. 'Czech experience with bilateral investment treaties: somewhat bitter taste of investment protection', *Czech Yearbook of Public and Private International Law* 2, 233–67.

Feinberg, Richard E. 2003. 'The political economy of United States' free trade arrangements', *The World Economy* 26, 1019–40.

Fekl, Matthias. 2015. 'Vers un nouveau moyen de régler les différends entre États et investis-seurs', Paris: Ministère des Affaires étrangères, May. Available at https://www.data.gouv.fr/s/resources/corpus-de-documents-relatif-aux-negocations-commerciales-internationales-en-cours-ttip-et-ceta/20151022-154940/20150530_ISDS_Papier_FR_VF.pdf.

Feldman, Mark. 2010. 'The standing of state-owned entities under investment treaties' in Karl P. Sauvant (ed.), *Yearbook on International Investment Law & Policy 2011*. Oxford University Press.

Feldman, Mark. 2016. 'State-owned enterprises as claimants in international investment arbi-tration'. *ICSID Review* 31, 24–35.

Feldstein, Martin. 1995. 'The effects of outbound foreign direct investment on the domestic capital stock' in Martin Feldstein, James Hines, and Glenn Hubbard (eds.), *The Effects of Taxation on Multinational Corporations*. University of Chicago Press.

Fergusson, Ian F. 2015. 'Trade Promotion Authority (TPA) and the role of congress in trade policy', Congressional Research Service (CRS) Report prepared for members and committees of Congress, Washington, DC.

Ferreira, Miguel and Paul Laux. 2009. 'Portfolio flows, volatility and growth', *Journal of Inter-national Money and Finance* 28, 271–92.

Fiezzoni, Silvia Karina. 2011. 'Challenge of UNASUR member countries to replace ICSID arbitration', *The Beijing Law Review* 2, 134–44.

Firth, Michael, Oliver M. Rui, and Wenfeng Wu. 2011. 'The effects of political connections and state ownership on corporate litigation in China', *The Journal of Law & Economics* 54, 573–607.

Fisher, Roger, William Ury, and Bruce Patton. 2011. *Getting to Yes: Negotiating Agreement without Giving In*. New York: Penguin Random House.

Fleming, Jeremy. 2014. 'ISDS clause: a gateway to future trade deals', *EurActiv*, 9 December.

Flynn, Sean M., Brook Baker, Margot Kaminski, and Jimmy Koo. 2013. 'The U.S. proposal for an intellectual property chapter in the Trans-Pacific Partnership Agreement', *American University International Law Review* 28, 105–202.

Follesdal, Andreas and Simon Hix. 2006. 'Why there is a democratic deficit in the EU: a response to Majone and Moravcsik', *Journal of Common Market Studies* 44, 533–62.

Foreign Broadcasting Information Service. 1990. 'Sub-Saharan Africa', *Daily Report*, FBIS-AFR-90–125, 28 June.

Fortier, L. Yves and Stephen L. Drymer. 2004. 'Indirect expropriation in the law of international investment: I know it when I see it, or caveat investor', *ICSID Review* 19, 293–327.

Fouchard, Philippe and others, 1999. *Fouchard, Gaillard, Goldman on International Commercial Arbitration*. Hague, London: Kluwer Law International.

Franck, Susan. 2005. 'The legitimacy crisis in investment arbitration: privatizing public international law through inconsistent decisions', *Fordham Law Review* 73, 1521–625.

Franck, Susan. 2007. 'Empirically evaluating claims about investment treaty arbitration', *North Carolina Law Review* 86, 1–88.

Franck, Susan. 2009. 'Development and outcomes of investment treaty arbitration', *Harvard International Law Journal* 50, 435–89.

Franck, Susan and Lindsey E. Wylie. 2015. 'Predicting outcomes in investment treaty arbitra-tion', *Duke Law Journal* 65, 459–526.

Franck, Susan D., James Freda, Kellen Lavin, Tobias Lehmann, and Anne van Aaken. 2015. 'The diversity challenge: exploring the invisible college of international arbitration', *Columbia Journal of Transnational Law* 53, 429–506.

Franck, Thomas M. 1990. *The Power of Legitimacy Among Nations*. Oxford University Press.

Franck, Thomas M. 2006. 'The power of legitimacy and the legitimacy of power: international law in an age of power disequilibrium', *The American Journal of International Law* 100, 88–106.

Frank, André Gunder. 1972. 'The development of underdevelopment' in James Cockcroft, André Gunder Frank, and Dale Johnson (eds.), *Dependence and Underdevelopment: Latin America's Political Economy*. Garden City: Anchor Books.

Freeman, Harry. 1999. 'The role of constituents in U.S. policy development towards trade in financial services' in Alan Deardorff and Robert Stern (eds.), *Constituent Interests and US Trade Policy*. Ann Arbor: University of Michigan Press.

Fujita, Masahisa. 2008. 'A critical assessment of FDI data and policy implications', *Transnational Corporations* 17, 107–26.

Gagné, Gilbert and Jean-Frédéric Morin. 2006. 'The evolving American policy on investment protection: evidence from recent FTAs and the 2004 Model BIT', *Journal of International Economic Law* 9, 357–82.

Gallagher, Kevin and Melissa Birch. 2006. 'Do investment agreements attract investment? Evidence from Latin America', *The Journal of World Trade and Investment* 7, 961–74.

Gallagher, Kevin P. and Leonardo E. Stanley. 2013. *Capital Account Regulations and the Trading System: A Compatibility Review*. Boston: Pardee Center Task Force.

Gallagher, Norah and Wenhua Shan. 2009. *Chinese Investment Treaties: Policies and Practice*. Oxford University Press.

Gallagher, Norah and Wenhua Shan. 2013. 'China' in Chester Brown (ed.), *Commentaries on Selected Model Investment Treaties*. Oxford University Press.

Garcia, Julian. 2012. 'Venezuela's Chavez: won't accept rulings by ICSID court'. *Wall Street Journal*, 8 January.

Gaukrodger, David. 2013. 'Investment treaties as corporate law: Shareholder claims and issues of consistency. A preliminary framework for policy analysis', *OECD Working Papers on International Investment*, No 2013/3.

Gaukrodger, David. 2014a. 'Investment treaties and shareholder claims for reflective loss: insights from advanced systems of corporate law', *OECD Working Papers on International Investment*, No 2014/02.

Gaukrodger, David. 2014b. 'Investment treaties and shareholder claims: analysis of treaty practice', *OECD Working Papers on International Investment*, No 2014/03.

Gaukrodger, David and Kathryn Gordon. 2012. 'Investor-state dispute settlement: a scoping paper for the investment policy community', *OECD Working Papers on International Investment*, No 2012/03.

Gehring, Thomas and Benjamin Faude. 2014. 'A theory of emerging order within institutional complexes: how competition among regulatory international institutions leads to institutional adaptation and division of labor', *The Review of International Organizations* 9, 471–98.

Geithner, Timothy. 2011. Letter by Timothy F. Geithner to Ricardo Hausmann, 12 April.

Gertz, Geoffrey, Srividya Jandhyala, and Lauge Poulsen. 2016. 'Legalization and diplomacy: American power and the investment regime'. *Working Paper*. On file with the authors.

Gillies, Alexandra. 2010. 'Reputational concerns and the emergence of oil sector transparency as an international norm', *International Studies Quarterly* 54, 103–26.

Gilpin, Robert. 2001. *Global Political Economy: Understanding the International Economic Order*. Princeton University Press.

Ginsburg, Tom. 2005. 'International substitutes for domestic institutions: bilateral investment treaties and governance', *International Review of Law and Economics* 25, 107–23.

Girma, Sourafel and Holger Görg. 2007. 'Evaluating the foreign ownership wage premium using a difference-in-differences matching approach'. *Journal of International Economics* 72, 97–112.

Girma, Sourafel, David Greenaway, and Katharine Wakelin. 2001. 'Who benefits from foreign direct investment in the UK?' *Scottish Journal of Political Economy* 48, 119–33.

Goldberg, Linda. 2007. 'Financial sector FDI and host countries: new and old lessons', *NBER Working Paper No.* 10441. Cambridge: National Bureau of Economic Research.

Goldberg, Linda and Charles Kolstad. 1995. 'Foreign direct investment, exchange rate variability and demand uncertainty', *International Economic Review* 36, 855–73.

Goldhaber, Michael D. 2016. 'The global lawyer: the first shoe drops in Argentina', *The American Lawyer Daily*, 4 February.

Gomar, José Octavio Velázquez, Lindsay C. Stringer, and Jouni Paavola. 2014. 'Regime complexes and national policy coherence: experiences in the biodiversity cluster', *Global Governance: A Review of Multilateralism and International Organizations* 20, 119–45.

Gomes, Erivaldo. 2013. Brazilian Investment Policy and IIAs: Forward Thinking. Presentation at 7th Annual IISD Forum of Developing Country Investment Negotiators, Jakarta, 5 November. On file with the authors.

Gómez-Mera, Laura. 2015. 'International regime complexity and regional governance: evidence from the Americas', *Global Governance: A Review of Multilateralism and International Organizations* 21, 19–42.

Goodman, Ryan and Derek Jinks. 2013. *Socializing States: Promoting Human Rights Through International Law.* Oxford University Press.

Görg, Holger and David Greenaway. 2004. 'Much ado about nothing? Do domestic firms really benefit from foreign direct investment?', *World Bank Research Observer* 19, 171–97.

Gowa, Joanne and Edward D. Mansfield. 1993. 'Power politics and international trade', *American Political Science Review* 87, 408–20.

Graham, Edward. 2000. 'Fighting the wrong enemy: antiglobal activists and multinational enterprises'. Washington, DC: Institute for International Economics.

Gray, Julia. 2015. The patronage function of dysfunctional international organizations. *Working Paper.* Available at https://sites.sas.upenn.edu/jcgray/files/patronage-2014_0.pdf.

Gresik, Thomas A. 2001. 'The taxing task of taxing transnationals', *Journal of Economic Literature* 39, 800–38.

Griffith, Rachel, Helen Simpson, and Frank Windmeijer. 2001. 'Understanding productivity differences between foreign and domestic firms', *Institute for Fiscal Studies Working Paper WP 01/10.* London: Institute for Fiscal Studies.

Gross, Stuart G. 2003. 'Inordinate chill: BITs, non-NAFTA MITS, and host-state regulatory freedom—an Indonesian case study', *Michigan Journal of International Law* 24, 893–959.

Grosse, Robert and Len Trevino. 2009. 'New institutional economics and FDI location in Central and Eastern Europe' in Kark Sauvant and Lisa Sachs (eds.), *The Effect of Treaties on Foreign Direct Investment: Bilateral Investment Treaties, Double Taxation Treaties and Investment Flows.* Oxford University Press.

Grossman, Gene and Elhanan Helpman. 1994. 'Protection for sale', *The American Economic Review* 84, 833–50.

Grossman, Gene and Elhanan Helpman. 1996. 'Foreign investment with endogenous protection' in Robert Feenstra, Gene Grossman, and Douglas Irwin (eds.), *The Political Economy of Trade Policy: Papers in Honor of Jagdish Bhagwati*. Cambridge: MIT Press.

Grossman, Nienke. 2016. 'Achieving sex-representative international court benches', *The American Journal of International Law* 110, 82–95.

Grossman, Sanford J. and Oliver D. Hart. 1986. 'The costs and benefits of ownership: A theory of vertical and lateral integration', *The Journal of Political Economy* 94, 691–719.

Gudgeon, K. Scott. 1986. 'United States bilateral investment treaties: comments on their origin, purposes, and general treatment standards', *International Tax and Business Lawyer* 4, 105–31.

Guerin, Selen. 2010. 'Do the European Union's bilateral investment treaties matter? The way forward after Lisbon', *CEPS Working Document No. 333, July*. Brussels: Centre for European Policy Studies.

Guisinger, Alexandra and Alastair Smith. 2002. 'Honest threats: the interaction of reputation and political institutions in international crises', *Journal of Conflict Resolution* 46, 175–200.

Guzman, Andrew. 1998. 'Why LDCs sign treaties that hurt them: explaining the popularity of bilateral investment treaties', *Virginia Journal of International Law* 38, 639–88.

Guzman, Andrew. 2008. *How International Law Works: A Rational Choice Theory*. Oxford University Press.

Guzman, Andrew. 2009. 'Determining the appropriate standard of review in WTO dispute resolution', *Cornell International Law Journal* 42, 45–76.

Hafner-Burton, Emilie, Sergio Puig, and David G. Victor. 2016. 'Against international settlement? Secrecy, adjudication and the transformation of international law', *Arizona Legal Studies Discussion Paper No. 16–33, August*.

Hafner-Burton, Emilie M., Zachary C. Steinert-Threlkeld, and David G. Victor. 2016. 'Predictability versus flexibility', *World Politics* 68, 413–53.

Haftel, Yoram. 2010. 'Ratification counts: US investment treaties and FDI flows into developing countries', *Review of International Political Economy* 17, 348–77.

Haftel, Yoram and Hila Levi. 2016. 'Neither in nor out: Argentina's curious response to the global investment regime', paper presented at Hebrew University of Jerusalem, 25 May. On file with the authors.

Haftel, Yoram and Alex Thompson. 2015. 'When do states renegotiate agreements? The case of bilateral investment treaties', *Working Paper, February*. On file with the authors.

Haggard, Stephan and Lydia Tiede. 2011. 'The Rule of Law and economic growth: where are we?', *World Development* 39, 673–85.

Hale, Thomas. 2015. *Between Interests and Law: The Politics of Transnational Commercial Disputes*. Cambridge University Press.

Hale, Thomas, David Held, and Kevin Young. 2013. *Gridlock: Why Global Cooperation Is Failing When We Need It Most*. Cambridge: Polity Press.

Hall, Peter A. and David Soskice (eds.). 2001. *Varieties of Capitalism: The Institutional Foundations of Comparative Advantage*. Oxford University Press.

Hallward-Driemeier, Mary. 2003. 'Do bilateral investment treaties attract FDI? Only a bit and they could bite', *World Bank Policy Research Paper WPS 3121*. Washington, DC: World Bank.

Hamamoto, Shotaro. 2016. 'Debates in Japan over investor-state arbitration with developed states', *CIGI Investor-State Arbitration Series, Paper No. 5*. Available at cigionline.org.

Hamby, Chris. 2016a. 'The Court that Rules the World', *BuzzFeed*, Part One, 28 August.

Hamby, Chris. 2016b. 'The Billion Dollar Ultimatum', *BuzzFeed*, Part Two, 30 August.

Hamby, Chris. 2016c. 'Let's Make Them Poorer, And We'll Get Rich', *BuzzFeed*, Part Three, 31 August.

Hamby, Chris. 2016d. 'Elizabeth Warren Squares Off Against Global Super Court', *BuzzFeed*, 9 September.

Hamilton, Calvin and Paula Rochwerger. 2005. 'Trade and investment: foreign direct investment through bilateral and multilateral treaties', *New York International Law Review* 18, 1–59.

Hamilton, Dan and Jacques Pelkmans (eds.). 2015. *Rule-Makers or Rule-Takers? Exploring the Transatlantic Trade and Investment Partnership*. London: Rowman & Littlefield.

Hanson, Gordon H., Raymond J. Mataloni Jr, and Matthew J. Slaughter. 2001. 'Expansion strategies of US multinational firms', *NBER Working* Paper No. 8433. Cambridge: National Bureau of Economic Research.

Harding, Torfinn and Beata Javorcik. 2011. 'Roll out the red carpet and they will come: investment promotion and FDI inflows', *The Economic Journal* 121, 1445–76.

Harms, Philipp and Pierre-Guillaume Méon. 2011. 'An FDI is an FDI is an FDI? The growth effects of greenfield investment and mergers and acquisitions in developing countries', *Study Center Gerzensee Working Paper No 11.10*.

Harrison, James. 2012. 'The life and death of BITs: legal issues concerning survival clauses and the termination of investment treaties', *The Journal of World Investment and Trade* 13, 928–50.

Hart, Oliver and John Moore. 1990. 'Property rights and the nature of the firm', *Journal of Political Economy* 98, 1119–58.

Hasenclever, Andreas, Peter Mayer, and Volker Rittberger. 1996. 'Interests, power, knowledge: the study of international regimes', *Mershon International Studies Review* 40, 177–228.

Haskel, Jonathan, Sonia Pereira, and Matthew Slaughter. 2002. 'Does inward foreign direct investment boost the productivity of domestic firms', *NBER Working Paper No. 8724*, Cambridge: National Bureau of Economic Research.

Haslam, Paul Alexander. 2007. 'A "flexibility for development" index: can international investment agreements be compared quantitatively?', *European Journal of Development Research* 19, 251–73.

Hausmann, Ricardo, Dani Rodrik, Joseph Stiglitz, et al. 2011. Letter by 250 economists to Secretaries Clinton, Geithner, Ambassador Kirk, 31 January 2011. Available at http://www.ase.tufts.edu/gdae/policy_research/CapCtrlsLetter.html#statement.

Havránek, Tomáš and Zuzana Iršová. 2010. 'Which foreigners are worth wooing? A meta-analysis of vertical spillovers from FDI', *Working Paper Series 3*. Prague: Czech National Bank.

Helfer, Lawrence R. 2004. 'Regime shifting: the TRIPS agreement and the new dynamics of international intellectual property lawmaking', *Yale Journal of International Law* 29, 1–83.

Helfer, Lawrence R. 2009. 'Regime shifting in the international intellectual property system', *Perspectives on Politics* 7, 39–44.

Helpman, Elhanan. 1984. 'A simple theory of international trade with multinational corporations', *The Journal of Political Economy* 92, 451–71.

Helpman, Elhanan. 1999. 'The structure of foreign trade', *Journal of Economic Perspectives* 13, 121–44.

Helpman, Elhanan and Paul R. Krugman. 1985. *Market Structure and Foreign Trade: Increasing Returns, Imperfect Competition, and the International Economy*. Cambridge: MIT Press.

Helpman, Elhanan, Marc Melitz, and Stephen Yeaple. 2004. 'Export versus FDI with heterogeneous firms', *The American Economic Review* 94, 300–16.

Henckels, Caroline. 2012. 'Indirect expropriation and the right to regulate: revisiting proportionality analysis and the standard of review in investor-state arbitration', *Journal of International Economic Law* 15, 223–55.

Henckels, Caroline. 2013. 'Balancing investment protection and the public interest: the role of the standard of review and the importance of deference in investor–state arbitration', *Journal of International Dispute Settlement* 4, 197–215.

Henckels, Caroline. 2015. *Proportionality and Deference in Investor-State Arbitration.* Cambridge University Press.

Henckels, Caroline. 2016. 'Protecting regulatory autonomy through greater precision in investment treaties: the TPP, CETA, and TTIP', *Journal of International Economic Law* 19, 27–50.

Henderson, Keith E. 2006. 'Global lessons and best practices: corruption and judicial independence—a framework for an annual state of the judiciary report' in Guy Canivet, Mads Andenas, and Duncan Fairgrieve (eds.), *Independence, Accountability and the Judiciary.* London: British Institute of International and Comparative Law.

Hendrix, Cullen and Marcus Noland. 2014. *Confronting the Curse: The Economics and Geopolitics of Natural Resource Governance.* Washington, DC: Peterson Institute for International Economics.

Henisz, Witold. 2000. 'The institutional environment for multinational investment', *Journal of Law, Economics and Organization* 16, 334–64.

Henry, Peter Blair. 2007. 'Capital account liberalization: theory, evidence, and speculation', *Journal of Economic Literature* 45, 887–935.

Hepburn, Jarrod. 2015. 'Poland claims round-up: at least a dozen investment treaty arbitrations', *Investment Arbitration Reporter*, 29 July.

Hermes, Niels and Robert Lensink. 2003. 'Foreign direct investment, financial development and economic growth', *The Journal of Development Studies* 40, 142–63.

Hershey, Amos S. 1907. 'The Calvo and Drago Doctrines', *The American Journal of International Law* 1, 26–45.

Herzer, Dierk and Mechthild Schrooten. 2007. 'Outward FDI and domestic investment', *Discussion Paper No. 679.* Berlin: German Institute of Economic Research.

Hindelang, Steffen. 2011. 'Restitution and compensation—reconstructing the relationship in investment treaty law' in Rainer Hofmann and Christian J. Tams (eds.), *International Investment Law and General International Law: From Clinical Isolation to Systemic Integration?* Baden-Baden: Nomos.

Hindelang, Steffen. 2014. *Study on Investor-State Dispute Settlement ('ISDS') and Alternatives of Dispute Resolution in International Investment Law*, EXPO/B/INTA/2014/08-09-10, September. Brussels: European Parliament.

Hindelang, Steffen and Carl-Philipp Sassenrath. 2015. *The Investment Chapters of the EU's International Trade and Investment Agreements in a Comparative Perspective.* Brussels, Strasbourg: European Parliament.

Hines Jr, James R. 1999. 'Lessons from behavioral responses to international taxation', *National Tax Journal* 53, 305–22.

Hirschman, Albert O. 1970. *Exit, Voice, and Loyalty: Responses to Decline in Firms, Organizations, and States.* Cambridge: Harvard University Press.

Hiscox, Michael J. 2001. 'Class versus industry cleavages: inter-industry factor mobility and the politics of trade', *International Organization* 55, 1–46.

Ho, Jean. 2013. 'Singapore' in Chester Brown (ed.) *Commentaries on Selected Model Investment Treaties*. Oxford University Press.

Hodgson, Matthew. 2014. 'Counting the costs of investment treaty arbitration', *Global Arbitration Review*, 24 March.

Hoekman, Bernard M. and Michel M. Kostecki. 1995. *The Political Economy of the World Trading System: From GATT to WTO*. Oxford University Press.

Hoekman, Bernard M. and Michel M. Kostecki. 2009. *The Political Economy of the World Trading System: The WTO and Beyond*, 3rd edn. Oxford University Press.

Hoekman, Bernard M. and Petros C. Mavroidis. 2015. 'WTO 'à la carte' or 'menu du jour'? Assessing the case for more plurilateral agreements', *European Journal of International Law* 26, 319–43.

Hoffmann, Anne K. 2008. 'Indirect expropriation' in Reinisch August (ed.), *Standards of Investment Protection*. Oxford University Press.

Hoffmann, Anne K. 2013. 'Counterclaims in investment arbitration', *ICSID Review* 28, 438–53.

Hogan Lovells, Bingham Centre for the Rule of Law, and the British Institute of International and Comparative Law. 2015. *Risk and Return: Foreign Direct Investment and the Rule of Law*. Report. London.

Horst, Thomas. 1972. 'Firm and industry determinants of the decision to invest abroad: an empirical study', *The Review of Economics and Statistics* 54, 258–66.

Horstmann, Ignatius and James R. Markusen. 1987. 'Licensing versus direct investment: A model of internalization by the multinational enterprise', *Canadian Journal of Economics* 20, 464–81.

Howse, Rob. 1999. 'The house that Jackson built: restructuring the GATT System', *Michigan Law Review* 20, 107–19.

Howse, Rob. 2017. 'International investment law and arbitration: a conceptual framework' forthcoming in Helene Ruiz-Fabri (ed) *International Law and Litigation*: Baden-Baden: Nomos.

Hurd, Ian. 1999. 'Legitimacy and authority in international politics', *International Organization* 53, 379–408.

Hurrell, Andrew. 2005. 'Legitimacy and the use of force: can the circle be squared?', *Review of International Studies* 31, 15–32.

Hymer, Stephen. 1976. *The International Operations of National Firms: A Study of Direct Foreign Investment*. Cambridge: MIT Press.

Ingraham, Christopher and Howard Schneider. 2014. 'Industry voices dominate the trade advisory system', *The Washington Post*, 27 February.

Inland Revenue Authority of Singapore. 2016. 'Stamp duty for property'. Available at https://www.iras.gov.sg/IRASHome/Other-Taxes/Stamp-Duty-for-Property/.

International Centre for the Settlement of Investment Disputes (ICSID). 1970. *History of the ICSID Convention: Documents Concerning the Origin and the Formulation of the Convention on the Settlement of Investment Disputes between States and Nationals of Other States*. Volume II-1. Washington, DC: ICSID.

International Centre for the Settlement of Investment Disputes (ICSID). 2015. *The ICSID Caseload—Statistics. Special Focus: South & East Asia & The Pacific*. Washington, DC: ICSID.

International Centre for the Settlement of Investment Disputes (ICSID). 2016a. *The ICSID Caseload—Statistics. Special Focus: Africa*. Washington, DC: ICSID.

International Centre for the Settlement of Investment Disputes (ICSID). 2016b. *The ICSID Caseload—Statistics. Special Focus: European Union.* Washington, DC: ICSID.

International Centre for the Settlement of Investment Disputes (ICSID). 2017. *The ICSD Caseload - Statistics. Issue 2017-1.* Washington, DC: ICSID.

International Comparative Legal Guides (ICLG). 2016. Litigation and Disputes Resolution. Available at https://www.iclg.co.uk/practice-areas/litigation-and-dispute-resolution/litigation-and-dispute-resolution-2016.

International Institute for Sustainable Development (IISD). 2005. IISD Model International Agreement on Investment for Sustainable Development, April 2005. Available at https://www.iisd.org/pdf/2005/investment_model_int_agreement.pdf.

International Law Commission. 2007. 'Commentary to the articles on state responsibility', A/56/10, *Yearbook of the International Law Commission, 2001*, Vol II, Part Two.

International Monetary Fund. 2012. Liberalizing Capital Flows and Managing Outflows, 13 March. Available at http://www.imf.org/external/np/pp/eng/2012/031312.pdf.

Iršová, Zuzana and Tomáš Havránek. 2013. 'Determinants of horizontal spillovers from FDI: evidence from a large meta-analysis', *World Development* 42, 1–15.

Iversen, Karl. 1935. *Aspect of the Theory of International Capital Movements.* Copenhagen: Levin & Munsgaard and Oxford University Press.

Jackson, Rupert. 2010. *Review of Civil Litigation Costs: Final Report.* London: The Stationary Office.

Jandhyala, Srividya, Witold J. Henisz, and Edward D. Mansfield. 2011. 'Three waves of BITs: the global diffusion of foreign investment policy', *Journal of Conflict Resolution* 55, 1047–73.

Jandhyala, Srividya and Robert Weiner. 2014. 'Institutions sans frontières: international agreements and foreign investment', *Journal of International Business Studies* 45, 649–69.

Javorcik, Beata. 2004. 'Does foreign direct investment increase the productivity of domestic firms? In search of spillovers through backward linkages', *The American Economic Review* 94, 605–27.

Javorcik, Beata and Mariana Spatareanu. 2005. 'Do foreign investors care about labor market regulations?', *Review of World Economics* 141, 375–403.

Javorcik, Beata and Mariana Spatareanu. 2009. 'Liquidity constraints and firms' linkages with multinationals', *The World Bank Economic Review* 23, 323–46.

Javorcik, Beata and Mariana Spatareanu. 2011. 'Does it matter where you come from? Vertical spillovers from foreign direct investment and the origin of investors', *Journal of Development Economics* 96, 126–38.

Javorcik, Beata and Shang-Jin Wei. 2004. 'Pollution havens and foreign direct investment: dirty secret or popular myth?', *Contributions in Economic Analysis & Policy* 3(2), Article 8.

Jensen, Nathan M. 2003. 'Democratic governance and multinational corporations: Political regimes and inflows of foreign direct investment', *International Organization* 57, 587–616.

Jensen, Nathan M. 2008. 'Political risk, democratic institutions, and foreign direct investment', *The Journal of Politics* 70, 1040–52.

Jensen, Nathan M., Edmund Malesky, Mariana Medina, and Ugur Ozdemir. 2014. 'Pass the bucks: credit, blame, and the global competition for investment', *International Studies Quarterly* 58, 433–47.

Jinnah, Sikina. 2011a. 'Climate change bandwagoning: the impacts of strategic linkages on regime design, maintenance, and death', *Global Environmental Politics* 11, 1–9.

Jinnah, Sikina. 2011b. 'Strategic linkages: the evolving role of trade agreements in global environmental governance', *The Journal of Environment & Development* 20, 191–215.

Johns, Leslie and Rachel Wellhausen. 2016. 'Under one roof: supply chains and the protection of foreign investment', *American Political Science Review* 110, 31–51.

Johnson, Lise, Perrine Toledano, Ilan Strauss, and Sebastian James. 2013. *Background Paper on Investment Incentives: The Good, the Bad and the Ugly: Assessing the Costs, Benefits and Options for Policy Reform*. Columbia University Academic Commons.

Johnson, Lise, Ana Teresa Tavares-Lehmann, Perrine Toledano, and Lisa Sachs. 2016. *Rethinking Investment Incentives: Trends and Policy Options*. New York: Columbia University Press.

Johnson, Lise and Oleksandr Volkov. 2013. 'Investor-state contracts, host-state "commitments" and the myth of stability in international law', *American Review of International Arbitration* 24, 361–415.

Johnson, Tana and Johannes Urpelainen. 2012. 'A strategic theory of regime integration and separation', *International Organization* 66, 645–77.

Johnston, Adrian M. and Michael J. Trebilcock. 2013. 'Fragmentation in international trade law: insights from the global investment regime', *World Trade Review* 12, 621–52.

Jones, Geoffrey. 1996. *The Evolution of International Business: An Introduction*. London: Routledge.

Joubin-Bret, Anna. 2008. 'Admission and establishment in the context of investment' in Reinisch August (ed.), *Standards of Investment Protection*. Oxford University Press.

Jude, Cristina and Grégory Levieuge. 2015. 'Growth effect of FDI in developing economies: the role of institutional quality', *Document de Travail No. 559*. Paris: Banque de France.

Jupille, Joseph, Walter Mattli, and Duncan Snidal. 2013. *Institutional Choice in Global Commerce: Governance Strategies from the 19th Century to the Present*. Cambridge University Press.

Justice Not Profit. 2015. 'Third party litigation funding in the United Kingdom: a market analysis'. Available at http://www.justicenotprofit.co.uk/wp-content/uploads/2015/09/Final-TPLF-Paper.pdf.

Kaldor, Nicholas. 1940. 'A note on tariffs and the terms of trade', *Economica* 7, 377–80.

Kant, Chander. 1996. 'Foreign direct investment and capital flight', *Princeton Studies in International Finance No. 80*, March.

Kantor, Mark. 2008. *Valuation for Arbitration: Compensation Standards, Valuation Methods and Expert Evidence*. Alphen aan den Rijn: Kluwer Law International.

Kantor, Mark. 2014. 'Essays in International Economic Law, Development and Arbitration in Honor of Don Wallace, Jr' in Borzu Sabahi, Nichals J. Birch, Ian A. Laird, and Antonio Rivas (eds.), *Comparing Political Risk Insurance and Investment Treaty Arbitration*. Huntington: Juris Publishing.

Kapeliuk, Daphna. 2010. 'The repeat appointment factor: exploring decision patterns of elite investment arbitrators', *Cornell Law Review* 96, 47–90.

Kapeliuk, Daphna. 2012. 'Collegial games analyzing the effect of panel composition on outcome in investment arbitration', *The Review of Litigation* 31, 267–311.

Kaplow, Louis. 1986. 'An economic analysis of legal transactions', *Harvard Law Review* 99, 511–617.

Kaplow, Louis. 1992. 'Rules versus standards: an economic analysis', *Duke Law Journal* 42, 557–629.

Karl, Joachim. 2015. 'An appellate body for international investment disputes: how appealing is it?', *Columbia FDI Perspectives* No. 147, 11 May. New York: Columbia University Vale Columbia Center on Sustainable International Investment.

Karton, Joshua. 2014. 'International arbitration culture and global governance' in Walter Mattli and Thomas Dietz (eds.), *International Arbitration and Global Governance*. Oxford University Press.

Kathuria, Vinish. 2000. 'Productivity spillovers from technology transfer to Indian manufacturing firms', *Journal of International Development* 12, 343–69.

Katzenstein, Suzanne. 2013. *Why Surrender Sovereignty? Empowering Non-State Actors to Protect the Status Quo*. PhD. New York: Columbia University.

Kaufmann, Daniel, Aart Kraay, and Massimo Mastruzzi. 2007. 'Governance matters VI: aggregate and individual governance indicators 1996–2006', *World Bank Policy Research Working Paper 4280*, July 2007.

Kaufmann-Kohler, Gabrielle. 2008. 'Is consistency a myth?' in Emmanuel Gaillard and Yas Banifatemi (eds.), *Precedent in International Arbitration*. Huntington: JurisNet.

Keidenren. 1997. Keidenren's views on the MAI negotiations. Available at https://www.keidanren.or.jp/english/policy/pol057.html.

Kennedy, David. 2001. 'The international human rights movement: part of the problem?', *European Human Rights Law Review* 3, 245–67.

Keohane, Robert O. 1984. *After Hegemony: Cooperation and Discord in the World Political Economy*. Princeton University Press.

Keohane, Robert O. 2011. 'Global governance and legitimacy', *Review of International Political Economy* 18, 99–109.

Keohane, Robert and Van Doom Ooms. 1975. 'The multinational firm and international regulation', *International Organization* 29, 169–209.

Keohane, Robert O. and Joseph E. Nye Jr. 2001. 'The club model of multilateral cooperation and problems of democratic legitimacy' in Roger B. Porter and others (eds.), *Efficiency, Equity, and Legitimacy: The Multilateral Trading System at the Millennium*. Washington, DC: Brookings Institution Press.

Keohane, Robert O. and David G. Victor. 2011. 'The regime complex for climate change', *Perspectives on Politics* 9, 7–23.

Kerner, Andrew. 2009. 'Why should I believe you? The costs and consequences of bilateral investment treaties', *International Studies Quarterly* 53, 73–102.

Kerner, Andrew. 2014. 'What we talk about when we talk about foreign direct investment', *International Studies Quarterly* 58, 804–15.

Kerner, Andrew and Jane Lawrence. 2014. 'What's the risk? Bilateral investment treaties, political risk and fixed capital accumulation', *British Journal of Political Science* 44, 107–21.

Kim, Jae Hoon. 2011. 'Korea's development of a better investor-state dispute resolution system' in Susan D. Franck and Anna Joubin-Bret (eds.), *Investor-State Disputes: Prevention and Alternatives to Arbitration II*. Geneva: United Nations.

Kindleberger, Charles P. 1969. 'American business abroad', *The International Executive* 11, 11–12.

Kingsbury, Benedict. 2012. 'International courts: uneven judicialization in global order' in James Crawford and Marti Koskenniemi (eds.), *The Cambridge Companion to International Law*. Cambridge University Press.

Kingshuk, Nag. 1999. 'Austria delegation comes scouting for Indian investors', *The Times of India*, 11 February 1999.

Kläger, Roland. 2011. *'Fair and Equitable Treatment' in International Investment Law*. Cambridge University Press.

Klein, Benjamin and Keith Leffler. 1981. 'The role of market forces in assuring contractual performance', *Journal of Political Economy* 89, 615–41.

Klein, Naomi. 2001. 'Time to fight free trade laws that benefit multinationals', *Guardian Weekly*, 14 March.

Kleinheisterkamp, Jan. 2014. 'Financial responsibility in european international investment policy', *International and Comparative Law Quarterly* 63, 449–76.

Kleinheisterkamp, Jan. 2015. 'Investment treaty law and the fear for sovereignty: transnational challenges and solutions', *The Modern Law Review* 78, 793–825.

Kleinheisterkamp, Jan and Lauge Poulsen. 2014. 'Investment protection in TTIP: three feasible proposals', *Global Economic Governance Programme*, Policy Brief, December. University of Oxford.

Klerman, Daniel. 2009. 'The emergence of English commercial law: Analysis inspired by the Ottoman experience', *Journal of Economic Behavior & Organization* 71, 638–46.

Knauer, Sebastian. 2009. 'Vattenfall vs Germany: power plant battle goes to international arbitration', *Spiegel Online,* 15 July. Available at http://www.spiegel.de/international/germany/vattenfall-vs-germany-power-plant-battle-goes-to-international-arbitration-a-636334. html.

Knickerbocker, Frederick T. 1973. *Oligopolistic Reaction and Multinational Enterprise.* Cambridge: Harvard University Press.

Kobrin, Stephen J. 1987. 'Testing the bargaining hypothesis in the manufacturing sector in developing countries', *International Organization* 41, 609–38.

Kogut, Bruce and Sea Jin Chang. 1991. 'Technological capabilities and Japanese foreign direct investment in the United States', *The Review of Economics and Statistics* 73, 401–13.

Koh, Harold. 1997. 'Review essay: why do nations obey international law?', *Yale Law Journal* 106, 2599–659.

Kohler, Wilhelm and Frank Stähler. 2016. 'The economics of investor protection: ISDS versus national treatment', *CESifo Working Paper Series No. 5766*, 11 April. Available at https://www.cesifo-group.de/de/ifoHome/publications/working-papers/CESifoWP/CESifoWPdetails?wp_id=19189938.

Kolo, Abba and Thomas Wälde. 2000. 'Renegotiation and contract adaptation in international investment projects: applicable legal principles and industry practices', *Journal of World Investment and Trade* 1, 5–57.

Konings, Jozef. 2001. 'The effects of foreign direct investment on domestic firms', *Economics of Transition* 9, 619–33.

Korinek, Anton. 2011. 'The new economics of prudential capital controls: a research agenda', *IMF Economic Review* 59, 523–61.

Kose, M. Ayhan, Eswar Prasad, Kenneth Rogoff, and Shang-Jin Wei. 2009. 'Financial globalization: a reappraisal', *IMF Staff Papers* 56, 8–62.

Koskenniemi, Martti. 1989. *From Apology to Utopia: The Structure of International Legal Argument.* Helsinki: Finnish Lawyers Publishing Company.

Koskenniemi, Martti. 2002. *The Gentle Civilizer of Nations: The Rise and Fall of International Law, 1870–1960.* Cambridge University Press.

Koskenniemi, Martti. 2009. 'Miserable comforters: international relations as new natural law', *European Journal of International Relations* 15, 395–422.

Koskenniemi, Martti. 2017. 'It's not the cases, it's the system', *The Journal of World Investment and Trade* 18, 343–53.

Krasner, Stephen D. 1978. *Defending the National Interest: Raw Materials Investments and US Foreign Policy*. Princeton University Press.

Krasner, Stephen D. 2009. *Power, the State, and Sovereignty: Essays on International Relations*. London: Routledge.

Kravis, Irving and Robert Lipsey. 1992. 'Sources of competitiveness of the U.S. and of its multinational firms', *Review of Economics and Statistics* 74, 193–201.

Krisch, Nico. 2005. 'International law in times of hegemony: unequal power and the shaping of the international legal order', *European Journal of International Law* 16, 369–408.

Krisch, Nico. 2010. *Beyond Constitutionalism: The Pluralist Structure of Postnational Law*. Oxford University Press.

Kronstein, Heinrich. 1944. 'Business arbitration. instrument of private government', *The Yale Law Journal* 54, 36–69.

Krugman, Paul, Maurice Obstfeld, and Marc Melitz. 2014. *International Economics: Theory and Policy*, 10th edn. London, New York: Pearson.

Kugler, Maurice. 2006. 'Spillover from foreign direct investment: within or between industries?', *Journal of Development Economics* 80, 444–77.

Kurtz, Jürgen. 2009. 'The use and abuse of WTO law in investor–state arbitration: competition and its discontents', *European Journal of International Law* 20, 749–71.

Kurtz, Jürgen. 2012. 'Australia's rejection of investor-state arbitration: causation, omission and implication', *ICSID Review* 27, 65–86.

Kurtz, Jürgen. 2014. 'Building legitimacy through interpretation in investor-state arbitration: on consistency, coherence, and the identification of applicable law' in Zachery Douglas, Joost Pauwelyn, and Jorge E. Viñuales (eds.), *The Foundations of International Investment Law: Bringing Theory into Practice*. Oxford University Press.

Kurtz, Jürgen. 2016. *The WTO and International Investment Law: Converging Systems*. Cambridge University Press.

Kurtz, Marcus J. and Andrew Schrank. 2007a. 'Growth and governance: models, measures, and mechanisms', *Journal of Politics* 69, 538–54.

Kurtz, Marcus J. and Andrew Schrank. 2007b. 'Growth and governance: a defense', *Journal of Politics* 69, 563–69.

Kryvoi, Yaraslau. 2012. 'Counterclaims in investor-state arbitration', *Minnesota Journal of International Law* 21, 216–52.

Laborde, Gustavo. 2010. 'The case for host state claims in investment arbitration', *Journal of International Dispute Settlement* 1, 97–122.

Langford, Malcolm and Daniel Behn. 2016. 'Managing backlash: the evolving investment treaty arbitrator?', September. On file with the authors.

Lasser, Mitchel. 2004. *Judicial Deliberations: A Comparative Analysis of Transparency and Legitimacy*. Oxford University Press.

Law Commission of India. 2015. *Law Commission of India Report No.260 Analysis of the 2015 Draft Model Indian Bilateral Investment Treaty*, New Delhi.

Lawyers for Civil Justice, Civil Justice Reform Group, U.S. Chamber Institute for Legal Reform. 2010. 'Litigation cost survey of major companies', statement to Committee on Rules of Practice and Procedure Judicial Conference of the United States 2010 Conference on Civil Litigation, Duke Law School, 10–11 May.

Lazareff, Serge. 2005. 'L'arbitre singe ou comment assasiner l'arbitrage' in Gerald Aksen (ed.), *Global Reflections on International Law, Commerce and Dispute Resolution: Liber Amicorum in Honour of Robert Briner*, vol. 477–89. Paris: ICC Publishing.

Lee, Chew Ging. 2010. 'Outward foreign direct investment and economic growth: evidence from Japan', *Global Economic Review* 39, 317–26.

Legg, Andrew. 2012. *The Margin of Appreciation in International Human Rights Law: Deference and Proportionality*. Oxford University Press.

Legum, Barton. 2006. 'Defining investment and investor: who is entitled to claim?', *Arbitration International* 22, 521–6.

Lejour, Arjan and Maria Salfi. 2015. 'The Regional Impact of Bilateral Investment Treaties on Foreign Direct Investment', *CPB Discussion Paper No. 298*, January. The Hague: CPB Netherlands Bureau for Economic Policy Analysis.

Lenin, Vladimir. 1917. *Imperialism: The Highest Stage of Capitalism*. Petrograd. Translated and reissued in 2010 by Penguin (London) as a mass market paperback.

Leontief, Wassily. 1953. 'Domestic production and foreign trade: the American capital position re-examined', *Proceedings of the American Philosophical Society* 97, 332–49.

Lesher, Molly and Sébastien Miroudot. 2006. 'Analysis of the economic impact of investment provisions in regional trade agreements', *OECD Trade Policy Papers No. 36*. Paris: OECD.

Lester, Simon. 2015. 'Rethinking the international investment law system', *Journal of World Trade* 49, 211–21.

Letsas, George. 2006. 'Two concepts of the margin of appreciation', *Oxford Journal of Legal Studies* 26, 705–32.

Levinson, David. 2000. 'Making government pay: markets, politics, and the allocation of constitutional costs', *University of Chicago Law Review* 67, 345–420.

Levy, Marc A., Oran R. Young, and Michael Zürn. 1995. 'The study of international regimes', *European Journal of International Relations* 1, 267–330.

Levy, Philip I. and Thirukodikaval Nilakanta Srinivasan. 1996. 'Regionalism and the (dis) advantage of dispute-settlement access', *The American Economic Review* 86, 93–8.

Lew, Julian D. M., Loukas A. Mistelis, and Stefan Kröll. 2003. *Comparative International Commercial Arbitration*. The Hague, London: Kluwer Law International.

Lewis, Clive. 2015. *Judicial Remedies in Public Law*, 5th ed. London: Sweet & Maxwell/Thomson Reuters.

Li, Quan. 2009. 'Democracy, autocracy, and expropriation of foreign direct investment', *Comparative Political Studies* 42, 1098–127.

Li, Quan and Adam Resnick. 2003. 'Reversal of fortunes: democratic institutions and foreign direct investment inflows to developing countries', *International Organization* 57, 175–211.

Li, Xiaoying and Xiaming Liu. 2005. 'Foreign direct investment and economic growth: an increasingly endogenous relationship', *World Development* 33, 393–407.

Liberman, Jonathan. 2013. 'Plainly constitutional: the upholding of plain tobacco packaging by the High Court of Australia', *American Journal of Law & Medicine* 39, 361–81.

Lipsey, Robert. 1999. 'The role of foreign direct investment in international capital flows', *NBER Working Paper No. 7094*, Cambridge: National Bureau of Economic Research.

Lipsey, Robert and Fredrik Sjöholm. 2001. 'Foreign direct investment and wages in Indonesian manufacturing', *NBER Working Paper No. 8299*. Cambridge: National Bureau of Economic Research.

Lipsey, Robert. 2005. 'The impact of inward FDI on host countries: why such different answers?' in Theodore Moran, Edward Graham, and Magnus Blomström (eds.), *Does Foreign Direct Investment Promote Development?* Washington, DC: Center for Global Development and Institute for International Economics.

Lipsey, Richard and Kelvin Lancaster. 1956. 'The general theory of the second best', *The Review of Economic Studies* 24, 11–32.

Lipson, Charles. 1985. *Standing Guard: Protecting Foreign Capital in the Nineteenth and Twentieth Centuries*. Berkeley: University of California Press.

Liptak, Adam. 2004. 'Review of U.S. rulings by NAFTA tribunals stirs worries', *The New York Times*, 18 April.

Loree, David W. and Stephen E. Guisinger. 1995. 'Policy and non-policy determinants of US equity foreign direct investment', *Journal of International Business Studies* 26, 281–99.

Lowenfeld, Andreas F. 2003. 'Investment Agreements and International Law', *Columbia Journal of Transnational Law* 42, 123–30.

Lucas, Robert. 1990. 'Why doesn't capital flow from rich to poor countries?', *The American Economic Review* 80, 92–6.

Lustig, Doreen and Eyal Benvenisti. 2014. 'The multinational corporation as "the good despot": the democratic cost of privatization in global settings', *Theoretical Inquiries in Law* 15, 125–57.

Lutz, Ellen L. and Kathryn Sikkink. 2000. 'International human rights law and practice in Latin America', *International Organization* 54, 633–59.

Maass, Peter. 2009. *Crude World: The Violent Twilight of Oil*. London: Vintage.

MacDougall, Donald. 1960. 'The benefits and costs of private investment from abroad', *Economic Record* 36, 13–35.

Mackenzie, Ruth. 2010. *Selecting International Judges: Principle, Process, and Politics*. Oxford University Press.

Madiès, Thierry and Jean-Jacques Dethier. 2012. 'Fiscal competition in developing countries: a survey of the theoretical and empirical literature', *Journal of International Commerce, Economics and Policy* 3, 1250013-1-31.

Majone, Giandomenico. 1998. 'Europe's "democratic deficit": the question of standards', *European Law Journal* 4, 5–28.

Makino, Shige, Chung-Ming Lau, and Rhy-Song Yeh. 2002. 'Asset-exploitation versus asset-seeking: implications for location choice of foreign direct investment from newly industrialized economies', *Journal of International Business Studies* 33, 403–21.

Malvesi, Lara. 2017. 'Malmström: CETA done, Mexico and Mercosur next up', *EurActiv*, 16 February.

Manger, Mark. 2009. *Investing in Protection: The Politics of Preferential Trade Agreements Between North and South*. Cambridge University Press.

Manger, Mark. 2008. 'International investment agreements and services markets: locking in market failure?', *World Development* 36, 2456–69.

Manger, Mark and Clint Peinhardt. 2017. 'Learning and the Precision of International Investment Agreements' *International Interactions* 43.

Mangklatanakul, Vilawan. 2012. 'Thailand's first treaty arbitration: gain from pain' in UNCTAD, *Investor-State Disputes: Prevention and Alternatives to Arbitration II*. Geneva: United Nations.

Mann, Howard. 2007. 'Investment agreements and the regulatory state: can exceptions clauses create a safe haven for governments?', International Institute for Sustainable Development. Available at www.iisd.org/pdf/2007/inv_agreements_reg_state.pdf.

Mann, Howard. 2008. 'International investment agreements, business and human rights: key issues and opportunities', International Institute for Sustainable Development. Available at https://www.iisd.org/pdf/2008/iia_business_human_rights.pdf.

Mansfield, Edward D. and Helen V. Milner. 2012. *Votes, Vetoes, and the Political Economy of International Trade Agreements*. Princeton University Press.

Marboe, Irmgard. 2009. *Calculation of Compensation and Damages in International Investment Law*. Oxford University Press.

March, James G. and Johan P. Olsen. 1998. 'The institutional dynamics of international political orders', *International Organization* 52, 943–69.

Markus, Stanislav. 2012. 'Secure property as a bottom-up process: firms, stakeholders, and predators in weak states', *World Politics* 64, 242–77.

Markusen, James R. 1984. 'Multinationals, multi-plant economies, and the gains from trade', *Journal of International Economics* 16, 205–26.

Markusen, James R. 2001. 'Commitment to rules on investment: the developing countries' stake', *Review of International Economics* 9, 287–302.

Markusen, James R. 2002. *Multinational Firms and the Theory of International Trade*. Cambridge: MIT Press.

Markusen, James R. 2008. 'Foreign direct investment', in Kenneth Reinhart and Ramkishen Ranjan (eds.), *The Princeton Encyclopedia of the World Economy*. Princeton University Press.

Markusen, James R. and Keith E. Maskus. 2002. 'Discriminating among alternative theories of the multinational enterprise', *Review of International Economics* 10, 694–707.

Markusen, James R., Anthony Venables, Denise Konan, and Kevin Zhang. 1996. 'A unified treatment of horizontal direct investment, vertical direct investment, and the pattern of trade in goods and services', *NBER Working Paper No. 5696*, Cambridge: National Bureau of Economic Research.

Mattli, Walter. 2001. 'Private justice in a global economy: from litigation to arbitration', *International Organization* 55, 919–47.

Mattli, Walter and Thomas Dietz. 2014. *International Arbitration and Global Governance: Contending Theories and Evidence*. Oxford University Press.

Mattli, Walter and Anne-Marie Slaughter. 1995. 'Law and politics in the European Union: a reply to Garrett', *International Organization* 49, 183–90.

Maupin, Julie A. 2011. 'MFN-based jurisdiction in investor–state arbitration: is there any hope for a consistent approach?', *Journal of International Economic Law* 14, 157–90.

Maurer, Noel. 2013. *The Empire Trap: The Rise and Fall of US Intervention to Protect American Property Overseas, 1893–2013*. Princeton University Press.

Mazumder, Soumyajit. 2016. 'Can I stay a BIT longer? The effect of bilateral investment treaties on political survival', *The Review of International Organizations* 11, 477–521.

McLachlan, Campbell. 2009. *Lis Pendens in International Litigation*. Leiden, Boston: Martinus Nijhoff.

McLachlan, Campbell, Laurence Shore, and Matthew Weiniger. 2017. *International Investment Arbitration: Substantive Principles*, 2nd edn. Oxford University Press.

McRae, Donald. 2012. 'MFN in the GATT and WTO', *Asian Journal of WTO and International Health Law and Policy* 7, 1–24.

Medvedev, Denis. 2012. 'Beyond trade: the impact of preferential trade agreements on FDI inflows', *World Development* 40, 49–61.

Meeker, Leonard. Undated. Circular 175 Authority for Signature of World Bank Convention on Settlement of Investment Disputes.

Melitz, Marc J. 2003. 'The impact of trade on intra-industry reallocations and aggregate industry productivity', *Econometrica* 71, 1695–725.

Melitz, Marc J. 2005. 'When and how should infant industries be protected?', *Journal of International Economics* 66, 177–96.

Merrills, John Graham. 2011. *International Dispute Settlement*, 5th edn. Cambridge University Press.

Meshel, Tamar. 2015. 'Human rights in investor-state arbitration: the human right to water and beyond', *Journal of International Dispute Settlement* 6, 277–307.

Miceli, Thomas J. 2011. *The Economic Theory of Eminent Domain: Private Property, Public Use.* Cambridge University Press.

Miceli, Thomas J. and Kathleen Segerson. 1994. 'Regulatory takings: when should compensation be paid?', *The Journal of Legal Studies* 23, 749–76.

Milanović, Branko. 2005. *Worlds Apart: Measuring International and Global Inequality.* Princeton University Press.

Miles, Kate. 2013. *The Origins of International Investment Law: Empire, Environment, and the Safeguarding of Capital.* Cambridge University Press.

Milner, Helen V. 1988. *Resisting Protectionism: Global Industries and the Politics of International Trade.* Princeton University Press.

Milner, Helen V. 1997. 'Industries, governments, and regional trade blocs' in Edward D. Mansfield and Helen V. Milner (eds.), *The Political Economy of Regionalism.* New York: Columbia University Press.

Mina, Wasseem. 2009. 'External commitment mechanisms, institutions, and FDI in GCC countries', *International Financial Markets, Institutions and Money* 19, 371–86.

Mnookin, Robert H. and Lewis Kornhauser. 1979. 'Bargaining in the shadow of the law: the case of divorce', *The Yale Law Journal* 88, 950–97.

Mody, Ashoka and Antu Murshid. 2011. 'Growth from international capital flows: the role of volatility regimes', *IMF Working Paper No. 11/90*, Washington, DC: International Monetary Fund.

Moloo, Rahim and Justin Jacinto. 2011. 'Environmental and health regulation: assessing liability under investment treaties', *Berkeley Journal of International Law* 29, 1–65.

Moloo, Rahim and Justin Jacinto. 2013. 'Standards of review and reviewing standards: public interest regulation in international investment law' in Karl P. Sauvant (ed.), *Yearbook on International Investment Law and Policy 2011–2012.* Oxford University Press.

Montt, Santiago. 2009. *State Liability in Investment Treaty Arbitration: Global Constitutional and Administrative Law in the BIT Generation.* Oxford, Portland: Hart.

Moon, Chungshik. 2014. 'Credible commitment institutions and foreign direct investment: how are autocratic countries able to attract FDI?', PhD Thesis, Tallahassee: Florida State University. Available at http://diginole.lib.fsu.edu/islandora/object/fsu%3A185291.

Moore, Kimberely A. 2003. 'Xenophobia in American courts', *Northwestern University Law Review* 97, 1497–550.

Moran, Theodore. 2007. *Harnessing Foreign Direct Investment for Development: Policies for Developed and Developing Countries*. Washington, DC: Center for Global Development.

Moran, Theodore. 2011. *Foreign Direct Investment and Development: Launching a Second Generation of Policy Research: Avoiding the Mistakes of the First, Reevaluating Policies for Developed and Developing Countries*. Washington, DC: Peterson Institute for International Economics.

Moravcsik, Andrew. 1998. *The Choice for Europe: Social Purpose and State Power from Rome to Maastricht*. Ithaca: Cornell University Press.

Moravcsik, Andrew. 2000. 'The origins of human rights regimes: democratic delegation in postwar Europe', *International Organization* 54, 217–52.

Morgenthau, Hans Joachim. 1948. *Politics among Nations; The Struggle for Power and Peace*. New York: A. A. Knopf.

Moyers, Bill. 2002. *Reports: Trading Democracy*. PBS television broadcast, 4 February. Available at http://www.gwu.edu/~nsarchiv/NSAEBB/NSAEBB65/transcript.html.

Muchlinski, Peter. 2011. 'Regulating multinationals: foreign investment, development, and the balance of corporate and home country rights and responsibilities in a globalizing world' in José E. Alvarez and Karl P. Sauvant (eds.), *The Evolving International Investment Regime: Expectations, Realities, Options*. Oxford University Press.

Mukherjee, Bumba and David Andrew Singer. 2010. 'International institutions and domestic compensation: the IMF and the politics of capital account liberalization', *American Journal of Political Science* 54, 45–60.

Muir Watt, Horatia. 2014. 'The contested legitimacy of investment arbitration and the human rights ordeal: the missing link' in Walter Mattli and Thomas Dietz (eds.), *International Arbitration and Global Governance: Contending Theories and Evidence*. Oxford University Press.

Multilateral Investment Guarantee Agency (MIGA PAS). 1991a. *Industrialized Countries' Policies Affecting Foreign Direct Investment in Developing Countries*, Vol I. Washington, DC: World Bank.

Multilateral Investment Guarantee Agency (MIGA PAS). 1991b. *Annual Report*. Washington, DC: World Bank.

Multilateral Investment Guarantee Agency (MIGA PAS). 2002. *Ethiopia Negotiate with Investors to Resolve Investment Claims*, 18 December.

Multilateral Investment Guarantee Agency (MIGA PAS). 2011. *World Investment and Political Risk*. Washington, DC: World Bank.

Mundell, Robert. 1957. 'International trade and factor mobility', *The American Economic Review* 47, 321–35.

Mustill, Michael J. 2004. 'It is a bird' in Reymond Henri (ed.), *Liber amicorum Claude Reymond: Autour de l'arbitrage: mélanges offerts à Claude Reymond*. Paris: Litec.

Nair-Reichert, Usha and Diana Weinhold. 2001. 'Causality tests for cross-country panels: a new look at FDI and economic growth in developing countries', *Oxford Bulletin of Economics and Statistics* 63, 153–71.

Nappert, Sophie and Nikos Lavranos. 2016. 'Brexit: implications for the EU reform of investor-state dispute settlement'. Available at https://efilablog.org/2016/04/12/brexit-implications-for-the-eu-reform-of-investor-state-dispute-settlement/.

Navaretti, Giorgio Barba, Anthony Venables, and Frank Barry. 2006. *Multinational Firms in the World Economy*. Princeton University Press.

Neslen, Arthur. 2016. 'TTIP: Chevron lobbied for controversial legal right as "environmental deterrent"', *The Guardian*, 26 April.

Neto, Paula, Antonio Brandão, and Antonio Cerqueira. 2010. 'The impact of FDI, cross border mergers and acquisitions and greenfield investments on economic growth', *The IUP Journal of Business Strategy* 7, 24–44.

Neumayer, Eric. 2006. Self-interest, foreign need and good governance: are bilateral investment treaty programs similar to aid allocation?, *Foreign Policy Analysis* 2, 245–68.

Neumayer, Eric and Laura Spess. 2005. 'Do bilateral investment treaties increase foreign direct investment to developing countries?', *World Development* 33, 1567–85.

Neven, Damien and Georges Siotis. 1993. 'Foreign direct investment in the European community: some policy issues', *Oxford Review of Economic Policy* 9, 72–93.

Newcombe, Andrew Paul and Lluis Paradell. 2009. *Law and Practice of Investment Treaties: Standards of Treatment*. Alphen aan den Rijn: Kluwer Law International.

Newman, Carol, John Rand, Theodore Talbot, and Finn Tarp. 2015. 'Technology transfers, foreign investment and productivity spillovers', *European Economic Review* 76, 168–87.

Nickell, Stephen J. 1996. 'Competition and corporate performance', *Journal of Political Economy* 104, 724–46.

Nicolson, Harold. 1963. *Diplomacy*, 3rd edn. Oxford University Press.

Nikièma, Suzy H. 2012, March. 'Best practices: indirect expropriation', The International Institute for Sustainable Development. Available at http://www.iisd.org/pdf/2012/best_prac tice_indirect_expropriation.pdf.

Nolan, Beth and others. 2000. 'Memorandum for John D. Podesta: urgent need for policy guidance to resolve interagency litigation strategy dispute in Loewen NAFTA arbitration', Clinton Presidential Records, Box Number 18426.

North, Douglass. 1990. *Institutions, Institutional Change and Economic Performance*. Cambridge University Press.

North, Douglas and Weingast Barry. 1989. 'Constitutions and commitment: the evolution of institutions governing public choice in seventeenth century England', *Journal of Economic History* 49, 803–32.

Nottage, Luke R. and Sakda Thanitcul. 2016. 'The past, present and future of international investment arbitration in Thailand', *Sydney Law School Research Paper 16/31*.

Nunnenkamp, Peter and Julius Spatz. 2002. 'Determinants of FDI in developing countries: has globalization changed the rules of the game?' *Kiel Working Paper No. 1122*. Kiel Institute for World Economics.

Nunnenkamp, Peter and Julius Spatz. 2004. 'FDI and economic growth in developing economies: how relevant are host-economy and industry characteristics', *Transnational Corporations* 13, 53–86.

Nwogugu, Edwin I. 1965. *The Legal Problems of Foreign Investment in Developing Countries*. Manchester University Press.

Oatley, Thomas. 2010. *International Political Economy*, 4th edn. New York: Longman.

Obama, Barack. 2015. Statement by the President on Senate passage of trade promotion authority and trade adjustment assistance, The White House, 22 May. Available at https://

www.whitehouse.gov/the-press-office/2015/05/22/statement-president-senate-passage-trade-promotion-authority-and-trade-a.

Oberdorfer, Dan. 1992. 'Kazakhstan agrees to give up a-arms: START treaty roadblock is cleared,' *The Washington Post*, 20 May.

O'Donnell, Guillermo, Philippe C. Schmitter, and Laurence Whitehead. 1986. *Transitions from authoritarian rule: comparative perspectives*. Baltimore: John Hopkins University Press.

Odell, John S. 2000. *Negotiating the World Economy*. Ithaca: Cornell University Press.

OECD, Giuliana Palumbo, Giulia Giupponi, Luca Nunziata, and Juan S. Mora Sanguinetti. 2013. 'The Economics of Civil Justice: New Cross-country Data and Empirics', OECD Economics Department Working Papers No. 1060.

Office of the Historian, U.S. Department of State. 2015. 'Bretton Woods-GATT 1941–1947'. Available at https://history.state.gov/milestones/1937-1945/bretton-woods.

Office of the Historian, U.S. Department of State. 2015. 'Bilateral investment treaties and related agreements'. Available at www.state.gov/e/eb/ifd/bit.

Oh, Chang Hoon and Michele Fratianni. 2010. 'Do additional bilateral investment treaties boost foreign direct investment?' *Working Paper*, Indiana University, Department of Business Economics and Public Policy.

Olson, Mancur. 1965. *The Logic of Collective Action: Public Goods and the Theory of Groups*. Cambridge: Harvard University Press.

Olson, Mancur. 1993. 'Dictatorship, democracy, and development', *American Political Science Review* 87, 567–76.

Organisation for Economic Cooperation and Development. 2002. *Foreign Direct Investment for Development: Maximising Benefits, Minimising Costs*. Paris: OECD.

Organisation for Economic Cooperation and Development. 2005. 'Transparency and Third Party Participation in Investor-State Dispute Settlement Procedures', *OECD Working Papers on International Investment*, 2005/01. Paris: OECD.

Organisation for Economic Cooperation and Development. 2008. *OECD Benchmark Definition of Foreign Direct Investment*, 4th edn. Paris: OECD. Available at http://www.oecd.org/daf/inv/investmentstatisticsandanalysis/40193734.pdf.

Organisation for Economic Cooperation and Development. 2015a. 'FDI positions by partner countries—2012'. Available at https://stats.oecd.org/Index.aspx?DataSetCode=FDI_FLOW_PARTNER.

Organisation for Economic Cooperation and Development. 2015b. 'FDI regulatory restrictiveness index—2014'. Available at http://stats.oecd.org/Index.aspx?datasetcode=FDIINDEX#.

Orsini, Amandine, Jean-Frédéric Morin, and Oran Young. 2013. 'Regime complexes: A buzz, a boom, or a boost for global governance?', *Global Governance* 19, 27–39.

Ortino, Federico. 2012. 'From 'non-discrimination' to 'reasonableness': a paradigm shift in international economic law?' in Francesco Palermo and others (eds.), *Globalization, Technologies and Legal Revolution: The Impact of Global Changes on Territorial and Cultural Diversities, on Supranational Integration and Constitutional Theory*. Baden-Baden: Nomos.

Ostrom, Elinor. 1990. *Governing the Commons: The Evolution of Institutions for Collective Action*. Cambridge University Press.

Ostry, Jonathan, Atish R. Ghosh, Karl Habermeier, Marcos Chamon, Mahvash S. Qureshi, and Dennis B.S. Reinhardt. 2010. 'Capital inflows: the role of controls', *IMF Staff Position Note* SPN/10/04, Washington, DC: International Monetary Fund.

Pack, Howard and Kamal Saggi. 2006. 'Is there a case for industrial policy? A critical survey', *World Bank Research Observer* 21, 267–97.

Paddeu, Federica I. 2014. 'Circumstances precluding wrongfulness' in Rüdiger Wolfrum (ed.), *Max Planck Encyclopedia of Public International Law*. Oxford University Press.

Pahuja, Sundhya. 2011. *Decolonising International Law: Development, Economic Growth and the Politics of Universality*. Cambridge University Press.

Paine, Josh. 2015. 'The project of system-internal reform in international investment law: an appraisal', *Journal of International Dispute Settlement* 6, 332–54.

Pandya, Sonal. 2014. 'Democratization and foreign direct investment liberalization, 1970–2000', *International Studies Quarterly* 58, 475–88.

Paparinskis, Martins. 2010. 'The limits of depoliticisation in contemporary investor-state arbitration' in James Crawford and Sarah Nouwen (eds.), *Select Proceedings of the European Society of International Law*. Oxford: Hart.

Paparinskis, Martins. 2013. *The International Minimum Standard and Fair and Equitable Treatment*. Oxford University Press.

Paparinskis, Martins, Lauge Poulsen, and Michael Waibel. forthcoming. 'Investment law before arbitration'. On file with the authors.

Park, William W. 2001. 'Arbitration and the Fisc: NAFTA's "Tax Veto"', *Chicago Journal of International Law* 2, 231–41.

Park, William W. 2009. 'Investment claims and arbitrator comportment' in Thomas Wälde, Jacques Werner, and Arif Hyder Ali (eds.), *A Liber Amicorum: Thomas Wälde: Law Beyond Conventional Thought*. London: Cameron May.

Parra, Antonio. 2012. *The History of ICSID*. Oxford: Oxford University Press.

Parvanov, Parvan and Mark Kantor. 2012. 'Comparing U.S. law and recent U.S. investment agreements: much more similar than you might expect' in Karl Sauvant (ed.), *Yearbook on International Investment Law & Policy 2010–2011*. Oxford University Press.

Pastor, Manuel and Carol Wise. 1994. 'The origins and sustainability of Mexico's free trade policy', *International Organization* 48, 459–89.

Paulsson, Jan. 1995. 'Arbitration without privity', *ICSID Review—Foreign Investment Law Journal* 10, 232–56.

Paulsson, Jan. 2005. *Denial of Justice in International Law*. Cambridge University Press.

Paulsson, Jan. 2010. 'Moral hazard in international dispute resolution', *ICSID Review* 25, 339–55.

Pauwelyn, Joost. 2003. *Conflict of Norms in Public International Law: How WTO Law Relates to Other Rules of International Law*. Cambridge University Press.

Pauwelyn, Joost. 2005. 'The transformation of world trade', *Michigan Law Review* 104, 1–65.

Pauwelyn, Joost. 2015. 'The rule of law without the rule of lawyers? Why investment arbitrators are from Mars, trade adjudicators from Venus', *The American Journal of International Law* 109, 761–805.

Pauwelyn, Joost and Luiz Eduardo Salles. 2009. 'Forum shopping before international tribunals: (real) concerns, (im)possible solutions', *Cornell International Law Journal* 42, 77–118.

Peters, Anne. 2013. 'Towards transparency as a global norm' in Andrea Bianchi and Anne Peters (eds.), *Transparency in International Law*. Cambridge University Press.

Peinhardt, Clint and Todd Allee. 2012a. 'Failure to deliver: the investment effects of US preferential economic agreements', *The World Economy* 35, 757–83.

Peinhardt, Clint and Todd Allee. 2012b. 'Devil in the details? The investment effects of dispute settlement variation in BITs' in Karl Sauvant (ed.), *Yearbook on International Investment Law & Policy 2010–2011*. Oxford University Press.

Peinhardt, Clint and Todd Allee. 2016. 'Political risk insurance as dispute resolution', *Journal of International Dispute Settlement* 7, 205–24.

Peinhardt, Clint and Rachel Wellhausen. 2016. 'Withdrawing from investment treaties but protecting investment', *Global Policy* 7, 571–6.

Pelc, Krzysztof J. 2016. 'Does the international investment regime induce frivolous litigation?'. *International Organization*. Forthcoming. On file with the authors.

Pelc, Krzysztof J. and Johannes Urpelainen. 2015. 'When do international economic agreements allow countries to pay to breach?', *The Review of International Organizations* 10, 231–64.

Perera, Sriral. 2008. 'Arbitration under the convention establishing the multilateral investment guarantee agency and its mediation services', in Association for International Arbitration, *Arbitration and Mediation in the ACP-EU Relations* 103, 112. Antwerpen, Apeldoorn: Maklu.

Pinto, Pablo, Santiago Pinto, and Nicolas Stier-Moses. 2012. 'Regulating foreign investment: a study of the properties of bilateral investment regimes', *Paper prepared for the Annual Meeting of the International Political Economy Society*, Cambridge, MA, 20 April 2012. On file with the authors.

Pogge, Thomas W. 2014. 'International law between two futures', *Journal of International Dispute Settlement* 5, 432–37.

Pohl, Joachim, Kekeletso Mashigo, and Alexis Nohen. 2012. 'Dispute Settlement Provisions in International Investment Agreements: A Large Sample Survey', *OECD Working Papers on International Investment No. 2012/02*. Paris: OECD.

Polanco Lazo, Rodrigo. 2015. 'The no of Tokyo revisited: or how developed countries learned to start worrying and love the Calvo Doctrine', *ICSID Review* 30, 172–93.

Porter, Michael E. 1998. *Competitive Advantage: Creating and Sustaining Superior Performance*. New York: The Free Press.

Porterfield, Matthew C. 2004. 'International expropriation rules and federalism', *Stanford Environmental Law Journal* 23, 3–90.

Posner, Eric A. and John C. Yoo. 2005. 'Judicial independence in international tribunals', *California Law Review* 93, 1–74.

Posner, Eric A. and Sykes Alan O. 2011. 'Efficient breach of international law: optimal remedies, legalized noncompliance, and related issues', *Michigan Law Review* 110, 243–94.

Post, Alison E. 2014. *Foreign and Domestic Investment in Argentina: The Politics of Privatized Infrastructure*. Cambridge University Press.

Potestà, Michele. 2011. 'The interpretation of consent to ICSID arbitration contained in domestic investment laws', *Arbitration International* 27, 149–70.

Poulsen, Lauge. 2010. 'The importance of BITs for foreign direct investment and political risk insurance: revisiting the evidence' in Karl P. Sauvant (ed.), *Yearbook on International Investment Law & Policy 2009/2010*. Oxford University Press.

Poulsen, Lauge. 2011a. 'Sacrificing Sovereignty by Chance: Investment Treaties, Developing Countries, and Bounded Rationality', PhD Thesis, London School of Economics and Political Science. Available at http://etheses.lse.ac.uk/141/.

Poulsen, Lauge. 2011b. 'The politics of south-south bilateral investment treaties' in Tomer Broude, Marc Busch, and Amelia Porges (eds.), *The Politics of International Economic Law.* Cambridge University Press.

Poulsen, Lauge. 2014. 'Bounded rationality and the diffusion of modern investment treaties', *International Studies Quarterly* 58, 1–14.

Poulsen, Lauge. 2015. *Bounded Rationality and Economic Diplomacy: The Politics of Investment Treaties in Developing Countries.* Cambridge University Press.

Poulsen, Lauge. 2016. 'States as foreign investors: diplomatic disputes and legal fictions', *ICSID Review* 31, 12–23.

Poulsen, Lauge. 2017. 'Property Rights Through Focal Points: The Early Investment Treaty Regime'. Working Paper on file with the authors.

Poulsen, Lauge and Emma Aisbett. 2013. 'When the claim hits: bilateral investment treaties and bounded rational learning', *World Politics* 65, 273–313.

Poulsen, Lauge and Emma Aisbett. 2016. 'Diplomats want treaties: diplomatic agendas and perks in the investment regime', *Journal of International Dispute Settlement* 7, 72–91.

Poulsen, Lauge, Jonathan Bonnitcha, and Jason Webb Yackee. 2015. *Transatlantic Investment Treaty Protection*, Paper No. 3 in the CEPS-CTR Project on 'TTIP in the Balance', CEPS Special Report No 102, March 2015, London.

Poulsen, Lauge and Gary Hufbauer. 2011. 'Foreign Direct Investment in Times of Crisis', *Working Paper Series No. 11–3, 19.* Washington, DC: Peterson Institute for International Economics.

Poulsen, Lauge and Jason Yackee. 2016. 'Measurement Error in the Empirical Research Study of Investment Treaties'. Working paper on file with authors.

Prasad, Eswar, Raghuram Rajan, and Arvind Subramanian. 2006. 'Patterns of international capital flows and their implications for economic development', in *Proceedings.* Federal Reserve Bank of Kansas City, 119–58.

Prebisch, Raúl. 1959. 'Commercial policy in the underdeveloped countries', *The American Economic Review* 49, 251–73.

Price, Daniel M. and Christy P. Brian. 1996. 'Agreement on trade related investment measures (TRIMS): limitations and prospects for the future' in P. Stewart Terence (ed.), *The World Trade Organization: The Multilateral Trade Framework for the 21st Century and US Implementing Legislation.* Chicago: American Bar Association.

Priest, Dana. 1991. 'Menem signs "revolutionary" treaty with US to protect investments', *The Washington Post*, 15 November.

Productivity Commission. 2010. *Bilateral Trade and Regional Trade Agreements, Research Report.* Canberra: Commonwealth of Australia.

Proehl, Paul. O. 1960. 'Private investments abroad', *Journal of Public Law* 9, 362–73.

Puig, Sergio. 2014. 'Social capital in the arbitration market', *European Journal of International Law* 25, 387–424.

Puig, Sergio. 2015. 'The merging of international trade and investment law', *Berkeley Journal of International Law* 33, 1–59.

Puig, Sergio. 2016. 'Tobacco litigation in international courts', *Harvard International Law Journal* 64, 383–432.

Puig, Sergio and Anton Strezhnev. 2016a. 'Affiliation bias in arbitration: an experimental approach'. Paper on file with the authors.

Puig, Sergio and Anton Strezhnev. 2016b. The David effect. On file with the authors.

Putnam, Robert D. 1988. 'Diplomacy and domestic politics: the logic of two-level games', *International Organization* 42, 427–60.

Queen Mary School of Arbitration. 2010. *2010 International Arbitration Survey: Choices in International Arbitration*. London: Queen Mary School of Arbitration.

Ræder, Anton Henrik and Magnus Synnestvedt. 1912. *L'arbitrage international chez les Hellènes*. New York: G. P. Putnam.

Ramamurti, Ravi. 2003. 'Can governments make credible promises? Insights from infrastructure projects in emerging economies', *Journal of International Management* 9, 253–69.

Ranganathan, Surabhi. 2014. *Strategically Created Treaty Conflicts and the Politics of International Law*. Cambridge University Press.

Ranjan, Prabash. 2014. 'India and bilateral investment treaties—a changing landscape', *ICSID Review* 29, 419–50.

Ratner, Steven R. 2008. 'Regulatory takings in institutional context: beyond the fear of fragmented international law', *The American Journal of International Law* 102, 475–528.

Raustiala, Kal and David G. Victor. 2004. 'The regime complex for plant genetic resources', *International Organization* 58, 277–309.

Ravenhill, John. 2008. 'The move to preferential trade on the Western Pacific Rim: some initial conclusions', *Australian Journal of International Affairs* 62, 129–50.

Ravenhill, John. 2011. *Global Political Economy*, 3rd edn. Oxford University Press.

Raz, Joseph. 1979. *The Authority of Law: Essays on Law and Morality*. Oxford: Clarendon Press.

Reed, Lucy, Jan Paulsson, and Nigel Blackaby. 2011. *Guide to ICSID Arbitration*, 2nd edn. Alphen aan den Rijn: Kluwer Law International.

Reinhart, Carmen and Vincent Reinhart. 2008. 'Capital flow bonanzas: an encompassing view of the past and present' in Jeffrey Frankel and Christopher Pissaridis (eds.), *NBER International Seminar on Macroeconomics*. University of Chicago Press.

Reinisch, August. 2010. 'The issues raised by parallel proceedings and possible solutions' in Michael Waibel, Asha Kaushal, Kwo-Hwa Liz Chung, and Claire Balchin (eds.), *The Backlash against Investment Arbitration: Perceptions and Reality*. Alphen aan den Rijn: Kluwer Law International.

Reinisch, August. 2013. 'Austria' in Chester Brown (ed.), *Commentaries on Selected Model Investment Treaties*. Oxford University Press.

Reinisch, August. 2016. 'The European Union and investor-state dispute settlement: from investor-state arbitration to a permanent investment court', *Investor-State Arbitration Series, Paper No 2*. Ontario: Centre for International Governance Innovation (CIGI).

Reisman, W. Michael. 2009. 'International investment arbitration and ADR: married but best living apart', *ICSID Review* 24, 185–92.

Reisman, W. Michael and Robert Sloane. 2004. 'Indirect expropriation and its valuation in the BIT generation', *British Yearbook of International Law* 74, 115–50.

Ripinsky, Sergey. 2013. 'Russia' in Chester Brown (ed.), *Commentaries on Selected Model Investment Treaties*. Oxford University Press.

Ripinsky, Sergey and Kevin Williams. 2008. *Damages in International Investment Law*. London: British Institute of International and Comparative Law.

Roberts, Anthea. 2010. 'Power and persuasion in investment treaty interpretation: the dual role of states', *The American Journal of International Law* 104, 179–225.

Roberts, Anthea. 2013. 'Clash of paradigms: actors and analogies shaping the investment treaty system', *The American Journal of International Law* 107, 45–94.

Roberts, Anthea. 2014. 'State-to-state investment treaty arbitration: a hybrid theory of inter-dependent rights and shared interpretive authority', *Harvard International Law Journal* 55, 1–70.

Roberts, Anthea. 2015. 'Triangular treaties: the extent and limits of investment treaty rights', *Harvard International Law Journal* 56, 353–417.

Rodrik, Dani. 1995. 'Political economy of trade policy' in Gene M. Grossman and Kenneth Rogoff (eds.), *Handbook of International Economics*, Volume 3. Amsterdam, New York: Elsevier.

Rodrik, Dani. 2006. 'What's so special about China's exports?', *China and World Economy* 14, 1–19.

Rodrik, Dani. 2008. 'Normalizing industrial policy', *Working Paper 3*, Washington, DC: Commission on Growth and Development.

Rodrik, Dani. 2010. 'The end of an era in finance', *Project Syndicate*, 11 March 2010. Available at http://www.project-syndicate.org/commentary/the-end-of-an-era-in-finance.

Rodrik, Dani. 2011. *The Globalization Paradox: Why Global Markets, States, and Democracy Can't Coexist*. Oxford University Press.

Rodrik, Dani, Arvind Subramanian, and Francesco Trebbi. 2004. 'Institutions rule: the primacy of institutions over geography and integration in economic development', *Journal of Economic Growth* 9, 131–65.

Röller, Lars-Hendrik and Leonard Waverman. 2001. 'Telecommunications infrastructure and economic development: a simultaneous approach', *The American Economic Review* 91, 909–23.

Rose-Ackerman, Susan and Rory Truex. 2013. 'Corruption and policy reform' in Bjørn Lomborg (ed.), *Global Problems, Smart Solutions: Costs and Benefits*. Cambridge University Press.

Rosenberg, Charles B. 2013. 'The intersection of international trade and international arbitration: the use of trade benefits to secure compliance with arbitral awards', *Georgetown Journal of International Law* 44, 503–30.

Rosendorff, Peter B. and Kongjoo Shin. 2012. 'Importing transparency: the political economy of BITs and FDI flows', *Working Paper*, 4 August 2012, New York University. Available at https://wp.nyu.edu/faculty-rosendorff/wp-content/uploads/sites/1510/2015/03/RosendorffShinAPSA2012.pdf.

Ross, Michael. 2012. *The Oil Curse: How Petroleum Wealth Shapes the Development of Nations*. Princeton University Press.

Rostow, Eugene. 1952. 'The democratic character of judicial review', *Harvard Law Review* 66, 193–224.

Roth, Andreas Hans. 1949. *The Minimum Standard of International Law Applied to Aliens*. Leiden: AW Sijthoff.

Rowley, Anthony. 2013. 'TPP's thick veil of secrecy', *The Business Times*, 15 June.

Rugman, Alan. 1977. 'Risk, direct investment and International diversification', *Review of World Economics* 113, 487–500.

Rugman, Alan. 1980. 'Internalization as a general theory of foreign direct investment: A re-appraisal of the literature', *Review of World Economics* 116, 365–79.

Rugman, Alan. 1981. *Inside the Multinationals: The Economics of Internal Markets*. New York: Columbia University Press.

Rugman, Alan. 2005. *The Regional Multinationals: MNEs and 'Global' Strategic Management*. Cambridge University Press.

Rugman, Alan M. and Alain Verbeke. 1990. *Global Corporate Strategy and Trade Policy*. London: Routledge.

Rugman, Alan M. and Alain Verbeke. 2004. 'A perspective on regional and global strategies of multinational enterprises', *Journal of International Business Studies* 35, 3–18.

Rui, Huaichuan and George S. Yip. 2008. 'Foreign acquisitions by Chinese firms: A strategic intent perspective', *Journal of World Business* 43, 213–26.

Russo, Deborah. 2015. 'Addressing the relation between treaties by means of "saving clauses"', *British Yearbook of International Law*, 133–70.

Sabahi, Borzu. 2011. *Compensation and Restitution in Investor-State Arbitration: Principles and Practice*. Oxford University Press.

Sacerdoti, Giorgio. 1997. 'Bilateral treaties and multilateral instruments in investment protection', in *Collected Courses of the Hague Academy of International Law*, vol. 269. Leiden, Boston: Brill Nijhoff.

Sachs, Lisa. 2009. 'Bilateral investment treaties and FDI flows', World Association of Investment Promotion Agencies (WAIPA) Newsletter 5.

Salacuse, Jeswald W. 2003. *The Global Negotiator: Making, Managing, and Mending Deals around the World in the Twenty-First Century*. New York: Palgrave Macmillan.

Salacuse, Jeswald W. 2007. 'Is there a better way? Alternative methods of treaty-based, investor-state dispute resolution', *Fordham International Law Journal* 31, 138–85.

Salacuse, Jeswald W. 2010. *The Law of International Investment Treaties*. Oxford University Press.

Salacuse, Jeswald W. 2013. *The Three Laws of International Investment: National, Contractual, and International Frameworks for Foreign Capital*. Oxford University Press.

Salacuse, Jeswald W. and Nicholas Sullivan. 2005. 'Do BITs really work? An evaluation of bilateral investment treaties and their grand bargain', *Harvard International Law Journal* 46, 67–130.

Sally, Razeen. 2002. *Classical Liberalism and International Economic Order: Studies in Theory and Intellectual History* London: Routledge.

Sanders, Anthony B. 2010. 'Of all things made in America why are we exporting the Penn Central Test?', *Northwestern Journal of International Law & Business* 30, 339–81.

Sands, Philippe. 2006. *Lawless World: Making and Breaking Global Rules*. London: Penguin.

Sasse, Jan Peter. 2011. *An Economic Analysis of Bilateral Investment Treaties*. Wiesbaden: Gabler.

Sattorova, Mavluda. 2014. 'The impact of investment treaty law on host state behavior: some doctrinal, empirical and interdisciplinary insights' in Shaheeza Lalani and Rodrigo Polanco Lazo (eds.), *The Role of the State in Investor-State Arbitration*. Leiden, Boston: Brill Nijhoff.

Sattorova, Mavluda. 2016. *The Impact of Investment Treaty Law on Government Conduct: Enabling Good Governance*. Oxford: Hart.

Sattorova, Mavluda, Ohio Omiunu, and Erkan Mustafa. 2016. 'How do host states respond to investment treaty law? Some empirical observations', *European Yearbook of International Economic Law*.

Sauvant, Karl P. 2015. 'The negotiations of the United Nations code of conduct on transnational corporations: experience and lessons learned', *Journal of World Investment and Trade* 16, 11–87.

Sauvé, Pierre and Karsten Steinfatt. 2001. 'Financial services and the WTO: what next?' in Robert E. Litan, Paul Masson, and Michael Pomerleano (eds.), *Open Doors: Foreign Participation in Financial Systems in Developing Countries*. Washington, DC: Brookings Institution Press.

Scharpf, Fritz Wilhelm. 1999. *Governing in Europe: Effective and Democratic?* Oxford University Press.

Schill, Stephan W. 2007. 'Tearing down the Great Wall: The new generation investment treaties of The People's Republic of China', *Cardozo Journal of International and Comparative Law* 15, 73–118.

Schill, Stephan W. 2009. *The Multilateralization of International Investment Law*. Cambridge University Press.

Schill, Stephan W. 2010. 'International investment law and comparative public law—an introduction' in Stephan W. Schill (ed.), *International Investment Law and Comparative Public Law*. Oxford University Press.

Schill, Stephan W. 2011. 'W(h)ither fragmentation? On the literature and sociology of international investment law', *European Journal of International Law* 22, 875–908.

Schill, Stephan W. 2012. 'System-building in investment treaty arbitration and lawmaking' in Armin von Bogdandy and Ingo Venzke (eds.), *International Judicial Lawmaking*. Berlin, Heidelberg: Springer.

Schill, Stephan W. 2015. 'Conceptions of legitimacy' in David D. Caron and others (eds.), *Practising Virtue: Inside International Arbitration*. Oxford University Press.

Schill, Stephan W. 2016. 'In defense of international investment law', *European Yearbook of International Economic Law* 7, 309–41.

Schneiderman, David. 2008. *Constitutionalizing Economic Globalization: Investment Rules and Democracy's Promise*. Cambridge University Press.

Schneiderman, David. 2010. 'Investing in democracy? Political process and international investment law', *Toronto Law Journal* 60, 909–40.

Schneiderman, David, Kyla Tienhaara, and Gus Van Harten. 2015. 'Reply to European Federation of Investment Law and Arbitration (EFILA)', 6 July. Available at https://gusvanharten.wordpress.com/tag/efila/.

Schreiber, Will. 2008. 'Realizing the right to water in international investment law', *Natural Resources Journal* 48, 431–78.

Schreuer, Christoph. 2004a. 'Non-pecuniary remedies in ICSID arbitration', *Arbitration International* 20, 325–32.

Schreuer, Christoph. 2004b. 'Travelling the BIT route: of waiting periods, umbrella clauses and forks in the road', *Journal of World Investment* 5, 231–56.

Schreuer, Christoph. 2006. 'The concept of expropriation under the ECT and other investment protection treaties' in Ribeiro Clarisse (ed.), *Investment Arbitration and The Energy Charter Treaty*. Huntington: Huntington Juris, 108–59.

Schreuer, Christoph. 2011. 'Interaction of international tribunals and domestic courts in investment law' in Arthur W. Rovine (ed.), *Contemporary Issues in International Arbitration and Mediation: The Fordham Papers (2010)*. Leiden: Martinus Nijhoff, 71–94.

Schreuer, Christoph. 2013. 'Coherence and consistency in international investment law' in Roberto Echandi and Pierre Sauvé (eds.), *Prospects in International Investment Law and Policy*. Cambridge University Press.

Schreuer, Christoph H. and others. 2009. *The ICSID Convention: A Commentary*, 2nd edn. Cambridge University Press.

Schrijver, Nico and Prislan Vid. 2013. 'Netherlands' in Chester Brown (ed.), *Commentaries on Selected Model Investment Treaties*. Oxford University Press.

Schudson, Michael. 2015. *The Rise of the Right to Know: Politics and the Culture of Transparency, 1945–1975*. Cambridge: The Belknap Press of Harvard University Press.

Schultz, Thomas. 2014. 'Against consistency in investment arbitration?' in Zachary Douglas, Joost Pauwelyn, and Jorge E. Viñuales (eds.), *The Foundations of International Investment Law: Bringing Theory into Practice*. Oxford University Press.

Schwebel, Stephen M. 1987. *International Arbitration: Three Salient Problems*. Cambridge: Grotius.

Schwebel, Stephen. 2004. 'The influence of bilateral investment treaties on customary international law', *Proceedings of the Annual Meeting of the American Society of International Law* 98, 27–30.

Schwebel, Stephen. 2007. 'Is mediation of foreign investment disputes plausible?', *ICSID Review* 22, 237–41.

Schwebel, Stephen. 2009. 'The overwhelming merits of bilateral investment treaties', *Suffolk Transnational Law Review* 32, 263–9.

Sell, Susan K. 2000. 'Big business and the new trade agreements: the future of the WTO', *Political Economy and the Changing Global Order* 2, 174–83.

Sethi, Deepak and William Judge. 2009. 'Reappraising liabilities of foreignness within an integrated perspective of the costs and benefits of doing business abroad', *International Business Review* 18, 404–16.

Shaffer, Gregory, Manfred Elsig, and Sergio Puig. 2014. 'The extensive (but fragile) authority of the WTO Appellate Body', *Law and Comtemporary Problems* 79, 237–73.

Shany, Yuval. 2008. 'Squaring the circle-independence and impartiality of party-appointed adjudicators in international legal proceedings', *Loyola LA International and Comparative Law Review* 30, 473–90.

Shaw, Malcolm N. 2008. *International Law*, 6th edn. Cambridge University Press.

Shawcross, Hartley. 1995. *Life Sentence: The Memoirs of Hartley Shawcross*. London: Constable.

Shea, Donald Richard. 1955. *The Calvo Clause: A Problem of Inter-American and International Law and Diplomacy*. Minneapolis: University of Minnesota Press.

Shelton, Dinah. 2004. *Remedies in International Human Rights Law*, 2nd edn. Oxford University Press.

Shihata, Ibrahim F. I. 1986. 'Towards a greater depoliticization of investment disputes: the roles of ICSID and MIGA', *ICSID Review* 1, 1–25.

Shihata, Ibrahim F. I. 1993. *Legal Treatment of Foreign Investment: 'The World Bank Guidelines'*. Dordrecht: Martinus Nijhoff.

Shihata, Ibrahim F. I. 1995. 'Judicial reform in developing countries and the role of the world bank' in Ibrahim F. I. Shihata (ed.), *The World Bank in a Changing World: Selected Essays and Lectures*. Volume II. Leiden: Martinus Nijhoff.

Shirlow, Esmé. 2016. 'Dawn of a new era? The UNCITRAL rules and UN convention on transparency in treaty-based investor-state arbitration', *ICSID Review* 31, 622–54.

Siegel, Deborah E. 2013. 'Using free trade agreements to control capital account restrictions: relationship to the mandate of the IMF' in Kevin P. Gallagher and Leonardo E. Stanley (eds.), *Capital Account Regulations and the Trading System: A Compatibility Review*. Boston: Pardee Center Task Force.

Siegmann, Till. 2008. 'The impact of bilateral investment treaties and double taxation treaties on foreign direct investments', *Law and Economic Research Paper Series No. 2008-22*, University of St. Gallen Law School.

Simma, Bruno. 2011. 'Foreign investment arbitration: a place for human rights?' *International & Comparative Law Quarterly* 60, 573–96.

Simma, Bruno and Dirk Pulkowski. 2006. 'Of planets and the universe: self-contained regimes in international law', *European Journal of International Law* 17, 483–529.

Simmons, Beth A. 1998. 'Compliance with international agreements', *Annual Review of Political Science* 1, 75–93.

Simmons, Beth A. 2000. 'The legalization of international monetary affairs', *International Organization* 54, 573–602.

Simmons, Beth A. 2009. *Mobilizing for Human Rights: International Law in Domestic Politics*. Cambridge University Press.

Simmons, Beth A. 2014. 'Bargaining over BITs, arbitrating awards: the regime for protection and promotion of international investment', *World Politics* 66, 12–46.

Sinclair, Anthony C. 2004. 'The origins of the umbrella clause in the international law of investment protection', *Arbitration International* 20, 411–34.

Sinclair, Anthony C. 2009. 'ICSID arbitration: how long does it take?', *Global Arbitration Review* 5, 1–5.

Sinclair, Anthony C. 2013. *State Contracts in Investment Treaty Arbitration*, PhD Thesis, University of Cambridge. On file with the authors.

Sinclair, Scott. 2014. 'Trade agreements, the new constitutionalism and public services' in Stephen Gill and A. Claire Cutler (eds.), *New Constitutionalism and World Order*. Cambridge University Press.

Singh, Prabhakar. 2015. 'The rough and tumble of international courts and tribunals', *Indian Journal of International Law* 55, 1–38.

Shinkman, Matthew. 2007. 'The investors' view: economic opportunities versus political risks in 2007–11' in Laza Kekiz and Karl Sauvant (eds.), *World Investment Prospects to 2011: Foreign Direct Investment and the Challenge of Political Risk*. London: The Economist Intelligence Unit.

Shirlow, Esmé. 2014. 'Deference and indirect expropriation analysis in international investment law: observations on current approaches and frameworks for future analysis', *ICSID Review* 29, 595–626.

Slaughter, Anne-Marie. 1995. 'International law in a world of liberal states', *European Journal of International Law* 6, 503–38.

Smit, Hans. 2010. 'The pernicious institution of the party-appointed arbitrators', *Columbia FDI Perspectives No. 33*, 14 December. New York: Columbia University Vale Columbia Center on Sustainable International Investment.

Smith, Adam. 1776 (1981). *An Inquiry into the Nature and Causes of the Wealth of Nations*. Indianapolis: Liberty Classics, reprint.

Sokchea, Kim. 2007. 'Bilateral investment treaties, political risk and foreign direct investment', *Asia Pacific Journal of Economics & Business* 11, 6–24.

Soloway, Julie. 2003. 'NAFTA's Chapter 11: investment protection, integration and the public interest', *Choices* 9, 1–60.

Sornarajah, Muthucumaraswamy. 2006a. 'Power and justice third world resistance in international law', *Singapore Year Book of International Law* 10, 19–57.

Sornarajah, Muthucumaraswamy. 2006b. 'A law for need or a law for greed? Restoring the lost law in the international law of foreign investment', *International Environmental Agreements* 6, 329–57.

Sornarajah, Muthucumaraswamy. 2008. 'The neo-liberal agenda in investment arbitration' in Wenhua Shan, Penelope Simons, and Dalvinder Singh (eds.), *Redefining Sovereignty in International Economic Law*. Oxford: Hart.

Sornarajah, Muthucumaraswamy. 2010. *The International Law on Foreign Investment*, 3rd edn. Cambridge University Press.

Sornarajah, Muthucumaraswamy. 2011. 'Evolution or revolution in international investment arbitration? The descent into normlessness' in Chester Brown and Kate Miles (eds.), *Evolution in Investment Treaty Law and Arbitration*. Cambridge University Press.

Sornarajah, Muthucumaraswamy. 2015. *Resistance and Change in the International Law on Foreign Investment.* Cambridge University Press.

Spears, Suzanne A. 2010. 'The quest for policy space in a new generation of international investment agreements', *Journal of International Economic Law* 13, 1037–75.

Spence, Michael. 1973. 'Job market signaling', *The Quarterly Journal of Economics* 87, 355–74.

Spronk, Susan and Carlos Crespo. 2008. 'Water, national sovereignty and social resistance: bilateral investment treaties and the struggles against multinational water companies in Cochabamba and El Alto, Bolivia', *Law, Social Justice and Global Development* 1, 1–14.

St John, Taylor. 2017. *The Power of Modest Multilateralism: The International Centre for Settlement of Investment Disputes (ICSID), 1964–1980*, PhD thesis, University of Oxford. On file with the authors.

Staiger, Robert. 2003. 'A role for the WTO' in Kaushik Basu and others (eds.), *International Labor Standards: History, Theory and Public Options*. Oxford: Blackwell.

Steinitz, Maya. 2011. 'Whose claim is this anyway? Third-party litigation funding', *Minnesota Law Review* 95, 1268–338.

Stevens, Guy and Robert Lipsey. 1992. 'Interactions between domestic and foreign investment', *Journal of International Money and Finance* 11, 40–62.

Stewart, Richard and Michelle Sanchez-Badin. 2011. 'The World Trade Organization and Global Administrative Law' in Christian Joerges and Ernst-Ulrich Petersmann (eds.), *Constitutionalism, Multilevel Trade Governance and International Economic Law*. Oxford University Press.

Stigler, George. 1971. 'The theory of economic regulation', *Bell Journal of Economics and Management Science* 2, 3–21.

Stiglitz, Joseph. 2000. 'Capital market liberalization, economic growth, and instability', *World Development* 28, 1075–86.

Stiglitz, Joseph. 2007. 'Regulating multinational corporations: towards principles of cross-border legal frameworks in a globalized world balancing rights with responsibilities', *American University International Law Review* 23, 451–558.

Stiglitz, Joseph. 2013. 'Developing countries are right to resist restrictive trade agreements', *The Guardian*, November 8.

Strezhnev, Anton. 2016. 'Detecting bias in international investment arbitration', presented at the 57th Annual Convention of the International Studies Association—Atlanta, Georgia. 16–19 March. On file with the authors.

Stuyt, Alexander Marie. 1990. *Survey of International Arbitrations, 1794–1989*. 3rd edn., Dordrecht, Boston: Martinus Nijhoff.

Sunstein, Cass R., David Schkade, Lisa Michelle Ellman, and Andreas Sawicki. 2006. *Are Judges Political? An Empirical Analysis of the Federal Judiciary*. Washington DC: Brookings Institution Press.

Swenson, Deborah. 2005. 'Why do developing countries sign BITs?', *University of California Davis Journal of International Law and Policy* 12, 131–56.

Sykes, Alan. 2005. 'Public versus private enforcement of international economic law: standing and remedy', *The Journal of Legal Studies* 34, 631–66.

Tabarrok, Alexander and Eric Helland. 1999. 'Court politics: the political economy of tort awards', *The Journal of Law & Economics* 42, 157–88.

Tams, Christian. 2006. 'An appealing option? The debate about an ICSID appelate structure', *Essays in Transnational Economic Law* 57, 1–50.

Tavares-Lehmann, Ana Teresa, Lisa Sachs, Lise Johnson, and Perrine Toledano. 2016. 'Introduction' in Ana Teresa Tavares-Lehmann, Lisa Sachs, Lise Johnson, and Perrine Toledano (eds.), *Rethinking Investment Incentives: Trends and Policy Options*. New York: Columbia University Press.

Tavernise, Sabrina. 2013. 'Tobacco firms' strategy limits poorer nations' smoking laws', *New York Times*, 13 December.

te Velde, Dirk Willem. 2002. 'Government Policies for Inward Foreign Direct Investment in Developing Countries' OECD Development Centre, *Working Paper No 193*, CD/DOC(2002) 05, August, OECD: Paris.

The Economist. 2009. 'Behind closed doors—a hard struggle to shed some light on a legal grey area', *The Economist*, 23 April.

The Economist. 2014. 'The arbitration game—governments are souring on treaties to protect foreign investors', *The Economist*, 11 October.

The Economist. 2016. 'Baiting the bear: Russia is trying to impede enforcement of a massive damages award', *The Economist*, 16 April.

Thi Viet Hoa Nguyen, Thi Hong Vinh Cao, and Thi Thu Trang Lu. 2014. 'The impact of heterogeneous bilateral investment treaties (BIT) on foreign direct investment (FDI) inflows to Vietnam'. Available at http://www.wti.org/media/filer_public/b8/b2/b8b28529-f76f-4a47-88cc-a31679388a13/wti_seco_wp_03_2014.pdf.

Thomas, Christopher A. 2014. 'The uses and abuses of legitimacy in International Law', *Oxford Journal of Legal Studies* 34, 729–58.

Thomas, Jonathan and Tim Worrall. 1994. 'Foreign direct investment and the risk of expropriation', *Review of Economic Studies* 61, 81–108.

Thompson, Christopher. 2012. 'Big tobacco backs Australian law opposers', *Financial Times*, 29 April 2012.

Tienhaara, Kyla Susanne. 2011. 'Regulatory chill and the threat of arbitration: a view from political science' in Chester Brown and Kate Miles (eds.), *Evolution in Investment Treaty Law and Arbitration*. Cambridge University Press.

Tienhaara, Kyla Susanne. 2009. *The Expropriation of Environmental Governance: Protecting Foreign Investors at the Expense of Public Policy.* Cambridge University Press.

Tienhaara, Kyla Susanne and Patricia Ranald. 2011. 'Australia's rejection of investor-state dispute settlement: four potential contributing factors', *Investment Treaty News Quarterly.* Available at http://www.iisd.org/itn/2011/07/12/australias-rejection-of-investor-state-dispute-settlement-four-potential-contributing-factors/.

Tietje, Christian and Freya Baetens. 2014. 'The impact of investor-state-dispute settlement (ISDS) in the Transatlantic Trade and Investment Partnership', a study prepared for the Minister for Foreign Trade and Development Cooperation, Ministry of Foreign Affairs, The Netherlands, 24 June.

Titi, Aikaterini. 2014. *The Right to Regulate in International Investment Law.* Baden-Baden: Nomos.

Tobin, Jennifer and Susan Rose-Ackerman. 2005. 'Foreign direct investment and the business environment in developing countries: the impact of bilateral investment treaties', *Yale Law and Economics Research Paper No. 293.*

Tobin, Jennifer and Susan Rose-Ackerman. 2011. 'When BITs have some bite: the political-economic environment for bilateral investment treaties', *The Review of International Organizations* 6, 1–32.

Tomz, Michael. 2002. Democratic Default: Domestic Audiences and Compliance with International Agreements. Paper presented at the Annual Meeting of the American Political Science Association, Boston, 29 August–1 September. On file with the authors.

Tomz, Michael. 2007. *Reputation and International Cooperation: Sovereign Debt across Three Centuries.* Princeton University Press.

Toral, Mehmet and Thomas Schultz. 2010. 'The state, a perpetual respondent in investment arbitration? Some unorthodox considerations' in Michael Waibel, Asha Kaushal, Kwo-Hwa Liz Chung, and Claire Balchin (eds.), *The Backlash Against Investment Arbitration: Perceptions and Reality.* Alphen aan den Rijn: Kluwer Law International.

Trachtman, Joel P. 2008. *The Economic Structure of International Law.* Cambridge: Harvard University Press.

Trakman, Leon E. and David Musayelyan. 2016. 'The repudiation of investor–state arbitration and subsequent treaty practice: the resurgence of qualified investor–state arbitration', *ICSID Review* 31, 194–218.

Tremblay, Luc. 2005. 'The legitimacy of judicial review', *International Journal of Constitutional Law* 3, 617–48.

Trebilcock, Michael J. and Robert Howse. 2005. *The Regulation of International Trade*, 3rd edn. London: Routledge.

Tribe, Laurence H., Joseph Stiglitz, and Jeffrey D. Sachs. 2016. 220+ Law and Economics Professors Urge Congress to Reject the TPP and Other Prospective Deals that Include Investor-State Dispute Settlement (ISDS), letter to United States Congress, 7 September.

Trudeau, Justin. 2017. Address by Prime Minister Justin Trudeau to the European Parliament, Strasbourg, France, 16 February 2017. Available at http://pm.gc.ca/eng/news/2017/02/16/address-prime-minister-justin-trudeau-european-parliament.

Tucker, Todd. 2015. *Institutions and Development Ideologies in Investment Treaty Arbitration*, PhD, University of Cambridge. On file with the authors.

Tucker, Todd. 2016. 'Inside the black box: collegial patterns on investment tribunals', *Journal of International Dispute Settlement* 7, 183–204.

Turia, Tariana. 2013. 'Government moves forward with plain packaging of tobacco products', *New Zealand Government Official Website*, 19 February. Available at https://www.beehive. govt.nz/release/government-moves-forward-plain-packaging-tobacco-products.

United Nations. 2003. *Economic, Social and Cultural Rights: Human Rights, Trade and Investment*, Report of the United Nations High Commissioner for Human Rights, 2 July. Geneva.

United Nations Centre on Transnational Corporations. 1984. 'Bilateral, regional, and international arrangements on matters relating to transnational corporations'. *Official Records of the Economic and Social Council*, E.C. 10/1984/8.

United Nations Conference on Trade and Development (UNCTAD). 1992. *World Investment Report 1992*. Geneva: United Nations.

United Nations Conference on Trade and Development (UNCTAD). 1998. *World Investment Report: Trends and Determinants*. Geneva: United Nations.

United Nations Conference on Trade and Development (UNCTAD). 1999. *Foreign Direct Investment and Development*. Geneva: United Nations.

United Nations Conference on Trade and Development (UNCTAD). 2000. *World Investment Report: Cross-Border Mergers and Acquisitions and Development*. Geneva: United Nations.

United Nations Conference on Trade and Development (UNCTAD). 2001. *World Investment Report: Promoting Linkages*. Geneva: United Nations.

United Nations Conference on Trade and Development (UNCTAD). 2004. *World Investment Report: The Shift Towards Services*. Geneva: United Nations.

United Nations Conference on Trade and Development (UNCTAD). 2007. *Bilateral Investment Treaties 1995–2006: Trend in International Rulemaking*. Geneva: United Nations.

United Nations Conference on Trade and Development (UNCTAD). 2009a. 'The impact on foreign direct investment of BITs' in Karl Sauvant and Lisa Sachs (eds.), *The Effect of Treaties on Foreign Direct Investment: Bilateral Investment Treaties, Double Taxation Treaties and Investment Flows*. Oxford University Press.

United Nations Conference on Trade and Development (UNCTAD). 2009b. *The Impact of International Investment Agreements on Foreign Direct Investment to Developing Countries*. Geneva: United Nations.

United Nations Conference on Trade and Development (UNCTAD). 2009c. *The Role of International Investment Agreements in Attracting Foreign Direct Investment to Developing Countries*. Geneva: United Nations.

United Nations Conference on Trade and Development (UNCTAD). 2010. *Investor State Disputes: Prevention and Alternatives to Arbitration*. Geneva: United Nations.

United Nations Conference on Trade and Development (UNCTAD). 2011. *World Investment Report: Non-equity Modes of International Production and Development*. Geneva: United Nations.

United Nations Conference on Trade and Development (UNCTAD). 2012. *Transparency in IIAs. UNCTAD Series on Issues in International Investment Agreements II*. Geneva: United Nations.

United Nations Conference on Trade and Development (UNCTAD). 2013. *World Investment Report: Global Value Chains: Investment and Trade for Development*. Geneva: United Nations.

United Nations Conference on Trade and Development (UNCTAD). 2014. *World Investment Report: Investing in the SDGs: an Action Plan*. Geneva: United Nations.

United Nations Conference on Trade and Development (UNCTAD). 2015a. *World Investment Report: Reforming International Investment Governance*. Geneva: United Nations.

United Nations Conference on Trade and Development (UNCTAD). 2015b. *Recent Trends in IIAs and ISDS*. Geneva: United Nations.

United States. 2017. 'National Trade Policy Agenda for 2017', 28 February. Available at http://im.ft-static.com/content/images/1dd70b12-fe25-11e6-96f8-3700c5664d30.pdf.

United States Chamber of Commerce. 2013. 'Statement of the US Chamber of Commerce. On: The Transatlantic Trade and Investment Partnership. To: Office of the US Trade Representative', 10 May. Available at https://www.uschamber.com/sites/default/files/legacy/comments/USTR-2013-0019TTIP-U.S.ChamberofCommerceSubmission.pdf.

US Chamber of Commerce and Business Roundtable. 2011. Letter by US Business Organisations to Secretaries Clinton, Locke, Geithner, Chairman Bernanke, 7 February 2011.

US Department of State. 1960. *Foreign Relations of the United States, The Conference of Berlin 1945, Vol II*, Protocol of the proceedings of the Berlin Conference. Washington, DC: Government Printing Office, 1485–87.

US Trade Representative. 2013. Letter to the United States House of Representatives, March 20. Available at ustr.gov/sites/default/files/03202013%20TTIP%20Notification%20Letter.PDF.

US Trade Representative. 2014. 'Fact Sheet: U.S. Objectives, U.S. Benefits in the Transatlantic Trade and Investment Partnership: A Detailed View', March. Available at https://ustr.gov/about-us/policy-offices/press-office/press-releases/2014/March/US-Objectives-US-Benefits-In-the-TTIP-a-Detailed-View.

US Trade Representative. 2015. 'Fact Sheet: Investor-State Dispute Settlement', March. Available at https://ustr.gov/about-us/policy-offices/press-office/fact-sheets/2015/march/investor-state-dispute-settlement-isds.

Vadi, Valentina. 2012. *Public Health in International Investment Law and Arbitration*. London: Routledge.

Vadi, Valentina. 2015. *Analogies in International Investment Law and Arbitration*. Cambridge University Press.

van Aaken, Anne. 2009. 'International investment law between commitment and flexibility: a contract theory analysis', *Journal of International Economic Law* 12, 507-38.

van Aaken, Anne. 2010. 'Primary and secondary remedies in international investment law and national state liability: a functional and comparative view' in Stephan W. Schill (ed.), *International Investment Law and Comparative Public Law*. Oxford University Press.

van Aaken, Anne. 2011. 'Opportunities for and limits to an economic analysis of international law', *Transnational Corporations Review* 3, 27–46.

van Aaken, Anne. 2014a. 'Smart flexibility clauses in international investment treaties and sustainable development: a functional view', *The Journal of World Investment and Trade* 15, 827–61.

van Aaken, Anne. 2014b. 'Behavioral international law and economics', *Harvard International Law Journal* 55, 421–81.

van Aaken, Anne and Tobias Lehmann. 2013. 'Sustainable development and international investment law: a harmonious view from economics' in Roberto Echandi and Pierre Sauvé (eds.), *Prospects in International Investment Law and Policy*. Oxford University Press.

van den Berg, Albert Jan. 2011. 'Dissenting opinions by party-appointed arbitrators in investment arbitration' in Mahnoush Arsanjani et al. (eds.), *Looking to the Future: Essays on International Law in Honor of W. Michael Reisman*. Leiden: Martinus Nijhoff.

van der Ploeg, Frederick. 2011. 'Natural resources: curse or blessing?', *Journal of Economic Literature* 49, 366–420.

Van der Walt, André J. 2005. *Constitutional Property Law*. Cape Town: Juta.

Van Harten, Gus. 2000. 'Guatemala's peace accords in a free trade area of the Americas', *Yale Human Rights and Development Law Journal* 3, 112–58.

Van Harten, Gus. 2007. *Investment Treaty Arbitration and Public Law*. Oxford University Press.

Van Harten, Gus. 2010. 'Perceived bias in investment treaty arbitration' in Michael Waibel, Asha Kaushal, Kwo-Hwa Liz Chung, and Claire Balchin (eds.), *The Backlash against Investment Arbitration: Perceptions and Reality*. Alphen aan den Rijn: Kluwer Law International.

Van Harten, Gus. 2012. 'Arbitrator behaviour in asymmetrical adjudication: an empirical study of investment treaty arbitration', *Osgoode Hall Law Journal* 50, 211–68.

Van Harten, Gus. 2013. *Sovereign Choices and Sovereign Constraints: Judicial Restraint in Investment Treaty Arbitration*. Oxford University Press.

Van Harten, Gus. 2015. 'A report on the flawed proposals for investor-state dispute settlement (ISDS) in TTIP and CETA', *Osgoode Legal Studies Research Paper Series Paper 90*. Available at http://digitalcommons.osgoode.yorku.ca/olsrps/90.

Van Harten, Gus and Martin Loughlin. 2006. 'Investment treaty arbitration as a species of global administrative law', *European Journal of International Law* 17, 121–50.

Van Harten, Gus and Pavel Malysheuski. 2016. 'Who has benefited financially from investment treaty arbitration? An evaluation of the size and wealth of claimants', *Osgoode Hall Law Journal Legal Studies Research Paper Series Research Paper No 14/2016*.

Van Harten, Gus and Dayna Nadine Scott. 2016. 'Investment treaties and the internal vetting of regulatory proposals: a case study from Canada', *Journal of International Dispute Settlement* 7, 92–116.

Vandevelde, Kenneth. 1988. 'The bilateral investment program of the United States', *Cornell International Law Journal* 21, 201–76.

Vandevelde, Kenneth. 1992a. *United States Investment Treaties: Policy and Practice*. Alphen aan den Rijn: Kluwer Law International.

Vandevelde, Kenneth. 1992b. 'US bilateral investment treaties: the second wave', *Michigan Journal of International Law* 14, 621–704.

Vandevelde, Kenneth. 1998. 'The political economy of a bilateral investment treaty', *The American Journal of International Law* 82, 621–41.

Vandevelde, Kenneth. 2000. 'The economics of bilateral investment treaties', *Harvard International Law Journal* 41, 469–502.

Vandevelde, Kenneth. 2009. *U.S. International Investment Agreements*. Oxford University Press.

Vandevelde, Kenneth. 2010. *Bilateral Investment Treaties: History, Policy, and Interpretation*. Oxford University Press.

Vandevelde, Kenneth. 2011. 'Model bilateral investment treaties: the way forward', *Southwestern Journal of International Law* 18, 307–14.

Vandevelde, Kenneth. 2012. 'The First Bilateral Investment Treaties: U.S. Friendship, Commerce and Navigation Treaties in the Truman Administration', PhD Thesis, University of California San Diego. Available at http://gradworks.umi.com/35/47/3547346.html.

VanGrasstek, Craig. 2011. *The Political Economy of Services in Regional Trade Agreements*. Paris: OECD Publishing.

Varuhas, Jason N. E. 2016. *Damages and Human Rights*. Oxford, Portland: Hart.

Vasciannie, Stephen. 1999. 'The fair and equitable treatment standard in international investment law and practice', *British Yearbook of International Law* 70, 99–164.

Vaughan, Martin. 2013. 'Singapore's housing tax hits home', *The Wall Street Journal*, 29 January.

Veeder, Johnny. 2013. 'The historical keystone to international arbitration: the party-appointed arbitrator: from Miami to Geneva', *American Society of International Law Proceedings* 107, 387–405.

Venzke, Ingo. 2016. 'Investor-state dispute settlement in TTIP from the perspective of a public law theory of international adjudication', *Journal of World Investment and Trade* 17, 374–400.

Verheyen, Roda. 2012. Briefing Note: The Coal-fired Power Plant Hamburg-Moorburg, ICSID proceedings by Vattenfall under the Energy Charter Treaty and the result for environmental standards. Available at www.greenpeace.de/sites/www.greenpeace.de/files/publications/icsid_case_regarding_the_vattenfall_coal-fired_power_plant_hamburg-moorburg.pdf.

Vermeule, Adrian. 2006. *Judging Under Uncertainty: An Institutional Theory of Legal Interpretation*. Cambridge: Harvard University Press.

Vernon, Raymond. 1966. 'International investment and international trade in the product cycle', *The Quarterly Journal of Economics* 80, 190–207.

Vernon, Raymond. 1971. *Sovereignty at Bay; The Multinational Spread of U.S. Enterprises*. New York: Basic Books.

Vernon, Raymond. 1979. 'The product cycle hypothesis in a new international environment', *Oxford Bulletin of Economics and Statistics* 41, 255–67.

Viner, Jacob. 1950. *The Customs Union Issue*. New York: Carnegie Endowment for International Peace.

Veselá, Gita. 2009. 'Bilateral investment treaty overview—Czech Republic'. Available at www.investmentclaims.com.

Viñuales, Jorge E. 2012. *Foreign Investment and the Environment in International Law*. Cambridge University Press.

Voeten, Erik. 2008. 'The impartiality of international judges: evidence from the European Court of Human Rights', *American Political Science Review* 102, 417–33.

von Bogdandy, Armin and Ingo Venzke. 2014. *In Whose Name? A Public Law Theory of International Adjudication*. Oxford University Press.

Voon, Tania and Andrew D. Mitchell. 2016. 'Denunciation, termination and survival: the interplay of treaty law and international investment law', *ICSID Review* 31, 413–33.

Waibel, Michael. 2007a. 'Opening Pandora's box: sovereign bonds in international arbitration', *The American Journal of International Law* 101, 711–59.

Waibel, Michael. 2007b. 'Two worlds of necessity in ICSID arbitration: CMS vs. LG&E', *Leiden Journal of International Law* 20, 637–48.

Waibel, Michael. 2010a. 'The diplomatic channel' in James Crawford, Allain Pellet, and Simon Olleson (eds.), *Handbook on State Responsibility*. Oxford University Press.

Waibel, Michael. 2010b. 'BIT by BIT—The silent liberalisation of the capital account' in August Reinisch et al. (eds.), *International Investment Law for the 21st Century—Essays in Honour of Christoph Schreuer*. Oxford University Press.

Waibel, Michael. 2014. 'Coordinating adjudication processes' in Zachary Douglas, Joost Pauwelyn, and Jorge E. Viñuales (eds.), *The Foundations of International Investment Law: Bringing Theory Into Practice*. Oxford University Press.

Waibel, Michael, Asha Kaushal, Kwo-Hwa Liz Chung, and Claire Balchin (eds.). 2010. *The Backlash Against Investment Arbitration: Perceptions and Reality*. Alphen aan den Rijn: Kluwer Law International.

Waibel, Michael and Yanhui Wu. 2012. 'Are arbitrators political?', *Working Paper and Dataset on Arbitrator Characteristics*. On file with the authors.

Wälde, Thomas and Abba Kolo. 2001. 'Environmental regulation, investment protection and "regulatory takings" in international law', *International and Comparative Law Quarterly* 50, 811–48.

Wälde, Thomas and Todd Weiler. 2004. 'Investment arbitration under the Energy Charter Treaty in the light of new NAFTA precedents: towards a global code of conduct for economic regulation', *Transnational Dispute Management* 1.

Waldron, Jeremy. 2006. 'The core of the case against judicial review', *The Yale Law Journal* 115, 1346–60.

Wallach, Lori. 1999. 'Trade pacts accused of subverting U.S. policies', *Los Angeles Times*, 28 February.

Wallach, Lori and Ben Beachy. 2013. 'US shrouding TPP talks in secrecy: move represents a massive assault on democratic governance, which is untenable in this age of transparency', *The Business Times*, 6 August.

Walter, Andrew. 2001. 'NGOs, business, and international investment: the multilateral agreement on investment, Seattle, and beyond', *Global Governance* 7, 51–73.

Walter, Andrew and Gautam Sen. 2009. *Analyzing the Global Political Economy*. Princeton University Press.

Ware, Stephen J. 1999. 'Default rules from mandatory rules: privatizing law through arbitration', *Minnesota Law Review* 88, 703–54.

Warren, Elizabeth. 2014. Letter of Senator Warren to Ambassador Michael Froman, United States Trade Representative, 17 December. Available at http://www.warren.senate.gov/files/documents/TPP.pdf.

Wei, Shang-Jin. 2000. 'How taxing is corruption on international investors?' *Review of Economics and Statistics* 82, 1–11.

Weijia, Hu. 2015. 'US needs to show good faith in BIT negotiations by opening up its tech sectors', *Global Times*, 21 September. Available at www.globaltimes.cn/content/943649.shtml.

Weiler, Todd. 2004. 'Balancing human rights and investor protection', *Boston College International and Comparative Law Review* 27, 429–52.

Weingast, Barry R. 1993. 'Constitutions as governance structures: the political foundations of secure markets', *Journal of Institutional and Theoretical Economics* 149, 286–311.

Wellhausen, Rachel L. 2016a. 'Recent trends in investor–state dispute settlement', *Journal of International Dispute Settlement* 7, 117–35.

Wellhausen, Rachel L. 2016b. 'International Investment Law, Compliance, and Foreign Direct Reinvestment', May. On file with the authors.

Westermann, William Linn. 1907. 'Interstate arbitration in antiquity', *The Classical Journal* 2, 197–211.

Whitsitt, Elizabeth and Damon Vis-Dunbar. 2008. 'In focus: investment arbitration in Brazil: yes or no?' *Investment Treaty News*, December.

Wilcox, Clair. 1949. *A Charter for World Trade.* New York: Macmillan.

Williams, Zoe Philipps. 2016. *Risky Business or Risky Politics: What Explains Investor–State Disputes?* PhD, Hertie School of Governance. On file with the authors.

Williamson, John. 1990. 'What Washington means with policy reform' in John Williamson (ed.), *Latin American Adjustment: How Much has Happened?* Washington, DC: Institute for International Economics.

Williamson, John. 2008. 'Globalization and the great divergence: terms of trade booms and volatility in the poor periphery 1782–1913', *National Bureau of Economic Research Working Paper No. 13841.* Cambridge: NBER.

Williamson, Oliver. 1981. 'The economics of organization: the transaction cost approach', *American Journal of Sociology* 87, 548–77.

Williamson, Oliver. 1983. 'Credible commitments: using hostages to support exchange', *The American Economic Review* 73, 519–40.

Woll, Cornelia. 2008. *Firm Interests: How Governments Shape Business Lobbying on Global Trade.* Ithaca: Cornell University Press.

World Bank. 2009. *Knowledge in Development Note: Industrial Policy'.* Available at http://econ.worldbank.org/WBSITE/EXTERNAL/EXTDEC/EXTRESEARCH/0,,contentMDK:22447958~pagePK:64165401~piPK:64165026~theSitePK:469382,00.html.

World Bank. 2010. *Investment Law Reform: A Handbook for Development Practitioners*, June, Available at https://openknowledge.worldbank.org/handle/10986/25206.

World Bank. 2015. *Investment Climate: Investment Generation Toolkit.* Available at https://www.wbginvestmentclimate.org/toolkits/investment-generation-toolkit/.

World Bank. 2016. *Doing Business 2016.* Available at http://www.doingbusiness.org/.

World Economic Forum. 2014. 'Mega-regional trade agreements: game-changers or costly distractions for the world trading system?', Global Agenda Council on Trade & Foreign Direct Investment, 9 July. Washington, DC.

World Trade Organization. 2002. 'Concept Paper on Non-Discrimination', Communication from the European Community and Its Member States, WTO Doc WT/WGTI/W/122, 27 June.

World Trade Organization. 2011. Report on the Meeting of 7 and 8 March 2001, Note by the Secretariat, WT/WGTI/M/14.

World Trade Organization. 2016. Understanding the WTO: The Organization: Members and Observers. Available at http://www.wto.org/english/thewto_e/whatis_e/tif_e/org6_e.htm.

Wrobel, Sharon. 2010. 'Noble energy threatens to take disputer over raising gas royalties to International Court of Justice', *Jerusalem Post*, 6 October.

Wotipka, Christine Min and Francisco O. Ramirez. 2008. 'World society and human rights: an event history analysis of the Convention on the Elimination of All Forms of Discrimination against Women' in Beth A Simmons, Frank Dobbin, and Geoffrey Garrett (eds.), *The Global Diffusion of Markets and Democracy.* Cambridge University Press.

Xu, Bin. 2000. 'Multinational enterprises, technology diffusion, and host country productivity growth' *Journal of Development Economics* 62, 477–93.

Yackee, Jason Webb. 2007. *Sacrificing Sovereignty: Bilateral Investment Treaties, International Arbitration, and the Quest for Capital*, PhD, University of North Carolina-Chapel Hill.

Yackee, Jason Webb. 2008a. 'Bilateral investment treaties, credible commitment, and the rule of (international) law: Do BITs promote foreign direct investment?', *Law and Society Review* 42, 805–32.

Yackee, Jason Webb. 2008b. 'Conceptual difficulties in the empirical study of bilateral investment treaties', *Brooklyn Journal of International Law* 33, 405–62.

Yackee, Jason Webb. 2008c. 'Do we really need BITs? Toward a return to contract in international investment law', *Asian Journal of WTO and Health Law* 3, 121–46.

Yackee, Jason Webb. 2009. 'Do BITs really work? Revisiting the empirical link between investment treaties and foreign direct investment' in Karl Sauvant and Lisa Sachs (eds.), *The Effect of Treaties on Foreign Direct Investment: Bilateral Investment Treaties, Double Taxation Treaties and Investment Flows*. Oxford University Press.

Yackee, Jason Webb. 2011. 'Do bilateral investment treaties promote foreign direct investment? Some hints from alternative evidence', *Virginia Journal of International Law* 51, 397–442.

Yackee, Jason Webb. 2015. 'Do investment promotion agencies promote bilateral investment treaties?' in Andrea Bjorklund (ed.), *Yearbook on International Investment Law & Policy 2013-2014*. Oxford University Press.

Yackee, Jason Webb. 2016a. 'Do BITs "work"? Empirical evidence from France', *Journal of International Dispute Settlement* 7, 55–71.

Yackee, Jason Webb. 2016b. 'The first investor-state arbitration: The Suez Canal Company v. Egypt (1864)', *The Journal of World Investment and Trade* 17, 401–62.

Yeaple, Stephen Ross. 2003. 'The complex integration strategies of multinationals and cross country dependencies in the structure of foreign direct investment', *Journal of International Economics* 60, 293–314.

Young, Oran R. 1986. 'International regimes: toward a new theory of institutions', *World Politics* 39, 104–22.

Young, Oran R. 1989. 'The politics of international regime formation: managing natural resources and the environment', *International Organization* 43, 349–75.

Zaheer, Srilata. 1995. 'Overcoming the liability of foreignness', *Academy of Management Journal* 38, 341–63.

Zahrnt, Valentin. 2008. 'Domestic constituents and the formulation of WTO negotiating positions: what the delegates say', *World Trade Review* 7, 393–421.

Zangl, Bernhard. 2008. 'Judicialization matters! A comparison of dispute settlement under GATT and the WTO', *International Studies Quarterly* 52, 825–54.

Zeng, Ka and Yue Lu. 2016. 'Variation in bilateral investment treaty provisions and foreign direct investment flows to China, 1997–2011', *International Interactions* 42, 820–48.

■ INDEX

Note: The page numbers in bold indicate the main place(s) where the subject matter of the index term is discussed.

Printed in Great Britain
by Amazon

38170121R00196